A Text Book Of

BUSINESS INFORMATICS

For
BBA Semester - II (Course Code: 206)
As Per Revised Syllabus
Effective from June 2013

Gautam Bapat
M.C.A., P.G.D.B.M. (Marketing)
Asst. Professor, Computer Science & Applications
Mitsom College
Pune

N2916

Business Informatics ISBN 978-93-83525-99-7

Third Edition : January 2016
© : Author

The text of this publication, or any part thereof, should not be reproduced or transmitted in any form or stored in any computer storage system or device for distribution including photocopy, recording, taping or information retrieval system or reproduced on any disc, tape, perforated media or other information storage device etc., without the written permission of Author with whom the rights are reserved. Breach of this condition is liable for legal action.

Every effort has been made to avoid errors or omissions in this publication. In spite of this, errors may have crept in. Any mistake, error or discrepancy so noted and shall be brought to our notice shall be taken care of in the next edition. It is notified that neither the publisher nor the author or seller shall be responsible for any damage or loss of action to any one, of any kind, in any manner, therefrom.

Published By :
NIRALI PRAKASHAN
Abhyudaya Pragati, 1312, Shivaji Nagar
Off J.M. Road, PUNE – 411005
Tel - (020) 25512336/37/39, Fax - (020) 25511379
Email : niralipune@pragationline.com

Printed By :
Repro Knowledgecast Limited,
Thane

DISTRIBUTION CENTRES

PUNE
Nirali Prakashan : 119, Budhwar Peth, Jogeshwari Mandir Lane, Pune 411002, Maharashtra
Tel : (020) 2445 2044, 66022708, Fax : (020) 2445 1538
Email : bookorder@pragationline.com, niralilocal@pragationline.com

Nirali Prakashan : S. No. 28/27, Dhyari, Near Pari Company, Pune 411041
Tel : (020) 24690204 Fax : (020) 24690316
Email : dhyari@pragationline.com, bookorder@pragationline.com

MUMBAI
Nirali Prakashan : 385, S.V.P. Road, Rasdhara Co-op. Hsg. Society Ltd.,
Girgaum, Mumbai 400004, Maharashtra
Tel : (022) 2385 6339 / 2386 9976, Fax : (022) 2386 9976
Email : niralimumbai@pragationline.com

DISTRIBUTION BRANCHES

JALGAON
Nirali Prakashan : 34, V. V. Golani Market, Navi Peth, Jalgaon 425001,
Maharashtra, Tel : (0257) 222 0395, Mob : 94234 91860

KOLHAPUR
Nirali Prakashan : New Mahadvar Road, Kedar Plaza, 1st Floor Opp. IDBI Bank
Kolhapur 416 012, Maharashtra. Mob : 9850046155

NAGPUR
Pratibha Book Distributors : Above Maratha Mandir, Shop No. 3, First Floor,
Rani Jhanshi Square, Sitabuldi, Nagpur 440012, Maharashtra
Tel : (0712) 254 7129

DELHI
Nirali Prakashan : 4593/21, Basement, Aggarwal Lane 15, Ansari Road, Daryaganj
Near Times of India Building, New Delhi 110002
Mob : 08505972553

BENGALURU
Pragati Book House : House No. 1, Sanjeevappa Lane, Avenue Road Cross,
Opp. Rice Church, Bengaluru – 560002.
Tel : (080) 64513344, 64513355,Mob : 9880582331, 9845021552
Email:bharatsavla@yahoo.com

CHENNAI
Pragati Books : 9/1, Montieth Road, Behind Taas Mahal, Egmore,
Chennai 600008 Tamil Nadu, Tel : (044) 6518 3535,
Mob : 94440 01782 / 98450 21552 / 98805 82331,
Email : bharatsavla@yahoo.com

niralipune@pragationline.com | www.pragationline.com
Also find us on   www.facebook.com/niralibooks

Preface...

I take this opportunity to present this book entitled as **"Business Informatics"** to the students of Second Semester (BBA). The object of this book is to present the subject matter in a most concise and simple manner. The book is written strictly according to the Revised Syllabus.

The book has its own unique features. It brings out the subject in a very simple and lucid manner for easy and comprehensive understanding of the basic concepts, its intricacies, procedures and practices. This book will help the readers to have a broader view on Business Informatics. The language used in this book is easy and will help students to improve their vocabulary of Technical terms and understand the matter in a better and happier way.

I sincerely thank Shri. Dineshbhai Furia and Shri. Jignesh Furia of Nirali Prakashan, for the confidence reposed in me and giving me this opportunity to reach out to the students of management studies.

I thank Mr. Amar Salunkhe for his important inputs time to time and Mr. Akbar Shaikh who painstakingly attended to all the details to make this book appear good.

I also thank Ms. Chaitali Takale, Mr. Ravindra Walodare, Mr. Mahesh Swami, Mr. Vijay Shete, Mr. Sachin Shinde, Nikunj Joshi, Nilesh Deshmukh, Ashok Bodke, Moshin Sayyed and Nitin Thorat.

I have given my best inputs for this book. Any suggestions towards the improvement of this book and sincere comments are most welcome on niralipune@pragationline.com.

AUTHOR

Syllabus ...

1. **Introduction to Computers** [10 Lectures]
   1.1 Introduction
   1.2 Characteristics of Computers
   1.3 Block diagram of computer
   1.4 Booting Process
   1.5 Types of Programming Languages
      1.5.1 Machine Languages
      1.5.2 Assembly Languages
      1.5.3 High Level Languages
   1.6 Data Organization
      1.6.1 Drives
      1.6.2 Files
      1.6.3 Directories
   1.7 Storage Devices
      1.7.1 Primary Memory
         1.7.1.1 RAM
         1.7.1.2 ROM
      1.7.2 Secondary Storage Devices - FD, CD, HDD, Pen drive
   1.8 I/O Devices
      1.8.1 Monitor and types of monitor
      1.8.2 Printer and types of printer
      1.8.3 Scanners
      1.8.4 Digitizers
      1.8.5 Plotters
   1.9 Number Systems
      1.9.1 Introduction to Binary, Octal, Hexadecimal system
      1.9.2 Conversion
      1.9.3 Simple Addition, Subtraction, Multiplication, Division

2. **Operating System and Services in O.S.** [8 Lectures]
   2.1 Definition of operating system
   2.2 Services provided by OS
   2.3 Types of O.S.
   2.4 Features of Windows and Linux
   2.5 Files and Directories
   2.6 Internal and External Commands of DOS
   2.7 Batch Files

3. **Editors and Word Processors** [9 Lectures]
   3.1 Basic Concepts
   3.2 Examples : MS-Word2007
   3.3 Introduction to desktop publishing

Spreadsheets and Database packages
- 3.4 Purpose
- 3.5 MS-Excel2007
- 3.6 Creation of table in MS-Access2007
- 3.7 MS –PowerPoint2007

4. **Introduction to Networking** [15 Lectures]
    - 4.1 Basics of Computer Networks
    - 4.2 Definition
        - 4.2.1 Goals
        - 4.2.2 Applications
        - 4.2.3 Components
    - 4.3 Topology
        - 4.3.1 Types of Topology
    - 4.4 Types of Networks
        - 4.4.1 (LAN, MAN, WAN)
    - 4.5 Modes of Communication :
        - 4.5.1 (Simplex
        - 4.5.2 Half Duplex
        - 4.5.3 Full Duplex)
    - 4.6 Transmission media
        - 4.6.1 Twisted pair
        - 4.6.2 Coaxial cable
        - 4.6.3 Fiber optic cable
    - 4.7 Protocols and purpose
    - 4.8 Network Connectivity Devices
        - 4.8.1 Hubs
        - 4.8.2 Repeaters
        - 4.8.3 Bridges
        - 4.8.4 Switches
        - 4.8.5 Gateways

Internet Basics
- 4.9 Concept of Internet, Intranet and Extranet
- 4.10 Web Client
- 4.11 Web Server
- 4.12 WWW
- 4.13 Search Engine
- 4.14 Internet Service Providers (ISP)

5. **Introduction To R.D.B.M.S** [6 Lectures]
    - 5.1 Advantages and Limitations
    - 5.2 Normalization
    - 5.3 Entity Relationships
    - 5.4 Use Of simple SQL Commands involving both single table and joins.

●●●

Contents ...

1. Introduction to Computers — 1.1 – 1.104

2. Operating System and Services in Operating System — 2.1 – 2.46

3. Editors, Word Processors, Spreadsheet and Database Packages — 3.1 – 3.80

4. Introduction to Networking — 4.1 – 4.80

5. Introduction to R.D.B.M.S. — 5.1 – 5.60

Question Papers: October 2014, April 2015, October 2015 — P.1 – P.3

•••

Chapter 1...

Introduction to Computers

Contents ...

1.1 Introduction
    1.1.1 What is a Computer? / Meaning of Computer
    1.1.2 Definition
    1.1.3 Generations of Computers
    1.1.4 Types of Computers
    1.1.5 Advantages of Computers
    1.1.6 Disadvantages of Computers
    1.1.7 Computer Applications
1.2 Characteristics of Computers
1.3 Block Diagram of Computer
1.4 Booting Process
1.5 Types of Programming Languages
    1.5.1 Machine Language
    1.5.2 Assembly Language
    1.5.3 High Level Language
1.6 Data Organisation
    1.6.1 Drives
    1.6.2 Files
        1.6.2.1 Definition of File
        1.6.2.2 File Organisation
    1.6.3 Directories
1.7 Storage Devices
    1.7.1 Primary Memory
        1.7.1.1 RAM
        1.7.1.2 ROM
    1.7.2 Secondary Memory
    1.7.3 Secondary Storage Devices
        1.7.3.1 Magnetic Tape
        1.7.3.2 Magnetic Disks
        1.7.3.3 Optical Disks (CD and DVD)
        1.7.3.4 Pen Drive

1.8 I/O (Input/Output) Devices
    1.8.1 Input Devices
        1.8.1.1 Keyboard
        1.8.1.2 Mouse
        1.8.1.3 Scanner
        1.8.1.4 MICR
        1.8.1.5 OMR
        1.8.1.6 Digital Camera
        1.8.1.7 Digitizer
        1.8.1.8 Joystick
        1.8.1.9 Light Pen
        1.8.1.10 Trackball
        1.8.1.11 OCR
        1.8.1.12 Bar Code Readers
    1.8.2 Output Devices
        1.8.2.1 Monitor (CRT and LCD)
        1.8.2.2 Plasma Display
        1.8.2.3 Printers
        1.8.2.4 Plotters
1.9 Number Systems
    1.9.1 Binary Number System
    1.9.2 Octal Number System
    1.9.3 Decimal Number System
    1.9.4 Hexadecimal Number System
    1.9.5 Conversions
    1.9.6 Binary Arithmetic (Addition, Subtraction, Multiplication, Division)
- Questions

1.1 Introduction

- Now-a-days, computer are an integral part of our lives. They are used for the reservation of tickets for airplanes and railways, payment of telephone and electricity bills, deposit and withdrawal of money from banks, processing of business data, forecasting of weather conditions, diagnosis of diseases, searching for information on the internet, etc.
- Computer are also used extensively in schools, universities, organisations, music industry, movie industry, scientific research, law firms, fashion industry, etc.
- The term computer is derived from the Latin word 'compute'. The word 'compute' means to calculate.

- A computer is an electronic machine that accepts data from the user, processes the data by performing calculations and operations on it, and generates the desired output results.
- Computer performs both simple and complex operations, with speed and accuracy.
- A computer is a general purpose device that can be programmed to carry out a finite set of arithmetic or logical operations.
- A computer is an electronic device that manipulates information or data. It has the ability to store, retrieve, and process data.
- A computer is a programmable machine. The two **principal characteristics of a computer** are:
    1. Computer responds to a specific set of instructions in a well-defined manner, and
    2. Computer can execute a pre-recorded list of instructions (a program).

1.1.1 What is a Computer? / Meaning of Computer

- A computer is an advanced electronic device that takes raw data as input from the user and processes these data under the control of set of instructions (called program) and gives the result (output) and saves output for the future use.
- A computer can process both numerical and non-numerical (arithmetic and logical) calculations.
- A computer has following functions:
    1. **Input (Data):** Input is the raw information entered into a computer from the input devices. It is the collection of letters, numbers, images etc.
    2. **Process:** Process is the operation of data as per given instruction. It is totally internal process of the computer system.
    3. **Output and Storage:** Output is the processed data given by computer after data processing. Output is also called as Result. We can save these results in the storage devices for the future use.

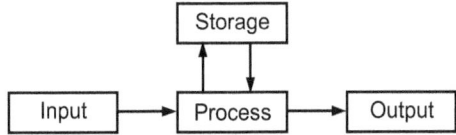

Fig. 1.1: Functions of a computer

1.1.2 Definition

- A computer is a programmable machine that can store, retrieve, and process data.

OR

- A computer is an extremely fast and accurate electronic data processing machine that receives data as input, performs arithmetic and logical operations on them according to a program stored in the memory and produces the desired output.

OR

- Computer is an electronic machine made up of various electronic devices (parts) to process the data to produce useful information.

OR

- A computer is an electronic device which is capable of receiving information (data) in a particular form and of performing a sequence of operations in accordance with a predetermined but variable set of procedural instructions (program) to produce a result in the form of information or signals.

1.1.3 Generations of Computers

- Generation in computer terminology is a change in technology a computer is/was being used.
- A generation in computer talk is a step in technology. Computer developed after ENIAC have been classified into five generations depending upon the technology used, processing techniques, computer languages, memory systems.

1. First Generation Computer (1942-1955):

- The first generation computer were using Vacuum Tubes and machine languages were used for giving instructions. The computer of this generation were very large in size and their programming was a difficult task.
- The first commercial electronic digital computer capable of using stored programs was called "Universal Automatic Calculator" (UNIVAC) built by Macuchy and Eckert in 1951. Punched cards were used for feeding and retrieving of information.
- The major first generation computer were UNIVAC-1, IBM-701, IBM-650, ENIAC, EDVAC, EDSAC, etc.

 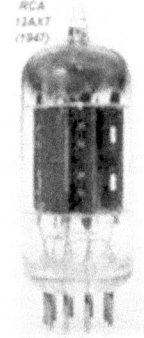

(a) 1st generation computer   (b) Vacuum tube

Fig. 1.2

- First generation computer were the fastest calculating devices of their time. They could perform computations in milliseconds. Vacuum tube technology made possible the advent of electronic digital computers.

Advantages:
   (i) First generation computer were fastest calculating devices of their time.
   (ii) Support parallel processing.

Disadvantages:
 (i) Air conditioning is required.
 (ii) Bulky in size (required large rooms) for assembly on installation.
 (iii) Vacuum tube required very high power consumption.
 (iv) Commercial production of these computer was difficult and costly.
 (v) Time consuming for assembling and installation.
 (vi) These computer required very high constant maintenance.
 (vii) Difficult to use and programming.

Application:
- They were used for scientific applications as they were the fastest computing device of their time.

2. Second Generation Computer (1955-1964):
- Computer are entered into second generation by the introduction of Transistors.
- Vacuum tubes were replaced by tiny solid-state components called transistors.
- Transistors were highly reliable, requires less power and faster than vacuum tubes. High Level Languages such as FORTRAN, COBOL, BASIC etc. were introduced.
- The practice of writing programs in Machine languages were replaced by High Level Languages.
- Punched cards were used for input-output operations.
- Major second generation computer were IBM-1400 series, 7000 series, Honeywell 200, CDC 3600, UNIVAC 1108 etc.

(a) 2nd generation computer   (b) Transistor

Fig. 1.3

Advantages:
 (i) They used transistor technology as transistor are faster than vacuum tube.
 (ii) More reliable.
 (iii) Cheaper.
 (iv) Smaller in size.
 (v) Less power consumption.
 (vi) Support parallel processing.

Disadvantages:
- (i) Time consuming for assembly and installation.
- (ii) Air-conditioning required.
- (iii) Difficult for commercial production.
- (iv) Costly for commercial production.
- (v) Maintenance is high.

3. Third Generation Computer (1964-1975):

- The third generation computer used the new technology, Transistor Integrated Circuits (IC) intended by Jack and Noyce in 1958.
- All electronic components like transistors, resistor and capacitor were fabricated on silicon chips. Computer were designed by making use of ICs.
- IC has higher speed, larger storage capacity and smaller size. Operating systems were introduced for use in computers.
- Significant advances in hardware technology made the introduction of keyboards and monitor for data input and output. More high level languages like Pascal, RPG were also introduced.
- Major third generation computer were IBM -360 series, ICL -1900 series, CDC's CYBER - 175, TDC-316, IBM 370/168 etc.

(a) 3rd generation computer   (b) ICs

Fig. 1.4

Advantages:
- (i) Required small space (portable).
- (ii) More reliable.
- (iii) Faster in speed.
- (iv) Support high level languages.
- (v) Commercial production is raised.
- (vi) Installation is required in less time.
- (vii) Low maintenance.

Disadvantages:
- (i) Air-conditioning required.
- (ii) Cost is more than fourth generation computers.
- (iii) Highly sophisticated technology required for the manufacturing chips.

Application:
- Computer became accessible to mass audience. Computer were produced commercially and were smaller and cheaper than their predecessors.

4. Fourth Generation Computer (1975-1989):

- The ICs used in third generation computer had about 10 to 100 transistor per unit.
- This technology was called Small-Scale Integration (SSI). Later, with the advancement of technology for manufacturing ICs, it is possible to integrate 10,000 transistor in an IC.
- This technology is called Large-Scale Integration (LSI). Very Large Scale Integration (VLSI) can pack a million or more transistor on a single chip. LSI and VLSI technologies led to the introduction of Microprocessors.
- Computer which are designed using Microprocessor become the fourth generation computers. Magnetic disks become the primary means for external storage.
- Intel introduced the first microprocessor 4004 using LSI. The languages C, LISP, Prolog become popular. Present day computer are fourth generation computers.
- Major fourth generation computer are IBM System 370, CRAY–MPC, WIPRO 860, IBM AS/400/B60, IBM ps/2 MODEL 80, HCL Magnum, etc.

(a) 4th generation computer   (b) Microprocessor

Fig. 1.5

Advantages:
(i) Portable in size.
(ii) Cheaper.
(iii) More reliable.
(iv) Easy for installation.
(v) Support high level language.
(vi) Support networking.
(vii) Support GUI (Graphical User Interface).
(viii) Less time required for manual assembly.

Disadvantages:
(i) Air-conditioning is required.
(ii) Expensive.
(iii) Single user oriented.

Application:
- They became widely available for commercial purposes. Personal computer became available to the home user.

5. Fifth Generation Computer (1989 onwards):

- Fifth generation computer are capable of parallel processing, high speed computing and artificial intelligence.
- They have an architecture which allows more neural problem solving ability. These machines uses the principle of Artificial Intelligence.
- They have the ability to understand natural languages like English, Malayalam, etc. it can converse with human beings.
- Computer languages such as LISP, PROLOG, C, C++, etc., are available to program such computers.
- The goal of fifth generation computing is to develop computer that are capable of learning and self-organisation. The fifth generation computer use Super Large Scale Integrated (SLSI) chips that are able to store millions of components on a single chip. These computer have large memory requirements.

Fig. 1.6: 5th generation computer

Advantages:
(i) More smaller and handy than computer of fourth generation, allowing user to use the computing facility even while travelling.
(ii) Very less power required.
(iii) No air-conditioning required.
(iv) Use for large scale organisations.
(v) Support standard HLL (High Level Language).
(vi) User friendly interface.
(vii) Faster in speed.
(viii) More reliable.
(ix) Easy for installation.
(x) Very short time required for manual assembly.
(xi) Support very high powerful applications (multimedia).

1.1.4 Types of Computers

- Computer can be classified based on their principles of operation or on their configuration.
- By configuration, we mean the size, speed of doing computation and storage capacity of a computer.

- Types of computer according to the principles of operation and configuration are shown in Fig. 1.7.

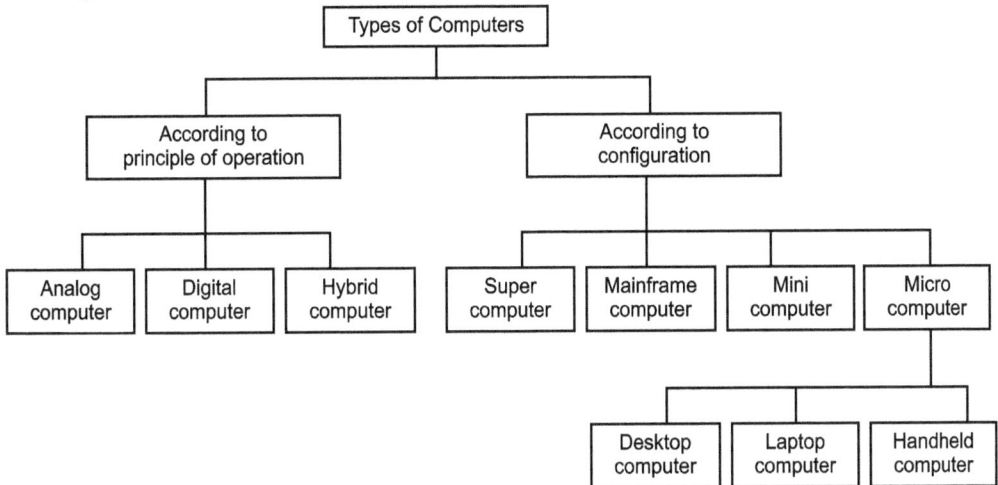

Fig. 1.7: Types of computers

1. **Analog Computers:**
- The earliest computer were analog computers. Analog computer is a computing device that works on continuous range of values. The results given by the analog computer will only be approximate since they deal with quantities that vary continuously.
- Analog computer generally deals with physical variables such as voltage, pressure, temperature, speed, etc.
- Analog computer are used for measuring parameter that vary continuously in real time, such as temperature, pressure and voltage.
- Analog computer may be more flexible but generally less precise than digital computers.
- Slide rule, Antikythera mechanism, astrolabe, differential analyzer, Deltar, Kerrison Predictor are the example of an analog computers.

Definition:
- An analog computer (spelled analogue) is a form of computer that uses electrical, mechanical or hydraulic phenomena to model the problem being solved.

OR

- Analog computer is a mechanical, electrical, or electronic computer that performs arithmetical operations by using some variable physical quantity, such as mechanical movement or voltage, to represent numbers.

Advantages:
  (i) Continuous representation of all data within the range of the machine.
  (ii) Fast and inexpensive when implemented with same technology as digital computer.
  (iii) Parallel and real-time operation many signal values can be computed simultaneously.
  (iv) Computation can be done for some applications without the requirement for transducer to convert the inputs/outputs to/from digital electronic form.

Disadvantages:

(i) Computation elements have a limited useful dynamic range, usually not much more than 120 dB, about 6 significant digits of accuracy.

(ii) Useful solution of problems of any size can take an inordinate amount of setup time.

(iii) For a given size (mass) and power consumption, digital computer can solve larger problems.

(iv) Solutions appear in real (or scaled) time, and may be difficult to record for later use or analysis.

(v) The range of useful time constants is limited. Problems that have components operating on vastly different time scales are difficult to deal with accuracy.

2. Digital Computers:

- A digital computer uses distinct values to represent the data internally. All information are represented using the digits 0s and 1s.
- The computer that we use at our homes and offices are digital computers.
- The digital computer is designed using digital circuits in which there are two levels for an input or output signal. These two levels are known as logic 0 and logic 1. Digital computer can give more accurate and faster results.
- Digital computer is well suited for solving complex problems in engineering and technology. Hence digital computer have an increasing use in the field of design, research and data processing.
- UNIVAC, IBM-360 and other mainframe computer are examples of digital computers.

Definition:

- A computer that performs calculations and logical operations with quantities represented as digits, usually in the binary number system.

OR

- Digital computer is an electronic computer in which the input is discrete rather than continuous, consisting of combinations of numbers, letters, and other character written in an appropriate programming language and represented internally in binary notation.

Advantages:

(i) Greater flexibility and precision.

(ii) It can store large amount of facts, instructions, and information.

Disadvantage:

(i) Its higher cost and complexity.

Difference between Digital and Analog Computers:

Terms	Digital computers	Analog computers
1. Definition	A computer that performs calculations and logical operations with quantities represented as digits, usually in the binary number system (0's and 1's).	Analog computer is a mechanical, electrical, or electronic computer that performs arithmetical operations by using some variable physical quantity, such as mechanical movement or voltage, to represent numbers.
2. Computing power	Digital computers, however, are not limited specific types of applications, but have a more general purpose in terms of usage.	Analog computer are limited to performing restrictive and specialized mathematical calculations such as the measurement and analysis of electrical voltages.
3. Output	Digital computer produce number as output. The computer uses display screens, printers, disc drives and other peripherals to capture this output.	Analog computer output voltage signals, and has sets of analog meter and oscilloscopes to display the voltages.
4. Electronic circuits	Digital computer use a variety of on-off switching circuits, such as microprocessors, clock pulse generator and logic gates.	Analog computer circuits use op-amps, signal generator and networks of resistor and capacitors. These circuits process continuous voltage signals.
5. Discrete versus Continuous signals	Digital signals have two discrete states, on or off. The off state is usually zero volts, and the on state is typically five volts.	Analog signals are continuous. They may have any value between two extremes, such as -15 and +15 volts. An analog signal's voltage may be constant or vary with time.
6. Size	Digital computer range from tiny microchips a few millimeter square to room-sized server installations.	Analog computer vary in size from small desktop systems the size of a large book to tall racks laden with equipment.
7. Data storage	The numeric, discrete nature of digital computer makes data storage simple. A memory circuit copies and retains the discrete states of another circuit.	For analog computers, storing data is more difficult, as they use continuous signals. A circuit that stores an analog signal is prone to drift over time.
8. Speed and Accuracy	Digital computer can give more accurate and faster results.	Analogue computer can give less accurate and slow results.
9. Cost	Cost is high.	Cost is low.

3. Hybrid Computers:

- A hybrid computer combines the desirable features of analog and digital computers.
- Hybrid computer is mostly used for automatic operations of complicated physical processes and machines.
- Now-a-days analog-to-digital and digital-to-analog converter are used for transforming the data into suitable form for either type of computation.

Definition:

- Hybrid computer is a computer that combines the characteristics of a digital computer and an analog computer by its capacity to accept input and provide output in either digital or analog form and to process information digitally.

OR

- Hybrid computer as the name suggests are a hybrid of analog and digital computers. The analog part of the hybrid computer computes higher mathematical calculations such as differential equations while the digital part takes care of the logical computation and also controls the overall process.

Advantages:

(i) Hybrid computer have tremendous computing speed enabled by the all-parallel configuration provided by the analog subsystem.

(ii) The results provided by hybrid computer are precise, accurate, more detailed and much more useful when compared to their earlier counterparts.

Uses:

(i) One of the most widespread uses of hybrid computer is in automated assembly lines. In radar and sonar applications, signals are received in the analog form and often need to be analyzed instantaneously so that the next signal can be interpreted.

(ii) Other entities that use hybrid computer include the military and defense organisations of all the countries and some research labs. These military devices are a form of hybrid computer since they process analog signals with digital logical circuits.

(I) Super Computers:

- Super computer are one of the fastest computer currently available.
- Super computer are very expensive and are employed for specialized applications that require immense amounts of mathematical calculations (number crunching), like weather forecasting, scientific simulations, (animated) graphics, analysis of geological data etc.
- They are the best in terms of processing capacity and also the most expensive ones. These computer can process billions of instructions per second.
- Perhaps the best known super computer manufacturer is Cray Research. Some of the traditional companies which produce super computer are Cray, IBM and Hewlett-Packard.
- As of July 2009, the IBM Roadrunner, located at Los Alamos National Laboratory, is the fastest super computer in the world.

Fig. 1.8: Super computer

Advantages:
1. Super computer can solve bigger problems.
2. Run more problems in shorter time i.e. they are very fast.
3. They have very high storage capacity.

Disadvantages:
1. They require very high power.
2. Takes up a lot of space i.e. they are larger in size.
3. May only be good for specific applications.
4. They are more costly.
5. Maintenance cost is very high.
6. Difficult to assembly.
7. Air-conditioning is required.

Applications of Super computers:
1. The machine can be used in both scientific and business applications, but used mainly in scientific applications. Few large multinational banks and corporations are using small super computers.
2. Applications of super computer includes, special effects in film, collecting and processing of weather data, processing of geological data, processing of data regarding genetic decoding, aerospace (aerodynamics and structural designing), simulation, and mass destruction weapons.
3. The user include Film makers, National weather forecasting agencies, Geological data processing agencies, Genetics research organisations, Space agencies, Government agencies, Scientific laboratories, Research groups, Military and defence systems, Large time-sharing network, and Large corporations.

(II) Mainframe Computers:
- Mainframe computers, created in the early 1940s, initially were bulky machines that required cooling-sensitive rooms.
- Mainframe computer can also process data at very high speeds i.e., hundreds of million instructions per second and they are also quite expensive.
- Normally, they are used in banking, airlines and railways etc. for their applications.

- Mainframe is a very large in size and is an expensive computer capable of supporting hundreds, or even thousands, of user simultaneously.
- Mainframe executes many programs concurrently. Mainframes support many simultaneous programs execution.
- Examples of mainframe computer are DEC-1090, IBM 308-580 series, IBM 4300, ICIM 2904, etc.

Characteristics of mainframe computers:
1. Ability to run multiple operating systems.
2. Mainframes can add system capacity non disruptively and granularly.
3. Mainframes are designed to handle very high volume input and output (I/O) and emphasize throughput computing.
4. Mainframe Return On Investment (ROI), like any other computing platform, is dependent on its ability to scale, support mixed workloads, reduce labor costs, deliver uninterrupted service for critical business applications, and several other risk-adjusted cost factors.
5. Mainframes also have execution integrity characteristics for fault tolerant computing.

Fig. 1.9: Mainframe computer

Advantages:
1. Huge memory.
2. High speed compared to volume of data.
3. No virus attack so far reported in last 50-60 years.
4. Superb virtualization.
5. Huge data processing.

Disadvantages:
1. Cost of hardware is high.
2. Special operating systems/software require so higher cost.
3. Intense human attention required.
4. Intense space occupied.
5. More resource consumption.

Applications of mainframe computers:
1. Both e-business and e-commerce use mainframe computer to perform business functions and exchange money over the internet.

2. The military one of the first user of mainframe computer continues employing this technology in combat and for keeping the country's border secure. All branches of the armed forces use mainframes for communication among ships, planes and land; for prediction of weather patterns; and for tracking strategic locations and positions using a Global Positioning System (GPS).
3. Satellites that were once a science fiction fantasy continue to operate mainframe computer in their intelligence and spying efforts.
4. Public and private libraries, as well as colleges and universities, use mainframe computer for storage of critical data.

(III) Mini Computers:
- Mini computer are computer that are somewhere, in between a micro computer and a mainframe computer.
- Mini computer are lower to mainframe computer in terms of speed and storage capacity.
- They are also less expensive than mainframe computers. Some of the features of mainframes will not be available in mini computers. Hence, their performance also will be less than that of mainframes.
- Mini computer is a class of multi-user computer that lies in the middle range of computing spectrum, in between mainframe computer and micro computer.
- Mini computer are designed for single user.
- Examples of mini computer are Control Data's CDC 160A and CDC 1700, DEC PDP and VAX series, Data General Nova, Hewlett-Packard HP3000 series, Honeywell-Bull Level 6/DPS 6/DPS 6000 series, IBM midrange computers.

Characteristics of mini computers:
1. Small in size and require small space.
2. More reliable and less power required.
3. Faster in speed.
4. Larger primary and secondary storage capacity.
5. Use for scientific and commercial use.
6. Standardization of high level language.

Fig. 1.10: Mini computer

Advantages:
1. They are faster and powerful than other computers.
2. Smaller in size.
3. Less power required.
4. Larger storage capacity.
5. Support high level language.
6. More reliable.
7. Support both scientific and commercial applications.
8. Support standardized high level languages.
9. Supports time sharing concept.

Disadvantages:
1. Air-conditioning required.
2. Cost is more than micro computer.

Applications of Minicomputers:
1. Mini computer were often used in manufacturing sector for process control. A mini computer used for process control has two primary functions. The first function of a process control minicomputer is data acquisition. The second function of a process control minicomputer is feedback, or, controlling a process.
2. Mini computer used for data management can be employed to acquire data, as in process control, generate data, or simply as a storage system for information.
3. Mini computer can be used as a communications tool in a larger system.

(IV) Micro Computers:
- The invention of microprocessor (single chip CPU) gave birth to the much cheaper micro computers.
- Micro computer are also known as Personal Computer (PC).
- A PC can be defined as a small, relatively inexpensive computer designed for an individual user. PCs are based on the microprocessor technology that enables manufacturer to put an entire CPU on one chip.
- Businesses use personal computer for word processing, accounting, desktop publishing, and for running spreadsheet and database management applications. At home, the most popular use for personal computer is for playing games and surfing the internet.
- Some examples of micro computer are HP 9100 A, Altair 8800 etc.
- Microcomputer is the term coined in the 1970s for a personal computer. Until that point, computer had been bulky room-sized electronics; even the smallest models were the size of large cars.
- The microcomputer has many uses, especially in the home, in business and in the medical field.

Characteristics of micro computers:
1. Support Graphical User Interface (GUI).
2. Speed is faster and larger storage capacity.
3. More powerful.
4. Smaller in size and cheaper.
5. Uses standard high level programming.
6. Use for office and homes.
7. Less power required.

Types of Micro Computers:

(i) Desktop Computers:
- Today the Desktop computer are the most popular computer systems.
- The desktop computer are also known as personal computer or simply PCs.
- They are usually easier to use and more affordable. They are normally intended for individual user for their word processing and other small application requirements.

Fig. 1.11: Desktop computer

(ii) Laptop Computers:
- Laptop computer are portable computers.
- They are lightweight computer with a thin screen. They are also called as notebook computer because of their small size.
- They can operate on batteries and hence are very popular with travellers. The screen folds down onto the keyboard when not in use.

Fig. 1.12: Laptop computer

(iii) Handheld Computers:
- Handheld computer or Personal Digital Assistants (PDAs) are pen-based and also battery-powered.
- They are small and can be carried anywhere. They use a pen like stylus and accept handwritten input directly on the screen.

- They are not as powerful as desktops or laptops but they are used for scheduling appointments, storing addresses and playing games.
- They have touch screens which we use with a finger or a stylus to be operated by user.

Fig. 1.13: Handheld computer

Advantages:
1. Smaller in size.
2. Cheaper.
3. More powerful and easy for installation.
4. Air-conditioning not required.
5. Faster in speed.
6. Larger primary and secondary storage.
7. Sharing resources in networking.
8. Does not require manual assembly.
9. More reliable and less hardware failure.

Disadvantages:
1. Non-portable.
2. Single user oriented.
3. More maintenance.

Applications of Micro computers:
1. Families use microcomputer for education; software can hold thousands of book volumes worth of information. Also, the first portable video games were built for the microcomputers. The home microcomputer paved the way for the invention of laptops.
2. Businesses took a huge leap forward in book-keeping, inventory and communication when microcomputer were made readily available.
3. The first microcomputer was built specifically for storing medical records. Before microcomputer were available, medical records were stored in paper form.

General Purpose and Special Purpose Computers:
- General purpose computer are designed to solve a large variety of problems. That is they can be given different program to solve different types of problems.
- General purpose computer can process business data as readily as they process complex mathematical formulas.
- General purpose computer can store large amount of data and the programmes necessary to process them. Because general purpose computer are so versatile, most businesses today use them.
- Special purpose computer are often used as training simulators.

- A simulator is a computer-controlled device for training people under simulated, or artificially created, conditions.
- The computer creates test conditions the trainee must respond to it then records and evaluates the responses, providing these results to both trainee and supervisor.
- Special purpose computer are simpler and cheaper than general purpose computer but have more limited logical and computational capabilities.

Difference between a Micro computer and a Mini computer:

Micro computer	Mini computer
1. A micro computer is a standard desktop computer used at a home and in business.	1. Mini computer are mid-sized computer used in universities, research labs and small corporations.
2. A micro computer is a computer with a microprocessor as its CPU.	2. Mini computer are faster than micro-computers.
3. They are cheap, compact and can be easily accommodated on a study table.	3. They are expensive and larger than microcomputer.
4. Microcomputer is a single-user computer.	4. Minicomputer is a multi-user computer.
5. The two most common types of storage devices used with microcomputer are tapes and disks.	5. For secondary storage, most minicomputer use magnetic disks or tapes.
6. Micro computer is not powerful or as fast as minicomputer.	6. Mini computer is powerful than microcomputer but not as super computer and mainframe computer.
7. Examples are: Modern computers like desktop, laptop etc.	7. Examples are: IBM 9375, Motorola 68040 etc.

Comparison between a Mainframe and Super computers:

Mainframe computer	Super computer
1. Low speed than super computer.	1. Very high speed computers. It can process trillions of instructions in one second.
2. Low storage capacity.	2. High storage capacity.
3. A Mainframe computer is a large computer that is used in large companies like insurance companies or the government.	3. A super computer is the largest computer with extremely high speed. Companies like Nasa use super computers.
4. Cost is low.	4. Cost is very high.
5. Examples: (i) IBM4381 (ii) NEC 610 (iii) DEC 10 etc.	5. Examples: (i) CRAY-XP (ii) ETA-10 etc.

1.1.5 Advantages of Computers

- Following list demonstrates the advantages of computer in today's arena:
    1. **High Speed:** Computer is a very fast device. It can perform millions of calculations in few seconds as compared to man who can spend many months for doing the same task.
    2. **Accuracy:** Computer are very accurate. The computer can perform calculations 100% error free.
    3. **Storage Capability:** Computer can store large amount of data using memory. Computer can store any type of data such as images, videos, text, audio and any other type.
    4. **Versatility:** A computer is a very versatile machine. Computer machine can be used to solve the problems relating to various different fields.
    5. **Automation:** Automation means ability to perform the task automatically. Computer is a automatic machine. Once, a program (instruction) is given to computer i.e. stored in computer memory, the program and instruction can control the program execution without human interaction.
    6. **Diligence:** Unlike human beings, a computer is free from monotony, tiredness and lack of concentration. Computer can work continuously without creating any error and boredom and it can do repeated work with same speed and accuracy.
    7. **Reliability:** A computer is a reliable machine and modern electronic components have failure free long lives. Computer are designed to make maintenance easy and simple.
    8. **Reduction in Cost:** Though the initial investment for installing a computer is high but it substantially reduces the cost of each of its transaction.
    9. **Reduction in Paper Work:** The use of computer for data processing in an organisation leads to reduction in paper work and speeds up the process.

1.1.6 Disadvantages of Computers

- Various disadvantage of computers are listed below:
    1. **No intelligence:** A computer is a machine and has no intelligence of its own to perform any task. Each and every instruction has to be given to computer. A computer can not take any decision on its own.
    2. **Environment:** The operating environment of computer should be dust free and suitable to it.
    3. **No feeling:** Computer has no feeling or emotions.
    4. **Dependency:** Computer can perform function as instructed by user, so it is fully dependent on human being. Computer cannot make Judgment based on feeling, taste, experience and knowledge unlike a human being.
    5. **Violation of Privacy:** It is crucial that personal and confidential records stored in computers be protected properly.

6. **Health Risks:** Prolonged or improper computer use can lead to disorders. Computer user can protect themselves from health risks through proper workplace design, good posture while at the computer and appropriately spaced work breaks.
7. **Impact on the Environment:** Computer manufacturing processes and computer waste are depleting natural resources and polluting the environment.

1.1.7 Computer Applications

- Various application of computer in various fields are listed below:

1. **Banking:**
- Today Banking is almost totally dependent on computer.
- Banks provide following facilities:
    (i) Banks, on-line accounting facility, which include current balances, deposits, overdrafts, interest charges, shares and trustee records.
    (ii) ATM machines are making it even easier for customer to deal with banks.

2. **Business:**
- Computer used in business organisation for payroll calculations, budgeting, sales analysis, financial forecasting, managing employees database and maintenance of stocks etc.

3. **Education:**
- The computer has provided a lot of facilities in the education system.
- The uses of computer provide a tool in the Education system is known as CBE (Computer Based Education).

4. **Marketing:**
- In Marketing uses of computer are following:
    (i) **Home Shopping:** Home shopping has been made possible through use of computerised catalogs that provide access to product information and permit direct entry of order to be filled by the customers.
    (ii) **Advertising:** With computers, advertising professionals create art and graphics, write and revise copy, and print and disseminate ads with the goal of selling more products.

5. **Insurance:**
- Insurance companies are keeping all records up to date with the help of computer.
- The insurance companies, finance houses and stock broking firms are widely using computer for their concerns.
- Insurance companies are maintaining a database of all clients with information showing how to continue with policies, starting date of the policies, next due installment of a policy, maturity date, interests due, survival benefits bonus and so on.

6. **Communication:**
   - Communication means to convey a message, an idea, a picture or speech that is received and understood clearly and correctly by the person for whom it is meant.
   - Some main areas in this category are: E-mail, Chatting, Usenet, FTP, Telnet, Video-conferencing and so on.

7. **Health Care:**
   - The computer are being used in hospitals to keep the record of patients and medicines. It is also used in scanning and diagnosing different diseases.
   - ECG, EEG, Ultrasounds and CT Scans etc. are also done by computerised machines. Some of major fields of health care in which computer are used:
     (i) **Pharma Information System:** Computer checks Drug-Labels, expiry dates, harmful drug side effects etc.
     (ii) **Diagnostic System:** Computer are used to collect data and identify cause of illness.
     (iii) **Patient Monitoring System:** These are used to check patient's signs for abnormality such as in cardiac arrest, ECG etc.
     (iv) Now-a-days, computer are also used in **performing surgery**.
     (v) **Lab-diagnostic System:** All tests can be done and reports are prepared by computer.

8. **Military:**
   - Computer are largely used in defence. Modern tanks, missiles, weapons etc. employ computerized control systems.
   - Some military areas where a computer has been used are: missile control, military communication, military operation and planning, smart weapons and so on.

9. **Government Applications:**
   - Computer play an important role in government applications.
   - Some major fields in this category are: budgets, sales tax department, income tax department, male/female ratio, computerization of voter lists, computerization of driving licensing system, computerization of pan card, weather forecasting and so on.

10. **Engineering Design:**
    - Computer are widely used in Engineering purposes. Some fields are:
      (i) **Industrial Engineering:** Computer deals with design, implementation and improvement of integrated systems of people, materials and equipments.
      (ii) **Architectural Engineering:** Computer help in planning towns, designing buildings, determining a range of buildings on a site using both 2D and 3D drawings.
      (iii) **Structural Engineering:** Requires stress and strain analysis required for design of ships, buildings, budgets, airplanes etc.

1.2 Characteristics of Computers

- The main characteristics (capabilities) of computer, which makes them powerful and useful are:
    1. **Automation:** Computer has automation power that means computer can perform the task automatically by using programs.
    2. **Speed:** Computer are of high speed in its operation. The speed is measured in terms of Instructions Per Second (IPS). All modern computer can process information at a speed of a couple of Million Instructions Per Second (MIPS).
    3. **Accuracy:** Computer are highly accurate in its operations. They either give correct answer or do not answer at all. Error can occur in computer but these are mainly due to human rather than technological weakness.
    4. **Reliability:** It is the ability of a computer to perform the same job exactly in the same way in any number of times.
    5. **Versatility:** A computer is capable of performing almost any task provided that the task can be reduced to a series of logical steps.
    6. **Integrity:** It is the ability of a computer to carry out a sequence of instructions.
    7. **No feelings:** Computer are devoid of emotions. They have no feeling because they are machines.
    8. **Diligence continuity:** A computer is free from monotony, tiredness, lack of concentration, etc. It can work for hour without creating any error.
    9. **Power of remembering:** Computer can store and recall any amount of information because of its storage capability.

1.3 Block Diagram of Computer

- Fig. 1.14 shows block diagram of a computer.

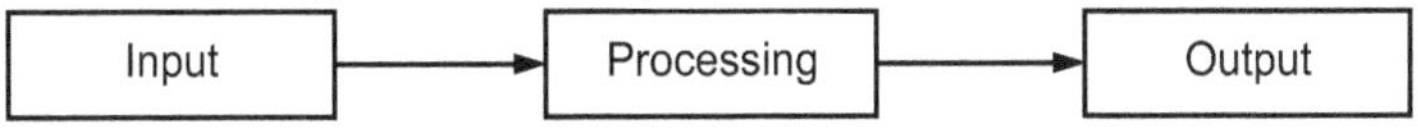

Input → Processing → Output

(a)

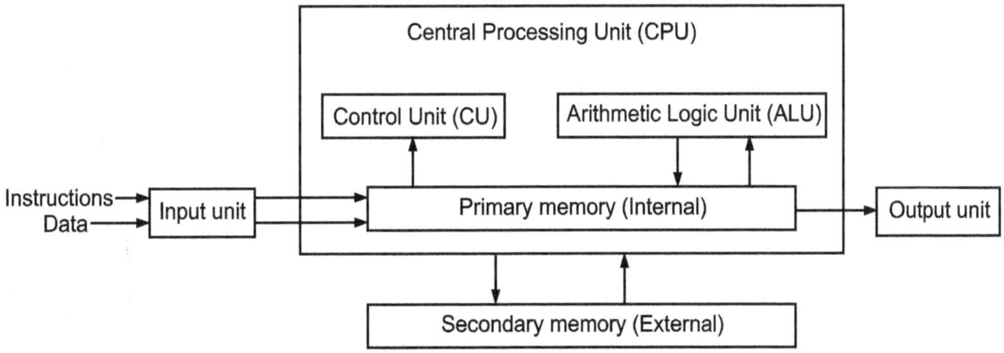

Central Processing Unit (CPU): Control Unit (CU), Arithmetic Logic Unit (ALU)

Instructions, Data → Input unit → Primary memory (Internal) → Output unit

Secondary memory (External)

(b) Block diagram of a computer

Fig. 1.14

- Various parts of computer are described below:

1. **Input Unit:**
- Input unit contains devices with the help of which we enter data into computer. This unit makes link between user and computer.
- The input devices translate the human readable information into the form understandable by computer.
- Some important input devices which are used in computer systems are: keyboard, mouse, joystick, light pen, track ball, scanner, graphic tablet, microphone, Magnetic Ink Card Reader (MICR), Optical Character Reader (OCR), bar code reader, optical mark reader (OMR).
- An input device performs the following functions:
  (i) It accepts (i.e. reads) the list of instruction and data from the user.
  (ii) It converts these instructions and data in binary form which is understood by the computer.
  (iii) It supplies the converted instructions and data to the computer for further processing.

2. **CPU:**
- The task of performing operations like arithmetic and logical operations is called processing.
- The Central Processing Unit (CPU) takes data and instructions from the storage unit and makes all sorts of calculations based on the instructions given and the type of data provided. It is then sent back to the storage unit.
- Central Processing Unit (CPU) is the heart of every computer system that performs the user instructions.
- The CPU is like brain performs the following functions:
  (i) It performs all calculations.
  (ii) It takes all decisions.
  (iii) It controls all units of the computer.
- CPU itself has following three components:

1. **Arithmetic Logical Unit (ALU):**
   After we enter data through the input device it is stored in the primary storage unit. The actual processing of the data and instruction are performed by Arithmetic Logical Unit (ALU). The major operations performed by the ALU is addition, subtraction, multiplication, division, logic and comparison. Data is transferred to ALU from storage unit when required. After processing the output is returned back to storage unit for further processing or getting stored. This unit consists of two subsection namely:

   (a) Arithmetic section: Function of arithmetic section is to perform arithmetic operations like addition, subtraction, multiplication and division. All complex operations are done by making repetitive use of above operations.

   (b) Logic Section: Function of logic section is to perform logic operations such as comparing, selecting, matching and merging of data.

Functions of ALU:
   (i) All calculations are performed in the Arithmetic Logic Unit (ALU) of the computer. The ALU can perform basic operations such as addition, subtraction, multiplication, division, etc and does logic operations viz, >, <, =, 'etc.
   (ii) It also supplies or gives out the information and results for computation to the outside world.

2. **Control Unit (CU):**

   It controls all other units in the computer. The control unit instructs the input unit, where to store the data after receiving it from the user. It controls the flow of data and instructions from the storage unit to ALU. It also controls the flow of results from the ALU to the storage unit. The control unit is generally referred as the central nervous system of the computer that control and synchronizes its working.

   The main function of control unit is to control all operations like input, processing, output etc. Control Unit (CU) acts as the supervisor seeing that things are done in proper fashion. Control Unit is responsible for coordinating various operations using time signal. The control unit determines the sequence in which computer programs and instructions are executed. Things like processing of programs stored in the main memory, interpretation of the instructions and issuing of signals for other units of the computer to execute them. It also acts as a switch board operator when several user access the computer simultaneously. Thereby it coordinates the activities of computer's peripheral equipments as they perform the input and output.

   Control unit controls the operations of all parts of computer. It does not carry out any actual data processing operations.

   Functions of control unit are:
   (i)   It is responsible for controlling the transfer of data and instructions among other units of a computer.
   (ii) It manages and coordinates all the units of the computer.
   (iii) It does not process or store data.
   (iv) It obtains the instructions from the memory, interprets them and directs the operation of the computer.
   (v)   It communicates with Input/Output (I/O) devices for transfer of data or results from storage.

3. **Memory or Storage Unit:**
   - Memory unit can store instruction, data and intermediate results. This unit supplies information to the other units of the computer when needed.
   - It is also known as internal storage unit or main memory or primary storage or Random Access Memory (RAM).
   - Its size affects speed, power and capability. There are two types of memories in the computer namely primary memory and secondary memory.

- **Function of memory unit** are:
  (i) It stores all the data to be processed and the instructions required for processing.
  (ii) It stores intermediate results of processing.
  (iii) It stores final results of processing before these results are released to an output device.
  (iv) All inputs and outputs are transmitted through main memory.

4. **Secondary Memory (Storage):**
- To supplement the limited storage capacity of the primary storage section, most computer have secondary storage capabilities.
- These devices are connected directly to the processor which accept data/program instructions for the processor, retain them, and then write them back to the processor as needed to complete the processing tasks.
- Magnetic tape, disks are the examples of secondary storage.

5. **Output Unit:**
- Output is the process of producing results from the data for getting useful information. Similarly the output produced by the computer after processing must also be kept somewhere inside the computer before being given to you in human readable form. Again the output is also stored inside the computer for further processing. The result of computer processing is called as output. This result is communicated to user through a device called output devices.
- Output unit consists of devices with the help of which we get the information from computer. This unit is a link between computer and users.
- Output devices translate the computer's output into the human readable form.
- Few of the important output devices which are used in computer systems are: Monitors, Graphic plotter, Printer etc.
- The following **functions are performed by an output** unit:
  (i) It accepts results produced by the computer which are in binary coded form and hence cannot be understood by user.
  (ii) It converts these coded results to human readable form.
  (iii) It supplies the converted form to the user.

1.4 Booting Process

- Booting (also known as booting up) is the initial set of operations that a computer system performs when electrical power to the CPU is switched ON.

Booting Process:
- The process begins when a computer is turned ON for the first time or is re-energized after being turned OFF, and ends when the computer is ready to perform its normal operations.

- On modern general purpose computers, this can take tens of seconds and typically involves performing a power-on self-test, locating and initializing peripheral devices, and then finding, loading and starting an operating system.
- Many computer systems also allow these operations to be initiated by a software command without cycling power, in what is known as a soft reboot, though some of the initial operations might be skipped on a soft reboot.
- A boot loader is a computer program that loads the main operating system or runtime environment for the computer after completion of the self-tests.
- The computer term boot is short for bootstrap or bootstrap load and derives from the phrase to pull oneself up by one's bootstraps.
- The usage calls attention to the requirement that, if most software is loaded onto a computer by other software already running on the computer, some mechanism must exist to load initial software onto the computer.
- Early computers used a variety of ad-hoc methods to get a small program into memory to solve this problem. The invention of integrated circuit read-only memory (ROM) of various types solved this paradox by allowing computers to be shipped with a start up program that could not be erased. Growth in the capacity of ROM has allowed ever more elaborate start up procedures to be implemented.

Definition:
- Booting is a process or set of operations that loads and hence starts the operating system, starting from the point when user switches on the power button.

OR
- Booting process is bootstrapping process (to pull oneself up by bootstraps) that's starts operating systems whenever the user turns on or switch on the computer system.

OR
- When we start our computer then there is an operation which is performed automatically by the computer which is also called as booting. In the booting, system will check all the hardware's and software's those are installed or attached with the system and this will also load all the files those are needed for running a system.

Types of Booting:
- There are two types of booting i.e. warm and cold bootings.
    1. **Warm Booting:** When the system starts from the starting or from initial state means when we starts our system this is called as warm booting. in the warm booting the system will be started from its beginning state means first of all, the user will press the power button, then this will read all the instructions from the ROM and the operating system will be automatically gets loaded into the system.
    2. **Cold Booting :** The cold booting is that in which system automatically starts when we are running the system, for example due to light fluctuation the system will automatically restarts so that in this chances damaging of system are more and the system will no be start from its initial state so may some files will be damaged because they are not properly stored into the system.

1.5 Types of Programming Languages

- A language is a source of communication. With the help of computer language the programmer tells the computer what he/she wants it to do.
- Computer language has its own set of symbols, each symbol tell the computer to perform a specific task.
- Each and every problem solved by the computer has to be broken down into logical steps which has the following basic operations – Input data, Process data and Output data.
- A programming language is a computer language programmers use to develop applications, scripts, or other set of instructions for a computer to execute.
- Computer languages are classified into following categories:
  1. Machine language,
  2. Assembly language, and
  3. High-level language.

1.5.1 Machine Language

- The most elementary and first type of computer language, which was invented, was machine language.
- Sometimes machine language is referred to as machine code or object code. Machine language is a collection of binary digits or bits that the computer reads and interprets.
- Machine language is the only language a computer is capable of understanding.
- Machine language was machine dependent.
- A program written in machine language cannot be run on another type of computer without significant alterations. Machine language is sometimes also referred as the binary language i.e., the language of 0 and 1 where 0 stands for the absence of electric pulse and 1 stands for the presence of electric pulse.
- Machine languages are sometimes referred to as 1st generation programming languages.
- The popular binary coding systems ASCII and EBCDIC use 8-bits. The 'Unicode' is new system, uses 16-bits.
  1. **ASCII:** ASCII stands for "American Standard Code for Information Interchange". This binary coded system is widely used for microcomputers. The ASCII character set values are fixed to 0 to 9 numbers, A to Z and a to z alphabets and other symbols like +, – etc.
  2. **EBCDIC:** EBCDIC stands for "Extended Binary Coded Decimal Interchange Code". It is developed by IBM company for main frame computers.
  3. **UNICODE:** It is 16-bit binary coding system. It is designed for Chinese and Japanese languages. These languages use many symbols and 8-bits are not sufficient for all the symbols in it. Hence, apple corporation, IBM and Microsoft developed this Unicode by their combined efforts.

Advantages of Machine Language:
1. It makes fast and efficient use of the computer.
2. It requires no translator to translate the code that is directly understood by the computer.
3. The performance and efficiency of CPU increases if instructions are given in machine language.

Disadvantages of Machine Language:
1. All operation codes have to be remembered.
2. All memory addresses have to be remembered.
3. It is hard to amend or find errors in a program written in the machine language.
4. These languages are machine dependent i.e. a particular machine language can be used on only one type of computer.
5. Many days are required to complete the program coding so it is time consuming.

1.5.2 Assembly Language

- As computer became more popular, it became quite apparent that machine language programming was simply too slow, tedious for most programmers.
- Sometimes, assembly language referred to as assembly or ASL. Assembly language is a low-level programming language used to interface with computer hardware.
- Assembly language uses structured commands as substitutions for numbers allowing humans to read the code easier than looking at binary. Although easier to read than binary, assembly language is a difficult language and is usually substituted for a higher language such as C.
- Assembly languages are also called as low level language instead of using the string of members programmers began using English like abbreviation to represent the elementary operation. The language provided an opportunity to the programmers to use English like words that were called MNEMONICS.
- It is low level programming language in which the sequence of 0s and 1s are replaced by mnemonic (ni-monic) codes. Typical instruction for addition and subtraction.
  Example: ADD for addition, SUB for subtraction etc.
- Since, our system only understand the language of 0s and 1s, therefore a system program is known as assembler.

Advantages Assembly Language:
1. Easy to understand: As compared to the machine language it is easier to understand.
2. Easy to remove errors: Because of the codes use English alphabets, its easy to locate and correct errors in an assembly language program.
3. Easy to modify: As the program written in assembly language is easy to understand, it is easy to modify this program as compared to the machine language program.
4. It saves time and reduces work.

Disadvantages Assembly Language:
1. Like machine language it is also machine dependent.
2. Since, it is machine dependent, the programmer should have the knowledge of the hardware also.
3. Coding is time consuming.

1.5.3 High Level Language

- The syntax that means rules and words used are close to English language. The research in computing field developed new types of assembler and translators.
- Initially for one command of the source programme, one instruction of machine language was developed. The advance assemblers can write more lines of code in machine level language.
- The required set of instructions can be stored and used whenever requested for it. This facility is used in higher level languages which saves time.
- High level languages are the computer languages in which it is much easier to write a program than the low level language.
- A program written in high level language is just like giving instruction to person in daily life.
- A high-level language is an advanced computer programming language that isn't limited by the computer, designed for a specific job, and is easier to understand.
- Today, there are dozens of high-level languages; some examples include BASIC, C, FORTRAN, Java, and Pascal.

Advantages:
1. High level languages require less time to write.
2. High level languages use words and symbols like English language, hence it is easier to learn it as compared to assembly level language.
3. Language is machine independent but programming is for the problem, hence can be used on any computer.
4. The length of programme i.e. lines of code are less than the assembly language code, hence less time is required.
5. Maintenance is easier.
6. Documentation is good as compared to other languages.
7. Machine independent languages.

Disadvantages:
1. The language processors required for these languages are of bigger size as these languages use many words.
2. The internal memory required is more due to bigger size.
3. During compilation, more time is required to find a match for word from big list.

1.6 Data Organization

- A group of symbol used to express a value of characteristic of an object is called data. Data can be defined as "a representation of facts, concepts or instruction in a formalized manner which should be suitable for communication, interpretation or processing by human or electronic machine".
- Data is represented with the help of character like alphabets (A-Z,a-z), digits (0-9) or special characters(+,-,/,*,<,>,= etc).
- A data which has been processed and organized so that it can be used to draw meaningful conclusion is called information.
- Information is organised or classified data so that it has some meaningful values to the receiver.
- Example: 2225860 is a number data. When we say that it is a telephone number, then we get information from the data.

Difference between Data and Information:

Data	Information
1. It is the information which processing is done.	1. An organized fact is called information.
2. A data has neither fixed nor define meaning.	2. An information has not only fixed but also define meaning.
3. Data is similar to raw material.	3. Information is similar to finish goods.

Data Processing:

- Data processing is the re-structuring or re-ordering of data by people or machine to increase their usefulness and add values for particular purpose.
- Data processing is "a sequence of operations performed on data, especially by a computer, in order to extract information, reorder files, etc."
- Data processing may involve various processes, including:
  1. **Data validation:** Ensuring that supplied data is "clean, correct and useful."
  2. **Sorting:** "Arranging items in some sequence and/or in different sets."
  3. **Data aggregation:** Combining multiple pieces of data.
  4. **Statistical analysis:** The "collection, organization, analysis, interpretation and presentation of data".
  5. **Reporting:** List detail or summary data or computed information.

1.6.1 Drives

- A disk driver is a device driver that allows a specific disk drive to communicate with the remainder of the computer.
- It is a machine that reads data from and writes data onto a disk. A disk drive rotates the disk very fast and has one or more heads that read and write data.

- There are different types of disk drives for different types of disks.

1. Hard Disk Drive (HDD):
- The mechanism that reads and writes data on a hard disk. Hard disk drives (HDDs) for PCs generally have seek times of about 12 milliseconds or less. Many disk drives improve their performance through a technique called caching.
- There are several interface standards for passing data between a hard disk and a computer. The most common are IDE and SCSI.
- Hard disk drives are sometimes called Winchester drives, Winchester being the name of one of the first popular hard disk drive technologies developed by IBM in 1973.

2. Floppy Disk Drive (FDDs):
- A Floppy Disk Drive, or FDD or FD for short, is a computer disk drive that enables a user to save data to removable diskettes.
- Although 8" disk drives were first made available in 1971, the first real disk drives used were the $5^{1/4}$" floppy disk drives, which were later replaced with $3^{1/2}$" floppy disk drives.
- Today, because of the limited capacity and reliability of floppy diskettes many computer no longer come equipped with floppy disk drives and are being replaced with CD-R, other writable discs, and flash drives.

1.6.2 Files
- A file is a collection of related records. In other words, a file is a collection of data or information usually stored on disk.
- A record is a collection of data items arranged for processing by a program.
- The files can be viewed as logical files and physical files.
- Logical file is a very viewed in terms of what data items, its record contain and what processing operations may be performed upon the file. The user of the file will normally adopt such a view.
- Physical file is a file viewed in terms of how the data is stored on a storage device and how the processing operations are made possible.

1.6.2.1 Definition of File
- File is a structured collection of data i.e., a collection of related records.

OR

- We can define file as "A set of logically related records".

1.6.2.2 File Organisation
- File organisation refer to the way records are physically arranged on a storage device.
- The term "file organisation" refer to the way in which data is stored in a file and consequently the methods by which it can be accessed.
- File organisation refer to the relationship of the key of the record to the physical location of that record in the computer file.

Definition of File Organisation:
- File organisation refer to the way records are physically arranged on a storage device. File organisation refer to the arrangement of records within a database.

OR

- "File organisation" refer to the logical relationships among the various records that constitute the file, particularly with respect to the means of identification and access to any specific record. "File structure" refer to the format of the label and data blocks and of any logical record control information.
- File organisation may be either **physical file** or a **logical file**.
- A physical file is a physical unit, such as magnetic tape or a disk.
- A logical file on the other hand is a complete set of records for a specific application or purpose.
- A logical file may occupy a part of physical file or may extend over more than one physical files.
- **The objectives of computer based file organisation are:**
    1. Ease of file creation and maintenance
    2. Efficient means of storing and retrieving information.
- The organisation of a given file may be sequential, relative, or indexed.

1. **Sequential File Organisation:**
- In sequential file organisation, records are arranged sequentially.
- A sequential file is a file whose records can be accessed on the order of their appearance in the file.
- The order in which the records are stored is determined by the order in which they are written when the file was prepared. This order does not change. Records may be added at the end of file only.
- The records may be accessed in the order on which they were originally written into a file.
- A magnetic tape file, such as printer, can only have a sequential organisation.
- A sequentially organized file may be stored on either a serial–access or direct access storage medium.
- The task of file handling is the responsibility of the system software known as Input-Output Control System (IOCS). Block is used to group a number of consecutive records. IOCS takes care of blocking. IOCS reserves a memory space equal to the size of a block of the file.
- Sequential files may be recorded in variable-length of fixed-length record form. If a file consists of variable-length records, each logical record is preceded by control information that indicates the size of the logical record.

- If a file consists of fixed-length records, the record size is established at the time the file is opened and is the same for every logical record on the file. Therefore, there is no need to record any control information with the logical record.
- Sequential files are normally created and stored on magnetic tape using batch processing method.

Advantages:
   (i) Simple to understand and implement.
   (ii) Easy to maintain and organize.
   (iii) Loading a record requires only the record key.
   (iv) Relatively inexpensive I/O media and devices can be used.
   (v) Easy to reconstruct the files.
   (vi) The proportion of file records to be processed is high.

Disadvantages:
   (i) Entire file must be processed, to get specific information.
   (ii) Very low activity rate stored.
   (iii) Transactions must be stored and placed in sequence prior to processing.
   (iv) Data redundancy is high, as same data can be stored at different places with different keys.
   (v) Impossible to handle random enquiries.

Area of Use:
- Sequential files are most frequently used in commercial batch oriented data processing applications where there is the concept of a master file to which details are added periodically. Example: Payroll applications.

2. Index Sequential File Organisation:
- When there is need to access records sequentially by some key value and also to access records directly by the same key value, the collection of records may be organized in an effective manner called index sequential file organisation.
- In index sequential file organisation, the records are stored in the key sequence order usually in ascending order. Some index tables are also created and maintained with the file.
- Index table provide to identify the groups of records in the file. When an indexed file is accessed randomly, the programmer control the sequence on which the records are accessed by specifying the value of a data item called record key.
- When the new records are inserted in the data file, the sequence of records needs to be preserved and also the index is accordingly updated.

Advantages:
   (i) In indexed sequential file organisation, the item in the table can be examined sequentially if all the records in the file must be accessed.
   (ii) Indexed sequential file organisation is very useful when a random access or records by specifying the key is required.
   (iii) Updating is easily accommodated.
   (iv) Random access is possible.

Area of Use:
- Index sequential file organisation support applications that selectively access individual records rather than searching through the entire collection in sequence.
- Example: Train Enquiry System, Reservation Enquiry System and so on.

3. Direct/Random/Relative File Organisation:
- In direct access file organisation, records are placed randomly throughout the file.
- Records need not be in sequence because they are updated directly and rewritten back in the same location.
- New records are added at the end of the file or inserted in specific locations based on software commands.
- Records are accessed by addresses that specify their disk locations. An address is required for locating a record, for linking records, or for establishing relationships.
- Addresses are of two types:
   - **(i) An absolute address** represents the physical location of the record. It is usually stated in the format of sector/track/record number. One problem with absolute address is that they become invalid when the file that contains the records is relocated on the disk.
   - **(ii) A relative address** gives a record location relative to the beginning of the file. There must be fixed length records for reference. Another way of locating a record is by the number of bytes it is from the beginning of the file. When the file is moved, pointer need not be updated because the relative location remains the same.

Advantages:
   (i) Records can be immediately accessed for updation.
   (ii) Several files can be simultaneously updated during transaction processing.
   (iii) Transaction need not be sorted.
   (iv) Existing records can be amended or modified.
   (v) Very easy to handle random enquiries.
   (vi) Most suitable for interactive online applications.

Disadvantages:
   (i) Data may be accidentally erased or over written unless special precautions are taken.
   (ii) Risk of loss of accuracy and breach of security. Special backup and reconstruction procedures must be established.
   (iii) Less efficient use of storage space.
   (iv) Expensive hardware and software are required.
   (v) High complexity in programming.
   (vi) File updation is more difficult when compared to that of sequential method.

Area of Use:
- Relative (Random/Direct) file organisation is used where the records of a file are updated for a number of times during a working day. Price list can be a file, which is to be constantly interrogated during a billing run.

4. **Indexed Files:**
- An indexed file, which must be allocated in the execution activity to two or more random mass storage files (one for the index, and one or more for the data) is organized such that each record is uniquely identified by the value of key within the record.
- An index is a data structure that organizes data records on disk to optimize certain file operations. An index allows us to efficiently search or retrieve all records. Using an index, we can achieve a fast search of data records.
- In order to create and maintain index files a computer create a data file and an index file. The data file contains the actual contents (data) of the record and index file contains the index entries. The one field in a file is the primary key, which identifies a record uniquely.
- Files are organized in the following ways:
    (i) The data file is stored in the order of the primary key values.
    (ii) The index file contains two fields: the key value and the pointer to the data record.
    (iii) One record in the index file thus, consists of a key value and a pointer to the corresponding data record. The pointer points to the first entry within the range of data records.

Example:

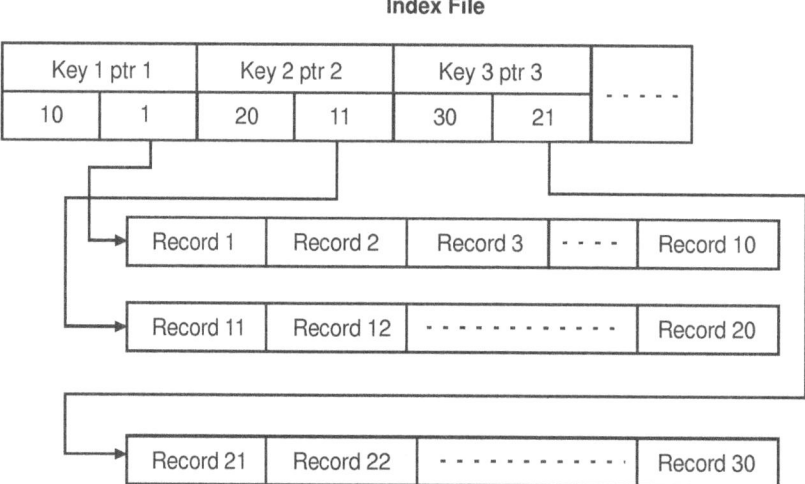

Fig. 1.15: Index file organisation

- Generally, the key value is the largest primary key value in a given range of records.
- In the Fig. 1.15, the first index entry is 10, which is highest primary key value in the first data block of 1 to 10. The pointer from this index entry points to the start of this range i.e. 1.

- There are several types of ordered indexes:
  1. **Primary Index:** A primary index is an index specified on the ordering key field of an ordered records. Every record has unique value for that field.
  2. **Clustering Index:** If the ordering field is not a key field i.e. if several records in the file can have the same value for the ordering field then a clustering index can be used. Notice that, a file can have atmost one physical ordering field, so it can have at most one primary index or one clustering index, but not both.
  3. **Secondary Index:** The third type of index, called a secondary index, can be specified on any non-ordering field of a file. A file can have several secondary indexes in addition to its primary access method.

1.6.3 Directories

- Files contain text or data. Directories contain files. Directories should be organized in hierarchical manner.
- A directory is a named group of related files that are separated by the naming convention from other groups of files.
- A directory is file system cataloging structure in which references to other computer files, and possibly other directories, are kept.
- Consequently we can identify:
  1. Parent directories, and
  2. Child directories.
- Top most directory is the root directory. The directory you are in is you current directory.
- When you log in the OS places you in your home directory (usually a child of the directory users).

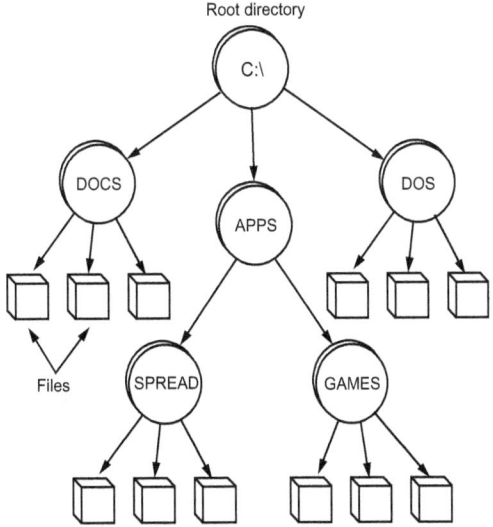

Fig. 1.16: Directory structure

- Directories contain bookkeeping information about files that are, figuratively speaking, beneath them in the hierarchy. You can think of a directory as a file cabinet that contains folder that contain files. Many graphical user interfaces use the term folder instead of directory.

- Computer manuals often describe directories and file structures in terms of an inverted tree. The files and directories at any level are contained in the directory above them. To access a file, you may need to specify the names of all the directories above it. You do this by specifying a path.
- The topmost directory in any file is called the root directory. A directory that is below another directory is called a subdirectory. A directory above a subdirectory is called the parent directory. Under DOS and Windows, the root directory is a back slash (\).
- To read information from, or write information into, a directory, you must use an operating system command. You cannot directly edit directory files.
- For example, the DIR command in DOS reads a directory file and displays its contents.

1.7 Storage Devices

- Computer memory or storage is any physical device capable of storing information temporarily or permanently.
- Computer data storage, often called storage or memory, is a technology consisting of computer components and recording media used to retain digital data.
- Memory refer to the physical devices used to store programs (sequences of instructions) or data (e.g. program state information) on a temporary or permanent basis for use in a computer or other digital electronic device.
- The main function of memory is to store the information or data.
- There are two types of memories:
    1. **Volatile memory** is a type of memory (storage) whose contents are erased when the system's power is turned off or interrupted.
    2. **Non-volatile memory** is any memory or storage that will be saved regardless if the power to the computer is on or off.

Comparison between Volatile and Non-volatile memories:

Volatile Memories	Non-volatile Memories
1. Information stored is lost when power is switched OFF.	1. Information stored is retained even after power is switched OFF.
2. All RAMs are volatile memories.	2. ROMs, EPROMS are non-volatile memories.
3. Stored information is retained as long as power is ON.	3. No effect of power, on stored information.
4. Used for temporary storage of information.	4. Used for permanent storage of information.

- Fig. 1.17 shows classification of memories.

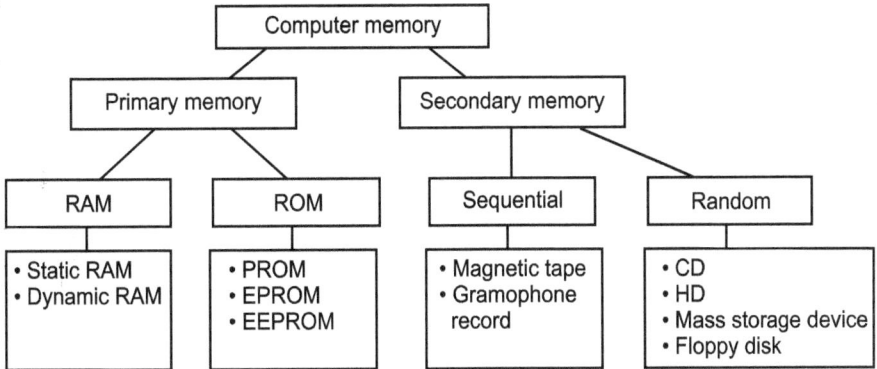

Fig. 1.17: Classification of computer memories

1.7.1 Primary Memory

- Primary memory (primary storage or main memory or internal memory), often referred to simply as memory, is the only one, directly accessible to the CPU.
- The CPU continuously reads instructions stored there and executes them as required.
- Any data actively operated on is also stored there in uniform manner.
- Primary memory holds only those data and instructions on which computer is currently working. It has limited capacity and data get lost when power is switched off.
- It is generally made up of semiconductor device. These memories are not as fast as registers. The data and instruction required to be processed earlier reside in main memory.
- Primary memory is divided into two subcategories RAM and ROM.

Characteristic of main (Primary) memory:
1. Primary memories are semiconductor memories.
2. Usually volatile memory.
3. Data is lost in case power is switched off.
4. It is working memory of the computer.
5. Faster than secondary memories.
6. A computer cannot run without primary memory.

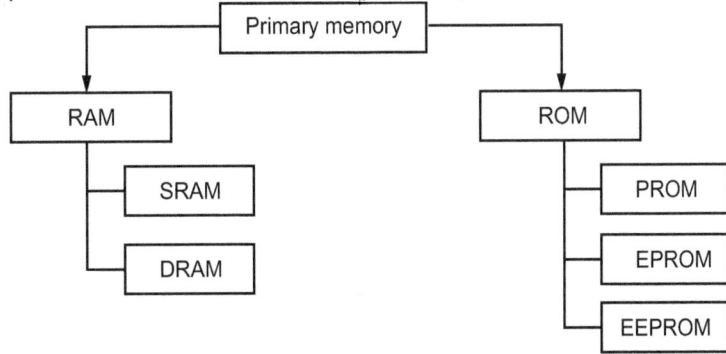

Fig. 1.18

1.7.1.1 RAM

- RAM stands for Random Access Memory.
- A RAM constitutes the internal memory of the CPU for storing data, program and program result. It is read/write memory.
- RAM is volatile, i.e. data stored in it is lost when we switch off the computer or if there is a power failure. Hence, a backup Uninterruptible Power System (UPS) is often used with computers. RAM is small, both in terms of its physical size and in the amount of data it can hold.
- This memory is accessible from any memory location anytime. one can switch to one place to another place in memory randomly.
- RAM is of two types i.e. Static RAM (SRAM) and Dynamic RAM (DRAM).

1. SRAM:

- SRAM (Static Random Access Memory) is a type of semiconductor memory where the word static indicates that, it does not need to be periodically refreshed, as SRAM uses bistable latching circuitry to store each bit.
- SRAM is volatile in the conventional sense that data is eventually lost when the memory is not powered.
- Static RAM is used as cache memory needs to be very fast and small.

Characteristic of the Static RAM:

  (i) It has long data lifetime.
  (ii) There is no need to refresh.
  (iii) Faster.
  (iv) Used as cache memory.
  (v) Large size.
  (vi) Expensive.
  (vii) High power consumption.

2. DRAM:

- DRAM (Dynamic Random Access Memory) is a type of random access memory that stores each bit of data in a separate capacitor within an integrated circuit.
- Since, real capacitor leak charge, the information eventually fades unless the capacitor charge is refreshed periodically. Because of this refresh requirement, it is a dynamic memory as opposed to SRAM and other static memory.

Characteristic of the Dynamic RAM:
(i) It has short data lifetime.
(ii) Need to refresh continuously.
(iii) Slower as compared to SRAM.
(iv) Used as RAM.
(v) Lesser in size.
(vi) Less expensive.
(vii) Less power consumption.

Comparison between Static RAM and Dynamic RAM:

Static RAM (SRAM)	Dynamic RAM (DRAM)
1. Each static RAM cell is a flip-flop.	1. A dynamic RAM cell consists of a MOSFET and a capacitor.
2. Less number of memory cells/unit area.	2. More number of memory cells/unit area.
3. More number of components per cell.	3. Only two components per cell.
4. Does not require refreshing.	4. Require refreshing.
5. Faster memories.	5. Slower memories.
6. Power consumption is less.	6. More power consumption.

1.7.1.2 ROM

- ROM stands for Read Only Memory.
- The memory from which we can only read but cannot write on it.
- This type of memory is non-volatile. The information is stored permanently in such memories during manufacture.
- Read only memory, also known as firmware, is an integrated circuit programmed with specific data when it is manufactured. ROM chips are used not only in computers, but in most other electronic items as well like washing machine and microwave oven.
- A ROM, stores such instruction as are required to start computer when electricity is first turned on, this operation is referred to as bootstrap.

Advantages of ROM:
1. Non-volatile in nature.
2. These can not be accidentally changed.
3. Cheaper than RAMs.
4. Easy to test.
5. More Reliable than RAMs.
6. These are static and do not require refreshing.
7. Its contents are always known and can be verified.

Types of ROMs:

1. MROM:
- MROM stands for Masked ROM.
- The very first ROMs were hard-wired devices that contained a pre-programmed set of data or instructions.
- These kind of ROMs are known as masked ROMs.
- MROM is inexpensive ROM.

2. PROM:
- PROM stands for Programmable Read Only Memory.
- PROM is read-only memory that can be modified only once by a user. The user buys a blank PROM and enter the desired contents using a PROM programmer.
- Inside the PROM chip there are small fuses which are burnt open during programming. It can be programmed only once and is not erasable.
- A Programmable Read-Only Memory or Field Programmable Read-Only Memory (FPROM) is a form of digital memory where the setting of each bit is locked by a fuse or antifuse.

3. EPROM:
- EPROM stands for Erasable and Programmable Read Only Memory.
- An EPROM is a type of memory chip that retains its data when its power supply is switched off. The EPROM can be erased by exposing it to ultra-violet light for a duration of up to 40 minutes. Usually, a EPROM eraser achieves this function.
- During programming an electrical charge is trapped in an insulated gate region. The charge is retained for more than ten year because the charge has no leakage path.
- For erasing this charge, ultra-violet light is passed through a quartz crystal window (lid). This exposure to ultra-violet light dissipates the charge. During normal use the quartz lid is sealed with a sticker.

4. EEPROM:
- EEPROM stands for Electrically Erasable and Programmable Read Only Memory. EEPROM also written as E^2PROM.
- EEPROM is a type of non-volatile memory used in computer and other electronic devices to store small amounts of data that must be saved when power is removed,
- The EEPROM is programmed and erased electrically. It can be erased and reprogrammed about ten thousand times. Both erasing and programming take about 4 to 10 ms (milli second).
- In EEPROM, any location can be selectively erased and programmed. EEPROMs can be erased one byte at a time, rather than erasing the entire chip. Hence, the process of re-programming is flexible but slow.

Comparison between E²PROM and EPROM:

E²PROM	EPROM
1. E²PROM stands for Electrically Erasable Programmable Read Only Memory.	1. EPROM stands for Erasable Programmable Read Only Memory.
2. Can be programmed and erased electrically.	2. Cannot be erased electrically and require UV rays to erase the EPROM.
3. Can be erased in a small time of 10 ms.	3. Requires 20 to 30 min. for erasing the contents.
4. Not required to remove the chip from the circuit for erasing and reprogramming.	4. Chip has to be removed from the circuit for erasing and reprogram-ming.
5. Low density	5. High density
6. Expensive than EPROM.	6. Cheaper than E²PROM.

Difference between RAM and ROM:

RAM	ROM
1. RAM stands for Random Access Memory.	1. ROM stands for Read Only Memory.
2. It is temporary memory.	2. It is permanent memory.
3. RAM is volatile memory.	3. ROM is non-volatile memory.
4. Information stored by user.	4. Information stored by manufacturer.
5. Read/write operations can be performed.	5. Only read can be performed.
6. Every location can be accessed directly or randomly.	6. Longer access time.
7. RAM stores data, program instructions during program execution.	7. ROM stores system software are programs for basic operations.

Cache Memory:

- Cache memory is a very high speed memory placed in between RAM and CPU. Cache memory increases the speed of processing.
- Cache memory is a storage buffer that stores the data that is used more often, temporarily, and makes them available to CPU at a fast rate.
- During processing, CPU first checks cache for the required data. If data is not found in cache, then it looks in the RAM for data.
- To access the cache memory, CPU does not have to use the motherboard's system bus for data transfer.
- Cache memory is built into the processor, and may also be located next to it on a separate chip between the CPU and RAM.
- Cache built into the CPU is faster than separate cache, running at the speed of the microprocessor itself. However, separate cache is roughly twice as fast as RAM.

Flash Memory:
- It is an extension of EEPROMs.
- It uses floating gate principle.
- It is designed such that large blocks of memory can be erased all at once rather than just one word at a time.

Applications of Flash Memory:
1. To store photograph in a digital camera.
2. To store voice in compressed form in a voice recorder.
3. To store message in mobile phone.

1.7.2 Secondary Memory

- Secondary storage (also known as external memory or auxiliary storage or secondary storage), differ from primary storage in that it is not directly accessible by the CPU.
- The computer usually uses its input/output channels to access secondary storage and transfer the desired data using intermediate area in primary storage.
- Secondary storage does not lose the data when the device is powered down—it is non-volatile. Per unit, it is typically also two order of magnitude less expensive than primary storage.
- Consequently, modern computer systems typically have two order of magnitude more secondary storage than primary storage and data are kept for a longer time there.
- Secondary memory is slower than main memory.
- CPU directly does not access these memories instead they are accessed via input-output routines.
- Contents of secondary memories are first transferred to main memory, and then CPU can access it. For example: disk, CD-ROM, DVD etc.

Characteristic of secondary memory:
1. These are magnetic and optical memories.
2. It is known as backup memory.
3. It is non-volatile memory.
4. Data is permanently stored even if power is switched off.
5. It is used for storage of the data in the computer.
6. Computer may run without secondary memory.
7. Slower than primary memories.

Comparison between Primary and Secondary Memories:

Primary Memory	Secondary Memory
1. It is a part of CPU.	1. It is not a part of CPU.
2. It is the internal or main memory.	2. It is the external memory and resides on disk.
3. The access time is less a few nanoseconds.	3. The access time is more a few milliseconds.
4. It is a medium capacity memory.	4. It is a high capacity memory.
5. It is further classified as RAM and ROM.	5. There are different types of secondary storage devices such as hard disk, floppy disk, CD-ROM etc.
6. Most Primary Storage is temporary.	6. All secondary storage is permanent.
7. Primary storage is expensive and smaller.	7. Secondary storage is usually cheaper and large.
8. Primary storage is usually faster therefore more expensive.	8. Secondary storage connects to the CPU via cables and therefore is slower.

1.7.3 Secondary Storage Devices
1.7.3.1 Magnetic Tape

- Magnetic tape is now principally used only as a backup medium. It is also used to archive records of past transactions for long-term storage, as it is cheap, robust and easily used to store large quantities of data.
- Magnetic tape is a recording medium consisting of a thin tape with a coating of a fine magnetic material, used for recording analog or digital data.
- A device that stores computer data on magnetic tape is a tape drive.

Fig. 1.19 (a): Magnetic tape

- The magnetic tape drive is similar to the audio tape recorders. Before the data on magnetic tape can be processed, the tape must be placed in a machine called tape drive or tape transport.
- We can read/write data from the tape. Writing data on the tape destroys the previous tape contents.
- When the tape is accelerated to its full speed no recording can be done. The distance traversed by the tape during this time is called as Inter Block Gap (IBG). The beginning of the tape is indicated by a metal foil called a marker.
- When a write command is given, the block of data is written on the tape and after the IBG the next block of data is written. A metal foil is used again to indicate the end of tape. The data which is stored on the tape has to be accessed sequentially.

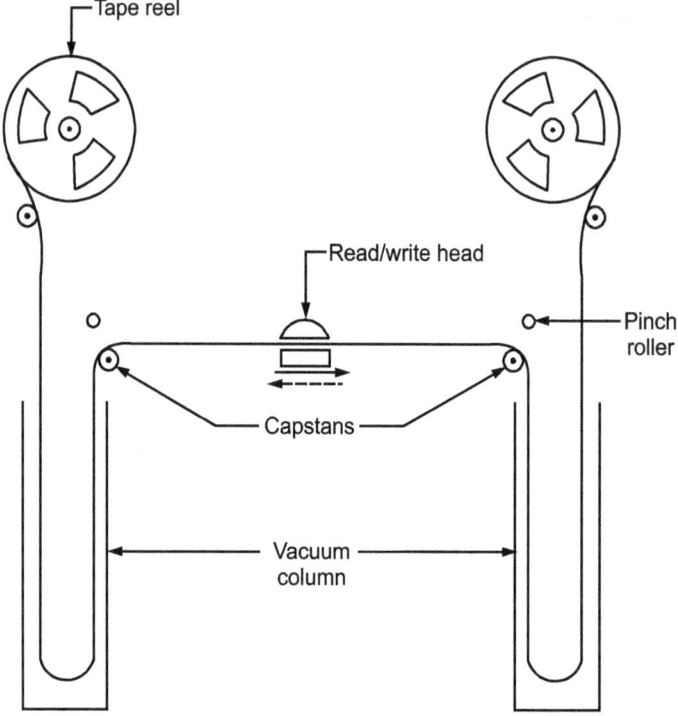

Fig. 1.19 (b): Magnetic tape drive

- Advantages of magnetic tape include the fact that it's generally the cheapest option for memory storage and it holds plenty of data (often 1 terabyte per tape). The disadvantages include that readers are becoming more obsolete over time, processing is slow, and searching within the data is cumbersome.

1.7.3.2 Magnetic Disks

1. Floppy Disk:
- The floppy disk is made up of thin flexible plastic (Mylar) material of circular shape. As the thickness of the Mylar is few thousands of an inch it is called floppy.
- The information can be stored on single side or both sides of the disk. Depending on the recording technique used, they are classified as single density and double density diskettes.
- The different sizes available are:
  (i) 8" disk which is used in order computer which is presently obsolete.
  (ii) $5^{1/4}$" disk having capacity 1.2 MB called mini floppy.
  (iii) $3^{1/2}$" disk having capacity 1.44 MB called micro floppy.

Fig. 1.20 (a): A floppy

Characteristics of a Floppy Disk:
- A "track" is a narrow recording band that forms a full circle on the surface of the disk.
- The disk's storage locations are then divided into pie-shaped sections, which break the tracks into small arcs called sectors (can hold 512 bytes of data).
- Floppy Disks store data on both sides. Each side consists of 80 tracks with 18 sectors per track.
- To read from and write on the disk, sectors are grouped into clusters (consist of 2 to 8 sectors).
- A cluster is the smallest unit of space used to store data.

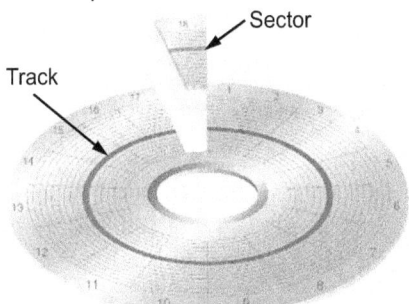

Fig. 1.20 (b)

- **Construction of floppy disk:** The floppy disk is coated with magnetic material and enclosed in a protective jacket. There is a large slot on jacket through which head reads and writes data on the disk.

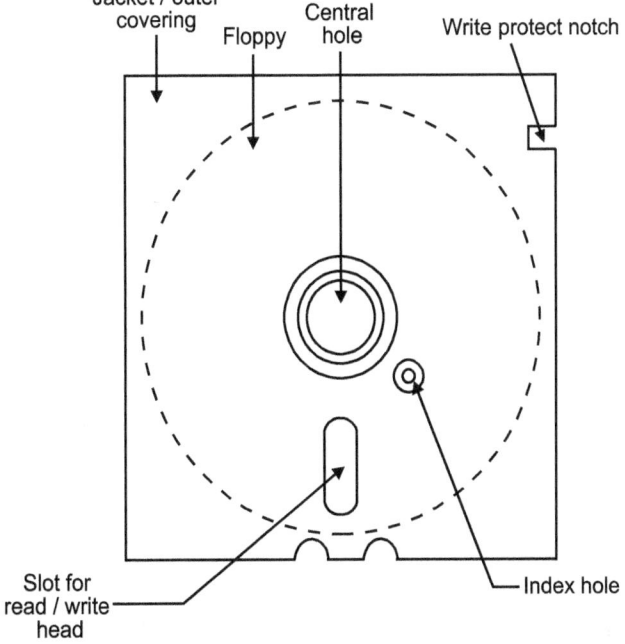

Fig. 1.21: Parts of a floppy

- A hole is provided at the centre called hub for clamping the floppy so that it can rotate easily without slipping. Near the centre a small hole is punched on the diskette called index hole.
- This hole indicates the beginning of a track. Writing is done on the floppy disk only after sensing the index hole.
- A write protect notch is provided. If this notch is open, writing on diskette is permitted. If this notch is covered by a paper or sticker then writing is not permitted.
- **Principle of working:** Floppy is made of number of tracks and each track is divided into a number of sectors. Data is stored on the track bit by bit using electromagnetic techniques, the data is read (or stored) from (on) the disk.
- There are two heads, one for writing on the top side of the disk and the other on the bottom side of the disk. In a write operation the write data line contains both clock pulses and data pulses.
- Current is passed through read/write head and flux transition is created for each clock or data pulse. In read operation e.m.f. is induced into the read head because of rotation of floppy disk which causes flux transitions. The induced e.m.f. is amplified and shaped by the amplifier circuit in FDD.
- In a write operation the data pulses as well as the clock pulses are stored on the disk or else it becomes difficult to differentiate between no data and zero data.

(i) Micro Floppy:

- It is of the size $3^{1/2}$ inch and its capacity is 1.44 MB. The 3.5" is so designed that one end is truncated which prevents improper insertion of the diskette.
- There is a round plastic sheet (mylar), coated with magnetic material and is enclosed in a hard plastic jacket. It uses a more finely grained medium with buffer magnetic properties so its capacity is more.
- A hole with slider is provided along the side of the plastic jacket. One can read/write if the hole is blocked by the slider. One can only read the data if the hole is visible.

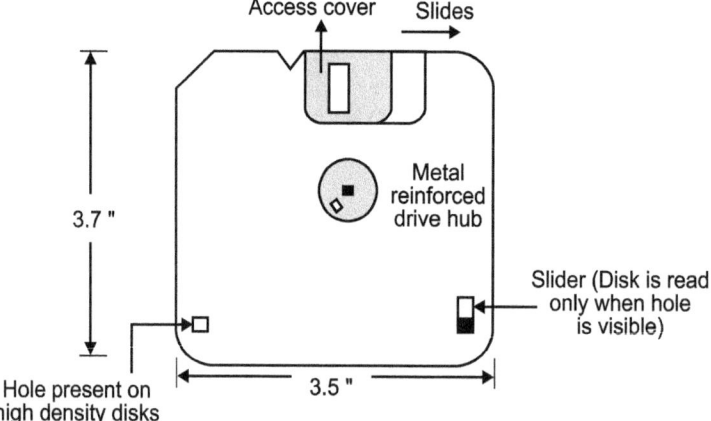

Fig. 1.22: Micro floppy

- It uses a metal hub so the disk can be centered very easily. If one more hole is provided it indicates the diskette has double density.

(ii) Mini Floppy:

- A mini floppy is of size of $5^{1/4}$ inch floppy disk. A floppy diskette is an ultra thin plastic piece in circular shape.
- It is coated with a magnetic material and enclosed in a protective jacket. An oval access hole is made on the jacket so as to provide contact between the read/write head and the diskette.
- On floppy there is write protect notch. If this notch is kept uncovered then you can write to the floppy, but if it is covered by a sticker then floppy becomes read only and you cannot write on to it.
- When index hole of upper cover and mini floppy matches each other then there is first block/sector on read/write head slot. It is widely used in present day computer including PCs, PC-XTs, PC-ATs, etc.

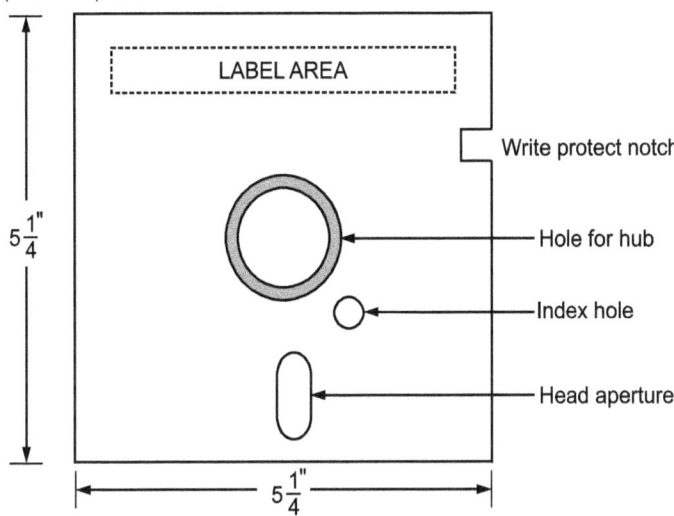

Fig. 1.23: Mini floppy

Advantages of Floppy Disk:
(i) Information can be directly encoded onto the disk.
(ii) Bulky media is not used, so ease in handling and transportation.
(iii) Used for storage, input and output.
(iv) It is cheap.
(v) Density is high.
(vi) It can be reused many times.

Disadvantages of Floppy Disk:
(i) It should be handled carefully.
(ii) It is sensitive to environment conditions such as heat, dust etc.

2. Hard Disk:

- The hard disk is the most widely used mass storage device for PCs. On the hard disk all the programs and data are stored which can be accessed instantly thus making the system faster.
- The hard disk drive or hard disk is the main, and usually largest data storage device in a computer.
- It is a non-volatile, random access digital magnetic data storage device.
- A hard drive is made up of platter which stored the data, and read/write heads to transfer data.
- A hard drive is generally the fastest of the secondary storage devices, and has the largest data storage capacity, approximately the same as magnetic tapes. Hard drives however, are not very portable and are primarily used internally in a computer system.

Construction of Hard Disk:

- Hard disks use a circular hard platter to store data on. They are in pristine condition with a mirror like finish to them. These platter are locked away inside a steel casing as unclean air can easily ruin a hard disk.
- This is why we should never remove the casing from the hard disk as it is very unlikely that we will be able to put it back together as a working component.

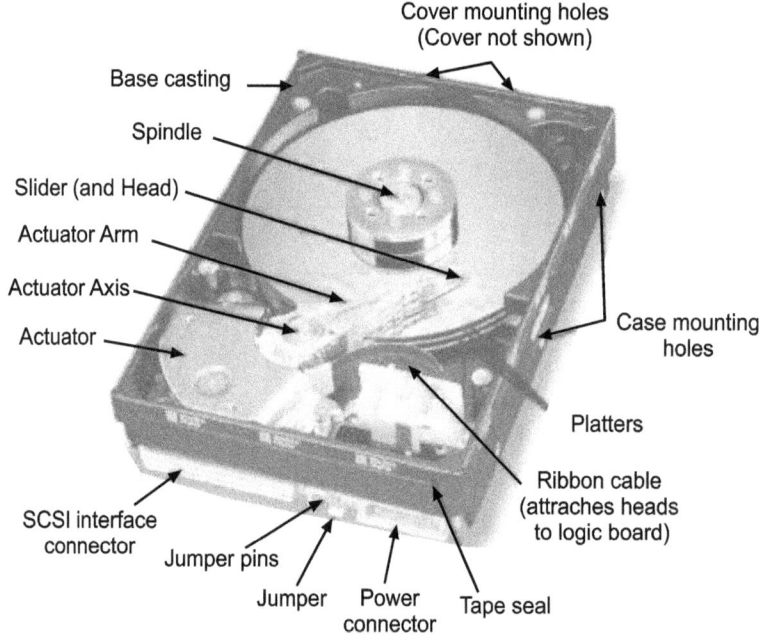

Fig. 1.24: Parts of hard disk

- Fig. 1.24 shows a labelled diagram of a hard disk.
- The model is a SCSI (Small Computer Scientific Interface) shows the hard platter on top of each other with a set of arms which hold the read/write head.

- The speed of the arm is truly amazing as well as the accuracy of the head which can read and write to perfection on a platter which is rotating around 7200 rpm.
- The hard disk looks a very simple idea and probably is, however a lot goes on before the simple writing to the disk itsself.
- Hard disk should have two parts i.e. physical part like platter read/write head.
- Logical parts like track, sector, pie, shape and cylinder.
- A hard disk is divided into tracks and sectors, data on this hard disk is positioned into these tracks and sector so they can be easily read by the heads and also to help reduce fragmentation on the hard disk.
- Fig. 1.25 depicts how a hard disk is divided into tracks and sectors.

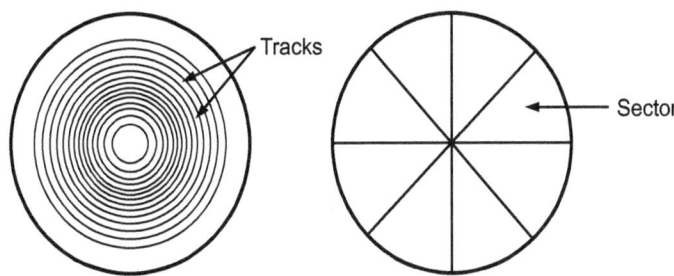

Fig. 1.25: Track and sector in harddisk

- Data on a hard drive are accessed by two methods:
  1. **Fixed Head:** Hard disks with fixed heads have a read/write head for each track on the hard disk, since there is no moving of heads to access data, the data access time is generally faster for fixed head hard drives.
  2. **Moving Head:** A moving head hard disk is one in which one or more read-write heads are attached to a movable arm which allows each head to cover many tracks of information.
- Each access to the hard drive to read or write data causes the read/write heads to burst into a furious flurry of movement – which must be performed with microscopic precision. The tolerances in a disk drive are equivalent to a jumbo jet flying at an altitude of less than a centimetre.
- Data is stored in a very orderly pattern on each platter. Bits of data are arranged in concentric, circular paths called tracks. Each track is broken up into smaller areas called sectors. Part of the hard drive stores a map of sector that have already been used up and other that are still free.
- When the computer wants to store new information, it takes a look at the map to find some free sectors
- Typically, data up to 100 GB's can be stored on single platter.
- With so much information stored in such a tiny amount of space, a hard drive is a remarkable piece of engineering.

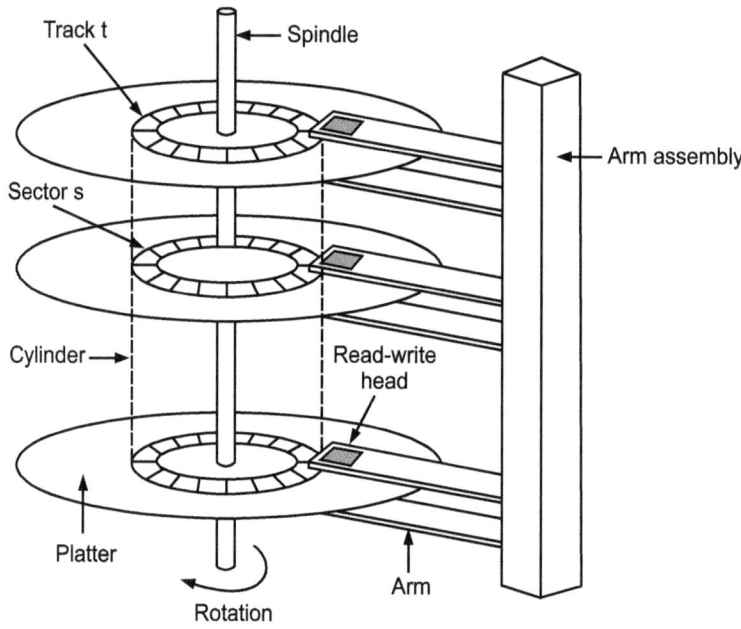

Fig. 1.26: Hard disk cylinder, R/W head spindle assembly

Comparison between Tape drive and Hard disk/Floppy disk:

Tape drive	Hard disk/Floppy disk
1. Data cannot be accessed directly, it has to be accessed sequentially.	1. Data can be accessed directly or sequentially
2. The data cannot be accessed and immediately updated.	2. The data can be accessed and updated in a few milliseconds.
3. It is cheaper than magnetic disks.	3. It is nearly 20 times more expensive than tape drive.
4. Easy to maintain security of tape files than files stored on a disk.	4. Security of files is less compared to tape drive.

Difference between Floppy disk and CD-ROM:

Floppy disk	CD-ROM
1. It has lower storage capacity 1.44 MB.	1. It has higher storage capacity upto 700 MB.
2. It uses magnetic technology.	2. It uses laser technology.
3. Data is recorded on both sides.	3. Data is recorded on one side.
4. It is affected by dust, moisture.	4. It is not affected by dust, mositure.
5. It is read/write medium.	5. It is read only medium.
6. Used to store low volumes of data.	6. Used to store high volumes of data such as encyclopaedia, telephone, directory etc.

Difference between Floppy disk and Hard disk:

Floppy disk	Hard disk
1. It is a removable, low storage capacity secondary storage medium.	1. It is not easily removable, high capacity secondary storage medium.
2. It provides off-line storage of data.	2. It can provide on-line storage of data.
3. It has more access time, but it is cheaper.	3. The access time is less but it is costly.
4. It has a write-protect notch.	4. It does not have a notch.
5. There are two read/write heads in the drive, one for each side of the floppy.	5. There are many read/write heads in the drive because the disk contains many plotters.
6. The read/write head touches the surface of floppy.	6. The read/write head never touches the surface.

1.7.3.3 Optical Disks (CD and DVD)

- Optical disk is an electronic data storage medium from which data is read and written to by using a low-powered laser beam.
- It is flat, circular, plastic or glass disk on which data is stored in the form of light and dark pits.
- There are three basic types of optical disks: Read-Only Optical Disks, Write Once Read Many Optical Disks and Rewritable Optical Disks.
- Two main types of optical disks are CD and DVD.

1. **CD:**
- CD stands for Compact Disk.

Fig. 1.27: A CD

- CD is an abbreviation of Compact Disk, and is a form of data storage that can transfer data up to the speed of 7800 KB/s.
- A standard 120 mm CD holds up to 700 MB of data, or about 70 minutes of audio. There are two types of CD: CD-ROM and CD-RW.
- CD-ROM are stands for CD-Read Only Memory and they function the same way Read Only Memory does.

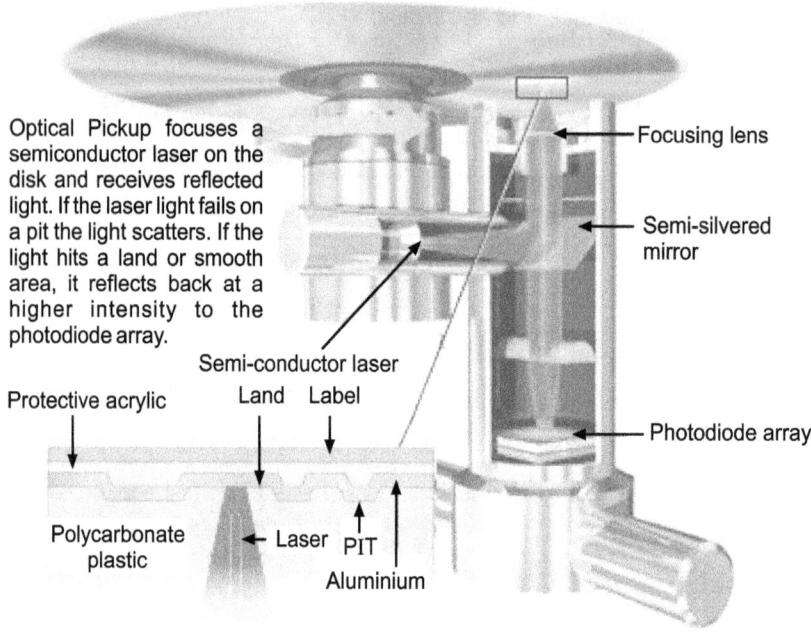

Fig. 1.28: Working of CD

- CD-RW stands for CD-Rewritable, these disks can be erased and rewritten at any time.
- The Compact Disk (CD) is storage media that hold content in digital form and that are written and read by a laser; these media include all the CD and DVD variations, as well as optical jukeboxes and autochangers.
- Optical media have a number of advantages over magnetic media such as the floppy disk. Optical disk capacity ranges up to 6 gigabytes; that's 6 billion bytes compared to 1.44 megabytes (MB) – 1,440,000 bytes – of the floppy.
- One optical disk holds about the equivalent of 500 floppies worth of data. Durability is another feature of optical media; they last up to seven times as long as traditional storage media.

2. **DVD:**
- DVD is an abbreviation of Digital Versatile Disc, and is an optical disc storage media format that can be used for data storage.
- The DVD supports disks with capacities of 4.7 GB to 17 GB and access rates of 600 Kbps to 1.3 mbps.
- A standard DVD disc store up to 4.7 GB of data. There are two types of DVD's: DVD-ROM and DVD-RW.
- DVD-ROM are stands for DVD-Read Only Memory and they function the same way Read Only Memory does.
- DVD-RW stands for DVD-Rewritable, these disks can be erased and rewritten at any time.

Fig. 1.29: DVDs

- A DVD is composed of several layer of plastic, polycarbonate base, totaling about 1.2 millimeter thick. Writing data to the DVD is done by a red laser beam modulated by the serial data stream. When the beam turns on and hits the dye layer, a distortion (known as a pit) on the surface is made.
- Dual layer recording allows DVD-R and DVD+R discs to store significantly more data, up to 8.54 GB's per side, per disc, compared with 4.7 GB's for single-layer discs. While you will need as much as 300 DVD's to be able to store that data.

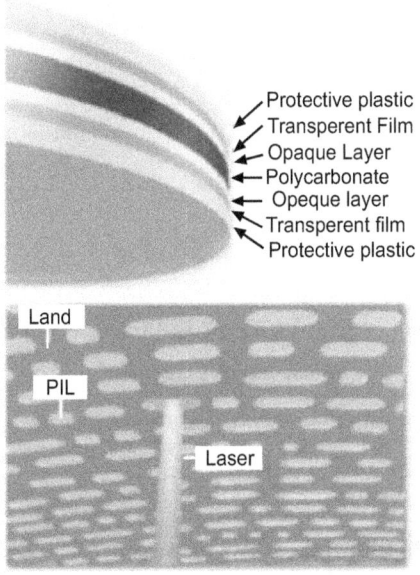

Fig. 1.30: Working of DVD

Comparison of CD and DVD:

Terms	CD	DVD
Stands for	Compact Disc	Digital Versatile Disc
Purpose	CDs are made with the purpose of holding audio files as well as program files.	DVDs are made with the purpose of holding video files, movies, substantial amount of programs, etc.

contd. ...

Media type	Optical disc	Optical disc
Encoding	Various	Various
Capacity	Typically up to 700 MiB (up to 80 minutes audio)	DVD can range from 4.7 GB to 17.08 GB.
Read mechanism	780 nm wavelength (infrared and red edge) semiconductor laser, 1200 Kib/s (1×)	650 nm laser, 10.5 Mbit/s (1×)
Write mechanism	1200 Kib/s (1×)	10.5 Mbit/s (1×)
Types	CD-R, CD-RW, CD-Text, CD + Graphics, CD + Extended Graphics, Super Audio CD, CD-MIDI, CD-ROM, Video CD, Super Video CD, Photo CD, CD-I, Enhanced CD, VinylDisc and Bootable CD.	DVD-RW, DVD+RW, DVD-RAM and Blu-Ray.
Developed by:	Philips, Sony	Philips, Sony, Toshiba, and Panasonic

1.7.3.4 Pen Drive

- Pen drive is type of Universal Serial Cable (USB) flash drive.
- It is a kind of memory card that can be plugged into a computer's USB port.
- It is termed "Pen drive" with reference to its size.
- It is a small and compact thus naming it fit into the palm of our hand. It is often flat and rectangular like a highlighter pen.
- A pen drive is used to store data and has a storage capacity of 64 MB to 32 GB.
- It is removable and rewritable. It is mostly used as a backup for CD-ROMs or floppy disks.

Technical Mechanism:

- Pen drive consists of a small printed circuit board. This circuit board provides a strong base for the pen drive's form and also serves as a means to collection information.
- The circuit board consists of a small microchip within it. This microchip enables the pen drive to extract or feed in data. This process requires relatively low electrical power compared to CD-R's or Floppy. It based on EEP-ROMS technology that allows writing and ensure process in a computer system.
- The data that is to be transferred is connected through a computer programme. It is then read, transmitted or rewritten from a pen drive to a computer or vice versa. Thus the required data gets copied to any selected derive on the computer for further use.

- When a pen drive is connected to a USB port, it is activated. The USB parts gives the pen drive access to the information on a specific computer drive. Most of the open drives are designed in such a way that they are compatible with any USB port of a computer.
- The data that is to be transferred is connected through a computer programme. It is then read, transmitted or rewritten from a pen drive to a computer or vice versa. Thus the required data gets copied to any selected drive on the computer for further use.
- Internal parts of a typical USB flash drive are shown in Fig. 1.31.
    1. US connector.
    2. USB mass storage controller device.
    3. Test points.
    4. Flash memory chip.
    5. Crystal oscillator.
    6. LED.
    7. Write-protect switch (Optional)
    8. Space for second flash memory chip.

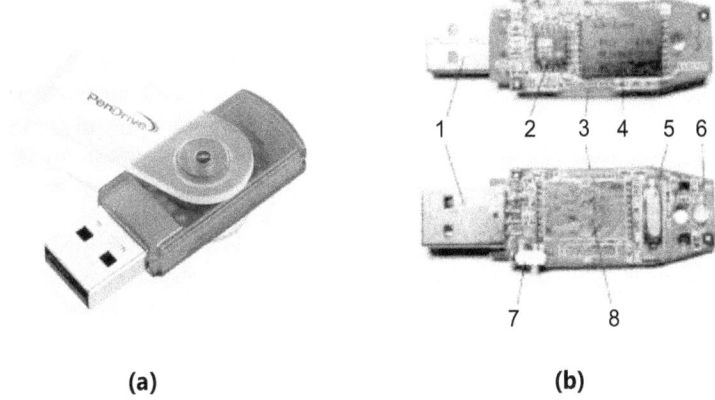

(a)   (b)

Fig. 1.31

Advantages:
1. Reliable than make external storage devices like CD, floppy etc.
2. Cost effective.
3. Easily Transportable in case of CD we need a pouch.
4. Can be used as a bootable device.
5. No prior software needed to write or read data, in case of CD writing we need software like Nero etc.

Disadvantages:
1. It does have a cyclic life span.
2. If items like dust goes inside then it will not work properly.
3. While the pen drive is portable and convenient, it also has the risk of being easily lost, as well as the fact that it has a limited number of write and erase cycles.

1.8 I/O (Input/Output) Devices

- The terms input and output are used both as verbs to describe the process of entering or displaying the data, and as nouns referring to the data itself entered into or displayed by the computer.
- Input devices allow us to enter raw data into a computer. The computer processes the data and then produces outputs that we can understand using an output device.

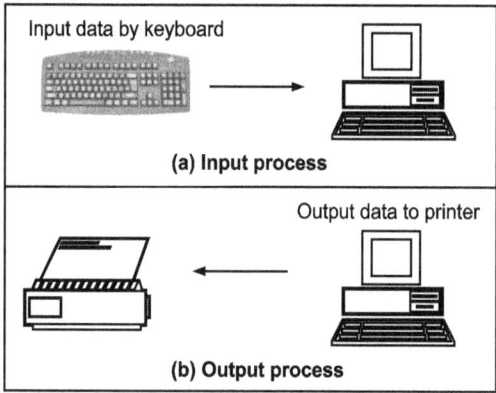

Fig. 1.32: I/O (Input/Output) process

- Any information or data that is entered or sent to the computer to be processed is considered input and anything that is displayed from the computer is output.
- Therefore, an input device such as a computer keyboard is capable of having information sent to the computer, but does not display (output) any information.
- An output device such as a computer printer can print information from the computer but does not send any information (input) to the computer.

1.8.1 Input Devices

- The devices which are used to input the data and the programs in the computer are known as Input Devices.
- Input device can read data and convert them to a form that a computer can understand and use.
- An input device is equipment used to capture information and commands.

1.8.1.1 Keyboard

- Keyboard is most common input device is used today. Keyboard are used for inputting data to computer.
- The data and instructions are input by typing on the keyboard. The message typed on the keyboard reaches the memory unit of a computer. It is connected to a computer via a cable. Apart from alphabet and numeral keys, it has other function keys for performing different functions.
- The layout of the keyboard is like that of traditional typewriter, although there are some additional keys provided for performing some additional functions.
- Keyboard are of two sizes 84 keys or 101/102 keys, but now 104 keys or 108 keys keyboard is also available for Windows and Internet.

- The keys are following:

Sr. No.	Keys	Description
1.	Typing Keys	These keys include the letter keys (A-Z) and digits keys (0-9) which are generally arranged in same layout as that of typewriters.
2.	Numeric Keypad	It is used to enter numeric data or cursor movement. Generally, it consists of a set of 17 keys that are laid out in the same configuration used by most adding machine and calculators.
3.	Function Keys	The twelve functions keys are present on the keyboard. These are arranged in a row along the top of the keyboard. Each function key has unique meaning and is used for some specific purpose.
4.	Control keys	These keys provides cursor and screen control. It includes four directional arrow key. Control keys also include Home, End, Insert, Delete, Page Up, Page Down, Control (Ctrl), Alternate (Alt), Escape(Esc).
5.	Special Purpose Keys	Keyboard also contains some special purpose keys such as Enter, Shift, Caps Lock, Num Lock, Space bar, Tab, and Print Screen.

- Fig. 1.33 shows a keyboard with its keys.

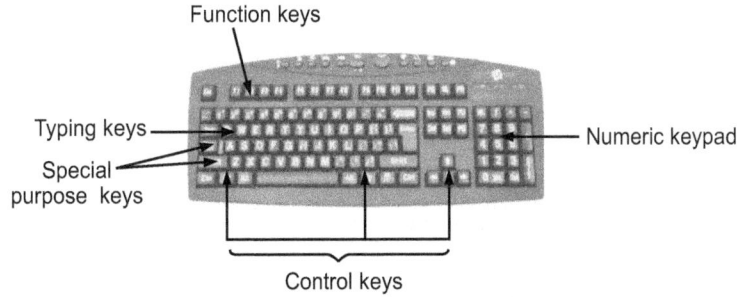

Fig. 1.33: Computer keyboard with different types of keys

Advantages of keyboards:
1. Cheaper in cost.
2. Using keyboard we can enter data very quickly.
3. Easy to use and handle.
4. Specialist keyboards are available e.g. ergonomic, gaming keyboards.

Disadvantages of keyboards:
1. It is easy to make mistakes when typing in data.
2. If you cannot touch type, it can be time consuming to enter data.
3. Keyboards are not suitable for creating diagrams.
4. Disabled people often find keyboards difficult to use.
5. Excessive use can lead to health problems such as Repetitive Strain Injury (R.S.I.).
6. Keyboards are easily damaged.

1.8.1.2 Mouse

- Mouse is most popular pointing device.
- Mouse is a very famous cursor-control device.
- Mouse is a small palm size box with a round ball at its base which senses the movement of mouse and sends corresponding signals to CPU on pressing the buttons.
- Generally it has two buttons called left and right button and scroll bar is present at the mid wheel, (See Fig. 1.34).
- Mouse can be used to control the position of cursor on screen, but it cannot be used to enter text into the computer.

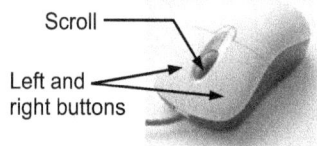

Fig. 1.34: Mouse

Advantages:
1. Easy to use.
2. Not very expensive.
3. Moves the cursor faster than the arrow keys of keyboard.

1.8.1.3 Scanner

- Scanner is an input device which works more like a photocopy (Xerox) machine.
- Scanners are used to enter information directly into the computer's memory.
- The scanner converts any type of printed or written information including photographs into digital pulses, which can be manipulated by the computer.
- Scanner is used when some information is available on a paper and it is to be transferred to the hard disc of the computer for further manipulation.
- Scanner captures images from the source which are then converted into the digital form that can be stored on the disc. These images can be edited before they are printed.
- There are several types of scanners, all of which serve a variety of functions:
    1. **Flatbed scanner:** This versatile scanner is usually found on a desktop. You lay the document on a glass panel, and a scan head moves beneath it. These scanners are great for scanning the occasional newspaper article, book chapter, or photograph; or for those who may need to scan or bulky items such as the cover of a DVD.

2. **Sheet-fed scanner:** With this scanner, you place documents into a feeder, and they move through the scanner while the scan head remains still.
3. **Handheld scanner:** In this case, the scan head is passed over the documents. These scanners don't usually produce high-quality images.
4. **Drum scanner:** This kind of scanner uses a photomultiplier tube to reproduce very detailed images. Drum scanners are often used in the publishing industry.

Fig. 1.35: Scanner

Advantages:
1. A scanner is not having to go to the printers or library to make a copy of documents when you are in need of a copy.
2. It also makes keeping records of your finances and important documents a great deal less time consuming because you can make a digital copy of them.
3. Using scanner fast and convenient to have a copy done.

Disadvantages:
1. One of the biggest disadvantages of having a scanner is that they are relatively slow.
2. A good scanner is a little on the expensive side.
3. Quality of scan not the same as original.
4. In scanner we only can scan on the surface but not above it.

1.8.1.4 MICR

- MICR is an input device.
- MICR is a very fast and reliable as a means of entering data into a computer.
- Magnetic Ink Card Reader (MICR) input device is generally used in banks because of a large number of cheques to be processed every day.
- The bank's code number and cheque number are printed on the cheques with a special type of ink that contains particles of magnetic material that are machine readable.
- This reading process is called Magnetic Ink Character Recognition (MICR). The main advantage of MICR is that it is fast and less error prone.
- MICR is a character recognition system that uses special ink and characters.

Fig. 1.36: MICR

Advantage:
1. The use of iron oxide-based ink ensures MICR characters are readable even if a document is obscured by miscellaneous marks or overprinted.
2. MICR systems provide a high level of security since MICR characters are required to follow a stringent format and use precise iron oxide ink, which makes the documents difficult to forge.
3. The error rate for reading MICR characters is small as compared to other character recognition systems.

Disadvantages:
1. MICR readers are expensive and capable of recognizing only MICR fonts written in a specific format.
2. The printing of MICR is demanding, setting precise but difficult-to-achieve standards, which is a distinct disadvantage in terms of time consumption.

1.8.1.5 OMR

- Optical Mark Reader (OMR) is the process of gathering data with an optical scanner by measuring the reflectivity of light at predetermined positions on a surface.
- OMR is a special type of optical scanner used to recognize the type of mark made by pen or pencil.
- OMR is used where one out of a few alternatives is to be selected and marked.
- OMR is specially used for checking the answer sheets of examinations having multiple choice questions.

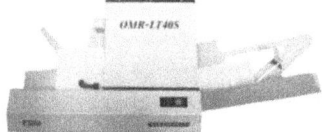

Fig. 1.37

Advantages:
1. A fast method of inputting large amount of data.
2. OMR is much accurate than data being keyed in by a user.
3. There is a large number of document to justify designing and printing them.
4. The user can only make marks and cannot write any information.

Disadvantages:
1. Document for mark reader are complicated to design.
2. Input of the data to computer is slow.
3. It is difficult for a computer to check marked data.
4. The person putting the marks on the document has to follow the instruction.

1.8.1.6 Digital Camera

- Digital camera is an input device.
- Digital cameras are becoming increasingly popular as they become cheaper and photo sharing websites become common.
- Digital camera is a device that captures digital photographs. Most digital cameras do not directly input data into a computer - they store photographs on memory cards.
- The photographs can later be transferred to a computer. A modern digital camera can capture 10 Megapixels or more per photograph - that's 10,000,000 colored dots (pixels) in every photo.

Fig. 1.38: Digital camera

1.8.1.7 Digitizer

- Digitizer is an input device which converts analog information into a digital form.
- Digitizer can convert a signal from the television camera into a series of number that could be stored in a computer.
- Digitizer can be used by the computer to create a picture of whatever the camera had been pointed at.
- Digitizer is also known as Tablet or Graphics Tablet because it converts graphics and pictorial data into binary inputs.
- A graphic tablet as digitizer is used for doing fine works of drawing and image manipulation applications.
- A digitizer tablet (also known as a digitizer or graphics tablet) is a tool used to convert hand-drawn images into a format suitable for computer processing.
- Images are usually drawn onto a flat surface with a stylus and then appear on a computer monitor or screen.
- Digitizer tablets can also be used as an input device, receiving information represented in drawings and sending output to a CAD (computer aided design) application and PC-based software like AutoCAD.

Fig. 1.39: Digitizer

1.8.1.8 Joystick

- Joystick is also a pointing device which is used to move cursor position on a monitor screen.
- Joystick is a stick having a spherical ball at its both lower and upper ends. The lower spherical ball moves in a socket. The Joystick can be moved in all four directions.
- The function of joystick is similar to that of a mouse.
- Joystick is mainly used in Computer Aided Designing (CAD) and playing computer games.

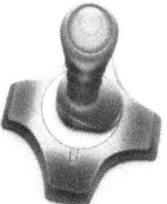

Fig. 1.40: Joystick

Advantages:
1. A joystick is that it is very easy to learn to use and they have a very simple design so they can be inexpensive.
2. The advantage of joystick is that it gives the player a real-time or virtual experience of the game.

Disadvantage:
1. A joystick is that some player finds it more difficult to control than using a mouse.
2. Joysticks are only limited to forward, backward, left and right.

1.8.1.9 Light Pen

- Light pen is an input device which is used to draw lines or figures on a computer screen.
- Light pen is a pointing device which is similar to a pen. It is used to select a displayed menu item or draw pictures on the monitor screen.
- Light pen consists of a photocell and an optical system placed in a small tube.
- When light pen's tip is moved over the monitor screen and pen button is pressed, its photocell sensing element detects the screen location and sends the corresponding signal to the CPU.

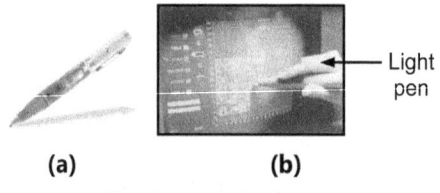

(a)   (b)

Fig. 1.41: Light pen

Advantages:
  (i) Light pens are easy to use.
  (ii) They have extremely good positional accuracy on a computer screen, much more than is possible with a mouse or a touch screen.
  (iii) They are ergonomically designed for ease of hand movement and are excellent for all drawing and pointing tasks.
  (iv) They don't require extra desk space and are easily modified for use by people with disabilities.
  (v) When used for bar code reading, they are lightweight, able to come in direct contact with the bar codes and have no moving parts.

Disadvantages:
  (i) Light pens are easily damaged.
  (ii) They can only be used on some computer screens; they do not work with LCD screens.
  (iii) They usually lack high resolution capability.
  (iv) They can be fatiguing to the hand if overused.
  (v) They can impair viewing of the computer screen on which they're being used. When used as bar code readers, they have a high error rate.

1.8.1.10 Track Ball

- Track ball is an input device that is mostly used in notebook or laptop computer, instead of a mouse.
- A trackball mouse is stationary, with a moveable ball. Users control the cursor on the screen by scrolling the ball, instead of moving their entire hand.
- This is a ball which is half inserted and by moving finger on ball, pointer can be moved.
- Since, the whole device is not moved, a track ball requires less space than a mouse. A track ball comes in various shapes like a ball, a button and a square.
- Track ball is similar to the upside- down design of the mouse.
- The user moves the ball directly, while the device itself remains stationary. The user spins the ball in various directions to effect the screen movements.

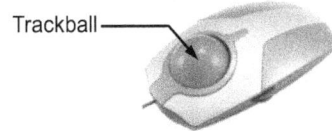

Fig. 1.42: Track ball

Advantages:
  1. **Small footprint:** Even the largest trackball takes less work surface space than is required to effectively use the smallest mouse.
  2. **Stationary use:** Not having to move means a trackball never runs out of work surface, never requires re-positioning, allows fast, continuous scrolling, never needs to be picked up and put it back on the mouse pad.

3. **Precise control:** Most modern trackballs allow you to control cursor movement with your finger tips or thumb. Much more precise than the hand and wrist movement required to move a mouse.
4. **Self cleaning:** While some are better than others, most trackballs require little or no cleaning in normal use.

Disadvantages:
1. Given that users are controlling the cursor with a ball, movements are not completely precise.
2. For designers and those who work in graphics, the customary mouse may have greater accuracy.
3. Another disadvantage is that the ball mechanism requires more cleaning and maintenance than a regular mouse.

1.8.1.11 OCR

- OCR stands for Optical Character Reader.
- OCR is a device which detects alpha numeric character printed or written on a paper.
- The text which is to be scanned is illuminated by a low frequency light source.
- The light is absorbed by the dark areas but reflected from the bright areas. The reflected light is received by the photocells.
- OCR is an input device used to read a printed text.
- OCR scans text optically character by character, converts them into a machine readable code and stores the text on the system memory.

Fig. 1.43: OCR

Advantages of OCR:
1. Cheaper than payment someone to manually enter large amounts of text.
2. Must faster than someone manually entering large amounts of text.
3. The latest software can recreate tables and the original layout.

Disadvantages of OCR:
1. Not 100% accurate, there are likely to be some mistakes made during the process.
2. All documents need to be checked over carefully and then manually corrected.
3. If the original document is of poor quality or the handwriting difficult to read, more mistakes will occur.
4. Not worth doing for small amounts of text.

1.8.1.12 Bar Code Readers

- A bar code reader reads bar codes and coverts them into electric pulses to be processed by a computer. A bar code is nothing but data coded in form of light and dark bars.
- Bar coded data is generally used in labelling goods, numbering the books etc. It may be a hand held scanner or may be embedded in a stationary scanner.
- Bar code reader scans a bar code image, converts it into an alphanumeric value which is then fed to the computer to which bar code reader is connected.

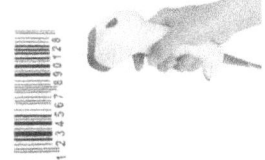

Fig. 1.44: Barcode reader

Advantages:
  (i) Much smaller in size.
  (ii) Less expensive i.e. barcodes are directly printed onto plastic or paper materials, therefore the only cost involved is the ink; a tiny overall cost.
  (iii) Barcodes work with the same accuracy on various materials in which they are placed.
  (iv) Barcode readers are helpful in stores in order to maintain accurate and updated inventory monitoring.

Disadvantages:
  (i) Barcode scanners need a direct line of sight to the barcode to be able to read.
  (ii) They are very labour intensive; as they must be scanned individually.
  (iii) Barcodes are more easily damaged; as the line of sight is needed to scan, the printed bar code has to be exposed on the outside of the product.
  (iv) Scratched or crumpled barcodes may cause problems.
  (v) Data must be coded in the barcode.
  (vi) In laser scanning, durability and cost are the two disadvantages.

1.8.2 Output Devices

- Output device can produce the final product of machine processing into a form usable by users. It provides machine to man communication.
- The output devices accept the results after processed by the CPU, converts it into human acceptable form and supplies it to the user.
- An output device is equipment used to see, hear, or otherwise accept the results of information processing requests.

1.8.2.1 Monitor (CRT and LCD)

- Monitor commonly called as Visual Display Unit (VDU) is the main output device of a computer.
- Monitor forms images from tiny dots, called pixels, that are arranged in a rectangular form. The sharpness of the image depends upon the no. of the pixels.
- The monitor displays the video and graphics information generated by the computer through the video card.
- Monitors are very similar to televisions but usually display information at a much higher resolution.
- The monitor is also known as screen, display, video display or video screen.
- Monitors come in two major types i.e. LCD and CRT.

1. CRT (Cathode Ray Tube):

- CRT monitor look much like old-fashioned televisions and are very deep in size. A monitor contains a Cathode Ray Tube (CRT), hardware to control an electronics beam and a power supply.
- A CRT is used to display numbers, letter and graphics.
- In the CRT display is made up of small picture elements called pixels for short. The smaller the pixels, the better the image clarity, or resolution. It takes more than one illuminated pixel to form whole character, such as the letter e in the word help.
- A finite number of character can be displayed on a screen at once. The screen can be divided into a series of character boxes - fixed location on the screen where a standard character can be placed.
- The most screens are capable of displaying 80 character of data horizontally and 25 lines vertically.

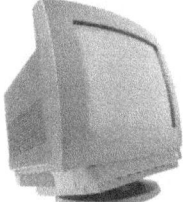

Fig. 1.45: CRT monitor

How CRT Monitor works?

- CRT monitor looks like TV screen. This kind of screen uses the Cathode Ray Tube (CRT) technology.
- CRT is a partially evacuated glass tube which is filled with an inert gas at very low pressure.
- Images are formed in this CRT by an electron gun shooting a stream of electrons at the surface of phosphorescent. Deflection coils are used to divert electron beam and strike on the exact position of phosphorescent surface.

- The CRT screen can be classified into two types in terms of color capability:
  (i) Monochrome Monitor: Monochrome monitor actually displays only two colors, one for the background and other for the foreground.
  (ii) Color Monitor: Color Monitor display color but the number of color they can display depends on the video adaptor capabilities as well as the monitors. Color monitor can display from 1 to 16 million different colors. Color monitor are sometime called RGB monitor because they accept three separate signal RED, GREEN and BLUE.
- Fig. 1.46 shows structure of CRT.

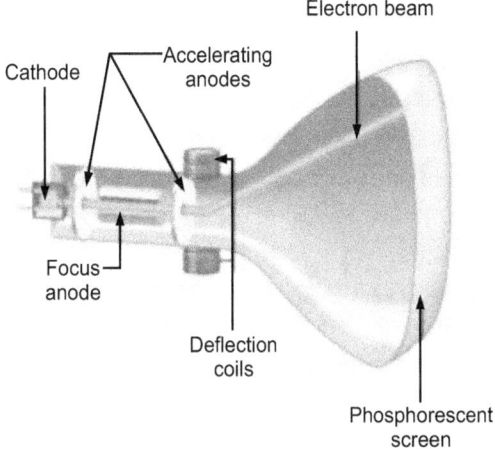

Fig. 1.46: Structure of CRT (internal)

- There are some disadvantage of CRT:
  (i) Large in size, and
  (ii) High power consumption.

2. LCD (Liquid Crystal Display):

- LCD monitor are much thinner, use less energy, and provide a greater graphics quality.
- LCD monitor have completely obsoleted CRT monitor due to their higher quality, smaller footprint on the desk, and decreasing price.
- The flat-panel display refer to a class of video devices that have reduced volume, weight and power requirement compared to the CRT.
- We can hang them on walls or wear them on your wrists. Current uses for flat-panel displays include calculators, videogames, monitors, laptop computer, graphics display.

Fig. 1.47: LCD monitor

- The flat-panel display are divided into two categories:
  - **(i) Emissive Displays:** The emissive displays are devices that convert electrical energy into light. Example are plasma panel and LED (Light-Emitting Diodes).
  - **(ii) Non-Emissive Displays:** The Non-emissive displays use optical effects to convert sunlight or light from some other source into graphics patterns. Example is LCD (Liquid-Crystal Device).

How LCD Monitor Works?

- In LCD or liquid crystalline material is sandwich between two glass or plates as shown in Fig. 1.48 (LCD monitor). The front plate is transparent and the back plate is reflective.
- The less expensive LCD's are called passive matrix LCD's. The expensive LCD's are called active matrix LCD's (also called thinfil transistor - TFT) used transistor to control the color of each screen pixel. Speed and color quality is improved on passive matrix LCD's.

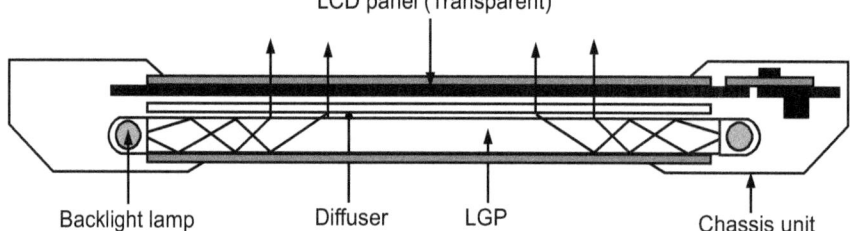

Fig. 1.48: Working of LCD monitor

Advantages:
  (i) Power consumption is low.
  (ii) Cost is less.

Disadvantages:
  (i) Turn-on and Turn-off is large hence they are slow devices.
  (ii) Their life span is less when used on DC.
  (iii) They occupy large area.
  (iv) Most monitor are in a widescreen format and range in size from 17" to 24" or more. This size is a diagonal measurement from one corner of the screen to the other.

1.8.2.2 Plasma Display

- A plasma display is a computer video display in which each pixel on the screen is illuminated by a tiny bit of plasma or charged gas, somewhat like a tiny neon light.
- Plasma displays are thinner than Cathode Ray Tube (CRT) displays and brighter than Liquid Crystal Displays (LCD).
- Plasma displays are sometimes marketed as "thin-panel" displays and can be used to display either analog video signals or display modes digital computer input.

Fig. 1.49: Plasma display

1.8.2.3 Printers

- Printer is a peripheral which produces a hard copy (permanent readable text and/or graphics) of documents stored in electronic form, usually on physical print media such as paper or transparencies.
- Printer is the most important output device, which is used to print information on paper.
- The quality of printer depends on following factors:
    1. **Speed:** The impact printer is slower than non-impact printer. The speed of dot matrix printer depends on number of pins. The expensive printer is faster than non-expensive printers. Generally, color printer is also slow.
    2. **Resolution:** The sharpness of text and image per inch is called resolution of computer. The quality of output depends on resolution. The high-resolution computer is expensive than low-resolution computers.
    3. **Memory:** The costly input/output device has own local memory to hold data at the time of processing. The printer is slower than the processor so, if it has its own memory to hold processed data, the speed can be increased. So, high memory printer is preferred for quality and fast printings.
    4. **Color:** The color is a part of information. The colorful text and graphics are more attractive than plain text and graphics. So, color printer is also a part of quality printings.
- Fig. 1.50 shows types of printers.

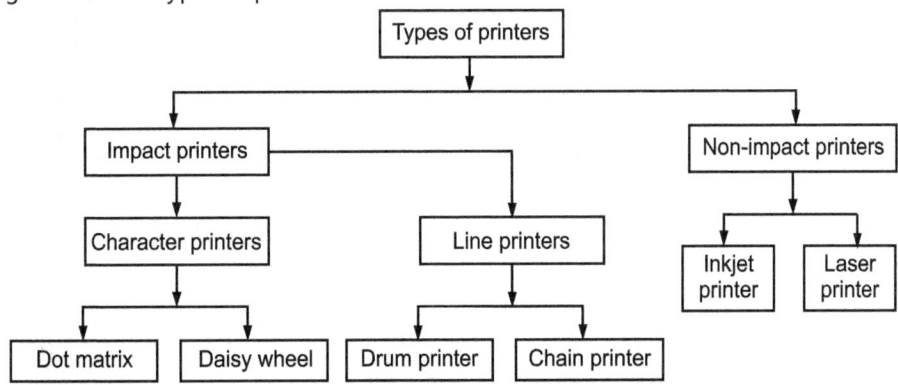

Fig. 1.50: Types of computer printer

1. **Impact Printers:**
   - The printer that print the character by striking against the ribbon and onto the paper, are called impact printers.
   - An impact printer is like a typewriter and the character are formed by physically striking the type devices against an inked ribbon.
   - Impact printer can produce a page, a line, or a character at a time. Print quality is low, but these printer are mainly used for printing backup copies of large amounts of data.
   - Some of the examples of impact printer are: Dot matrix printer, Daisy wheel printers, Drum printer and Chain printers.

   Characteristics of Impact Printers:
   (i) Very low consumable costs.
   (ii) Impact printer are very noisy.
   (iii) Useful for bulk printing due to low cost.
   (iv) There is physical contact with the paper to produce an image.
   - Impact printer are of two types:
     (i) Character printers: Character printer are printer which print one character at a time. These are of further two types Dot Matrix Printer (DMP) and Daisy wheel printer.
     (ii) Line printers: A line printer is a high-speed printing device that is able to store and print a complete line of information at a time. Line printer are printer which print one line at a time. Large computer system typically use line printer. Line printer are of further two types Drum printer and Chain printer.

   Advantages of Impact Printers:
   (i) Design and functioning of this kind of printer is easier than that of non-impact printer.
   (ii) Since, the image is produced as a result of impact, multiple copies can be produced by the use of carbon paper.

   Disadvantages of Impact Printer:
   (i) They are noisy in operation.
   (ii) The wear and tear of printer head causes the periodical replacement of the printer head.

2. **Non-impact Printers:**
   - Non-impact printer generally, use specially coated or sensitized paper that respond to thermal or electrostatic stimuli to form an image.
   - The printer that print the character without striking against the ribbon and onto the paper, are called non-impact printers.
   - Non-impact printer print a complete page at a time, also called as page printers.
   - Non-impact printers, used almost everywhere now, are faster and more quiet than impact printer because they have fewer moving parts.
   - Non-impact printer are of two types Laser printer and Inkjet printers.

Characteristics of Non-impact printers:
   (i) Faster than impact printers.
   (ii) They are not noisy.
   (iii) High quality.
   (iv) Support many fonts and different character size.

Advantages of non-impact printer:
   (i) Soundless operation.
   (ii) High quality output.

Disadvantages of non-impact printer:
   (i) Multiple copies cannot be produced in a single pass.
   (ii) They are costly.

Comparison between Impact and Non-impact printers:

Impact printer	Non-impact printer
1. Impact printer are usually cheap.	1. Non-impact printer are usually more expensive that impact printer.
2. Impact printer is not quiet.	2. Non-impact printer is quitter.
3. Produce poor quality print.	3. Produce better quality print.
4. Its prints non-electrically.	4. Its prints electrically.
5. **Example:** Dot-matrix, daisy wheel etc.	5. **Example:** Inkjet, thermal, Laser etc.

(i) Character Printer:
- These printers prints one character at a time. Dot matrix printer and Daisy wheel printers are the character printers.

1. Dot Matrix Printer:
- In the general sense many printer rely on a matrix of pixels, or dots, that together form the larger image. However, the term dot matrix printer is specifically used for impact printer that use a matrix of small pins to create precise dots.
- A dot matrix printer or impact matrix printer refer to a type of computer printer with a print head that runs back and forth on the page and prints by impact, striking an ink-soaked cloth ribbon against the paper, much like a typewriter.
- Dot matrix technology uses a series or matrix of pins to create printed dots arranged to form character on a piece of paper. Because the printing involves mechanical pressure, these printer can create carbon copies and carbonless copies.
- The print head mechanism pushes each pin into the ribbon, which then strikes the paper. Many offices and government agencies use them because they can make multiple copies at lowest cost.

Fig. 1.51: Dot matrix printer

Working of Dot Matrix Printers:
- Fig. 1.52 shows working of dot matrix printer.
- Dot matrix refer to the way the printer creates character or images on paper.
- This is done by several tiny pins, aligned in a column, striking an ink ribbon positioned between the pins and the paper, creating dots on the paper.
- Character are composed of patterns of these dots by moving the printhead laterally across the page in very small increments.
- The pins, contained in the printhead, are about one inch long and are driven by several hammer which force each pin into contact with the ink ribbon (and paper) at a certain time.
- The force on these hammer comes from the magnetic pull of small wire coils (solenoids) which are energized at a particular time, depending on the character to be printed.
- Timing of the signals sent to the solenoids is programmed into the printer for each character, and translated from information sent by the computer about which character to print.

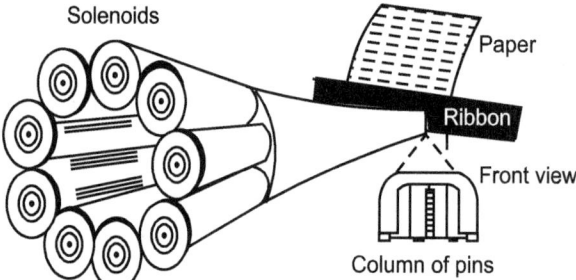

Fig. 1.52: Working of dot matrix printer

Advantages:
    (i) They can print on multi-part stationary or make carbon copies.
    (ii) Low printing cost.
    (iii) They can bear environmental conditions.
    (iv) Long life.

Disadvantages:
    (i) These printer are noisy.
    (ii) Low resolution.
    (iii) Very limited color performance.
    (iv) Low speed.
    (v) Servicing cost of this printer is more than buying a new one.

2. Daisy Wheel Printer:

- A daisy wheel printer is an electronic device that can be connected to a word processor or computer to allow documents to be printed from that machine.
- The basic functionality of these devices is similar to other printers, such as dot matrix or inkjet printers, though the way in which a document is printed is quite different.
- A daisy wheel printer uses a printing mechanism known as a "daisy wheel," which consists of numerous raised letter and number arrayed in a circle.
- Head is lying on a wheel and Pins corresponding to character are like petals of Daisy (flower name) that is why it is called Daisy Wheel Printer.
- These printer are generally used for word-processing in offices which require a few letter to be send here and there with very nice quality representation.

Fig. 1.53: Daisy wheel

Working of Daisy wheel printer:

- Daisy wheel printer operate in much the same fashion as a typewriter. A hammer strikes a wheel with petals (the daisy wheel), each petal containing a letter form at its tip.
- The letter form strikes a ribbon of ink, depositing the ink on the page and thus printing a character.
- By rotating the daisy wheel, different character are selected for printing.
- These printer were also referred to as letter-quality printer because, during their heyday, they could produce text which was as clear and crisp as a typewriter (though they were nowhere near the quality of printing presses). The fastest letter-quality printer printed 30 character per second.

Advantages:
1. More reliable than dot matrix printers.
2. Better quality.
3. The fonts of character can be easily changed.

Disadvantages:
1. Slower than dot matrix printers.
2. Noisy in operation.
3. More expensive than dot matrix printers.

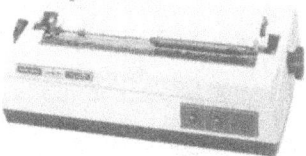

Fig. 1.54: Daisy wheel printer

(ii) Line Printers:
- Line printer are print one line at a time.

1. Drum Printer:
- Drum printer is like a drum in shape so it called drum printer.
- Drum Printer consists of a drum which consists of a number of characters; those are printed on the drum. And the number of character or number of tracks are divided, after examining the width of the paper.
- The surface of drum is divided into number of tracks. Total tracks are equal to size of paper i.e. for a paper width of 132 characters, drum will have 132 tracks.
- A character set is embossed on track. The different character sets are available in market 48 character set, 64 and 96 character set. One rotation of drum prints one line.
- Drum printer are fast in speed and speed is in between 300 to 2000 lines per minute.

Working of Drum Printer:
- In a typical drum printer design, a fixed font character set is engraved onto the periphery of a number of print wheels, the number equals the number of columns (letter in a line) the printer could print.
- The wheels, joined to form a large drum (cylinder), spin at high speed and paper and an inked ribbon are stepped (moved) past the print position.
- As the desired character for each column passes the print position, a hammer strikes the paper from the rear and presses the paper against the ribbon and the drum, causing the desired character to be recorded on the continuous paper.
- Because the drum carrying the letterforms (characters) remains in constant motion, the strike-and-retreat action of the hammer had to be very fast.

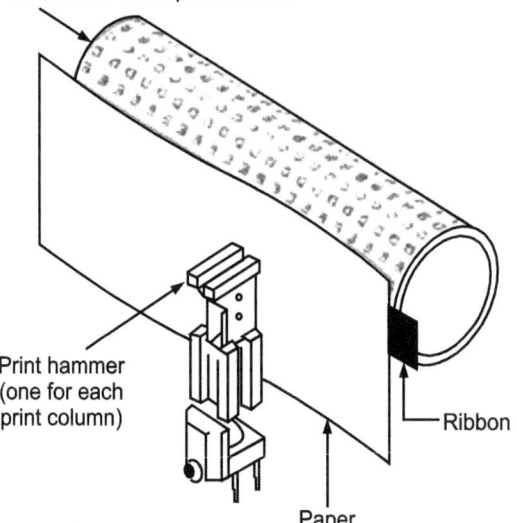

Fig. 1.55: Working of drum printer

Advantages:
   (i) Very high speed.

Disadvantages
   (i) Very expensive.
   (ii) Character fonts can not be changed.

2. Chain Printer:

- In this printer chain of character sets are used so it is called chain printers.
- A standard character set may have 48, 64, 96 characters.
- These are also line printers, which print one line at a time. All the character are printed on the chain and the set of character are placed on the chain.
- There are 48 and 64 and 96 character set printer are available. There are also some hammers, those are placed in front of the chain, and paper is placed between the hammer and the inked ribbon.
- The total number of hammer will be equal to the total number of print positions.

Working of Chain Printer:

- Chain printer (also known as train printers) placed the type on moving bar (a horizontally-moving chain).
- As with the drum printer, as the correct character passed by each column, a hammer was fired from behind the paper. Compared to drum printers, chain printer had the advantage that the type chain could usually be changed by the operator.
- By selecting chains that had a smaller character set (for example, just number and a few punctuation marks), the printer could print much faster than if the chain contained the entire upper - and lower - case alphabets, numbers, and all special symbols.

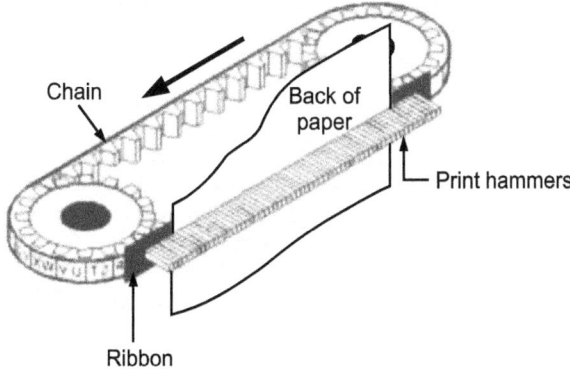

Fig. 1.56: Working of chain printer

Advantages:
   (i) Character fonts can easily be changed.
   (ii) Different languages can be used with the same printer.

Disadvantages:
   (i) Noisy in operation.
   (ii) Do not have the ability to print any shape of characters.

4. Inkjet Printers:

- Inkjet printer are non impact character printer based on a relatively new technology.
- Inkjet printer print character by spraying small drops of ink onto paper.
- Inkjet printer produce high quality output with presentable features.
- Inkjet printer make less noise because no hammering is done and these have many styles of printing modes available.
- Using inkjet printer, colour printing is also possible. Some models of Inkjet printer can produce multiple copies of printing also.

Fig. 1.57: Inkjet printer

- An inkjet printer is a type of computer printer that creates a digital image by propelling droplets of ink onto paper.
- Inkjet printer are the most commonly used type of printer and range from small inexpensive consumer models to very large professional machines that can cost up to thousands of dollars. Its consumable is called inkjet cartridge.

Working of Inkjet Printers:

- Inkjet printer operate by propelling variably-sized droplets of ink onto almost any sized page. They are the most common type of computer printer for the general consumer due to their low cost, high quality of output, capability of printing in different colors.
- A typical inkjet receives control info from your printer driver/PC, or may process the printout in its onboard electronics. Either way, roller advance a page from your paper tray (1) under a sliding printhead/cartridge assembly (2). Then, the printhead stepper motor (3), kicks in, drawing the assembly on a sliding rod (4), to its starting position, usually via a belt (5).
- The printhead (6) proper is an incredible piece of miniaturization, in some cases fabricated via an etching process similar to semiconductor manufacture. On some printers, the head and ink cartridge (7) are one unit.
- The head's microscopic nozzles (8) anywhere from dozens to literally thousands-are outlets for incredibly tiny ink chamber (9), which are fed by the cartridge's reservoirs. Microscopic droplets (10), measured in millionths of a millionth of a liter, fire through the nozzles.

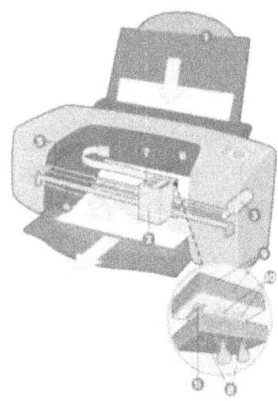

Fig. 1.58: Working of inkjet printer

Advantages:
- (i) High quality printing.
- (ii) More reliable.
- (iii) Low printer cost.
- (iv) Compact size.
- (v) Low noise.

Disadvantages:
- (i) Expensive as cost per page is high.
- (ii) Slow as compare to laser printer.
- (iii) The ink is often very expensive.
- (iv) Lifetime of inkjet prints produced by inkjet printer is limited. They will eventually fade and the color balance may change.
- (v) Easily get blur if get water drop.
- (vi) Easy to get clogging on inkjet nozzles.

5. **Laser Printer:**
- Laser printers are non impact printers.
- Laser printer use laser lights to produces the dots needed to form the character to be printed on a page.

Fig. 1.59: Laser printer

- Laser printing is the most advance technology.
- In laser printing, a computer sends data to the printer. Printer translates this data into printable image data. This kind of printer use xerographic principle.
- A laser beam discharges photo sensitive drum.
- A latent image is created on drum, during development process toner is attracted to the drum surface and then transferred to the paper. Its consumable called toner cartridge or laser toner.

Working of Laser Printer:
- Static electricity is the principle behind laser printers.
- A revolving drum or cylinder builds up an electrical charge.
- A tiny laser beam pointed at the drum discharges the surface in the pattern of the letter and images to be printed creating a surface with positive and negative areas.
- The surface is then coated with toner, a fine powder that is positively-charged so it clings only to the negatively-charged areas, and is then passed onto the paper to form the positive image.
- The paper then passes through heated roller fusing the toner to the paper. Color laser make multiple passes, in order to mix the different color toners.

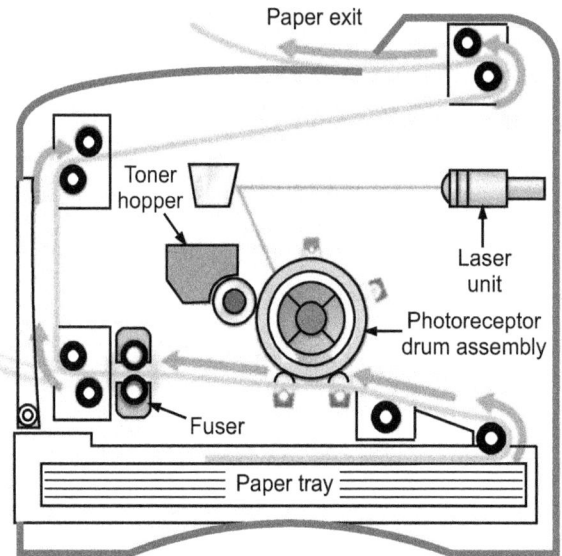

Fig. 1.60: Working of laser printer

Advantages:
  (i) Very high speed.
  (ii) Very high quality output.
  (iii) Low noise in printing operation.
  (iv) Support many fonts and different character size.
  (v) Low cost per page as compare to inkjet printer.
  (vi) Give good and high graphics quality.

Disadvantages:
  (i) Laser printer are more expensive, but getting more affordable these days.
  (ii) Cannot be used to produce multiple copies of a document in a single printing.
  (iii) Their size is generally larger.

Comparison between Laser, Inkjet and Dot Matrix Printers:

Terms	Laser Printers	Inkjet Printers	Dot Matrix Printers
Invented	1969 by Gary Starkweather.	Developed in the early 1950s.	Introduced by Digital Equipment Corporation in 1970.
How it works	Laser printer use fine ink powder and heat the powder on the paper.	Inkjet printer spray liquid ink on paper through microscopic nozzles.	Dot Matrix works having pins pushed against an ink soaked ribbon to paper.
Types	Personal and Office printers. Black and White or color printers.	Continuous (CIJ) and drop-on demand (DOD).	Serial Dot Matrix printer and Line Dot Matrix.
Price per page	USD 0.6 for black and white page. Much higher for a color page.	USD 0.20 color page; USD 0.4-0.5 black and white page.	Copies are quite cheap.
Cost for basic printer	Approximately USD 60-1000, depending on the size and use of the printer.	Approximately USD 100-150	Basic cost of printer is quite expensive. Compared to an inkjet, dot matrix can cost between two to ten times more.
Printing speed	20 pages a minute	6 pages a minute	30-550 character per second.
Quality	Printing quality is adequate. Best for black and white.	Printing quality is good, specially for smaller fonts.	Printing quality is bad if printing images. In terms of text, printing is fine.
Color Printing	Basic models only offer black and white, with higher models providing color printing.	Yes provides color printing.	Limited color printing.

contd. ...

Black and White Quality	Black and white quality is adequate, best for bulk printing.	Black and white quality is excellent, specially with small fonts.	Can print adequate quality images.
Color Quality	Color quality is a bit poor, with banding.	Color printing is sharp and excellent.	Only works best with low-res images.
Size	Smaller is available but is more common in larger sizes.	Smaller and more compact.	Size ranges depending on usage. New compact ones are also available.
Features	Offer scanner and faxing machines built in. Has bigger input trays, direct connecting facilities (wireless)	Can be used for wider range of paper (photo paper, vinyl, self-adhesive papers), accurate photographic images, ink is not waterproof.	Used for a variety of purposes. Can print on various types of papers.
Usage	Most commonly used for commercial purposes and places that require black and white printing.	More commonly used for homes as the unit is smaller and ink is cheaper.	Used to be used for office uses, but now only used by select places such as banks.
Maintenance	Expensive	Cheaper	Expensive, parts are hard to come by.
Advantages	Prints faster, bigger input trays.	Quieter in operation, high print quality, no warm up time, low cost per page	Cheaper to print as ribbon is cheap.
Disadvantages	More susceptible to paper jams. Toner is very expensive, print quality for color is adequate, device itself is expensive, has health hazards if not properly maintained.	Ink is expensive, issues with 'intelligent' ink cartridges, lifetime of inkjet prints produced by aqueous inks is shorter, ink is not waterproof, and nozzle is prone to clogging.	Initial purchase is expensive, maintenance is expensive, prints is not fast, makes noise.

1.8.2.4 Plotters

- A plotter is a device that draws images on paper after receiving a command from a computer.
- A plotter is a special output device used to produce hardcopies of graphs and designs on the paper.
- A plotter is typically used to print large-format graphs or maps such as construction maps, engineering drawings and big posters.
- Plotter are divided into two types drum plotter and flatbed plotter.

1. Drum Plotter:
- A drum plotter is also known as roller plotter.
- Drum plotter consists of a drum or roller on which a paper is placed and the drum rotates back and forth to produce the graph on the paper.
- Drum plotter also consists of mechanical device known as Robotic Drawing Arm that holds a set of colored ink pens or pencils.
- The robotic drawing arm moves side to side as the paper are rolled back and forth through the roller. In this way, a perfect graph or map is created on the paper. This work is done under the control of computer.
- Drum plotter are used to produce continuous output, such as plotting earthquake activity.

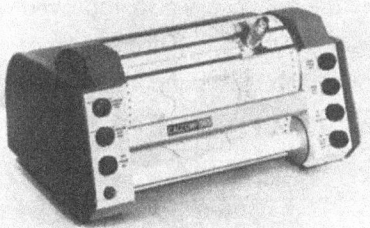

Fig. 1.61: Drum plotter

2. Flatbed Plotter:
- A flatbed plotter is also known as table plotter.
- Flatbed plotter plots on paper that is spread and fixed over a rectangular flatbed table.
- The flatbed plotter uses two robotic drawing arms, each of which holds a set of colored ink pens or pencils. The drawing arms move over the stationary paper and draw the graph on the paper. Typically, the plot size is equal to the area of a bed.
- The plot size may be 20 by 50 feet. It is used in the design of cars, ships, aircrafts, buildings, highways etc. Flatbed plotter is very slow in drawing or printing graphs. The large and complicated drawing can take several hour to print.
- The main reason of the slow printing is due to the movement mechanical devices.

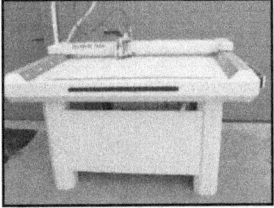

Fig. 1.62: Flatbed plotter

- Today, mechanical plotter have been replaced by thermal, electrostatic and inkjet plotters. These systems are faster and cheaper. They also produce large size drawings.

Advantages:
  (i) Plotters are faster than other types of printing machines, including the desktop printer.
  (ii) The versatility of plotter is another major advantage. A plotter can be hooked up to any computer. There are a number of plotter configuration options as well, depending on the model and series we buy.
  (iii) Plotter allows us to print and manipulate the plotter in a number of ways, and it also allows it to be connected to any type of machine. Plotter also have their own interfaces in some cases, which allow the user to operate and control them without resetting the paper or having to maintain the plotter during operation.
  (iv) The precision of the plotter is the main advantage for engineering drawings. Plotter have advanced technology that allows them to print more precise lines. When printing a set of drawings for a bridge or skyscraper, it is imperative that each line be precise.
  (v) Color accuracy and picture quality are also improved with the overall precision of the plotter. This is an advantage for a business looking for an inexpensive and efficient way to print promotional materials, banner and more.

Difference between Input and Output Devices:

Input devices	Output devices
1. An input device for a computer is anything that sends information to the CPU to perform a specific function.	1. Output is processed data or information.
2. A computer has the ability to use many different types of input devices to provide a unique experience to each user.	2. Output is data that has been processed into useful form, called information.
3. Computer input devices include many types of hardware such as a keyboard, mouse, webcam, scanner as well as a microphone.	3. The most common types of output are text, graphics, audio and video.
4. Input device are usually smaller.	4. Output device are large in size.
5. Cheaper in cost.	5. Costly in price.
6. Example: Keyboard, Microphone, Mouse etc.	6. Example: Speaker, Monitor, Printers etc.

1.9 Number Systems

- We are all familiar with number system which is an ordered set of ten (0, 1, 3, 4, 5, 6, 7, 8, 9) the symbols or digits.
- In computers we use data in numeric (0, 1, ... 9), alphabets (a, b, c, ... z, A, B, ... Z) or special characters (· ;, ,) etc.
- **The system in which an ordered set of digits are used to specify any number is called number system.**
- There are two types of number systems :
  1. Non-positional number system, and
  2. Positional number system.

1. **Positional Number Systems :**
- A positional number system in which each position is related to the next by a constant multiplier of that number system.
- For each position that the number is in, in that system has a relative symbol or meaning, relates to the number directly next to it.
- The total value of a positional number is the total of the resultant values of all positions.

2. **Non-Positional Number Systems :**
- In a non-positional number system, each number in each position does not have to be positional itself.
- Every system varies by country and it depends on symbols and values set by the people of that country.
- For example, the Egyptians use Hieroglyphics, and the Greeks use a numeral system.
- In this system, we have symbols, such as I for 1, II for 2, III for 3, IV for 4 etc.
- The various types of positional number systems are binary, ternary, octal, decimal, duo-decimal and hexadecimal.
- Some of the common radices used in digital system give rise to different positional number systems. They are summarized in following table.

Radix or Base 'b'	Number Systems	Basic digits (i.e. symbols) used in number systems
2	Binary	0, 1
3	Ternary	0, 1, 2
8	Octal	0, 1, 2, 3, 4, 5, 6, 7
10	Decimal	0, 1, 2, 3, 4, 5, 6, 7, 8, 9
12	Duo-decimal	0, 1, 2, 3, 4, 5, 6, 7, 8, 9, A, B
16	Hexadecimal	0, 1, 2, 3, 4, 5, 6, 7, 8, 9, A, B, C, D, E, F

1.9.1 Binary Number System

- The number system which uses only two digits or symbols, viz. 0 and 1 is called a binary number system.
- Naturally, the base (or radix) in this number system is 2. The symbols are 0 and 1 and the meaning associated with these symbols is the same as in the decimal number system.
- In binary number system, a binary number is called a bit, instead of binary digit. Incidentally, bit is a concatenation of the words binary digit.
- Binary number system, as the name indicates, is a number system in which the base (or radix) is 2 and numbers used are 0 and 1.
- From right to left, the successive positions of the binary number are weighted 1, 2, 4, 8, 16, 32, 64 etc. A list of the first several powers of 2 follows :

   $2^0 = 1$ $2^1 = 2$ $2^2 = 4$ $2^3 = 8$ $2^4 = 16$ $2^5 = 32$
   $2^6 = 64$ $2^7 = 128$ $2^8 = 256$ $2^9 = 512$ $2^{10} = 1024$ $2^{11} = 2048$

- For reference, the following table shows the decimal numbers 0 through 31 with their binary equivalents :

Decimal	Binary	Decimal	Binary
0	0	16	10000
1	1	17	10001
2	10	18	10010
3	11	19	10101
4	100	20	10100
5	101	21	10101
6	110	22	10110
7	111	23	10111
8	1000	24	11000
9	1001	25	11001
10	1010	26	11010
11	1011	27	11011
12	1100	28	11100
13	1101	29	11101
14	1110	30	11110
15	1111	31	11111

1.9.2 Octal Number System

- The number system which has the base (or radix) 8 and uses only eight digits or symbols, viz. 0, 1, 2, 3, 4, 5, 6 and 7 is called Octal number system.
- This system has 8 digits or symbols 0, 1, 2, 3, 4, 5, 6 and 7.
- Since, its base (or radix) is $8 = 2^3$, it is very simple to covert binary number to octal number system or vice versa.
- From right to left, the successive positions of the octal number are weighted 1, 8, 64, 512 etc. A list of the first several powers of 8 follows :
  $8^0 = 1$ $8^1 = 8$ $8^2 = 64$ $8^3 = 512$ $8^4 = 4096$ $8^5 = 32768$
- For reference, the following table shows the decimal numbers 0 through 31 with their octal equivalents :

Decimal	Octal	Decimal	Octal
0	0	16	20
1	1	17	21
2	2	18	22
3	3	19	23
4	4	20	24
5	5	21	25
6	6	22	26
7	7	23	27
8	10	24	30
9	11	25	31
10	12	26	32
11	13	27	33
12	14	28	34
13	15	29	35
14	16	30	36
15	17	31	37

1.9.3 Decimal Number System

- The number system which uses ten digits or symbols, viz. 0, 1, 2, 3, 4, 5, 6, 7, 8 and 9 is called a decimal number system.
- Decimal means 10. There are only 10 basic digits in this number system from 0 to 9.
- Decimal number system as the name indicates is a number system in which the base (or radix) is 10 and the digits or symbols used are : 0, 1, 2, 3, 4, 5, 6, 7, 8, 9.

- The weight associated with each symbol can be expressed as shown in following table.

MSD									LSD
10^4	10^3	10^2	10^1	10^0	.	10^{-1}	10^{-2}	10^{-3}	10^{-4}
10000	1000	100	10	1	.	1/10	1/100	1/1000	1/10000

↑ Weight   ↑ Decimal point

- In this case the Most Significant Digit (MSD) and Least Significant Digit (LSD) are the left most and the right most digit respectively.

- For example, the decimal number 1275 (written 1275_{10}) can be expanded as follows :

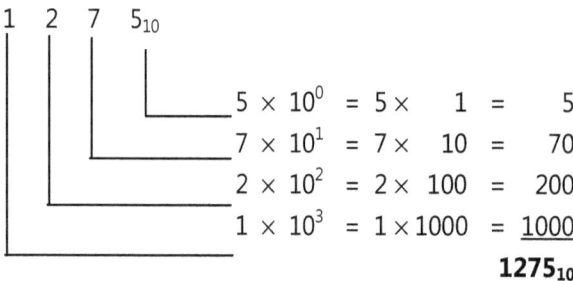

$$
\begin{aligned}
5 \times 10^0 &= 5 \times 1 = 5 \\
7 \times 10^1 &= 7 \times 10 = 70 \\
2 \times 10^2 &= 2 \times 100 = 200 \\
1 \times 10^3 &= 1 \times 1000 = \underline{1000} \\
&\qquad\qquad\qquad 1275_{10}
\end{aligned}
$$

- Remember the mathematical rule that $n^0 = 1$, or any number raised to the zero power is equal to 1.

- Here, is an another example of an expanded decimal number (10406_{10}).

$$
\begin{aligned}
6 \times 10^0 &= 6 \times 1 = 6 \\
0 \times 10^1 &= 0 \times 10 = 0 \\
4 \times 10^2 &= 4 \times 100 = 400 \\
0 \times 10^3 &= 0 \times 1000 = 0 \\
1 \times 10^4 &= 1 \times 10000 = \underline{10000} \\
&\qquad\qquad\qquad 10406_{10}
\end{aligned}
$$

1.9.4 Hexadecimal Number System

- Hexadecimal means 16. The number system which uses the radix (or base) 16 and 16 digits (or symbols), viz. 0, 1, 2, 3, 4, 5, 6, 7, 8, 9, A, B, C, D, E and F is called Hexadecimal number system.

- It is clear that number of digits corresponding to a given decimal or binary number is much less because the radix is 16. Thus, it is economical to use this system in digital computers and microprocessors.

- For reference, the following table shows the decimal numbers 0 through 31 with their hexadecimal equivalents :

Decimal	Hexadecimal	Decimal	Hexadecimal
0	0	16	10
1	1	17	11
2	2	18	12
3	3	19	13
4	4	20	14
5	5	21	15
6	6	22	16
7	7	23	17
8	8	24	18
9	9	25	19
10	A	26	1A
11	B	27	1B
12	C	28	1C
13	D	29	1D
14	E	30	1E
15	F	31	1F

- The same principles of positional number systems were applied to the decimal, binary and octal number systems can be applied to the hexadecimal number system.
- However, the base of the hexadecimal number system is 16, so each position of the hexadecimal number represents a successive power of 16.
- From right to left, the successive positions of the hexadecimal number are weighted 1, 16, 256, 4096, 65536, etc.

$16^0 = 1 \quad 16^1 = 16 \quad 16^2 = 256 \quad 16^3 = 4096 \quad 16^4 = 65536$

1.9.5 Conversions

1. **Binary To Decimal Conversion:**
- To determine the value of a binary number (1001_2, for example), we can expand the number using the positional weight as follows :

$1 \; 0 \; 0 \; 1_2$

$1 \times 2^0 = 1 \times 1 = 1$
$0 \times 2^1 = 0 \times 2 = 0$
$0 \times 2^2 = 0 \times 4 = 0$
$1 \times 2^3 = 1 \times 8 = \underline{8}$
$\qquad\qquad\qquad\qquad 9_{10}$

So, **(1001_2) = 9_{10}**

- Here's another example to determine the value of the binary number 1101010_2.

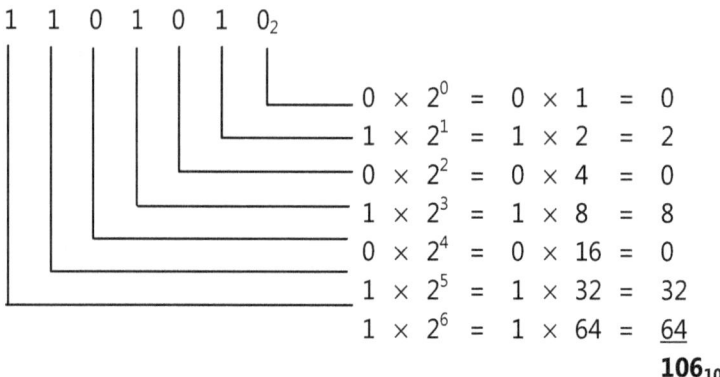

$$0 \times 2^0 = 0 \times 1 = 0$$
$$1 \times 2^1 = 1 \times 2 = 2$$
$$0 \times 2^2 = 0 \times 4 = 0$$
$$1 \times 2^3 = 1 \times 8 = 8$$
$$0 \times 2^4 = 0 \times 16 = 0$$
$$1 \times 2^5 = 1 \times 32 = 32$$
$$1 \times 2^6 = 1 \times 64 = \underline{64}$$
$$106_{10}$$

So, $(1101010_2) = 106_{10}$

2. **Decimal To Binary Conversion:**
- To convert a decimal number to its binary equivalent, the remainder method can be used. (This method can be used to convert a decimal number into any other base).
- The remainder method involves the following four steps:
   1. Divide the decimal number by the base (in the case of binary, divide by 2).
   2. Indicate the remainder to the right.
   3. Continue dividing into each quotient (and indicating the remainder) until the divide operation produces a zero quotient.
   4. The base 2 number is the numeric remainder reading from the last division to the first (if you start at the bottom, the answer will read from top to bottom).
- Convert the decimal number 99_{10} to its binary equivalent.

$2\overline{)1}\ \ 0$	1	(7) Divide 2 into 1. The quotient is 0 with a remainder of 1, as indicated. Since the quotient is 0, stop here.
$2\overline{)3}\ \ 1$	1	(6) Divide 2 into 3. The quotient is 1 with a remainder of 1, as indicated.
$2\overline{)6}\ \ 3$	0	(5) Divide 2 into 6. The quotient is 3 with a remainder of 0, as indicated.
$2\overline{)12}\ \ 6$	0	(4) Divide 2 into 12. The quotient is 6 with a remainder of 0, as indicated.
$2\overline{)24}\ \ 12$	0	(3) Divide 2 into 24. The quotient is 12 with a remainder of 0, as indicated.
$2\overline{)49}\ \ 24$	1	(2) Divide 2 into 49 (the quotient from the previous division). The quotient is 24 with a remainder of 1, indicated on the right.
START HERE ⇒ $2\overline{)99}\ \ 49$	1	(1) Divide 2 into 99. The quotient is 49 with a remainder of 1; indicate the 1 on the right.

- The answer, reading the remainders from top to bottom, is 1100011, so $99_{10} = 1100011_2$.
- Convert the decimal number 13_{10} to its binary equivalent.

$$\begin{array}{r|l} 2 & 1 \\ \hline & 0 \end{array} \quad 1 \qquad \text{(4) Divide 2 into 1. The quotient is 0 with a remainder of 1, as indicated.}$$

$$\begin{array}{r|l} 2 & 3 \\ \hline & 1 \end{array} \quad 1 \qquad \text{(3) Divide 2 into 3. The quotient is 1 with a remainder of 1, as indicated.}$$

$$\begin{array}{r|l} 2 & 6 \\ \hline & 3 \end{array} \quad 0 \qquad \text{(2) Divide 2 into 6. The quotient from the previous division). The quotient is 3 with a remainder of 0, indicated the right.}$$

START HERE $\Rightarrow$ $\begin{array}{r|l} 2 & 13 \\ \hline & 6 \end{array}$ 1 (1) Divide 2 into 13. The quotient is 6 with a remainder of 1; indicate the 1 on the right.

- The answer, reading the remainders from top to bottom, is 1101, so $13_{10} = 1101_2$.

3. Octal to Decimal Conversion:

- The conversion of octal to decimal is simple. It is similar to binary to decimal conversion. The only difference is that the radix (or base) is 8 instead of 2.
- An example will make the procedure more illustrative.
- Convert the octal number $(7204)_8$ to its decimal equivalent.

$$(7204)_8 = 7 \times 8^3 + 2 \times 8^2 + 0 \times 8^1 + 4 \times 8^0$$
$$= 7 \times 512 + 2 \times 64 + 0 \times 8 + 4 \times 1$$
$$= 3584 + 128 + 4 = (3716)_{10}$$

Thus, $(7204)_8 = (3716)_{10}$

- To determine the value of an octal number $(367)_8$, we can expand the number using the positional weight as follows :

$3 \quad 6 \quad 7_8$

$7 \times 8^0 = 7 \times 1 = 7$
$6 \times 8^1 = 6 \times 8 = 48$
$3 \times 8^2 = 3 \times 64 = \underline{192}$
247_{10}

So, $(367_8) = 247_{10}$

- Here's another example to determine the value of the octal number 1601_8.

$1 \quad 6 \quad 0 \quad 1_8$

$1 \times 8^0 = 1 \times 1 = 1$
$0 \times 8^1 = 0 \times 8 = 0$
$6 \times 8^2 = 6 \times 64 = 384$
$1 \times 8^3 = 1 \times 512 = \underline{512}$
897_{10}

So, $(1601_8) = 897_{10}$

4. Octal to Binary Conversion:

- Converting a binary number to its octal equivalent or vice-versa is a simple matter. Three binary digits are equivalent to one octal digit, as shown in the table below:

Binary	Octal
000	0
001	1
010	2
011	3
100	4
101	5
110	6
111	7

- To convert from binary to octal, divide the binary number into groups of 3 digits starting on the right of the binary number.
- If the leftmost group has less than 3 bits, put in the necessary number of leading zeroes on the left.
- For each group of three bits, write the corresponding single octal digit.

  For examples :
  1. $1101001101110111_2 = ?_8$
     Binary : 001 101 001 101 110 111
     Octal :   1   5   1   5   6   7
     So, $1101001101110111_2 = 151567_8$
  2. $101101111_2 = ?_8$
     Binary : 101 101 111
     Octal :   5   5   7
     So, $101101111_2 = 557_8$

- To convert from octal to binary, write the corresponding group of three binary digits for each octal digit.

  For examples :
  1. $1764_8 = ?_2$
     Binary : 1   7   6   4
     Octal :   001 111 110 100
     So, $1764_8 = 001111110100_2$
  2. $731_8 = ?_2$
     Binary : 7   3   1
     Octal :   111 011 001
     So, $731_8 = 111011001_2$

5. Decimal to Octal Conversion:

- To convert a decimal number to its octal equivalent, the remainder method (the same method used in converting a decimal number to its binary equivalent) can be used.
- To review, the remainder method involves the following four steps:
    1. Divide the decimal number by the base (in the case of octal, divide by 8).
    2. Indicate the remainder to the right.
    3. Continue dividing into each quotient (and indicating the remainder) until the divide operation produces a zero quotient.
    4. The base 8 number is the numeric remainder reading from the last division to the first (if you start at the bottom, the answer will read from top to bottom).

Example 1: Convert the decimal number 465_{10} to its octal equivalent:

$$8\overline{)7} = 0 \text{ r } 7$$

(3) Divide 8 into 7. The quotient is 0 with a remainder of 7, as indicated. Since, the quotient is 0, stop here.

$$8\overline{)58} = 7 \text{ r } 2$$

(2) Divide 8 into 58 (the quotient from the previous division). The quotient is 7 with a remainder of 2, indicated the right.

START HERE ⇒ $8\overline{)465} = 58 \text{ r } 1$

(1) Divide 8 into 465. The quotient is 58 with a remainder of 1; indicate the 1 on the right.

- The answer, reading the remainders from top to bottom, is 721, **so $465_{10} = 721_8$**.

Example 2: Convert the decimal number 2548_{10} to its octal equivalent:

$$8\overline{)4} = 0 \text{ r } 4$$

(4) Divide 8 into 4. The quotient is 0 with a remainder of 4, as indicated. Since, the quotient is 0, stop here.

$$8\overline{)39} = 4 \text{ r } 7$$

(3) Divide 8 into 39. The quotient is 4 with a remainder of 7, indicated on the right.

$$8\overline{)318} = 39 \text{ r } 6$$

(2) Divide 8 into 318 (the quotient from the previous division). The quotient is 39 with a remainder of 6, indicated on the right.

START HERE ⇒ $8\overline{)2548} = 318 \text{ r } 4$

(1) Divide 8 into 2548. The quotient is 318 with a remainder of 4; indicate the 4 on the right.

- The answer, reading the remainders from top to bottom, is 4764, **so $2548_{10} = 4764_8$**.

6. Decimal to Hexadecimal Conversion:

- To convert a decimal number to its hexadecimal equivalent, the remainder method (the same method used in converting a decimal number to its binary equivalent) can be used.

- To review, the remainder method involves the following four steps:
    1. Divide the decimal number by the base (in the case of hexadecimal, divide by 16).
    2. Indicate the remainder to the right. If the remainder is between 10 and 15, indicate the corresponding hex digit A through F.
    3. Continue dividing into each quotient (and indicating the remainder) until the divide operation produces a zero quotient.
    4. The base 16 number is the numeric remainder reading from the last division to the first (if you start at the bottom, the answer will read from top to bottom).

    Example 1: Convert 9263_{10} to its hexadecimal equivalent:

    $16 \overline{)2} = 0$ remainder 2   (4) Divide 16 into 2. The quotient is 0 with a remainder of 2, as indicated. Since, the quotient is 0, stop here.

    $16 \overline{)36} = 2$ remainder 4   (3) Divide 16 into 36. The quotient is 2 with a remainder of 4, indicated on the right.

    $16 \overline{)578} = 36$ remainder 2   (2) Divide 16 into 578 (the quotient from the previous division). The quotient is 36 with a remainder of 2, indicated on the right.

    START HERE ⇒ $16 \overline{)9263} = 578$ remainder F   (1) Divide 16 into 9263. The quotient is 578 with a remainder of 15; indicate the hex equivalent, "F", on the right.

- The answer, reading the remainders from top to bottom is 242F

    So, $9263_{10} = 242F_{16}$

    Example 2: Convert 4259_{10} to its hexadecimal equivalent:

    $16 \overline{)1} = 0$ remainder 1   (4) Divide 16 into 1. The quotient is 0 with a remainder of 1, as indicated. Since the quotient is 0, stop here.

    $16 \overline{)16} = 1$ remainder 0   (3) Divide 16 into 16. The quotient is 1 with a remainder of 0, indicated on the right.

    $16 \overline{)266} = 16$ remainder A   (2) Divide 16 into 266 (the quotient from the previous division). The quotient is 16 with a remainder of 10, so the hex equivalent "A" is indicated on the right.

    START HERE ⇒ $16 \overline{)4259} = 266$ remainder 3   (1) Divide 16 into 4259. The quotient is 266 with a remainder of 3; so indicate 3 on the right.

- The answer, reading the remainders from top to bottom, is 10A3, So **4259_{10} = $10A3_{16}$.**

7. Hexadecimal to Decimal Conversion:

- We can use the same method that we used to convert binary numbers and octal numbers to decimal numbers to convert a hexadecimal number to a decimal number, keeping in mind that we are now dealing with base 16.

- From right to left, we multiply each digit of the hexadecimal number by the value of 16 raised to successive powers, starting with the zero power, then sum the results of the multiplications.

- Remember that if one of the digits of the hexadecimal number happens to be a letter A through F, then the corresponding value of 10 through 15 must be used in the multiplication.

Example 1: Convert the hexadecimal number $20B3_{16}$ to its decimal equivalent.

2 0 B 3_{16}

$3 \times 16^0 = 3 \times 1 = 3$
$11 \times 16^1 = 11 \times 16 = 176$
$0 \times 16^2 = 0 \times 256 = 0$
$2 \times 16^3 = 1 \times 4096 = \underline{8192}$
8371_{10}

So, $20B3_{16} = 8371_{10}$

Example 2: Convert the hexadecimal number $12AE5_{16}$ to its decimal equivalent.

1 2 A E 5_{16}

$5 \times 16^0 = 5 \times 1 = 5$
$14 \times 16^1 = 14 \times 16 = 224$
$10 \times 16^2 = 10 \times 256 = 2560$
$2 \times 16^3 = 2 \times 4096 = 8192$
$1 \times 16^4 = 1 \times 65536 = \underline{65536}$
76517_{10}

So, $12AE5_{16} = 76517_{10}$

8. Binary to Hexadecimal Conversion:

- Converting a binary number to its hexadecimal equivalent or vice-versa is a simple matter.

- Four binary digits are equivalent to one hexadecimal digit, as shown in the table below:

Binary	Hexadecimal
0000	0
0001	1
0010	2
0011	3
0100	4
0101	5
0110	6
0111	7
1000	8
1001	9
1010	A
1011	B
1100	C
1101	D
1110	E
1111	F

- To convert from binary to hexadecimal, divide the binary number into groups of 4 digits starting on the right of the binary number.
- If the leftmost group has less than 4 bits, put in the necessary number of leading zeroes on the left.
- For each group of four bits, write the corresponding single hex digit.

  For example :

  1. $1101001101110111_2 = ?_{16}$

     Binary : 1101 0011 0111 0111

     Hexadecimal : D   3   7   7

     So, $1101001101110111_2 = D377_{16}$

  2. $101101111_2 = ?_{16}$

     Binary : 0001 0110 1111

     Hexadecimal : 1   6   F

     So, $101101111_2 = 16F_{16}$

- To convert from hexadecimal to binary, write the corresponding group of four binary digits for each hex digit.

  For example :

  1. $1BE9_{16} = ?_2$

Hexadecimal :	1	B	E	9
Binary :	0001	1011	1110	1001

  So, $1BE9_{16} = 0001101111101001_2$

  2. $B0A_{16} = ?_2$

Hexadecimal:	B	0	A
Binary :	1011	0000	1010

  So, $B0A_{16} = 101100001010_2$

9. Octal to Hexadecimal Conversion:

- For changing an octal number into a hexadecimal number, the octal number is first changed into a 3 bit binary number.
- Then the 4 bit binary number is converted into a hexadecimal number.
- Following example will make it more illustrative.
- Convert the following octal numbers to the hexadecimal equivalents :

  (a) 5634, (b) 7431.

  (a)   5   6   3   4   octal

         101 110   011 100   binary

         hexadecimal

  Hence, $(5634)_8 = (B9C)_{16}$

  (b)   7   4   3   1   octal

         111 100   011 001   binary

         hexadecimal

  Hence, $(7431)_8 = (F19)_{16}$

1's and 2's Complements:

- The numbers having either positive or negative signs are called signed numbers.
- Up till now, we have discussed only positive numbers.
- The representation of negative numbers is also equally important.
- There are two methods of representing signed numbers.
  1. Sign magnitude form.
  2. Complement form.
- There are two types of complement forms :
  1. 1's complement form.
  2. 2's complement form.

- Most digital computers do subtraction by the 2's complement method, but some it by the 1's complement method.
- The advantage of performing subtraction by the complement method is reduction in the hardware. Instead of having separate digital circuits for addition and subtraction, only adding circuits are needed.
- That is, subtraction is also performed by adders only. Instead of subtracting one number from the other, the complement of the subtrahend is added to the minuend.
- In sign-magnitude form, an additional bit called the sign bit is placed in front of the number. If the sign bit is zero (0), the number is positive. If it is one (1), the number is negative.

0	1	0	1	1	0	1	0	= + 90

sign bit — Magnitude

1	1	0	1	1	0	1	0	= – 90

sign bit — Magnitude

- Under the signed-magnitude system, a great deal of manipulation is necessary to add a positive number to a negative number. Thus, though the signed-magnitude number system is possible, but it is impractical.

(i) 1's Complement:

- The 1's complement system for representing signed numbers works as under:
  1. If the number is positive, the magnitude is represented in its binary form and a sign bit 0 is placed in front of the MSB.
  2. If the number is negative, the magnitude is represented in its 1's complement form and a sign bit 1 is placed in front of the MSB.
- That is, to represent the numbers in signed 1's complement form, determine the 1's complement of the magnitude of the number and then attach the sign bit to it.
- The 1's complement operation on a signed number will change a positive number to a negative number and vice-versa. The conversion of complement to true binary is the same as the process used to convert to a true binary to complement.
- The representation of – 90 in 1's complement form is shown below.

0	1	0	1	1	0	1	0	= + 90 (In sign magnitude form)

sign bit — Magnitude

1	1	0	1	1	0	1	0	= – 90 (In 1's complement form)

sign bit — Magnitude

(ii) 2's Complement:

- The 1's complement system for representing signed numbers works as under:
  1. If the number is positive, the magnitude is represented in its true binary form and a sign bit 0 is placed in front of the MSB.
  2. If the number is negative, the magnitude is represented in its 2's complement form and a sign bit 1 is placed in front of the MSB.

- That is, to represent the numbers in signed 2's complement form, determine the 2's complement of the magnitude of the number and then attach the sign bit.
- The 2's complement operation on a signed number will change a positive number to a negative number and vice-versa. The conversion of complement to true binary is the same as the process used to convert to a true binary to complement. The representation of – 90 in 2's complement form is shown below :

1	1	0	1	1	0	1	0	= – 90 (In sign magnitude form)

sign bit　　　　　　　　　Magnitude

1	0	1	0	0	1	1	1	= – 90 (In 2's complement form)

sign bit　　　　　　　　　Magnitude

- **Example :** Each of the following number is assigned a binary number. Determine the decimal value in each case, if they are (i) 1's complement form and (ii) 2's complement form : (a) 10101, (b) 011011, (c) 1100110 and (d) 001011.

Given Number	Sign magnitude form	1's complement form	2's complement form
(a) 10101	– 5	– 6	– 7
(b) 011011	+ 27	+ 4	+ 5
(c) 1100110	– 38	–25	– 26
(d) 001011	+ 11	+ 20	+ 21

- **Special case in 2's complement representation :** Whenever, a signed number has 1 in the sign bit place and all 0s for the magnitude bits, the decimal equivalent is – 2n, where n is the number of bits in magnitude.
- For example, 10 = – 2, 100 = – 4, 1000 = – 8 and 10000 = – 16.

1.9.6 Binary Arithmetic
(Addition, Subtraction, Multiplication, Division)

- Arithmetic is at the heart of the digital computer, and the majority of arithmetic performed by computers is binary arithmetic, i.e. arithmetic on base two numbers.
- Decimal and floating-point numbers, also used in computer arithmetic, depend on binary representations, and an understanding of binary arithmetic is necessary in order to understand either one.
- Computers perform arithmetic on fixed-size numbers. The arithmetic of fixedsize numbers is called finite-precision arithmetic. The rules for finite-precision arithmetic are different from the rules of ordinary arithmetic.
- There are four Binary Arithmetic Operations:
  1. Binary Addition,
  2. Binary Subtraction,
  3. Binary Multiplication, and
  4. Binary Division.

1. **Binary Addition :**
- Let's first take a look at decimal addition.
- As an example we have 26 plus 36,

    26
    +36

- To add these two numbers, we first consider the "ones" column and calculate 6 plus 6, which results in 12. Since, 12 is greater than 9 (remembering that base 10 operates with digits 0-9), we "carry" the 1 from the "ones" column to the "tens column" and leave the 2 in the "ones" column.
- Considering the "tens" column, we calculate 1 + (2 + 3), which results in 6. Since, 6 is less than 9, there is nothing to "carry" and we leave 6 in the "tens" column.

    26
    + 36
    62

- Binary addition works in the same way, except that only 0's and 1's can be used, instead of the whole spectrum of 0-9. This actually makes binary addition much simpler than decimal addition, as we only need to remember the following:

    0 + 0= 0
    0 + 1= 1
    1 + 0= 1
    1 + 1= 10

- As an example of binary addition we have,

    101
    + 101

    (a) To add these two numbers, we first consider the "ones" column and calculate 1 + 1, which (in binary) results in 10. We "carry" the 1 to the "tens" column, and the leave the 0 in the "ones" column.

    (b) Moving on to the "tens" column, we calculate 1 + (0 + 0), which gives 1. Nothing "carries" to the "hundreds" column, and we leave the 1 in the "tens" column.

    (c) Moving on to the "hundreds" column, we calculate 1 + 1, which gives 10. We "carry" the 1 to the "thousands" column, leaving the 0 in the "hundreds" column.

    101
    + 101
    1010

2. **Binary Subtraction :**
- Binary subtraction is simplified as well, as long as we remember how subtraction and the base 2 number system.

- As an example we have 26 plus 36,

    111
    - 10
    101

- Note that the difference is the same if this was decimal subtraction. Also similar to decimal subtraction is the concept of "borrowing." Watch as "borrowing" occurs when a larger digit, say 8, is subtracted from a smaller digit, say 5, as shown below in decimal subtraction.

    35
    - 8
    27

- For 10 minus 1, 1 is borrowed from the "tens" column for use in the "ones" column, leaving the "tens" column with only 2.
- The following examples show "borrowing" in binary subtraction.

    10100   1010
    - 1- 10   - 110
    110   100

3. **Binary Multiplication :**
- Binary multiplication is actually much simpler than decimal multiplication.
- In the case of decimal multiplication, we need to remember 3 x 9 = 27, 7 x 8 = 56, and so on.
- In binary multiplication, we only need to remember the following,

    0 × 0= 0
    0 × 1= 0
    1 × 0= 0
    1 × 1= 1

- Note that since binary operates in base 2, the multiplication rules we need to remember are those that involve 0 and 1 only. As an example of binary multiplication we have 101 times 11,

    101
    × 11

- First we multiply 101 by 1, which produces 101. Then we put a 0 as a placeholder as we would in decimal multiplication, and multiply 101 by 1, which produces 101.

    101
    × 11
    101
    1010   the 0 here is the placeholder.

- The next step, as with decimal multiplication, is to add. The results from our previous step indicates that we must add 101 and 1010, the sum of which is 1111.

```
   101
  × 11
   101
  1010
  1111
```

4. **Binary Division :**

- Binary division is almost as easy, and involves our knowledge of binary multiplication. Take for example the division of 1011 into 11.

```
       11   R = 10
    11 ) 1011
       - 11
         101
         -11
          10 ← remainder, R
```

- To check our answer, we first multiply our divisor 11 by our quotient 11. Then we add its' product to the remainder 10, and compare it to our dividend of 1011.

```
     11
   × 11
     11
     11
   1001 ← product of 11 and 11

   1001
   + 10
   1011 ← sum of product and remainder
```

- The sum is equal to our initial dividend, therefore our solution is correct.

Questions

1. What is computer? Explain generations of computer.
2. Define the following terms:
   (i) Computer,
   (ii) File.
3. What is analog computer? Explain its applications.
4. What is meant by programming languages?
5. What is booting? Explain its types.

6. What are the types of computers? Explain two of them in detail.
7. Describe general and special purpose computer in detail.
8. Enlist advantages of computers.
9. What is digital computer? State its applications and advantages.
10. Explain limitations of computer.
11. Enlist various application of computer in various fields like banking, business, military etc.
12. Write short note on: Data organisation.
13. Describe generations of computer with their advantages and disadvantages.
14. What is super computer? State its advantages and disadvantages.
15. What is mini computer? State its advantages and disadvantages.
16. What is mainframe computer? State its advantages and disadvantages.
17. What is micro computer? State its advantages and disadvantages.
18. Distinguish between:
    (i) Mini and micro computers.
    (ii) Super and mainframe computers.
19. What are the types of micro computer?
20. Explain hybrid computer in detail.
21. Describe functional block diagram of computer.
22. Define data and information.
23. Explain the following terms:
    (i) Input unit,
    (ii) Storage unit, and
    (iii) Output unit.
24. What is input and output? Explain meaning of input and output device.
25. What is scanner? What are its types?
26. What are the types of printers? Explain two of them in detail.
27. What is monitor? What are its types?
28. Explain the term keyboard in detail.
29. With the help of diagram describe working of following:
    (i) Laser printer,
    (ii) Daisy wheel printer, and
    (iii) Dot matrix printer.
30. Compare impact and non impact printers.
31. What is OMR? How it works? Explain in brief.
32. Write short note on: Plotter.
33. With the help of diagram describe working of drum printer.
34. Explain working of CRT and LCD diagrammatically.
35. Describe the term MICR in detail.
36. Explain working of inkjet printer in detail.
37. What are the types of line printers?
38. Distinguish between character printer and line printer.

39. Explain the following term:
    (i) Mouse, and
    (ii) Drum printer.
40. What is MICR? State its advantages.
41. With the help of diagram describe keyboard.
42. Compare printer and plotter.
43. Distinguish between inkjet and laser printers.
44. Explain the following terms in short:
    (i) Digitizer,
    (ii) Joystick,
    (iii) Digital camera,
    (iv) OCR.
45. Write short note on: Bar code reader.
46. What is computer memory?
47. What are the types of memory? Explain in detail.
48. With the help of diagram describe floppy disk.
49. Write short note on: Pen drive.
50. What is meant by primary and secondary memory? Compare them.
51. What is hard disk? Explain its construction in detail.
52. What is RAM and ROM? State its characteristics.
53. Enlist characteristics of primary and secondary memory.
54. What is CD? How it works? Explain diagrammatically.
55. Differentiate between RAM and ROM.
56. What is floppy disk? How it works?
57. Compare hard disk and floppy disk.
58. Write short note on: DVD.
59. Describe magnetic tape in detail.
60. With the help of diagram describe classification of memory.
61. Distinguish between magnetic tape and magnetic disks.
62. What is meant by volatile and non-volatile memories?
63. Explain booting process in detail.
64. Distinguish between hard disk and floppy disk.
65. Describe the number system : (i) Binary, (ii) Octal, (iii) Decimal, (iv) Hexadecimal.
66. Convert the following : (i) $1100110_2 = ?_{10}$, (ii) $1163_8 = ?_2$, (iii) $6252_{10} = ?_8$, (iv) $243F_{16} = ?_{10}$, (v) $114267_{10} = ?_{16}$, (vi) $101101111_2 = ?_8$
67. Explain the following programming language with its advantages and disadvantages:
    (i) Machine language,
    (ii) Assembly language, and
    (iii) High level language.

■■■

Chapter 2...

Operating System and Services in Operating System

Contents ...

2.1 Introduction
    2.1.1 Definition
    2.1.2 Objectives
    2.1.3 Characteristics
    2.1.4 Features
    2.1.5 Need
    2.1.6 Components of Operating System
    2.1.7 Operating System Services
    2.1.8 Advantages and Disadvantages
    2.1.9 Types of Operating Systems
    2.1.10 Examples of Operating Systems
2.2 Features of Windows and Linux
2.3 Files and Directories
    2.3.1 Files
    2.3.2 Directories
2.4 Introduction to DOS
    2.4.1 DOS History
    2.4.2 Internal and External Commands of DOS
        2.4.2.1 Internal DOS Commands
        2.4.2.2 External DOS Commands
2.5 Batch Files
    2.5.1 Creating Batch Files
    2.5.2 Batch File Commands
- Questions

2.1 Introduction

- An Operating System (OS) is a software program that enables the computer hardware to communicate and operate with the computer software.
- Without a computer operating system, a computer and software programs would be useless.

- An operating system is a program that acts as an interface between the software and the computer hardware.
- OS is an integration set of specialised programs that are used to manage overall resources and operations of the computer.
- An operating system is a collection of software that manages computer hardware resources and provides common services for computer programs.
- Most popular operating systems are Windows 7, Windows XP, Windows 8, Macintosh OSX, Linux, Unix, Windows Vista, Debian, Xandros Linux, Android, Solaris, etc.

2.1.1 Definition

- An operating system is a computer program that manages the resources of a computer.

OR

- An operating system is software that communicates with the hardware and allows other programs to run.

OR

- An operating system is a program that controls the execution of application programs and acts as an interface between the user of a computer and the computer hardware. In other words "the software that controls the hardware".

2.1.2 Objectives

- Objectives of operating system are listed below:
  1. To provide users a convenient interface to use the computer system.
  2. Manage the resources of a computer system.
  3. Making a computer system convenient to use in an efficient manner.
  4. The efficient and fair sharing of resources among users and programs.
  5. To hide the details of the hardware resources from the users.
  6. Keep the track of who is using which resource, granting resource requests, according to resource using and mediating conflicting requests from different programs and users.
  7. To act as an intermediary between the hardware and its users and making it easier for the users to access and use other resources.

2.1.3 Characteristics

- The operating system have the following characteristics:
  1. Operating system is a collection of programs those are responsible for the execution of other programs.
  2. Operating system is that which is responsible for controlling all the input and output devices those are connected to the system.
  3. Operating system is that which is responsible for running all the application software's.
  4. Operating system is that which provides scheduling to the various processes means allocates the memory to various process those want to execute.

5. Operating system is that which provides the communication between the user and the system.
6. Operating system is stored into the BIOS means in the Basic Input and Output System means when a user starts his system then this will read all the instructions those are necessary for executing the system means for running the operating system, operating system must be loaded into the computer this will use the floppy or hard disks which stores the operating system.

2.1.4 Features

- Some of the features of operating systems are detailed here:
    1. **Software and hardware management:** The operating system is the bridge between computer hardware and software and makes the communication between them possible. Also communication between different softwares in the computer is also taken care by operating system.
    2. **Constant API:** Application Program Interface (API) is a software that allows different applications that run on a computer to work on other computers also. But they should have same operating system. So it is very vital to have consistent API in the operating system.
    3. **Execution of programs:** Programs running in the computer are completely dependent on the operating system. But program execution is a tough process. The multitasking and multithreading features of the operating system are dependent upon the type of program execution feature of operating system.
    4. **Interruptions:** Interruption may happen at any time while using the computers. So the operating system should allow and handle many numbers of interrupts. Whenever, an interruption occurs, the operating system should respond to it by saving and stopping the current execution and work on the new execution. This is the most hard-hitting process for the operating system.
    5. **Managing memory:** The operating system provides the memory for the programs those are executed at any moment. So the operating system should have good memory allocation facility to execute the programs smoothly. The prioritization and allocation of memory to the applications running should be taken care by the operating systems.
    6. **Networking:** Today computers are nothing without internet connection or some network connection. This is the age of networking. So if computers are connected to a network, the there should be definitely communication between one computer and another. So the operating system is what makes it possible for one computer to communicate with other computers.
    7. **Security:** Security is the important feature that should be looked for in an operating system. An operating system in the computer takes care of all security issues of computer and data in it. Log in passwords, firewall settings, and every such aspect related to security depends on the ability of the operating system. Some of the computers in network may involve in file sharing, and other data sharing. So it is important in such cases to have powerful secured operating systems.

2.1.5 Need
- An operating system is an essential component of a computer system.
- The primary objectives of an operating system are to make computer system convenient to use and utilizes computer hardware in an efficient manner.
- Some of the important reasons why do we need an operating system are as follows:
    1. Operating system provides an environment for running user programs.
    2. Operating system provides an interface to the user to communicate with the system.
    3. User interacts with the computer through operating system in order to accomplish his/her task since it is his primary interface with a computer.
    4. It helps the user in understand the inner functions of a computer very closely.
    5. Operating system executes user programs and to make solving user problems easier.
    6. Operating system provides an overall control to the system.
    7. Many concepts and techniques found in operating system have general applicability in other applications.
    8. Operating system manages the computer resources in an efficient manner.
    9. Operating system uses hardware of the system in efficient manner.
- The positioning of operating system in overall computer system is shown in Fig. 3.1.

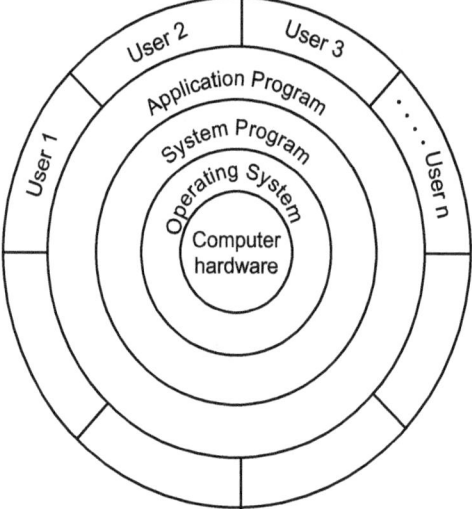

Fig. 2.1: Positioning of operating system in overall computer system

2.1.6 Components of Operating Systems
- Fig. 2.2 shows components of operating systems.
- A computer system can be divided roughly into four components:
    1. **The hardware:** The Central Processing Unit (CPU), memory and input/output devices constitute the basic hardware and provide the basic computing resources.
    2. **The application programs:** Word processors, spreadsheets, compilers, web browsers etc. are example of application programs that define the way in which these

resources are used to solve the computing problems of the users. The operating system controls and co-ordinates the use of the hardware among the various application programs for the various users.

3. **Operational Users:** Operational users are the users responsible for installation of the software, proper maintenance of software, making it available to the users, and housekeeping operations, taking regular backups, removing unnecessary files and directories, checking the disk space being used and space free.

4. **End Users:** End users are the actual users of the applications. Such users can perform limited tasks as defined by the application program they are using. Applications with user friendly environments and simplicity of operations are preferred in such cases.

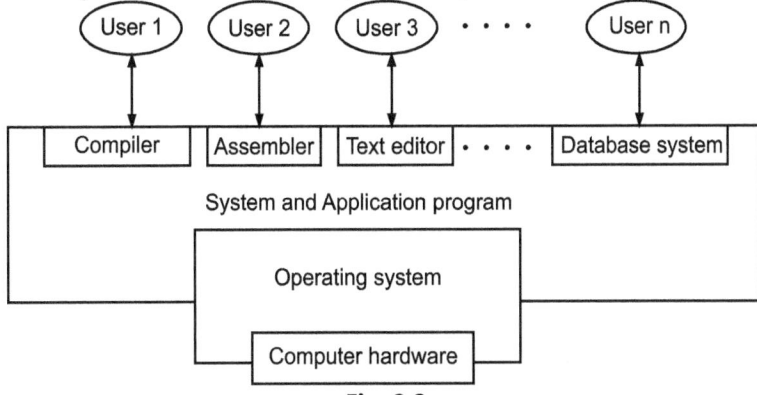

Fig. 2.2

2.1.7 Operating System Services

- The services provided by the operating system differs from one another. The quality of the operating system depends upon the amount at services that the user can exploit with the system.
- Fig. 2.3 shows one view of the various operating-system services and show they interrelate.

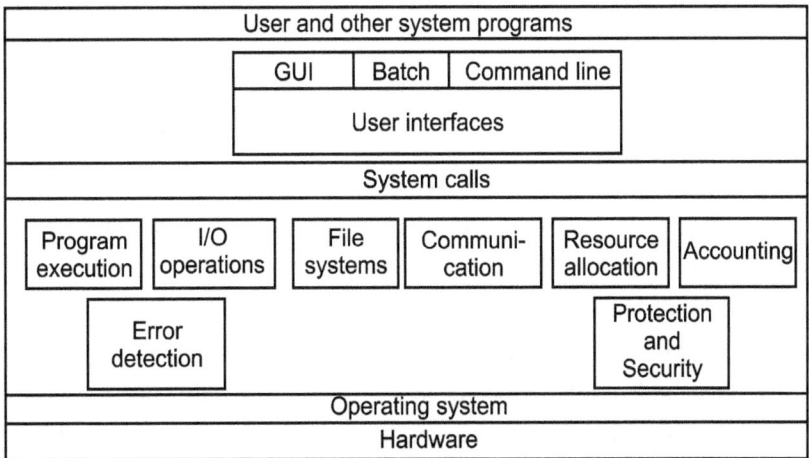

Fig. 2.3: A view of operating system services

- Following are the basic services which are provided by the operating system.
    1. **User interface:** Almost all operating systems have a User Interface (UI). This user interface can take several forms. One is a DTrace Command-Line Interface (CLI), which uses text commands and a method for entering them. Another is a batch interface, in which commands and directives to control those commands are entered into files, and those files are executed. Most commonly, a Graphical User Interface (GUI) is used. The GUI interface is a window system with a pointing device to direct I/O, choose from menus and make selections and a keyboard to enter text.
    2. **Program Execution:** The system must be able to load a program into memory and run the program. If due to some reason the program halts abruptly then an error is indicated by the operating system. Execution of program must end either normally or abnormally.
    3. **I/O Operations:** All the programs dealing with I/O operations relating to specific devices are to be dealt by the operating system. For example, if a user wants to print a page then operating system gives the command to I/O device for Printing the particular pages.
    4. **File System Implementation:** The file system is of particular interest. Programs need to read and write files. Files can also be detected by their unique names.
    5. **Communications:** The communication which takes place between the concurrent processes can be divided into two parts. The first one takes place between the processes that are running on the same computer and the other type of processes are those that are being executed on different computer systems through a computer network.
    6. **Protection:** In a multiuser environment, protection of valuable resources plays an important role. It ensures that all the access to system resource should be in a controlled manner. This is implemented by the help of security assigned at various levels.
    7. **Error detection:** There are various types of errors that occur when the process is running. These error may be caused by CPU, memory hardware, I/O devices etc. It is the job of the operating system to keep track of these errors, raise appropriate error's at the user's screen.
    8. **Accounting:** The record keeping work, as to which resource has been utilised by which process is being taken care at by the operating system. This record keeping also keeps track of the user who has used the resources and for how long so that he can be billed for that.
    9. **Resource allocation:** The operating system collects all the resources in the network environment and grants these resources to be requested process. Many different types of resources are managed by the operating system, these are CPU cycles, Main memory, I/O devices, File storage and so on.

2.1.8 Advantages and Disadvantages

- Operating system consists of following advantages:
    1. Operating system provides direct hardware access.
    2. Fast in speed because it provides direct access of computer hardware.
    3. Easy and complete memory use, and
    4. Efficiency use of computer hardware.
- Disadvantages of operating systems are given below:
    1. No back-up available.
    2. Unrestricted access.
    3. Deadlock problems, and
    4. Problems of memory data loss.

2.1.9 Types of Operating Systems

- Various types of operating systems are shown in Fig. 2.4.

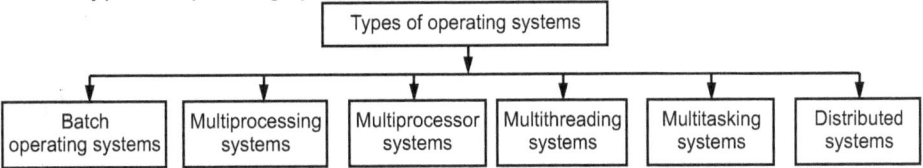

1. **Batch Operating System:**
- In old days the computers were large systems run from a console. The common input devices were card readers and tape drives and output devices were line printers, tape drives and card punches.
- The computer system did not directly interact with the users instead the computer users used to prepare a format that consisted of the programs, the data and some control information about the nature of the job and submitted it to the computer operator.
- The job was usually in the form of punch cards. The process as a whole took a lot of time and was slow. To speed up the processing jobs with similiar needs were batched together and were run through the computer as a group.
- Fig. 2.5 shows the memory layout for a simple batch system.

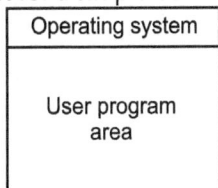

Fig. 2.5: Memory layout for a simple batch system

- A batch operating system, normally reads a stream of separate jobs, each with its own control cards that predefine what the job does. When the job is complete, its output is usually printed.
- The important feature of a batch system is lack of interaction between the user and the job while that job is being executed. The job is prepared and submitted and at some later time, the output appears.

- In a batch processing system, a job is described by a sequence of control statements stored in a machine-readable form.
- The operating system can read and execute a series of such jobs without human intervention except for such functions as tape and disk mounting. The order in which the jobs are selected and executed can be scheduled using appropriate algorithms.
- A batch is a sequence of user jobs.
- The batch monitor is responsible for:
    o Accepting command from the system operator,
    o Initiate the processing of a batch,
    o Sets up the processing of the first job,
    o At end of the job, terminates process and initiate execution of the next job,
    o At end of the batch, terminates batch and awaits initiation of the next batch by the operator.

Advantages of batch operating system:
(i) Move much of the work of the operator to the computer.
(ii) Increased performance since it was possible for job to start as soon as the previous job finished.

Disadvantages of batch operating system:
(i) Turn around time can be large from user standpoint.
(ii) Difficult to debug program.
(iii) Due to lack of protection scheme, one batch job can affect pending jobs.
(iv) A job could corrupt the monitor, thus affecting pending jobs.
(v) A job could enter an infinite loop.

Spooling Technique:
- In the batch operating system execution environment, the CPU is often idle. This idleness occurs because the speeds of the mechanical I/O devices are slower than those of electronic devices.
- As time passed, improvements in technology resulted in faster I/O devices and CPU speeds increased even faster, so the problem was not only unsolved but also increased.
- In the disk technology rather than the cards being read from the card reader directly into memory, and then the job being processed, cards are read directly from the card reader onto the disk.
- The location of the card images is recorded in a table kept by the operating system. When a job is executed, the operating system satisfied its request for card reader input by reading from the disk.
- Similarly, when the job requests the printer to output a line, that line is copied into a system buffer and is written to the disk. When the job is completed, the output is actually printed. This form of processing is called spooling.
- Spooling is used for data processing of remote sites. The CPU sends the data via communication paths to a remote printer. The remote processing is done at its own speed, with no CPU intervention.

Advantages of spooling:
  (i) Spooling overlaps the I/O of one job with the computation of other jobs.
  (ii) Spooling has a direct beneficial effect on the performance of the system.
  (iii) Spooling can keep both the CPU and the I/O devices working at much higher rates.
  (iv) Spooling operating uses a disk as a very large buffer.

2. **Multiprogramming:**
- Multiprogramming is a technique to execute number of programs simultaneously by a single processor.
- In multiprogramming number of processes reside is main memory at a time and the operating system picks and begins executing one of the jobs in the main memory.

Advantages of multiprogramming are:
  (i) Efficient memory utilization.
  (ii) CPU never sits idle, so it increases the CPU performance.
  (iii) Throughput of the CPU increases.
  (iv) In non-multiprogramming environment (mono programming) the user/ program has to wait for CPU much time. But waiting time is limited in multiprogramming.

3. **Multiprocessing (Multiprocessor) System:**
- Multiprogramming allows running a program on more than one CPU simultaneously.
- This system is similar to multiprogramming system, except that there is more than one CPU available.
- In most multiprocessor systems, the processors share a common memory. Thus, the user can view the system as if it were a powerful single processor.
- Below are some examples of multiprocessing operating systems.
    o Linux,
    o Unix, and
    o Windows 2000.

Advantages of multiprocessor systems:
  (i) Increases throughput: by increasing the number of processors, more work done in a shorter period of time.
  (ii) Multiprocessors can also save money compared to multiple single systems, because the processors can share peripherals, cabinets and power supplies.
  (iii) It increases reliability: if functions can be distributed properly among several processors, then the failure of one processor will not halt the system, but rather will only slow it down.
  (iv) Minimum hardware is required.

4. **Multithreading:**
   - Multithreading is a technique in which a process executing an application is divided into threads that can run concurrently.
     - **(i) Thread:** A dispatchable unit of work. It includes a processor context (which includes the program counter and stack pointer) and its own data area for stack.(to enable subroutine branching). A thread executes sequentially and is interruptable so that the processor can turn to another thread.
     - **(ii) Process:** A collection of one or more threads and associated system resources. (Such as memory containing both code and data, open files and devices).
   - Operating systems that would fall into this category are:
     - Linux
     - Unix
     - Windows 2000.
   - Multithreading refers to the ability of an operating system to support multiple threads of execution per process. The traditional approach of a single thread of execution per process is referred to as a single threaded approach.

   Advantages of multithreading:
   - (i) The efficiency of multithreading system is evident in multiprocessor system where parallel processing of thread is possible.
   - (ii) Thread switching is faster than process switching.
   - (iii) Threads are also useful for structuring processes that are part of the kernel.

   Disadvantages of multithreading:
   - (i) Multithreading is a complicated concept due to which operating system maintainability and designing are time consuming and expensive.
   - (ii) It is still evolving and requires multiprocessor machines, increased machine speed, high speed network attachments and increased size and variety of memory storage devices.

5. **Multitasking or Time Sharing:**
   - Time sharing or multitasking, is a logical extension of multiprogramming. Multiple jobs are executed by the CPU switching between them, but the switches occur so frequently that the users may interact with each program while running.
   - Time sharing systems were developed to provide interactive use of a computer at reasonable cost.
   - A time shared operating system uses CPU scheduling and multiprogramming to provide each user with a small portion of a time-shared computer. Each user has atleast one separate program in memory.
   - A program that is loaded into memory and is being executed is commonly referred to as a process.
   - Below are some examples of multitasking operating systems.
     - Unix
     - Windows 2000.

- A time shared operating system allows many uses to share the computer simultaneously. Since each action or command in, in a time-shared system tends to be short, only a little CPU time is needed for each user.
- Time sharing operating systems are even more complex than a multiprogrammed operating systems.

6. Distributed Systems:
- A distributed system is a collection of processors that do not share memory or a clock. Instead, each processor has its own local memory, and the processors communicate with each other through various communication lines.
- The purpose of distributed system is to provide an efficient and convenient environment for this type of sharing of resources.
- A distributed operating system allows a more complex type of network organization. This kind of operating system manages hardware and software resources, so that the user views the entire network as a simple system.
- The user is unaware of which machine on the network is actually running a program or storing data.

Advantages of distributed systems are:
   (i) Resource sharing,
   (ii) Reliability,
   (iii) Computation speed-up,
   (iv) Communication, and
   (v) Incremental growth.

7. Real Time Operating System (RTOS):
- Real Time Operating Systems are used to control machinery, scientific instruments and industrial systems.
- An RTOS typically has very little user-interface capability, and no end-user utilities, since the system will be a sealed box when delivered for use.
- A very important part of an RTOS is managing the resources of the computer so that a particular operation executes in precisely the same amount of time, every time it occurs.
- In a complex machine, having a part move more quickly just because system resources are available may be just as catastrophic as having it not move at all because the system is busy.

2.1.10 Examples of Operating Systems

1. Microsoft Windows:
- Microsoft Windows is a series of graphical interface operating systems developed, marketed, and sold by Microsoft.
- Microsoft introduced an operating environment named Windows on November 20, 1985 as a graphical operating system shell for MS-DOS in response to the growing interest in graphical user interfaces (GUI). Microsoft Windows came to dominate the world's personal computer market with over 90% market share, overtaking Mac OS, which had been introduced in 1984.

- As of April 2013, the most recent versions of Windows for personal computers, mobile devices, server computers and embedded devices are respectively Windows 8, Windows Phone 8, Windows Server 2012 and Windows Embedded 8.

Fig. 2.6: Microsoft Window 7

Fig. 2.7: Microsoft Window 8

Advantages of using Windows:
- (i) **Ease of use:** Users familiar with earlier versions of Windows will probably also find the more modern ones easy to work with.
- (ii) **Available software:** There is a huge selection of software available for Windows. This is both due to and the reason for Microsoft's dominance of the world market for PC computer operating systems and office software.

- **(iii) Backwards compatibility:** If you are currently using an older version of Windows and need something more up to date, but you don't want to loose the use of some older programs that are only available for Windows and are critical to your business needs, the chances are good (although not a certainty) that those programs will also work with a newer version of Windows.
- **(iv) Support for new hardware:** Virtually all hardware manufacturers will offer support for a recent version of Windows when they go to market with a new product. Again, Microsoft's dominance of the software market makes Windows impossible for hardware manufacturers to ignore. So, if you run off to a store today any buy some random new piece of computer hardware, you will find that it will probably work with the latest version of Windows.
- **(v) Plug and Play:** As an operating system for the average home user, Windows still has an edge over the competition in the area of Plug & Play support for PC hardware. As long as the right drivers are installed, Windows will usually do a good job at recognising new hardware. Other operating systems also offer Plug & Play functionality, but to a lesser degree and more frequently require manual intervention.

Disadvantages of using Windows:
- **(i) High resource requirements:** As opposed to the makers of other operating systems, Microsoft requires its customers to invest the most in their computer hardware: a faster processor (the CPU), more internal memory and a larger hard disk.
- **(ii) Virus susceptibility:** The susceptibility of any of Microsoft's operating systems to computer viruses has always been pronounced; nearly all computer viruses target Windows computers and regularly wreak newsworthy havoc.
- **(iii) Extortionist prices:** In the past, when Microsoft was asked on numerous occasions why it was raising the price of its Windows licenses yet again, the standard reply was that it was necessary to offset the development costs of their latest version.
- **(iv) Poor stability:** For people who are used to dealing with Windows, rebooting and re-installing are such a regular occurance that most don't even give it a second thought. However, that is by no means an excuse for such poor performance: Windows should not freeze up and reboot simply because Word or Internet Explorer was being used.
- **(v) Backwards incompatible file formats:** A well-known drawback of using Microsoft applications such as Office (Word, Excel, etc.), is that their file formats are not backwards compatible.

2. Mac Operating System:
- Mac operating system is a series of graphical user interface-based operating systems developed by Apple Inc. for their Macintosh line of computer systems.

- The original version was the integral and unnamed system software first introduced in 1984 with the original Macintosh, and referred to simply as the "System" software. The System was renamed to Mac OS in 1996 with version 7.6. The System is credited with popularizing the graphical user interface concept.
- Mac OS releases have existed in two major series. Up to major revision 9, from 1984 to 2000, it is historically known as Classic Mac OS. Major revision 10 (revisioned minorly, such as 10.0 through 10.9), from 2001 to present, has had the brand name of Mac OS X and now OS X. Both series share a general interface design and some shared application frameworks for compatibility, but also have deeply different architectures.

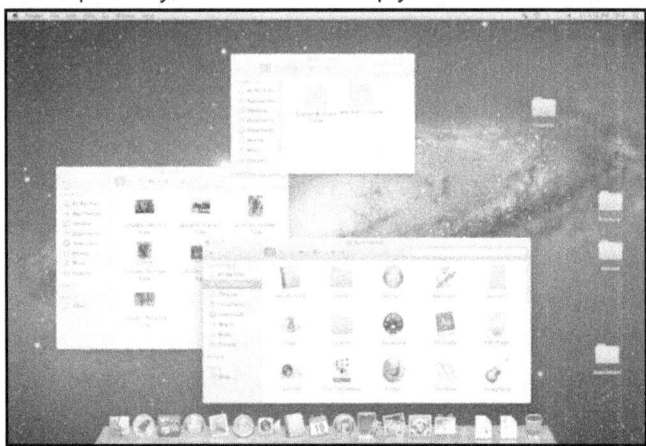

Fig. 2.8

Advantages:
   (i)   Easier to use for the non technical.
   (ii) Content creation is its strength.
   (iii) More secure than Windows due to its UNIX base
   (iv) More stable than Windows due to Apple's tighter control over the configuration options and its UNIX base.
   (v)   Almost no spyware or virus applications.
   (vi) More powerful than Windows due to its UNIX base.
   (vii) You have almost complete access to the enormous library of free open source applications.

Disadvantages:
   (i)   More expensive upfront than other choices.
   (ii) Less support. You have to goto Apple for all your hardware problems.
   (iii) Less hardware choices than Windows.
   (iv) More complex than Windows due to its UNIX base.

3. Linux:
- Linux is an operating system that evolved from a kernel created by Linus Torvalds when he was a student at the University of Helsinki.

- Generally, it is obvious to most people what Linux is. However, both for political and practical reasons, it needs to be explained further. To say that Linux is an operating system means that it's meant to be used as an alternative to other operating systems, Windows, Mac OS, MS-DOS, Solaris and others.
- Linux is not a program like a word processor and is not a set of programs like an office suite. Linux is an interface between computer/server hardware, and the programs which run on it.

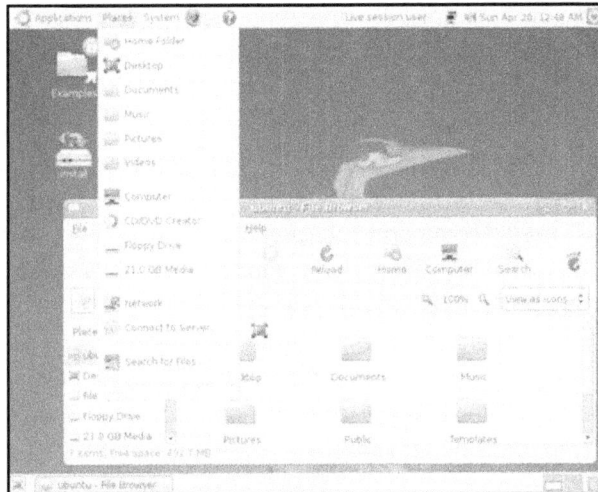

Fig. 2.9

Advantages:
   (i) The main advantage of Linux is that it is very flexible and it is highly adaptable for any kind of device.
   (ii) Linux is a free open source operating system. So it can be said, there is no license fee for buying or using Linux.
   (iii) Easy to use. In the past, they said that Linux is a difficult operating system, and only devoted to the hackers. But now, this opinion is wrong. Linux is easy to use and can be said that's almost as easy as using Windows.
   (iv) Almost all applications included in Windows, there have been alternative in Linux. We can access the Open Source website as Alternative to obtain useful fairly complete information about alternative of Windows applications on Linux.
   (v) Security is more superior than Windows.
   (vi) Linux is relatively stable. Computers that run on UNIX operating system is known to run stable indefinitely. Linux is a variant of UNIX, also inherits this stability.
   (vii) Linux is cheaper in cost as compare to windows.

Disadvantages:
   (i) The hardware support from certain vendors are not too good to Linux.
   (ii) The installation process of the software / application that is not as easy as in Windows. Installing software in Linux will be easier when connected to internet or if you have a CD / DVD repository.

(iii) For the system administrators who are not familiar with Unix-like systems (like Linux), inevitably have to learn more about this. So the requirements to become an administrator is a person who likes to learn new things and continually learning.
(iv) Linux does not have as much of a corporate backing as alternative operating systems.

4. Unix:

- UNIX is an operating system which was first developed in the 1960s, and has been under constant development ever since. By operating system, we mean the suite of programs which make the computer work. It is a stable, multi-user, multi-tasking system for servers, desktops and laptops.
- The Unix system is a multi-user, multi tasking operating system which means that it allows a single or multiprocessor computer to simultaneously execute several programs by one or several users.
- Unix has one or several command interpreters (shell) as well as a great number of commands and many utilities (assembler, compilers for many languages, text processing, email, etc.). Furthermore, it is highly portable, which means that it is possible to implement a Unix system on almost all hardware platforms.
- Currently, Unix systems have a strong foothold in professional and university environments thanks to their stability, their increased level of security and observance of standards, notably in terms of networks.

Advantages:

(i) Full multitasking with protected memory. Multiple users can run multiple programs each at the same time without interfering with each other or crashing the system.
(ii) Very efficient virtual memory, so many programs can run with a modest amount of physical memory.
(iii) Access controls and security. All users must be authenticated by a valid account and password to use the system at all. All files are owned by particular accounts. The owner can decide whether others have read or write access to his files.
(iv) A rich set of small commands and utilities that do specific tasks well -- not cluttered up with lots of special options. Unix is a well-stocked toolbox, not a giant do-it-all Swiss Army Knife.
(v) Ability to string commands and utilities together in unlimited ways to accomplish more complicated tasks -- not limited to preconfigured combinations or menus, as in personal computer systems.
(vi) A powerfully unified file system. Everything is a file: data, programs, and all physical devices. Entire file system appears as a single large tree of nested directories, regardless of how many different physical devices (disks) are included.
(vii) A lean kernel that does the basics for you but doesn't get in the way when you try to do the unusual.
(viii) Available on a wide variety of machines - the most truly portable operating system.
(ix) Optimized for program development, and thus for the unusual circumstances that are the rule in research.

Disadvantages:
  (i) The traditional command line shell interface is user hostile -- designed for the programmer, not the casual user.
  (ii) Commands often have cryptic names and give very little response to tell the user what they are doing. Much use of special keyboard characters - little typos have unexpected results.
  (iii) To use Unix well, you need to understand some of the main design features. Its power comes from knowing how to make commands and programs interact with each other, not just from treating each as a fixed black box.
  (iv) Richness of utilities (over 400 standard ones) often overwhelms novices. Documentation is short on examples and tutorials to help you figure out how to *use* the many tools provided to accomplish various kinds of tasks.

5. **Android:**
- Operating Systems have developed a lot in last 15 years. Starting from black and white phones to recent smart phones or mini computers, mobile OS has come far away.
- Especially for smart phones, Mobile OS has greatly evolved from Palm OS in 1996 to Windows pocket PC in 2000 then to Blackberry OS and Android.
- One of the most widely used mobile OS these days is ANDROID. Android is a software bunch comprising not only operating system but also middleware and key applications.
- Android Inc was founded in Palo Alto of California, U.S. by Andy Rubin, Rich miner, Nick sears and Chris White in 2003. Later Android Inc. was acquired by Google in 2005. After original release there have been number of updates in the original version of Android.

Android 1.1 Feb 2009	• Support for saving attachments for MMS • MArquee in layouts • API changes
Android 1.5 Cupcake April 2009	• Bluetooth A2DP and AVRCP support • Uploading videos to YouTube and pictures to Picasa
Android 1.6 Donut Sep. 2009	• WVGA screen revolution support • Google free turn by turn support
Android 2.0/1 Eclair Oct. 2009	• HTML5 file support • Microsoft exchange server • Bluetooth 2.1
Android 2.2 Froyo May 2010	• USB tethering and Wi-Fi hotspot functionality • Adobe flash 10.1 support
Android 2.3 Gingerbird Dec. 2010	• Multi touch software keyboard • Support for Extra Large screen sizes and resolution
Android 3.0 Honeycomb May 2011	• Optimized tablet support with a new user interface • 3D desktop • Video chat and Gtalk support

Fig. 2.10: Version of Android OS

Advantages of Android:
   (i) Android is open, because it is linux based open source so it can be developed by anyone.
   (ii) Easy access to the Android App Market: Android owners are people who love to learn the phone, with Google's Android App Market you can download applications for free.
   (iii) Populist Operating System: Android Phones, different from the iOS is limited to the iphone from Apple, then Android has many manufacturers, with their respective flagship gadget from HTC to Samsung.
   (iv) USB full facilities. You can replace the battery, mass storage, DiskDrive, and USB tethering.
   (v) Easy in terms of notification: The operating system is able to inform you of a new SMS, Email, or even the latest articles from an RSS Reader.
   (vi) Supports all Google services: Android operating system supports all of google services ranging from Gmail to Google reader. All google services can you have with one operating system, namely Android.
   (vii) Install ROM modification: There are many custom ROM that you can use on Android phones, and the guarantee will not harm your device.

Disadvantages of Android:
   (i) Connected to the Internet: Android can be said is in need of an active internet connection. At least there should be a GPRS internet connection in your area, so that the device is ready to go online to suit our needs.
   (ii) Sometimes slow device company issued an official version of Android your own.
   (iii) Android Market is less control of the manager, sometimes there are malware.
   (iv) As direct service providers, users sometimes very difficult to connect with the Google.
   (v) Sometimes there are ads: because it is easy and free, sometimes often a lot of advertising. In appearance it does not interfere with the performance of the application itself, as it sometimes is in the top or bottom of the application.
   (vi) Wasteful Batteries, This is because the OS is a lot of "process" in the background causing the battery quickly drains.

Android applications:
   1. Android applications are composed of one or more application components (activities, services, content providers, and broadcast receivers).
   2. Each component performs a different role in the overall application behavior, and each one can be activated individually (even by other applications).
   3. The manifest file must declare all components in the application and should also declare all application requirements, such as the minimum version of Android required and any hardware configurations required.
   4. Non-code application resources (images, strings, layout files, etc.) should include alternatives for different device configurations (such as different strings for different languages).

2.2 Features of Windows and Linux

1. **Windows Operating System:**
- Microsoft's line of Windows operating systems is the most used in the world. The original Windows operating system dates back to 1981.
- Windows is a personal computer operating system from Microsoft that, together with some commonly used business applications such as Microsoft Word and Excel, has become a de facto standard for individual users in most corporations as well as in most homes.
- The original 1985 version of Windows introduced to home and business PC users many of the Graphical User Interface (GUI) ideas that were developed at an experimental lab at Xerox and introduced commercially by Apple's Lisa and Macintosh computers.
- Some of the well-known versions of Windows have included: Windows 286, Windows 386, Windows 3.0 and 3.11, Windows 95, Windows 98, Windows NT, Windows 2000, Windows CE, Windows Me, Windows XP, Windows Vista, Windows 7, Windows 8.

Features of Windows:

(i) **Historical Features:** MS-DOS was the earliest consumer operating system that gained Microsoft worldwide attention. In the beginning, Windows was regarded primarily as a Graphical User Interface (GUI) that did little more than provide an easier and more visually pleasing way to use MS-DOS. What eventually made Windows a standout operating system was its ability to do what its name implies-- allow a computer user to have more than one program or process operating simultaneously in various "windows" on the computer screen.

(ii) **Advancements:** As Windows matured, Microsoft added advances to make the user experience more enjoyable and the development of software for the operating system easier. Windows 2.0 was the first to feature Control Panel, a tool that allowed the user to navigate a graphical interface to adjust settings on the computer. Subsequent advancements included peer-to-peer networking support, Internet support and dial-up networking capabilities. Software became "plug and play," which allowed users to insert diskettes (and eventually CD-ROM discs) into their computer and install software more easily, something that was still at the time difficult on other operating systems.

(iii) **Surface Features:** Windows 7, released in 2009, is Microsoft's most recent iteration of the Windows operating systems. On the surface, it features full 64-bit support, remote media streaming, and touchscreen functionality (when paired with a touchscreen monitor). It also features a new tool call Jump Lists, which makes accessing your most used media and programs easier. The desktop features Snap, a new way to organize, order and size the windows on your desktop so that they are easier to read and compare.

(iv) Advanced Features: Taking a cue from Apple's OS X operating system, Windows 7 features "Sleep" and "Resume" functionality. The search system has been made quicker and easier to navigate. Memory usage has also been optimized to ensure faster and more reliable performance. Windows 7 has also been redesigned for better power management through the reduction of background activities, less power-hungry media drives, automatic screen dimming and the intelligent and automated removal of power to unnecessary accessory ports.

2. Linux:

- Linux is an operating system that is evolved from a kernel created by Linus Torvalds.
- To say that Linux is an operating system means that it's meant to be used as an alternative to other operating systems, Windows, Mac OS, MS-DOS, Solaris and others.
- Linux is not a program like a word processor and is not a set of programs like an office suite. Linux is an interface between computer/server hardware, and the programs which run on it.

Features:

- Linux has evolved to have the following features as an outstanding operating system which is strong in security and networking.
    1. **Multitasking:** Several programs can run at the same time.
    2. **Multiuser:** Several users can logon to the same machine at the same time There is no need to have separate user licenses.
    3. **Multiplatform:** Linux runs on many different CPUs, that means it supports multiprocessor machine.
    4. **Multithreading:** Linux has native kernel support for multiple independent threads of control within a single process memory space.
    5. **Crash proof:** Linux has memory protection between processes, so that one program can't bring the whole system down.
    6. **Demand loads executables:** Linux only reads from those parts of a program that are actually used on the disk.
    7. **Shared copy-on-write pages among executables:** This means that multiple processes can use the same memory to run in. When one tries to write to that memory, that page (with 4KB piece of memory) is copied somewhere else. Copy-onwrite has two benefits that is increasing speed and decreasing memory use.
    8. Virtual memory uses paging (not swapping whole processes) to disk to a separate partition or a file in the file system, or both, with the possibility of adding more swapping areas during runtime. A total of 16 of these 128 MB (2GB in recent kernels) swapping areas can be used at the same time, for a theoretical total of 2 GB of usable swap space. It is simple to increase this if necessary, by changing a few lines of source code.

9. Linux has a unified memory pool for user programs and disk cache, so that all free memory can be used for caching, and the cache can be reduced when running large programs.
10. Linux does core dumps for post-mortem analysis, allowing the use of a debugger on a program not only while it is running but also after it has crashed.
11. Linux is mostly compatible with POSIX, System V, and BSD at the source level.
12. Free and Open source code for all: All source code of Linux is available, including the whole kernel and all drivers, the development tools and all user programs; also, all of it is freely distributable. Plenty of commercial programs are being provided for Linux without source, but everything that has been free, including the entire base operating system, is still free.
13. Linux supports pseudoterminals (pty's) and multiple virtual consoles: By several independent login sessions through the console, we can switch between by pressing a hot-key combination. These are dynamically allocated; we can use up to 64.

2.3 Files and Directories
2.3.1 Files
- A file is a collection of data that is stored on disk and that can be manipulated as a single unit by its name.
- We can define file as "a collection of logically related records".
- The way records are physically arranged on a storage device is termed as file organisation.
- File organisation refers to the arrangement of records within a database.
- The organisation of a given file may be sequential, relative, or indexed.

1. **Sequential File Organisation:**
- In these file organisation, records are arranged sequentially.
- A sequentially organized file may be stored on either a serial–access or direct access storage medium.
- Sequential files may be recorded in variable-length of fixed-length record form. If a file consists of variable-length records, each logical record is preceded by control information that indicates the size of the logical record.
- Sequential files are normally created and stored on magnetic tape using batch processing method.

Advantages:
   (i) Simple and easy to understand and implement.
   (ii) Easy and simple to maintain and organize.

Disadvantages:
   (i) Data redundancy is high.
   (ii) Very low activity rate stored.
   (iii) Impossible to handle random enquiries.

Index Sequential file organisation:
- In index this file organisation, the records are stored in the key sequence order usually in ascending order. Some index tables are also created and maintained with the file.
- Index table in this organisation provide to identify the groups of records in the file. When an indexed file is accessed randomly, the programmers control the sequence on which the records are accessed by specifying the value of a data item called record key.

Advantages:
   (i) Random access is possible.
   (ii) Updating is easily accommodated.

2. **Direct/Random File Organisation:**
- In this file organisation, records are placed randomly throughout the file.
- Records need not be in sequence because they are updated directly and rewritten back in the same location.
- New records in this organisation are added at the end of the file or inserted in specific locations based on software commands.
- In this organisation records are accessed by addresses that specify their disk locations. An address is required for locating a record, for linking records, or for establishing relationships.

Advantages:
   (i) Very easy and simple to handle random enquiries.
   (ii) Transaction need not be sorted.
   (iii) Several files can be simultaneously updated during transaction processing.
   (iv) Existing records can be amended or modified.

Disadvantages:
   (i) Expensive hardware and software are required.
   (ii) Risk of loss of accuracy and breach of security.
   (iii) High complexity in programming.

3. **Indexed Files:**
- An indexed file, which must be allocated in the execution activity to more than two random mass storage files is organized such that each record is uniquely identified by the value of key within the record.

- In index file an index is a data structure that organizes data records on disk to optimize certain file operations and it allows us to efficiently search or retrieve all records. Using an index, we can achieve a fast search of data records.
- In order to create and maintain index files a computer create a data file and an index file. The data file contains the actual contents (data) of the record and index file contains the index entries. The one field in a file is the primary key, which identifies a record uniquely.
- Files are organized in the following ways:
  1. The data file is stored in the order of the primary key values.
  2. The index file contains two fields: the key value and the pointer to the data record.
  3. One record in the index file thus, consists of a key value and a pointer to the corresponding data record. The pointer points to the first entry within the range of data records.

2.3.2 Directories

- A directory is a file that acts as a folder for other files. A directory can also contain other directories (subdirectories); a directory that contains another directory is called the parent directory of the directory it contains.
- A directory tree includes a directory and all of its files, including the contents of all subdirectories. (Each directory is a "branch" in the "tree.") A slash character alone ('/') is the name of the root directory at the base of the directory tree hierarchy; it is the trunk from which all other files or directories branch.
- Shows an abridged version of the directory hierarchy.

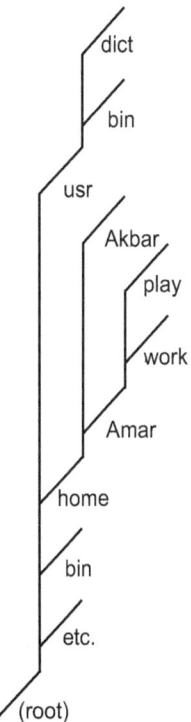

Fig. 2.11

- To represent a directory's place in the file hierarchy, specify all of the directories between it and the root directory, using a slash ('/') as the delimiter to separate directories. So the directory 'dict' as it appears in the preceding illustration would be represented as '/usr/dict'.
- Each user has a branch in the '/home' directory for their own files, called their home directory. The hierarchy in the previous illustration has two home directories:'Amar' and 'Akbar', both subdirectories of '/home'.

- When you are in a shell, you are always in a directory on the system, and that directory is called the current working directory. When you first log in to the system, your home directory is the current working directory.
- Whenever specifying a file name as an argument to a tool or application, you can give the slash-delimited path name relative to the current working directory. For example, if '/home/Amar' is the current working directory, you can use work to specify the directory '/home/Amar/work', and work/schedule to specify 'schedule', a file in the '/home/Amar/work' directory.
- Every directory has two special files whose names consist of one and two periods: '..' refers to the parent of the current working directory, and '.' refers to the current working directory itself. If the current working directory is '/home/Amar', you can use '.' to specify '/home/Amar' and '..' to specify '/home'. Furthermore, you can specify the '/home/Akbar' directory as ../Akbar.
- Another way to specify a file name is to specify a slash-delimited list of all of the directory branches from the root directory ('/') down to the file to specify. This unique, specific path from the root directory to a file is called the file's full path name, (When referring to a file that is not a directory, this is sometimes called the absolute file name).
- You can specify any file or directory on the system by giving its full path name. A file can have the same name as other files in different directories on the system, but no two files or directories can share a full path name. For example, user Amar can have a file 'schedule' in his '/home/Amar/work' directory and a file 'schedule' in his '/home/Amar/play' directory. While both files have the same name ('schedule'), they are contained in different directories, and each has a unique full path name--- '/home/Amar/work/schedule' and '/home/Amar/play/schedule'.
- However, you don't have to type the full path name of a tool or application in order to start it. The shell keeps a list of directories, called the *path*, where it searches for programs. If a program is "in your path," or in one of these directories, you can run it simply by typing its name.
- By default, the path includes '/bin' and '/usr/bin'. For example, the who command is in the '/usr/bin' directory, so its full path name is /usr/bin/who. Since the '/usr/bin' directory is in the path, you can type who to run /usr/bin/who, no matter what the current working directory is.

What is Directory?
- Files contain text or data. Directories contain files. Directories should be organized in hierarchical manner.
- A directory is a named group of related files that are separated by the naming convention from other groups of files.
- A directory is file system cataloging structure in which references to other computer files, and possibly other directories, are kept.

- The following extensions have become accepted standards.

Extension	Meaning
EXE	DOS executable file.
COM	DOS command file.
BAT	DOS Batch file.
SYS	DOS operating system file.
BAK	Back up file.
TXT	Text or word processing file.
DOC	A document file.
BAS	File containing Basic Program.
PAS	File containing Pascal Program.

- Files (program or data file) are usually stored on disks. DOS organizes these files by grouping related files into lists called directories. In addition to directories, DOS use an area called the File Allocation Table (FAT). When a disk is formatted (see FORMAT command explained later), this table is copied onto the disk and an empty directory, called root directory, is created.
- On every storage disk, files are stored in directories and File Allocation Table keeps the information about their location on the disk surface. The root directory is represented by the backslash character '\'.
- A pathname is a sequence of directory names followed by a filename. Each directory name is separated from the previous one by a backslash.
- A path is similar to pathname except that it does not include a filename. The pathname is specified in the following form:

    [\dir_name] [\dir_name ...] \filename

    For example, the pathname for RAVI's ABC.PAS file is,

    \STUDENT\RAVI\ABC.PAS

2.4 Introduction to DOS

- DOS (Disk Operating System) was the first widely-installed operating system for personal computers.
- The first personal computer version of DOS, called PC-DOS, was developed for IBM by Bill Gates and his new Microsoft Corporation. He retained the rights to market a Microsoft version, called MS-DOS.
- PC-DOS and MS-DOS are almost identical and most users have referred to either of them as just "DOS."
- DOS was (and still is) a non-graphical line-oriented command- or menu-driven operating system, with a relatively simple interface but not overly "friendly" user interface. Its prompt to enter a command looks like this:

    C:\>

2.4.1 DOS History

- MS-DOS is a non-graphical command line operating system derived from 86-DOS that was created for IBM compatible computers.
- MS-DOS originally written by Tim Patersonand introduced by Microsoft in August 1981 and was last updated in 1994 when MS-DOS 6.22 was released.
- Today, MS-DOS is no longer used; however, the command shell, more commonly known as the Windows command line is still used by many users.
- Fig. 2.12 shows DOS window.

Fig. 2.12

- Following table shows brief history of DOS:

Year	Event
1981	Microsoft buys the rights for QDOS from Seattle Computer Products (SCP) for $25,000 on July 1981.
1981	MS-DOS 1.0 was released August, 1981.
1982	MS-DOS 1.25 was released August, 1982.
1983	MS-DOS 2.0 was released March, 1983.
1984	Microsoft introduces MS-DOS 3.0 for the IBM PC AT and MS-DOS 3.1 for networks.
1986	MS-DOS 3.2 was released April, 1986.
1987	MS-DOS 3.3 was released April, 1987.
1988	MS-DOS 4.0 was released July, 1988.
1988	MS-DOS 4.01 was released November, 1988.
1991	MS-DOS 5.0 was released June, 1991.
1993	MS-DOS 6.0 was released August, 1993.
1993	MS-DOS 6.2 was released November, 1993
1994	MS-DOS 6.21 was released March, 1994
1994	MS-DOS 6.22 was released April, 1994

2.4.2 Internal and External Commands of DOS

- To be functional, each DOS command should be entered in a particular way. This command entry structure is known as the command's "syntax." Syntax notation is a way to reproduce a command syntax in print.
- For example, optional items can be determined by looking at the information printed inside square brackets. The notation [d:], for example, indicates an optional drive designation. The command syntax, on the other hand, is how you enter a command to make it work.

Elements of Command Syntax:

1. **Command Name:** The DOS command name is the name one enters into start a DOS program. A few of the DOS commands can be entered using shortcut names. DOS command name is always entered first. It should be kept in mind that one can enter command names in both lowercase and uppercase, or a mix of both.
2. **Drive Designation:** Drive designation (d:) is an option for many DOS commands. However, some commands are not related to disk drives and, therefore, do not require a drive designation. Whenever you enter a DOS command, it deals with disk drives. If you are already working in the drive in question, you do not have to enter the drive designator. For example, if you are working in drive A (when the DOS prompt A> is showing at the left side of the screen) and you want to use DIR command to display a directory listing of that same drive, you do not have to enter the drive designation. If you do not enter a drive designation, DOS always assumes you are referring to the drive you are currently working in.
3. **Filename:** A filename is the name of a file stored on disk. A filename can be of eight or fewer letters or other legal characters.
4. **Pathname:** A pathname (path) refers to the path you want DOS to follow in order to act on the DOS command. It indicates the path from the current directory or subdirectory to the files that are to be acted upon.
5. **Colon:** When referring to a drive in a DOS command, you should always follow the drive designator with a colon (:). This is how DOS recognizes it as a drive designation.
6. **Space:** One should always leave a space after command name.
7. **Brackets:** Items enclosed in square brackets are optional. In other words, a command will work in its basic form without entering the information inside the brackets.
8. **Filename Extension:** A filename extension is a string of characters added to the end of a filename. It is done usually to help specify what kind of information the file contains, or to distinguish between different versions of a file with the same name. A filename extension can follow the filename to further identify it. The extension follows a period and can be of three or fewer characters. A user does not actually have to type a filename extension.

9. **Ellipses:** Ellipses (...) indicate that an item in command syntax can be repeated as many times as needed.
10. **Switches:** The characters in command syntax that are represented by letters or numbers and preceded by forward slash (for example, "/P") are known as switches. Use of these options activates special operations as part of a DOS command's functions.
11. **Vertical Bar:** When items are separated by a vertical bar (|), it means that you are entering one of the separated items. For example, ON|OFF means that you can enter either ON or OFF, not both.

2.4.2.1 Internal DOS Commands

1. **BUFFERS Command:**

    It is used in the CONFIG.SYS file to set the number of disk buffers (number) that will be available for use during data input. It is also used to set a value for the number of sectors to be read in advance (read-ahead) during data input operations.

    ```
    BUFFERS = (number), (read-ahead number)
    ```

2. **CALL Command:**

    It calls another batch file and then returns to current batch file to continue.

    ```
    CALL [d:][path] batch filename [options]
    ```

3. **CLS Command:**

    It clears (erases) the screen.

    ```
    CLS
    ```

4. **CHOICE Command:**

    It is used to provide a prompt so that a user can make a choice while a batch program is running.

    ```
    CHOICE [/C [:] keys] [/N][/S][/T [:] c, nn] [text]
    ```

5. **CHCP Command:**

    It displays the current code page or changes the code page that DOS will use.

    ```
    CHCP (code page)
    ```

6. **CHDIR Command:**

    It displays working (current) directory and/or changes to a different directory.

    ```
    CHDIR (CD) [d:] path
    CHDIR (CD)[..]
    ```

7. **COPY Command:**

    It copies and appends files.

    ```
    COPY     [/Y|-Y]     [/A][/B]     [d:][path]     filename     [/A][/B]
    [d:][path][filename] [/V]
    or
    COPY    [/Y|-Y][/A][/B]    [d:][path]    filename+[d:][path]    filename
    [...][d:][path][filename] [/V]
    ```

8. **CTTY Command:**
   It changes the standard I/O (Input/Output) device to an auxiliary device.
   ```
   CITY (device)
   ```
9. **DATE Command:**
   It displays and/or sets the system date.
   ```
   DATE mm-dd-yy
   ```
10. **COUNTRY Command:**
    It is used in the CONFIG.SYS file to tell DOS to use country-specific text conventions during processing.
    ```
    COUNTRY=country code, [code page][,][d:][filename]
    ```
11. **DIR Command:**
    It displays directory of files and directories stored on disk.
    ```
    DIR     [d:][path][filename]      [/A:(attributes)]       [/O:(order)]
    [/B][/C][/CH][/L][/S][/P][/W]
    ```
12. **DEL (ERASE) Command:**
    It deletes (erases) files from disk.
    ```
    DEL (ERASE) [d:][path] filename [/P]
    ```
13. **DEVICEHIGH Command:**
    Like DEVICE, DEVICEHIGH is used in the CONFIG.SYS file to tell DOS which device driver software to use for devices. However, this option is used to install the device driver into the upper memory area.
    ```
    DEVICEHIGH=(driver name)
    ```
14. **DEVICE Command:**
    It is used in the CONFIG.SYS file to tell DOS which device driver to load.
    ```
    DEVICE=(driver name)
    ```
15. **DOS Command:**
    It is used in the CONFIG.SYS file to specify the memory location for DOS. It is used to load DOS into the upper memory area and to specify whether or not the upper memory blocks will be used.
    ```
    DOS = [high|low], [umb|noumb]
    ```
16. **ECHO Command:**
    It displays messages or turns on or off the display of commands in a batch file.
    ```
    ECHO on|off
    ECHO (message)
    ```
17. **DRIVPARM Command:**
    It is used in the CONFIG.SYS file to set parameters for a disk drive.
    ```
    DRIVPARM= /D:(number) [/C] [/F:(form factor)] [/H:(number)]
    [/I][/N][/S:(number)] [/T:(tracks)]
    ```
18. **EXIT Command:**
    It exits a secondary command processor.
    ```
    EXIT
    ```

19. **FILES Command:**

    It is used in the CONFIG.Sys file to specify the maximum number of files that can be open at the same time.

    ```
    FILES=(number)
    ```

20. **FOR Command:**

    It performs repeated execution of commands (for both batch processing and interactive processing).

    ```
    FOR %%(variable) IN (set) DO (command)
    or (for interactive processing)
    FOR %(variable) IN (set) DO (command)
    ```

21. **FCBS Command:**

    It is used in the CONFIG.SYS file to specify the number of file-control blocks for file sharing.

    ```
    FCBS=(number)
    ```

22. **GOTO Command:**

    It causes unconditional branch to the specified label.

    ```
    GOTO (label)
    ```

23. **INCLUDE Command:**

    It is used in the CONFIG.SYS file to allow one to use the commands from one CONFIG.SYS block within another.

    ```
    INCLUDE= block name
    ```

24. **IF Command:**

    It allows for conditional operations in batch processing.

    ```
    IF [NOT] EXIST filename (command) [parameters]
    IF [NOT] (string1)==(string2) (command) [parameters]
    IF [NOT] ERRORLEVEL (number) (command) [parameters]
    ```

25. **INSTALL Command:**

    It is used in the CONFIG.SYS file to load memory-resident programs into conventional memory.

    ```
    INSTALL=[d:][\path] filename [parameters]
    ```

26. **LASTDRIVE Command:**

    It is used in the CONFIG.SYS file to set the maximum number of drives that can be accessed.

    ```
    LASTDRIVE=(drive letter)
    ```

27. **LOADFIX Command:**

    It ensures that a program is loaded above the first 64K of conventional memory, and runs the program.

28. **LOADHIGH Command:**
    It loads memory resident application into reserved area of memory (between 640K-1M).
    ```
    LOADHIGH (LH) [d:][path]filename [parameters]
    ```
29. **MENUCOLOR Command:**
    It is used in the CONFIG.SYS file to set the colors that will be used by DOS to display text on the screen.
    ```
    MENUCOLOR=textcolor,[background]
    ```
30. **MENUDEFAULT Command:**
    It is used in the CONFIG.SYS file to set the startup configuration that will be used by DOS if no key is pressed within the specified timeout period.
    ```
    MENUDEFAULT=blockname, [timeout]
    ```
31. **MENUITEM Command:**
    It is used in the CONFIG.SYS file to create a start-up menu from which you can select a group of CONFIG.SYS commands to be processed upon reboot.
    ```
    MENUITEM=blockname, [menutext]
    ```
32. **MKDIR/ MD Command:**
    It creates a new subdirectory.
    ```
    MKDIR (MD) [d:]path
    ```
33. **MOVE Command:**
    It moves one or more files to the location you specify. Can also be used to rename directories.
    ```
    MOVE     [/Y|/-Y]     [d:][path]filename[,[d:][path]filename[...]] destination
    ```
34. **NUMLOCK Command:**
    It is used in the CONFIG.SYS file to specify the state of the NumLock key.
    ```
    NUMLOCK=on|off
    ```
35. **PATH Command:**
    It sets or displays directories that will be searched for programs not in the current directory.
    ```
    PATH;
    PATH [d:]path[;][d:]path[...]
    ```
36. **PAUSE Command:**
    It suspends execution of a batch file until a key is pressed.
    ```
    PAUSE [comment]
    ```
37. **PROMPT Command:**
    It changes the DOS command prompt.
    ```
    PROMPT [prompt text] [options]
    ```

38. **REM Command:**
    It is used in batch files and in the CONFIG.SYS file to insert remarks (that will not be acted on).
    ```
    REM [comment]
    ```
39. **RENAME (REN) Command:**
    It changes the filename under which a file is stored.
    ```
    RENAME (REN) [d:][path]filename [d:][path]filename
    ```
40. **SET Command:**
    It inserts strings into command environment. Programs can use the set values later.
    ```
    SET (string1)=(string2)
    ```
41. **SHELL Command:**
    It is used in the CONFIG.SYS file to specify the command interpreter that DOS should use.
    ```
    SHELL=[d:][path]filename [parameters]
    ```
42. **SHIFT Command:**
    It increases number of replaceable parameters to more than the standard ten for use in batch files.
    ```
    SHIFT
    ```
43. **STACKS Command:**
    It is used in the CONFIG.SYS file to set the number of stack frames and the size of each stack frame.
    ```
    STACKS=(number),(size)
    ```
44. **SUBMENU Command:**
    It is used in the CONFIG.SYS file to create a multilevel menu from which you can select start-up options.
    ```
    SUBMENU=blockname, [menutext]
    ```
45. **SWITCHES Command:**
    It is used in the CONFIG.SYS file to configure DOS in a special way; for example, to tell DOS to emulate different hardware configurations.
    ```
    SWITCHES= [/K][/F][/N][/W]
    ```
46. **TIME Command:**
    It displays current time setting of system clock and provides a way for you to reset the time.
    ```
    TIME hh:mm[:ss][.cc][A|P]
    ```
47. **TYPE Command:**
    It displays the contents of a file.
    ```
    TYPE [d:][path]filename
    ```
48. **VER Command:**
    It displays the DOS version number.
    ```
    VER
    ```

49. **VERIFY Command:**

    It turns on the verify mode; the program checks all copying operations to assure that files are copied correctly.

    ```
    VERIFY on|off
    ```

50. **VOL Command:**

    It displays a disk's volume label.

    ```
    VOL [d:]
    ```

2.4.2.2 External DOS Commands

1. **APPEND Command:**

   It displays or sets the search path for data files. DOS will search the specified path(s) in case the file is not found in the current path.

   ```
   APPEND;
   APPEND [d:] path [;][d:] path [...]
   APPEND [/X: on |off][/path: on |off] [/E]
   ```

2. **BACKUP Command:**

   It makes a backup copy of one or more files. In DOS Version 6, this program is stored on DOS supplemental disk.

   ```
   BACKUP  d:  [path][filename]  d:  [/S][/M][/A][/F:(size)]  [/P][/D:date] [/T: time] [/L: [path] filename]
   ```

3. **ASSIGN Command:**

   It redirects disk drive requests to a different drive.

   ```
   ASSIGN x=y [...] /sta
   ```

4. **ATTRIB Command:**

   It sets or displays the read only, archive, system and hidden attributes of a file or directory.

   ```
   ATTRIB [d:][path] filename [/S]
   ATTRIB [+R|-R] [+A|-A] [+S|-S] [+H|-H] [d:][path] filename [/S]
   ```

5. **BREAK Command:**

   It is used from the DOS prompt, or in a batch file, or in the CONFIG.SYS file to set (or display) whether or not DOS should check for a Ctrl + Break key combination.

   ```
   BREAK = on|off
   ```

6. **CHKDSK Command:**

   It checks a disk and provides a file and memory status report.

   ```
   CHKDSK [d:][path][filename] [/F][/V]
   ```

7. **COMP Command:**

   It compares two groups of files to find information that does not match. (See FC command).

   ```
   COMP [d:][path][filename] [d:][path][filename]
                           [/A][/C][/D][/L][/N:(number)]
   ```

8. **COMMAND Command:**

    It starts a new version of the DOS command processor, the program that loads the DOS Internal programs.

    ```
    COMMAND   [d:][path]   [device]   [/P][/E:(size)]   [/MSG][/Y   [/C
    (command)|
    /K (command)]
    ```

9. **DBLSPACE Command:**

    It is a program available with DOS 6.0 that allows you to compress information on a disk.

    ```
    DBLSPACE / automount=drives
    DBLSPACE /chkdsk [/F] [d:]
    DBLSPACE /compress d: [/newdrive=host:] [/reserve=size] [/F]
    DBLSPACE /create d: [/newdrive=host:] [/reserve=size] [/size=size]
    DBLSPACE /defragment [d:] ]/F]
    DBLSPACE /delete d:
    DBLSPACE /doubleguard=0|1
    DBLSPACE /format d:
    DBLSPACE [/info] [d:]
    DBLSPACE /list
    DBLSPACE /mount[=nnn] host: [/newdrive=d:]
    DBLSPACE /ratio[=ratio] [d:] [/all]
    DBLSPACE /size[=size] [/reserve=size] d:
    DBLSPACE /uncompress d:
    DBLSPACE /unmount [d:]
    ```

10. **DEBUG Command:**

    It is an MS-DOS utility used to test and edit programs.

    ```
    DEBUG [pathname] [parameters]
    ```

11. **DEFRAG Command:**

    It optimizes disk performance by reorganizing the files on the disk.

    ```
    DEFRAG [d:] [/F][/S[:]order] [/B][/skiphigh [/LCD|/BW|/GO] [/H]
    DEFRAG [d:] [/V][/B][/skiphigh] [/LCD]|/BW|/GO] [/H]
    ```

12. **DELOLDOS Command:**

    It deletes all files from previous versions of DOS after a 5.0 or 6.0 installation.

    ```
    DELOLDOS [/B]
    ```

13. **DISKCOMP Command:**

    It compares the contents of two diskettes.

    ```
    DISKCOMP [d:] [d:][/1][/8]
    ```

14. **DELTREE Command:**

    It deletes (erases) a directory including all files and subdirectories that are in it.

    ```
    DELTREE [/Y] [d:] path [d:] path [...]
    ```

15. DOSKEY Command:
It loads the DOSKEY program into memory which can be used to recall DOS commands so that you can edit them.
```
DOSKEY [reinstall] [/bufsize=size][/macros][/history]
                    [/insert|/overstrike] [macroname=[text]]
```

16. DISKCOPY Command:
It makes an exact copy of a diskette.
```
DISKCOPY [d:] [d:][/1][/V][/M]
```

17. DOSSHELL Command:
It initiates the graphic shell program using the specified screen resolution.
```
DOSSHELL [/B] [/G: [resolution][n]]|[/T: [resolution][n]]
```

18. EMM386 Command:
It enables or disables EMM386 expanded-memory support on a computer with an 80386 or higher processor.
```
EMM386 [on|off|auto] [w=on|off]
```

19. EXE2BIN Command:
It converts .EXE (executable) files to binary format.
```
EXE2BIN [d:][path] filename [d:][path] filename
```

20. EDIT Command:
It starts the MS-DOS editor, a text editor used to create and edit ASCII text files.
```
EDIT [d:][path] filename [/B][/G][/H][/NOHI]
```

21. FC Command:
It displays the differences between two files or sets of files.
```
FC  [/A][/C][/L][/Lb  n][/N][/T][/W][number]   [d:][path]   filename
[d:][path]
```
filename or (for binary comparisons)
```
FC [/B][/number] [d:][path] filename [d:][path] filename
```

22. FASTOPEN Command:
It keeps track of the locations of files for fast access.
```
FASTOPEN d: [=n][/X]
```

23. FASTHELP Command:
It displays a list of DOS commands with a brief explanation of each.
```
FASTHELP [command][command] /?
```

24. EXPAND Command:
It expands a compressed file.
```
EXPAND [d:][path] filename [[d:][path] filename [. . .]]
```

25. FDISK Command:
It prepares a fixed disk to accept DOS files for storage.
```
FDISK [/status]
```

26. **FIND Command:**

    It finds and reports the location of a specific string of text characters in one or more files.

    ```
    FIND [/V][/C][/I][/N] ÒstringÓ [d:][path] filename [...]
    ```

27. **GRAFTABL Command:**

    It loads a table of character data into memory (for use with a color/graphics adapter).

    ```
    GRAFTABL [(code page)]
    GRAFTABL [status]
    ```

28. **FORMAT Command:**

    It formats a disk to accept DOS files.

    ```
    FORMAT d: [/1][/4][/8][/F:(size)] [/N:(sectors)]
                [/T:(tracks)][/B|/S][/C][/V:(label)] [/Q][/U][/V]
    ```

29. **HELP Command:**

    It displays information about a DOS command.

    ```
    HELP [command] [/B][/G][/H][/NOHI]
    ```

30. **GRAPHICS Command:**

    It provides a way to print contents of a graphics screen display.

    ```
    GRAPHICS [printer type][profile] [/B][/R][/LCD][/PB:(id)]
                                          [/C][/F][/P (port)]
    ```

31. **JOIN Command:**

    It allows an access to the directory structure and files of a drive through a directory on a different drive.

    ```
    JOIN d: [d:path]
    JOIN d: [/D]
    ```

32. **INTERSVR Command:**

    It starts the interlink server.

    ```
    INTERSVR   [d:][...][/X=d:][...]   [/LPT:  [n|address]]   [/COM:
    [n|address]][/baud: rate] [/B][/V] INTERSVR /RCOPY
    ```

33. **INTERLINK Command:**

    It connects two computers via parallel or serial ports so that the computers can share disks and printer ports.

    ```
    INTERLINK [client [:]=[server][:]]
    ```

34. **LABEL Command:**

    It creates or changes or deletes a volume label for a disk.

    ```
    LABEL [d:][volume label]
    ```

35. **KEYB Command:**

    It loads a program that replaces the support program for U. S. keyboards.

    ```
    KEYB [xx][,][yyy][,][d:][path]filename [/E][/ID:(number)]
    LOADFIX [d:][path]filename [parameters]
    ```

36. **MEM Command:**
    It displays an amount of installed and available memory including extended, expanded and upper memory.
    ```
    MEM [/program|/debug|/classify|/free|/module(name)] [/page]
    ```
37. **MEMMAKER Command:**
    It starts the MemMaker program, a program that lets you optimize your computer's memory.
    ```
    MEMMAKER [/B][/batch][/session][/swap:d][/T][/undo][/W:size1,size2]
    ```
38. **MIRROR Command:**
    It saves disk storage information that can be used to recover accidentally erased files.
    ```
    MIRROR [d:]path [d:] path [...]
    MIRROR [d1:][d2:][...] [/T(drive)(files)] [/partn][/U][/1]
    ```
39. **MODE Command:**
    It sets mode of operation for devices or communications.
    ```
    MODE n
    MODE LPT#[:][n][,][m][,][P][retry]
    MODE [n],m[,T]
    MODE (displaytype,linetotal)
    MODE COMn[:]baud[,][parity][,][databits][,][stopbits][,][retry]
    MODE LPT#[:]=COMn [retry]
    MODE CON[RATE=(number)][DELAY=(number)]
    MODE (device) CODEPAGE PREPARE=(codepage) [d:][path]filename
    MODE (device) CODEPAGE PREPARE=(codepage list) [d:][path]filename
    MODE (device) CODEPAGE SELECT=(codepage)
    MODE (device) CODEPAGE [/STATUS]
    MODE (device) CODEPAGE REFRESH
    ```
40. **MORE Command:**
    It sends output to console, one screen at a time.
    ```
    MORE < (filename or command)
    (name)|MORE
    ```
41. **MSAV Command:**
    It scans your computer for known viruses.
    ```
    MSAV [d:] [/S|/C][/R][/A][/L][/N][/P][/F][/video][/mouse]
    MSAV /video
    ```
42. **MSBACKUP Command:**
    It is used to backup or restore one or more files from one disk to another.
    ```
    MSBACKUP [setupfile] [/BW|/LCD|/MDA]
    ```
43. **MSCDEX Command:**
    It is used to gain access to CD-ROM drives (new with DOS Version 6).
    ```
    MSCDEX  /D:driver   [/D:driver2. . .]   [/E][/K][/S][/V][/L:letter]
    [/M:number]
    ```

44. MSD Command:
It provides detailed technical information about your computer.
```
MSD [/B][/I]
MSD [/I] [/F[d:][path]filename [/P[d:][path]filename
                                          [/S[d:][path]filename
```

45. NLSFUNC Command:
It is used to load a file with country-specific information.
```
NLSFUNC [d:][path]filename
```

46. POWER Command:
It is used to turn power management on and off, report the status of power management, and set levels of power conservation.
```
POWER [adv:max|reg|min]|std|off]
```

47. PRINT Command:
It queues and prints data files.
```
PRINT [/B:(buffersize)] [/D:(device)] [/M:(maxtick)] [/Q:(value)]
[/S:(timeslice)][/U:(busytick)]
[/C][/P][/T] [d:][path][filename] [...]
```

48. RECOVER Command:
It resolves sector problems on a file or a disk. (Beginning with DOS Version 6, RECOVER is no longer available).
```
RECOVER [d:][path]filename
RECOVER d:
```

49. REPLACE Command:
It replaces stored files with files of the same name from a different storage location.
```
REPLACE [d:][path]filename [d:][path] [/A][/P][/R][/S][/U][/W]
```

50. RESTORE Command:
It restores to standard disk storage format files previously stored using the BACKUP command.
```
RESTORE d: [d:][path]filename [/P][/S][/B:mm-dd-yy]
[/A:mm-dd-yy][/E:hh:mm:ss]
[/L:hh:mm:ss] [/M][/N][/D]
RMDIR (RD) (Internal) - Removes a subdirectory.
RMDIR (RD) [d:]path
```

51. SCANDISK Command:
It starts the Microsoft ScanDisk program which is a disk analysis and repair tool used to check a drive for errors and correct any problems that it finds.
```
SCANDISK [d: [d: . . .]|/all][/checkonly|/autofix[/nosave]|/custom]
[/surface][/mono][/nosummay]
SCANDISK   volume-name[/checkonly|/autofix[/nosave]|/custom][/mono]
[/nosummary]
SCANDISK /fragment [d:][path]filename
SCANDISK /undo [undo-d:][/mono]
```

52. SELECT Command:
It formats a disk and installs country-specific information and keyboard codes (starting with DOS Version 6, this command is no longer available).
```
SELECT [d:] [d:][path] [country code][keyboard code]
```

53. SETVER Command:
It displays the version table and sets the version of DOS that is reported to programs.
```
SETVER [d:]:path][filename (number)][/delete][/quiet]
```

54. SHARE Command:
It installs support for file sharing and file locking.
```
SHARE [/F:space] [/L:locks]
```

55. SORT Command:
It sorts input and sends it to the screen or to a file.
```
SORT [/R][/+n] < (filename)
SORT [/R][/+n] > (filename2)
```

56. SUBST Command:
It substitutes a virtual drive letter for a path designation.
```
SUBST d: d:path
SUBST d: /D
```

57. SYS Command:
It transfers the operating system files to another disk.
```
SYS [source] d:
```

58. TREE Command:
It displays directory paths and (optionally) files in each subdirectory.
```
TREE [d:][path] [/A][/F]
```

59. UNDELETE Command:
It restores files deleted with the DELETE command.
```
UNDELETE [d:][path][filename] [/DT|/DS|/DOS]
UNDELETE [/list|/all|/purge[d:]|/status|/load|/U|/S[d:]|
                                        /Td:[-entries]]
```

60. UNFORMAT Command:
It is used to undo the effects of formatting a disk.
```
UNFORMAT d: [/J][/L][/test][/partn][/P][/U]
```

61. VSAFE Command:
VSAFE is a memory-resident program that continuously monitors your computer for viruses and displays a warning when it finds one.
```
VSAFE [/option [+|-]...] [/NE][/NX][Ax|/Cx] [/N][/D][/U]
```

62. XCOPY Command:
It copies directories, subdirectories and files.
```
XCOPY   [d:][path]filename   [d:][path][filename]   [/A][/D:(date)]
[/E][/M][/P][/S][/V][/W][Y\-Y]
```

2.5 Batch Files

- Batch file is the name given to a type of script file, a text file containing a series of commands to be executed by the command interpreter.
- A batch file may contain any command the interpreter accepts interactively at the command prompt. A batch file may also have constructs (IF, GOTO, Labels, CALL, etc.) that enable conditional branching and looping within the batch file.
- A file that contains a sequence, or batch, of commands. Batch files are useful for storing sets of commands that are always executed together because you can simply enter the name of the batch file instead of entering each command individually.
- In DOS systems, batch files end with a .BAT extension.
- MS-DOS allows you to put this command sequence into a special file called a batch file, and then run the whole sequence of commands by simply typing the name of the batch file.
- A batch file is simply a text file that contains one or more DOS commands and/or the names of application programs. Batch files are sometimes called batch commands. When batch command is executed, DOS locates that command on disk, reads the list of commands it contains, and executes them one at a time in the order in which they appear in the file.
- After the last command is executed, DOS is ready to accept another command. By using a batch file, we have to remember to type one command, instead of several. Thus, batch files allow us to extend and enhance the capabilities of DOS.

2.5.1 Creating Batch Files

- To create batch files, you will need to use a word processor or text editor. Batch files can also be created by using EDLIN, the MS-DOS editor, or by using simply the copy command.
- In this topic, we use the COPY command to create batch files. Suppose, we wish to create a batch file named TODAY.BAT to perform the following operations:
    1. Clear the screen (CLS command)
    2. Verify the date (DATE command), and
    3. Verify the time (TIME command)
- To do this simply follow the steps given below:
    1. Type the following
        ```
        A> COPY CON TODAY.BAT ↵
        ```
        This command instructs MS-DOS to copy the information from the console (keyboard) to the file TODAY.BAT.
    2. Now, type the following commands
        ```
        CLS ↵
        DATE ↵
        TIME ↵
        ```

3. At the end of last command (in this example, TIME) press CONTROL - Z and then press ← (RETURN KEY) to save the batch file. DOS then displays the message:
   ```
   1 FILE(s) copied
   ```
   to indicate that it created the file.
4. To execute the created batch file simply type the following command
   ```
   A> TODAY ←
   ```

- When this batch file command is executed, DOS executes, in order, each command the batch contains. In this example, DOS will first execute CLS clearing the display screen. Next it executes the second command DATE displaying current date and allowing you to change the date, if required. Finally, it executes TIME command displaying current time and giving a chance to change the time, if the displayed time is incorrect. This shows that the result is same as if the commands in the .BAT file were typed from the keyboard as individual commands.

Dummy Parameters:

- We discussed how to create a batch file. We can also create a batch file that takes parameters and does different operations depending upon the values of parameters at the execution time. This can be accomplished by using dummy parameters in the lines in the batch file.
- Each time the batch file is executed, DOS replaces the dummy parameters used in the batch file by the parameters used in the batch file by the parameter values expressed at the command line. For instance, let's consider a batch file named TEST.BAT having following lines in it:
  ```
  DIR %1
  CHKDSK %1
  TREE %1
  ```
- '%1' used in this batch file represents a dummy parameter. Dummy parameters are sometimes called replaceable parameters. Every dummy parameter consists of the percent sign (%) followed by a numeral. A batch file may have upto nine dummy parameters, '%1' through '%9'. The '%0' parameter always contains the name of the batch file. The remaining nine parameters receive command line values/arguments. Specifically, the '%1' parameter is replaced by the first command line argument, '%2' is replaced by the second argument, and so on. If the batch file TEST.BAT in our example is executed as:
  ```
  A> TEST C: ←
  ```
  then the DOS substitutes the parameter value (argument) 'C:' for the dummy parameter '%1' for its every occurrence in the batch file. This execution will result as if we entered the following commands:
  ```
  DIR C: ←
  CHKDSK C: ←
  TREE C: ←
  ```
- Executing the batch file TEST.BAT with no parameter value at command line will result in the substitution of null parameter in place of '%1'.

- While using batch file parameters following rules must be observed:
  1. There are ten dummy parameters, '%0' through '%9'.
  2. The ith argument (parameter value) in a batch file command relates to the dummy parameter '%i'.
  3. Executing batch file command results in temporarily replacing each dummy parameter with the corresponding argument. The batch file remains unchanged after its execution.
  4. Generally, the count of command line arguments and dummy parameters should be the same. If less number of arguments are specified while executing the batch file, null parameters are substituted for the excess dummy parameters.
- If a batch file command is to be terminated while it is running, press CONTROL + C keys. On pressing CONTROL + C, DOS displays a message asking you to confirm that you want to terminate the batch process. If you respond with the Y key (yes), DOS abandons the batch file and gives you next prompt. If you respond with the N key (NO), DOS continues with the next command in the batch file.

2.5.2 Batch File Commands

- MS-DOS supports several batch file commands that add power and flexibility to the batch files. Since several commands are included in a batch file, it is somewhat similar to programs.
- Table 2.1 shows the list of batch file commands.

Table 2.1: Batch File Commands

Command	Purpose
REM	Includes a remark in a batch file.
ECHO	Displays a message on the screen and can also be used to prevent screen output.
PAUSE	Temporarily suspends execution of a batch file.
CALL	Calls another batch file.
IF	Performs conditional execution of a command.
GOTO	Transfers execution of a batch file to a specified place in the file.
FOR	Allows a command sequence to be repeated.
SHIFT	Increase the number of command line arguments.

1. **REM:** The REM command allows you to place remarks or comments within batch file to explain the batch file processing. DOS does not execute lines containing the RPM command; instead, DOS simply ignores the line and continues the batch file's execution with next line.

    Syntax: REM [comment]
    where:
    comment - is string of characters of the length upto 123 characters.

Example: The following statements can be included in a batch file to add comment about the creation and purpose of a batch file.

```
REM Filename      : TODAY.BAT
REM Purpose       : To display current date and time and clear the
                    display screen.
REM Created By    : Mohankumar Zade
REM Date          : 08-16-1995
REM
```

The fifth REM statement in above example adds spaces to increase the readability.

2. **ECHO:** The ECHO command is used in batch files to display or suppress batch command messages. Normally, commands in a batch file are displayed/ echoed on the display screen when they are executed by MS-DOS. This feature can be controlled through the ECHO - ON/OFF options. Moreover, many batch files use ECHO to display messages to the user.

   Syntax: ECHO [ON | OFF | message]

   where:

   ON   : enables display of batch commands as they are executed.
   OFF   : prevents displays of batch commands as they are executed.
   message : text line to be displayed to the user.

   Example: To prevent each command in a batch file from being displayed, use the following command in a batch file:

   ECHO OFF

   Likewise, to cause commands to be displayed once again, use

   ECHO ON

   The following example shows how to use display user message in the batch file.

   ```
   @ ECHO OFF
   ECHO This batch file
   ECHO displays today's
   ECHO date and time.
   ```

3. **PAUSE:** The PAUSE command temporarily stops execution of a batch file. When the DOS encounters a PAUSE command within a batch file, it temporarily suspends the execution of a batch file and prints the message "strike a key when ready". On pressing any key, the execution of batch file resumes on the next command within the batch file. If you respond with CONTROL + C or CONTROL + BREAK, the batch file is terminated.

   Syntax: PAUSE [message]

   where:

   message : is a text upto 123 characters that is displayed by PAUSE when batch processing is suspended.

Example: In a batch processing, to instruct the user to insert a new disk in drive B, use the command:

PAUSE Insert a new disk in drive B

On encountering the above command, DOS will suspend batch processing, display the message, and will wait for user to strike any key to resume batch processing.

Similarly, the following command can be included in a batch file to suspend batch file processing without any user message:

    `PAUSE`

4. **CALL:** The CALL command is used to execute one batch file from within another. When the called batch file is executed, the calling batch file resumes execution at the line immediately following the CALL command.

   Syntax: `CALL [drive] [path] batch filename [argument(s)]`
   where:
   `batch filename` : is the name of a batch file to be called.
   `argument(s)` : is the command line parameters(s) for the called batch file.

   Example: Let's assume that, we are writing a batch file named DISKINFO.BAT to format a floppy disk and display information about the disk. To display today's date and time, we can include a call to the batch file TODAY.BAT by using the statement as:

       `CALL TODAY`

5. **IF:** The IF command is used to perform a specific command in a batch file based on the result of a condition.

   Syntax: `IF condition command`
   where:
   `condition` : can have one of the following three forms:
   `command` : any DOS command.

   ERRORLEVEL value is true if the previous program's exit status code is equal to, or greater than, value.
   EXIST filename   is true if specified file exists.
   string1 == string2 true if both strings are same.

   Example: The following command determines the existence of a file named INFO.TXT and displays a message if file is not found in the current directory:

       `IF NOT EXIST INFO.TXT ECHO File not found`

   Here NOT parameter is used before the condition to negate the result of the condition, i.e., ECHO command will be performed when the condition is false.

6. **GOTO:** The GOTO command transfers the execution to a specific place within the batch file. The GOTO command instructs the DOS to process commands starting with the line after the specified label. If the specified label does not exist, the execution of batch file is terminated.

   Syntax: `GOTO [:] label`
   where:
   `label` a character string, may include spaces, but not other separators such as ; or =.

Example: In the following example the existence of a file REPORT.DOC is checked. If the file exist it is displayed on the display screen, otherwise, a message is displayed on the screen.

```
@ ECHO OFF
IF NOT EXIST REPORT.DOC GOTO LBL1
TYPE REPORT.DOC
GOTO LBL2
: LBL1
ECHO REPORT.DOC not found
: LBL2
ECHO BATCH EXECUTION IS OVER
```

In the above example LBL1 and LBL2 are the labels. Note that any line that start with a colon (:) is ignored during batch processing.

Creating AUTOEXEC.BAT File:

- While working with DOS, one may find that several commands are always performed each time the system starts. For instance, defining the system prompt and setting the path for the most commonly used commands or applications.
- DOS lets you include such commands into a special batch file called AUTOEXEC.BAT. When computer is switched on, DOS searches the root directory of default disk drive for AUTOEXEC.BAT file. If AUTOEXEC.BAT file is found, DOS automatically executes it, by passing the date and time prompt. However, if AUTOEXEC.BAT file is not present, DOS automatically prompts for date and time.
- An example, let's create a AUTOEXEC.BAT file to perform:
  1. DATE command
  2. TIME command, and
  3. Set the PROMPT to display current drive and directory information.
  4. Clear display screen.
- To do so, follow the steps listed below:
  1. Enter the following command
     ```
     A> COPY CON AUTOEXEC.BAT ↵
     ```
  2. Include the required commands with appropriate options as below:
     ```
     DATE ↵
     TIME ↵
     PROMPT $P$G ↵
     CLS ↵
     ```
  3. Press CONTROL - Z and press ENTER key to copy the commands in step 2 into the AUTOEXEC.BAT file.
- Now, whenever you restart your computer, DOS will automatically locate AUTOEXEC.BAT file and executes it.

Questions

1. What is meant by operating system? List its features.
2. State advantages and disadvantages of operation system.
3. Define the following terms:
   (i) File
   (ii) Directory
4. Enlist various characteristics of operating system.
5. What are the types of operating systems? Explain two of them in detail.
6. Write short note on: Batch files.
7. What is DOS? Explain its history in detail.
8. Explain the following terms and state its advantages and disadvantages:
   (i) Linux
   (ii) Unix
   (iii) Android
   (iv) Windows
9. Explain following DOS commands with examples:
   (a) Break
   (b) CHDIR
   (c) MKDIR
   (d) CLS
   (e) COPY
   (f) DATE
   (g) DEBUG
   (h) DIR
   (i) ECHO
   (j) EDIT
   (k) EXIT
   (l) GOTO
   (m) FORMAT
   (n) MORE
   (o) MOVE
   (p) SORT.
10. Describe external commands of DOS.
11. Which different files make up the DOS Operating System?
12. What is file and file organisation? Explain its types.
13. Enlist various types of operating system.

■■■

Chapter 3...

Editors, Word Processors, Spreadsheet and Database Packages

Contents ...
3.1 Basic Concepts
    3.1.1 Features of MS-Office 2007
    3.1.2 Components of MS-Office 2007
3.2 MS-Word
3.3 Introduction to Desktop Publishing
3.4 MS-Excel
3.5 MS-PowerPoint
3.6 MS-Access
- Questions

3.1 Basic Concepts

- Microsoft Office 2007 is a version of Microsoft Office, a family of office suites and productivity software for Windows, developed and published by Microsoft.

3.1.1 Features of MS-Office 2007

1. **User interface:** The new user interface (UI), officially known as Fluent User Interface, has been implemented in the core Microsoft Office applications: Word, Excel, PowerPoint, Access, and in the item inspector used to create or edit individual items in Outlook. These applications have been selected for the UI overhaul because they center around document authoring.

2. **Office button:** The Office 2007 button, located on the top-left of the window, replaces the File menu and provides access to functionality common across all Office applications, including opening, saving, printing, and sharing a file. It can also close the application. Users can also choose color schemes for the interface.

3. **Ribbon:** The ribbon, a panel that houses a fixed arrangement of command buttons and icons, organizes commands as a set of tabs, each grouping relevant commands. The ribbon is present in Microsoft Word 2007, Excel 2007, PowerPoint 2007, Access 2007 and some Outlook 2007 windows. The ribbon is not user customizable in Office 2007. Each application has a different set of tabs which expose the functionality that application offers.

4. **Contextual Tabs:** Some tabs, called Contextual Tabs, appear only when certain objects are selected. Contextual Tabs expose functionality specific only to the object with focus. For example, selecting a picture brings up the Pictures tab, which presents options for dealing with the picture. Similarly, focusing on a table exposes table-related options in a specific tab. Contextual Tabs remain hidden except when an applicable object is selected.
5. **Mini Toolbar:** The new "Mini Toolbar" is a type of context menu that is automatically shown (by default) when text is selected. The purpose of this feature is to provide easy access to the most-used formatting commands without requiring a right-mouse-button click, as was necessary in older versions of the software.
6. **Quick Access Toolbar:** The Quick Access toolbar, which sits in the title bar, serves as a repository of most used functions, regardless of which application is being used, such as save, undo/redo and print. The Quick Access toolbar is customizable, although this feature is limited compared to toolbars in previous Office versions. Any command available in the entire Office application can be added to the Quick Access toolbar, including commands not available in the ribbon and macros.
7. **Super-tooltips or Screentips:** That can house formatted text and even images, are used to provide detailed descriptions of what most buttons do.
8. **Zoom slider:** It present in the bottom-right corner, allowing for dynamic and rapid magnification of documents.
9. **Status bar:** It is fully customizable. Users can right click the status bar and add or remove what they want the status bar to display.
10. **SmartArt:** It is found under the Insert tab in the ribbon in PowerPoint, Word, Excel, and Outlook, is a new group of editable and formatted diagrams.
11. **File formats:** Microsoft Office 2007 introduced a new file format, called Office Open XML, as the default file format. Such files are saved using an extra X letter in their extension (.docx/xlsx/pptx/etc.).

    Initially, Microsoft promised to support exporting to Portable Document Format (PDF) in Office 2007.

    Office 2007 documents can also be exported as XPS documents. This is part of service pack 2 and prior to that, was available as a free plug-in in a separate download.

    Microsoft backs an open-source effort to support OpenDocument in Office 2007, as well as earlier versions (up to Office 2000), through a converter add-in for Word, Excel and PowerPoint, and also a command-line utility.
12. **Themes and Quick Styles:** Microsoft Office 2007 places more emphasis on Document Themes and Quick Styles. The Document Theme defines the colors, fonts and graphic effects for a document.

    Quick Styles are galleries with a range of styles based on the current theme. There are quick styles galleries for text, tables, charts, SmartArt, WordArt and more. The style range goes from simple/light to more graphical/darker.

3.1.2 Components of MS-Office 2007
- Microsoft Office 2007 Professional Software contains five programs:
    1. **Word** is the word processing software that has replaced the typewriter. It is commonly used to create letters, mass mailings, resumes, newsletters and so on.
    2. **Excel** is a program used to create spread sheets. Spread sheets are commonly used to create payroll, balance a check book or track an organization's finances.
    3. **PowerPoint** is used to create a slideshow that helps address the topics being covered. It is commonly used to help discuss a topic or provide training.
    4. **Access** is a database management program. It allows large quantity of information to be easily searched, referenced, compared, changed or otherwise manipulated without a lot of work.
    5. **Outlook** is an e-mail software program that allows users to send and receive e-mail. It also allows you to keep a personal calendar and/or group schedule, personal contacts, personal tasks and has the ability to collaborate and schedule with other users.
- Table 3.1 shows file extensions of MS-Office 2007.

Table 3.1: File extensions in MS-Office

Program/Application	2003 Version	2007 Version
Word	.doc	.docx
Excel	.xls	.xlsx
PowerPoint	.ppt	.pptx
Access	.mdb	.accdb

3.2 MS-Word
- Microsoft Word is an example of a program called a "word processor."
- Word processors are used to create and print text documents in much the same way that you would use a typewriter.
- Microsoft Word can be used for the following purposes:
    1. To create business documents having various graphics including pictures, charts, and diagrams.
    2. To store and reuse ready-made content and formatted elements such as cover pages and sidebars.
    3. To create letters and letterheads for personal and business purpose.
    4. To design different documents such as resumes or invitation cards etc.
    5. To create a range of correspondence from a simple office memo to legal copies and reference documents.

Screen components of MS-Word:

- Fig. 3.1 shows various components of MS-Word screen.

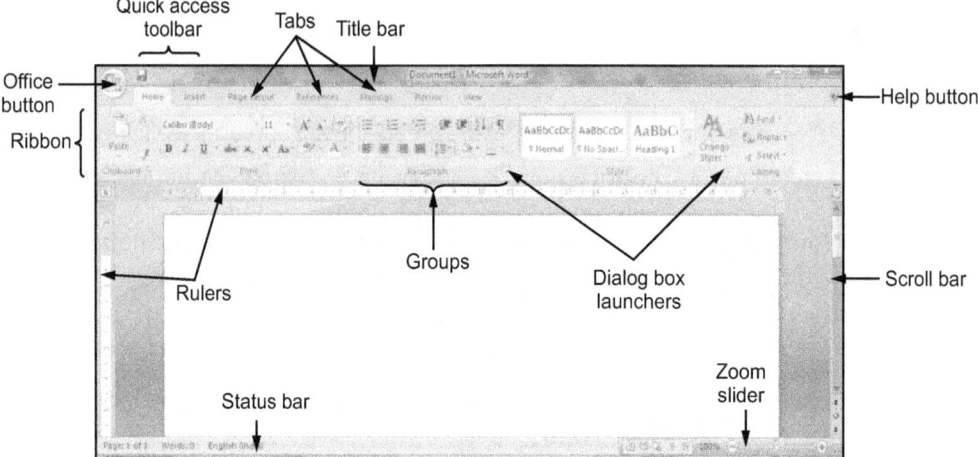

Fig. 3.1: Screen components

1. **Microsoft Office Button:** The Microsoft Office button performs many of the functions that were located in the File menu of older versions of Word. This button allows you to create a new document, open an existing document, save or save as, print, send (through email or fax), publish or close.

2. **Ribbon:** The Ribbon is the panel at the top portion of the document. It has seven tabs: Home, Insert, Page Layout, References, Mailings, Review, and View that contain many new and existing features of Word. Each tab is divided into groups. The groups are logical collections of features designed to perform functions that you will utilize in developing or editing your Word document. Commonly used features are displayed on the Ribbon, to view additional features within each group, click on the arrow at the bottom right of each group.

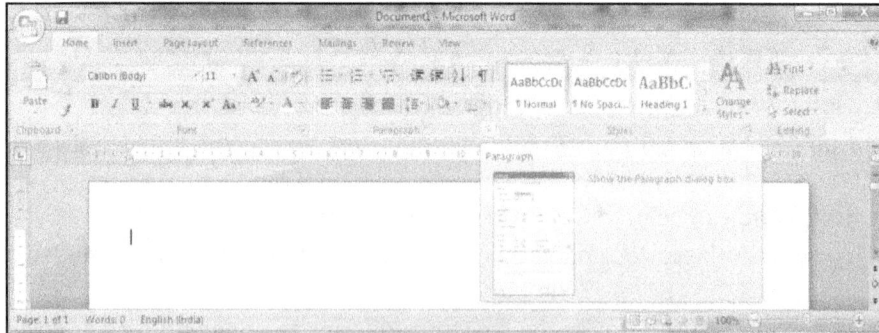

Fig. 3.2: Ribbon

3. **Quick Access Toolbar:** The quick access toolbar is a customizable toolbar that contains commands that you may want to use. You can place the quick access toolbar above or below the ribbon. To change the location of the quick access

toolbar, click on the arrow at the end of the toolbar and click on Show Below the Ribbon.

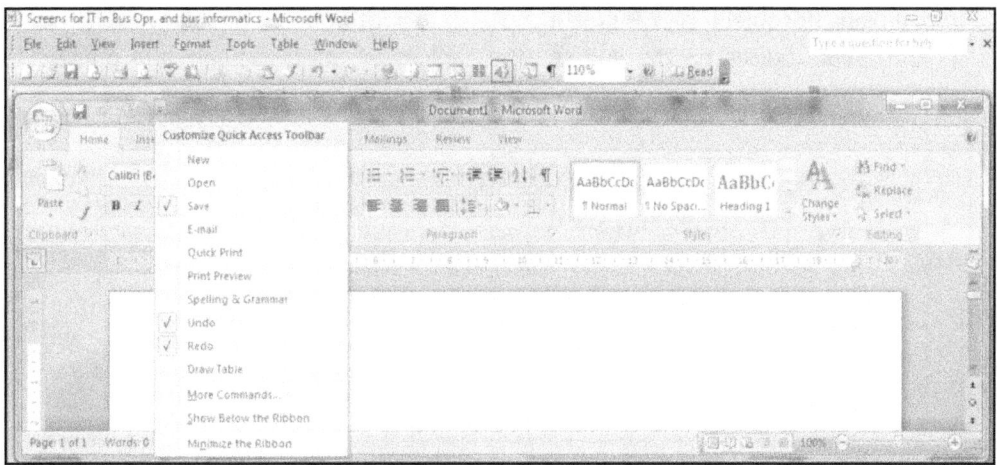

Fig. 3.3: Quick Access Toolbar (QAT)

4. **Title Bar:** The Title bar is located at the top of the screen. The Title bar displays the word Microsoft Word and the name of the document on which you are currently working.
5. **Menu Bar:** Located directly below the Title bar, the Menu bar displays the menu such as File and continues with Edit, View, Insert, Format, Tools, Table, Window, and Help. These menus are used to give instructions to the software.
6. **Toolbars:** Toolbars have buttons or shortcuts to menu commands. Toolbars are generally located just below the Menu bar but these toolbars can be move or customize if you want.
7. **The Vertical and Horizontal Ruler:** The ruler is located below the main toolbars. The ruler is used to change the format of your document quickly especially the margins.
8. **Scroll bars and Scroll buttons:** These elements are use to navigate your document quickly and easily. Scroll bars are use by dragging while scroll buttons is by clicking.
9. **Status bar:** This element is located at the bottom of horizontal scroll bar or the drawing toolbar. This indicates the current page, current section, total number of pages, inches from the top of the page, current line number, and current column number. The Status bar also provides options that enable you to track changes or turn on the Record mode, the Extension mode, the Overtype mode, and the Spelling and Grammar check.

Working with Documents:
1. **Create a New Document:** There are several ways to create new documents, open existing documents, and save documents in Word.
   Follow the following steps for creating new word document:
   (i) Click the Microsoft Office Button and Click New or
   (ii) Press CTRL+N (Depress the CTRL key while pressing the "N") on the keyboard

- You will notice that when you click on the Microsoft Office Button and Click **New**, you have many choices about the types of documents you can create. If you wish to start from a blank document, click **Blank**. If you wish to start from a template, you can browse through your choices on the left, see the choices on center screen, and preview the selection on the right screen.

Fig. 3.4: Creating new document

Opening an Existing Document

1. Click the Microsoft Office Button  and Click **Open**, or
2. Press CTRL+O (Depress the CTRL key while pressing the "O") on the keyboard, or
3. If you have recently used the document you can click the **Microsoft Office Button** and click the name of the document in the **Recent Documents** section of the window Insert picture of recent docs (documents).

Saving a Document:

1. Click the **Microsoft Office Button**  and Click **Save** or **Save As** (remember, if you're sending the document to someone who does not have Office 2007, you will need to click the **Office Button**, click **Save As**, and ClickWord 97-2003 Document), or
2. Press CTRL+S (Depress the CTRL key while pressing the "S") on the keyboard, or
3. Click the File icon on the Quick Access Toolbar.

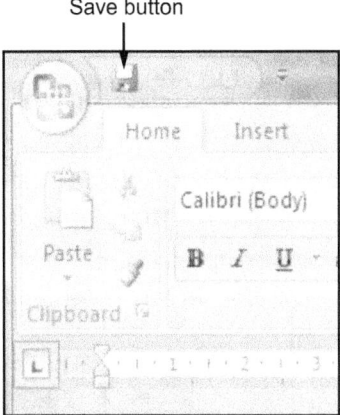

Fig. 3.5: Saving document

Close a Document:
- To close a document:
  1. Click the Office Button
  2. Click Close

Working with Text in MS-Word 2007:
1. **Inserting Text:** Text can be inserted in a document at any point using any of the following methods:
2. **Type Text:** Put your cursor where you want to add the text and begin typing.
3. **Copy and Paste Text:** Highlight the text you wish to copy and right click and click **Copy**, put your cursor where you want the text in the document and right click and click **Paste**.
4. **Cut and Paste Text:** Highlight the text you wish to copy, right click, and click **Cut**, put your cursor where you want the text in the document, right click, and click **Paste**.
5. **Drag Text:** Highlight the text you wish to move, click on it and drag it to the place where you want the text in the document.
- You will notice that you can also use the Clipboard group on the Ribbon.

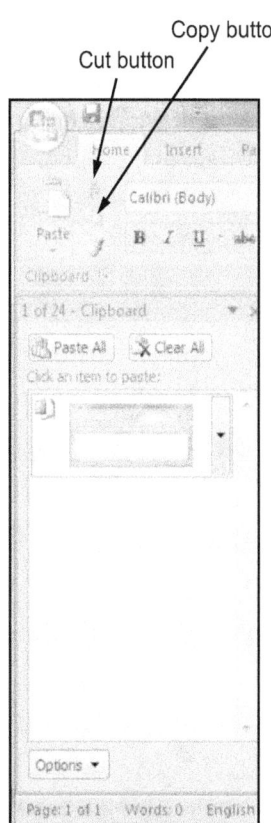

Fig. 3.6: Clipboard group

Rearranging Blocks of Text:
- To rearrange text within a document, you can utilize the Clipboard Group on the Home Tab of the Ribbon. Insert picture of clipboard group labeled,
    1. **Move text:** Cut and Paste or Drag as shown above.
    2. **Copy Text:** Copy and Paste as above or use the Clipboard group on the Ribbon.
    3. **Paste Text:** Ctrl + V (hold down the CTRL and the "V" key at the same time) or use the Clipboard group to Paste, Paste Special, or Paste as Hyperlink.

Fig. 3.7: Paste option

Search and Replace Text:
- To find a particular word or phrase in a document:
    1. Click **Find** on the **Editing Group** on the Ribbon.
    2. To find and replace a word or phrase in the document, click **Replace** on the Editing Group of the Ribbon.

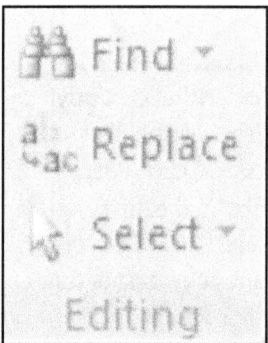

Fig. 3.8: Find and replace

Undo Changes:
- To undo changes; Click the **Undo Button** on the Quick Access Toolbar.

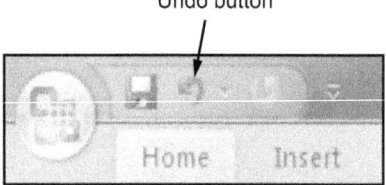

Fig. 3.9: Undo

Formatting Text in MS-Word 2007:

- **Styles:** A style is a format-enhancing tool that includes font typefaces, font size, effects (bold, italics, underline, etc.), colors and more. You will notice that on the Home Tab of the Ribbon, that you have several areas that will control the style of your document: Font, Paragraph, and Styles.

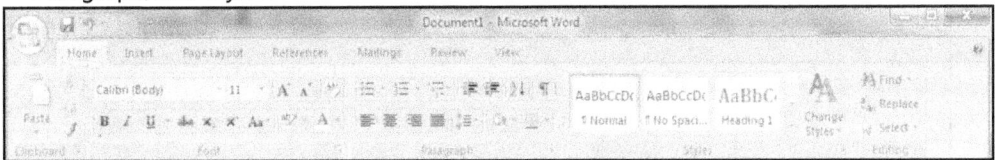

Fig. 3.10: Home tabs of Ribbon

- Fig. 3.11 shows font dialog box.

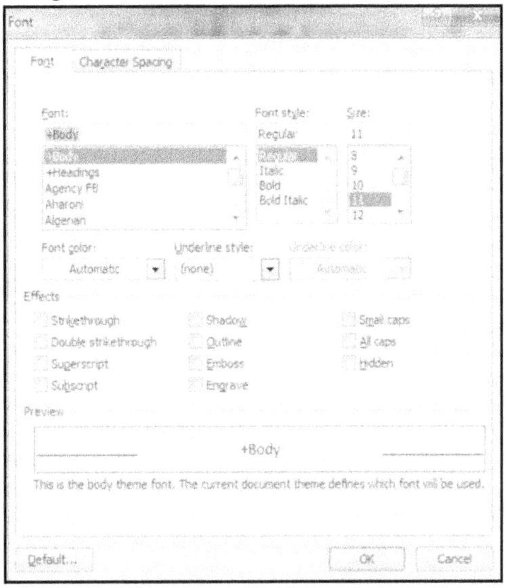

Fig. 3.11: Font dialog

Change Font Typeface and Size:

- **To change the font typeface:** Click the **arrow** next to the font name and choose a font.

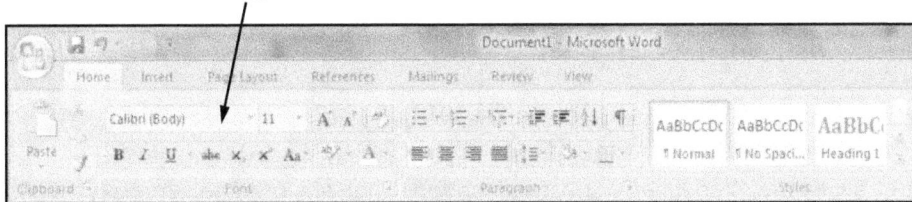

Fig. 3.12

- Remember that you can preview how the new font will look by highlighting the text, and hovering over the new font typeface.

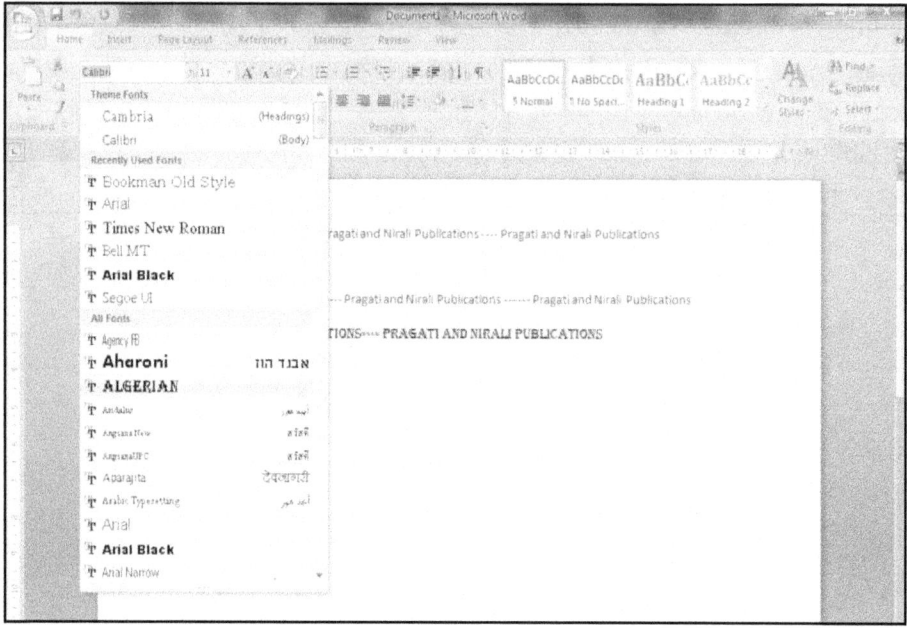

Fig. 3.13: Font list

To change the font size:
- Click the arrow next to the font size and choose the appropriate size, or
- Click the increase or decrease font size buttons.

Font size button

Fig. 3.14

Font Styles and Effects:
- Font styles are predefined formatting options that are used to emphasize text. They include: Bold, Italic, and Underline. To add these to text:
  1. Select the text and click the **Font Styles** included on the Font Group of the Ribbon, or
  2. Select the text and right click to display the font tools.

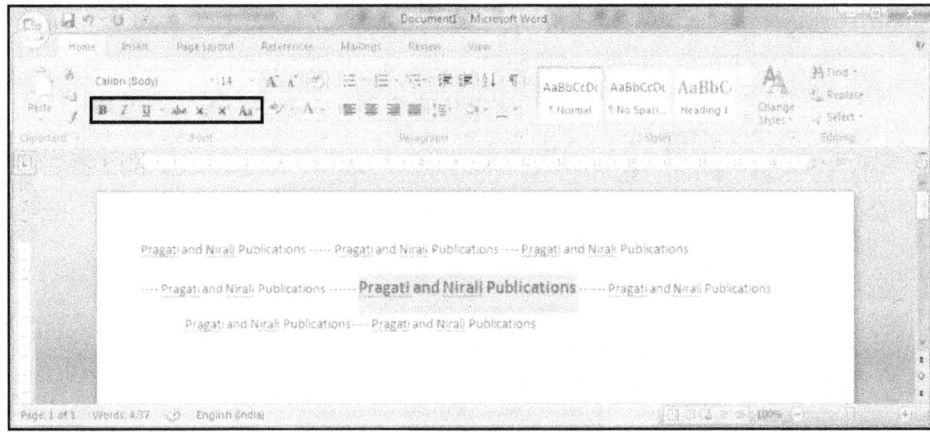

Fig. 3.15: Font tools

Change text color: To change the text color follow the following steps:
1. Select the text and click the **Colors** button included on the Font Group of the Ribbon, or
2. Highlight the text, right click, and choose the colors tool.
3. Select the color by clicking the down arrow next to the font color button.

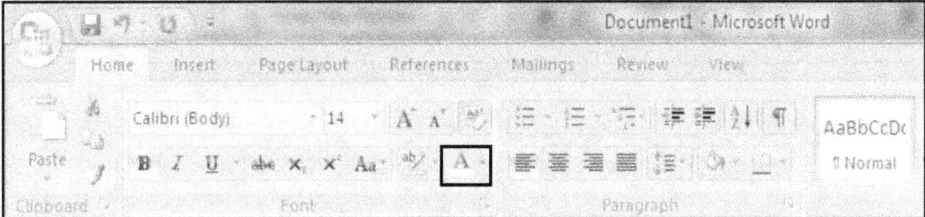

Fig. 3.16

Highlight Text:
- Highlighting text allows you to use emphasize text as you would if you had a marker. To highlight text:
    1. Select the text,
    2. Click the **Highlight Button** on the Font Group of the Ribbon, or
    3. Select the text and right click and select the highlight tool.
    4. To change the color of the highlighter click on down arrow next to the highlight button.

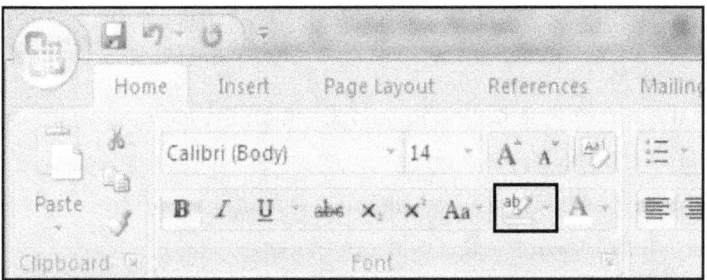

Fig. 3.17

Copy Formatting:
- If you have already formatted text the way you want it and would like another portion of the document to have the same formatting, you can copy the formatting. To copy the formatting, do the following:
  1. Select the text with the formatting you want to copy.
  2. Copy the format of the text selected by clicking the **Format Painter** button on the Clipboard Group of the Home Tab.
  3. Apply the copied format by selecting the text and clicking on it.

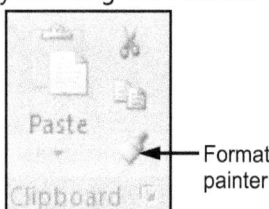

Fig. 3.18

Formatting Paragraphs:
- Formatting paragraphs allows you to change the look of the overall document.
- You can access many of the tools of paragraph formatting by clicking the **Page Layout** Tab of the Ribbon or the **Paragraph** Group on the Home Tab of the Ribbon.

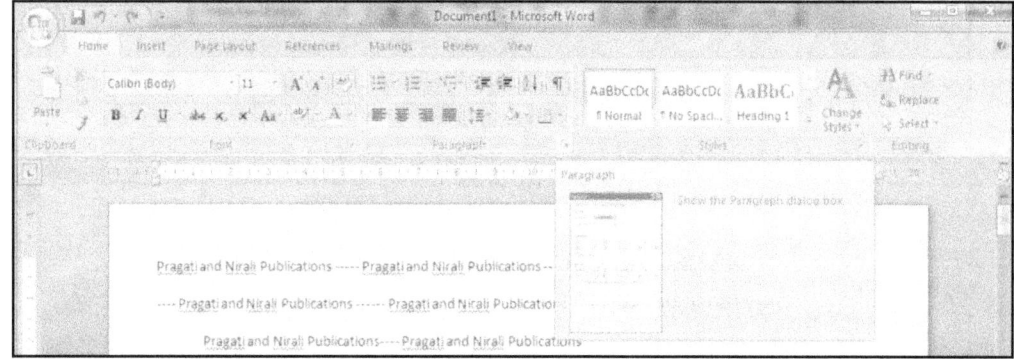

Fig. 3.19: Paragraph options of Ribbon

Change Paragraph Alignment:
- The paragraph alignment allows you to set how you want text to appear. To change the alignment:
  1. Click the **Home Tab**.
  2. Choose the appropriate button for alignment on the Paragraph Group.
     (i) **Align Left:** The text is aligned with your left margin
     (ii) **Center:** The text is centered within your margins
     (iii) **Align Right:** Aligns text with the right margin
     (iv) **Justify:** Aligns text to both the left and right margins.

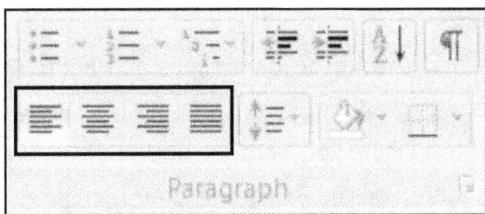

Fig. 3.20: Alignment options

Indent Paragraphs:
- Indenting paragraphs allows you set text within a paragraph at different margins. There are several options for indenting:
  (i) **First Line:** Controls the left boundary for the first line of a paragraph.
  (ii) **Hanging:** Controls the left boundary of every line in a paragraph except the first one.
  (iii) **Left:** Controls the left boundary for every line in a paragraph.
  (iv) **Right:** Controls the right boundary for every line in a paragraph.
- To indent paragraphs, you can do the following:
  (i) Click the Indent buttons to control the indent.
  (ii) Click the Indent button repeated times to increase the size of the indent.

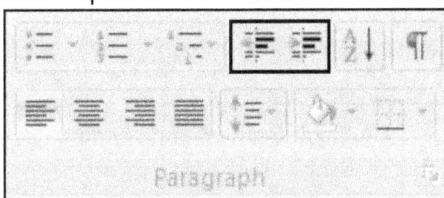

Fig. 3.21: Indenting options

(iii) Click the dialog box of the Paragraph Group.
(iv) Click the Indents and Spacing Tab.
(v) Select your indents.

Fig. 3.22: Paragraph dialog

Add Borders and Shading:
- You can add borders and shading to paragraphs and entire pages. To create a border around a paragraph or paragraphs:
    (i) Select the area of text where you want the border or shading.
    (ii) Click the Borders Button on the Paragraph Group on the Home Tab.
    (iii) Choose the Border and Shading.
    (iv) Choose the appropriate options.

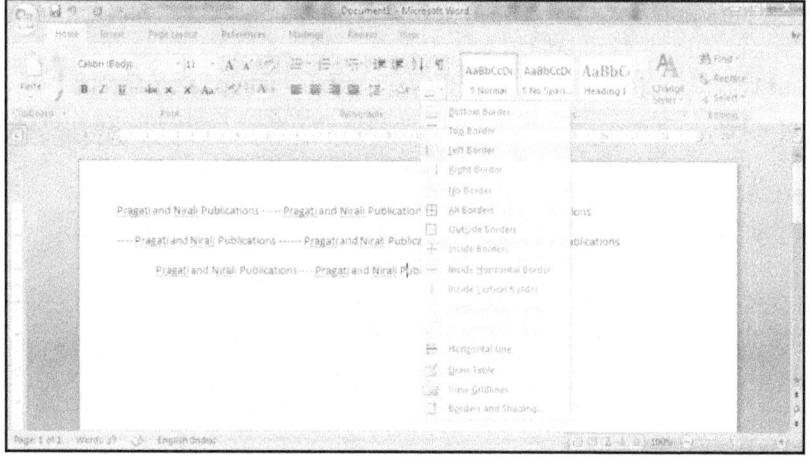

Fig. 3.23: Borders and shading

Apply Styles:
- Styles are a present collection of formatting that you can apply to text. To utilize Quick Styles:
    (i) Select the text you wish to format.
    (ii) Click the dialog box next to the **Styles Group** on the Home Tab.
    (iii) Click the style you wish to apply.

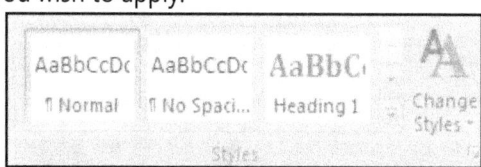

Fig. 3.24

Change Spacing Between Paragraphs and Lines:
- You can change the space between lines and paragraphs by doing the following:
    (i) Select the paragraph or paragraphs you wish to change.
    (ii) On the Home Tab, Click the **Paragraph** Dialog Box.
    (iii) Click the **Indents and Spacing** Tab.
    (iv) In the **Spacing** section, adjust your spacing accordingly.

Fig. 3.25

Adding Tables:
- Tables are used to display data in a table format.
- To create a table:
  (i) Place the cursor on the page where you want the new table.
  (ii) Click the **Insert** Tab of the Ribbon.
  (iii) Click the **Tables** Button on the Tables Group. You can create a table one of four ways:
  1. Highlight the number of row and columns.
  2. Click **Insert Table** and enter the number of rows and columns.
  3. Click the **Draw Table**, create your table by clicking and entering the rows and columns.
  4. Click **Quick Tables** and choose a table.

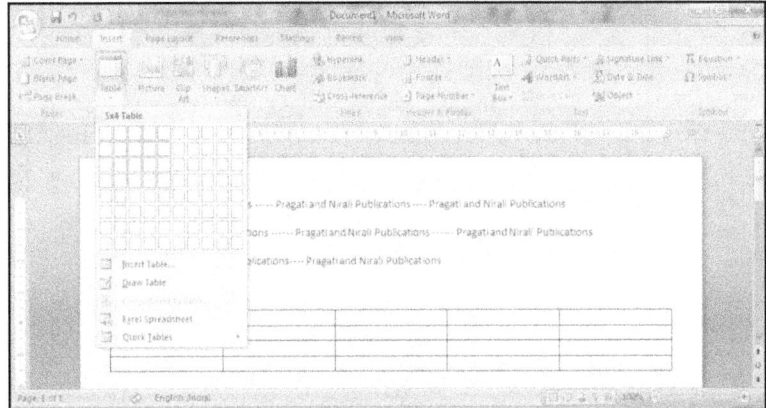

Fig. 3.26: Create a table

Symbols and Special Characters:
- Special characters are punctuation, spacing, or typographical characters that are not generally available on the standard keyboard.
- To insert symbols and special characters:
    (i) Place your cursor in the document where you want the symbol.
    (ii) Click the **Insert** Tab on the Ribbon.
    (iii) Click the **Symbol** button on the Symbols Group.
    (iv) Choose the appropriate symbol.

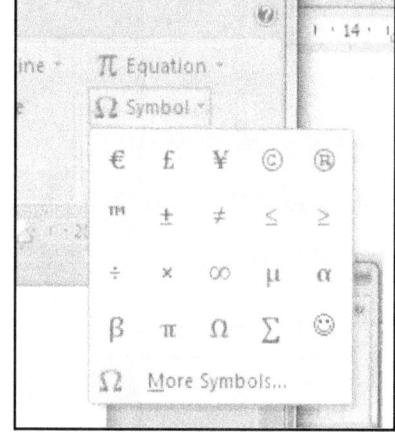

Fig. 3.27: Special character and symbols

Equations:
- Word 2007 also allows you to insert mathematical equations.
- To access the mathematical equations tool:
    (i) Place your cursor in the document where you want the symbol.
    (ii) Click the **Insert** Tab on the Ribbon.
    (iii) Click the **Equation** Button on the Symbols Group.
    (iv) Choose the appropriate equation and structure or click Insert New Equation.

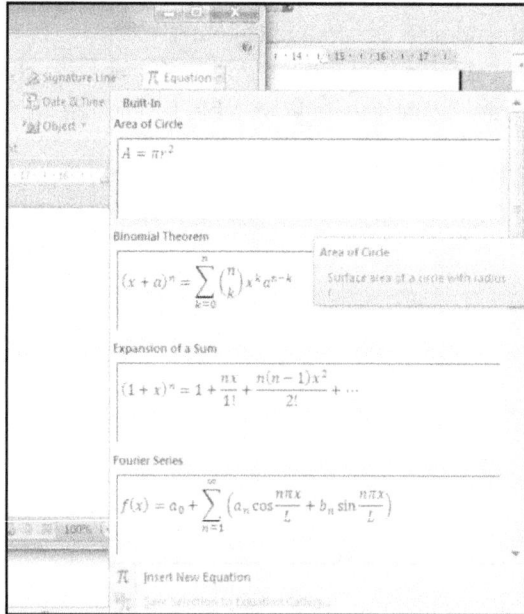

Fig. 3.28: Equations or mathematical symbols

- To edit the equation click the equation and the Design Tab will be available in the Ribbon.

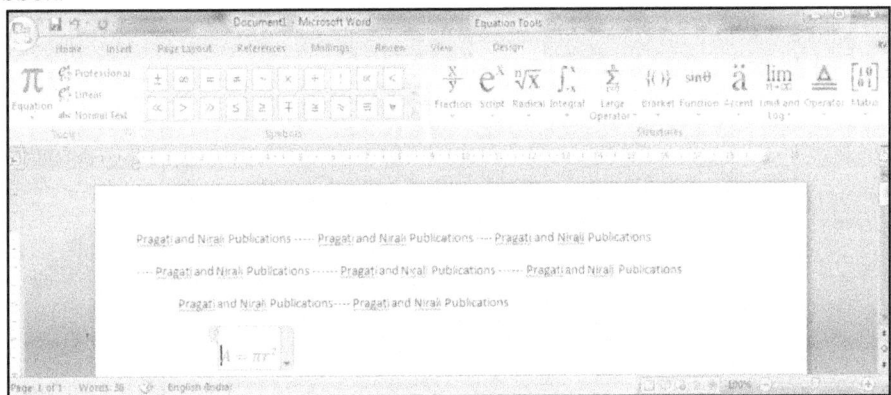

Fig. 3.29: Design tab

Pictures and Smart Art:
- Word 2007 allows you to insert illustrations and pictures into a document.

Inserting ClipArt:
- To insert illustrations:
    (i) Place your cursor in the document where you want the illustration/picture.
    (ii) Click the Insert Tab on the Ribbon.
    (iii) Click the Clip Art Button.
    (iv) The dialog box will open on the screen and you can search for clip art.
    (v) Choose the illustration you wish to include.

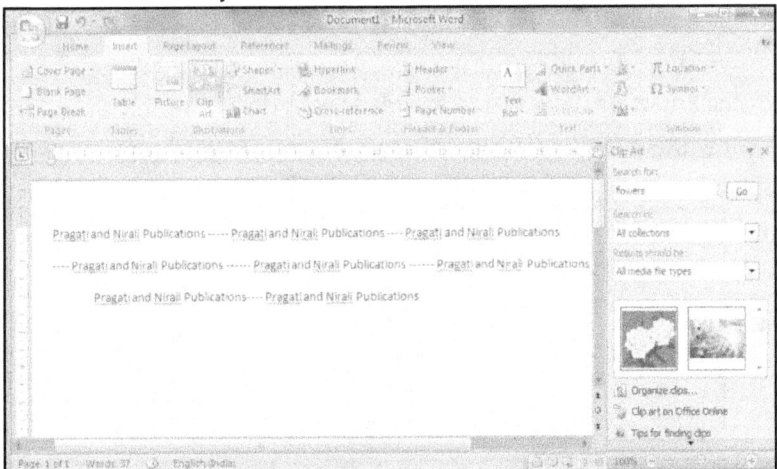

Fig. 3.30: Clip art option

Inserting Pictures:
- To insert a picture:
    (i) Place your cursor in the document where you want the illustration/picture.
    (ii) Click the **Insert** Tab on the Ribbon.

(iii) Click the **Picture** Button.
(iv) Browse to the picture you wish to include.
(v) Click the **Picture**.
(vi) Click **Insert**.

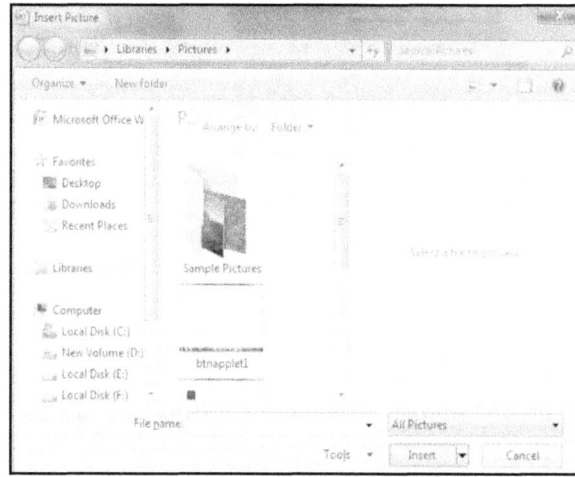

Fig. 3.31: Insert pictures dialog

- **Smart Art:** It is a collection of graphics you can utilize to organize information within your document. It includes timelines, processes, or workflow.
- To insert Smart Art:
    (i) Place your cursor in the document where you want the illustration/picture.
    (ii) Click the **Insert** Tab on the Ribbon.
    (iii) Click the **Smart Art** button.
    (iv) Click the **Smart Art** you wish to include in your document.
    (v) Click the arrow on the left side of the graphic to insert text or type the text in the graphic.

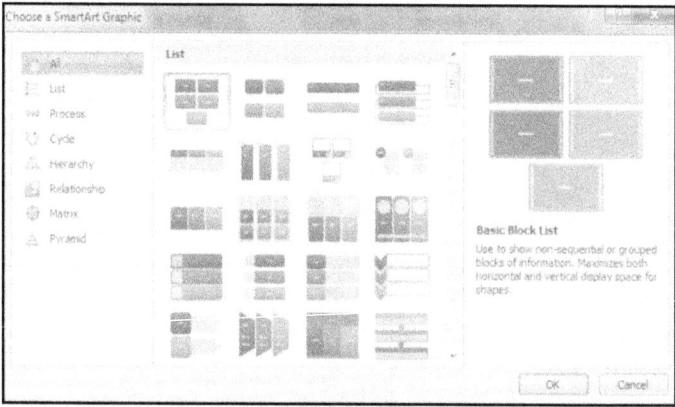

Fig. 3.32: Smart Art option

Proofing a Document:
- There are many features to help you proofread your document. These include: Spelling and Grammar, Thesaurus, AutoCorrect, Default Dictionary, and Word Count.

Spelling and Grammar:
- To check the spelling and grammar of a document:
    (i) Place the cursor at the beginning of the document or the beginning of the section that you want to check
    (ii) Click the **Review** Tab on the Ribbon
    (iii) Click **Spelling & Grammar** on the Proofing Group.

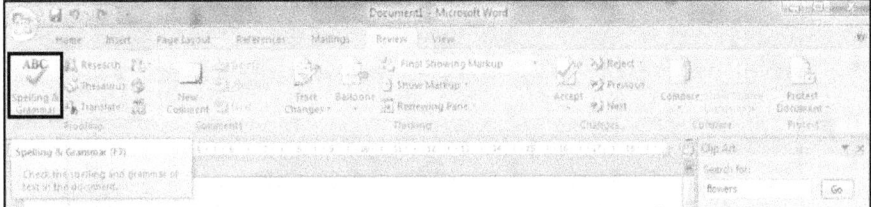

Fig. 3.33: Spelling and Grammar option

- Any errors will display a dialog box that allows you to choose a more appropriate spelling or phrasing.

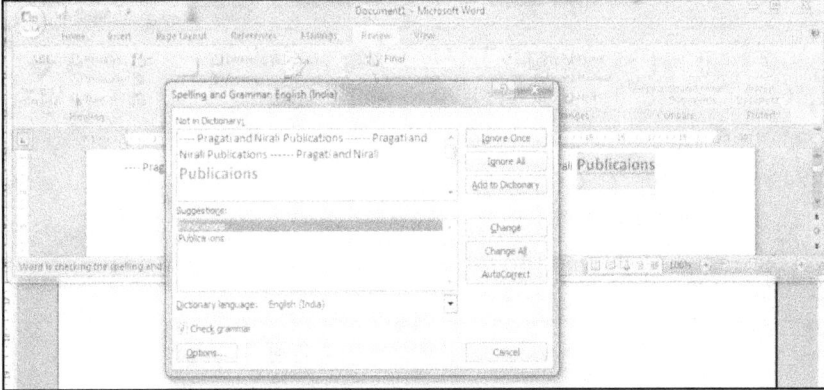

Fig. 3.34: Spelling and Grammar dialog

Page Formatting:
To Change Page Orientation:
   (i) Select the Page Layout tab.
   (ii) Click the Orientation command in the Page Setup group.

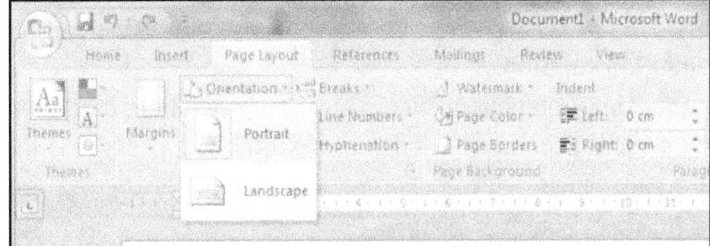

Fig. 3.35: Orientation option

   (iii) Left-click either Portrait or Landscape to change the page orientation.

Change the Paper Size:
  (i) Select the Page Layout tab.
  (ii) Left-click the Size command and a drop-down menu will appear. The current paper size is highlighted.

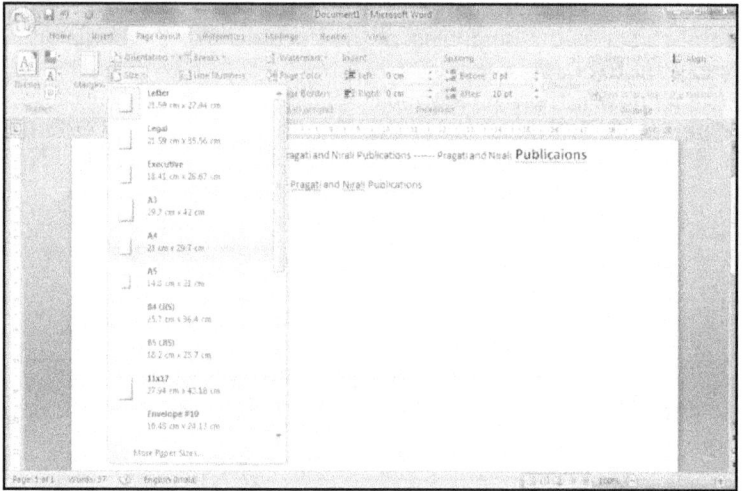

Fig. 3.36: Paper size option

  (iii) Left-click a size option to select it. The page size of the document changes.
- Apply a Page Border and Color.
- To apply a page border or color:
  (i) Click the **Page Layout** Tab on the Ribbon
  (ii) On the Page Background Group, click the **Page Colors** or **Page Borders** drop down menus

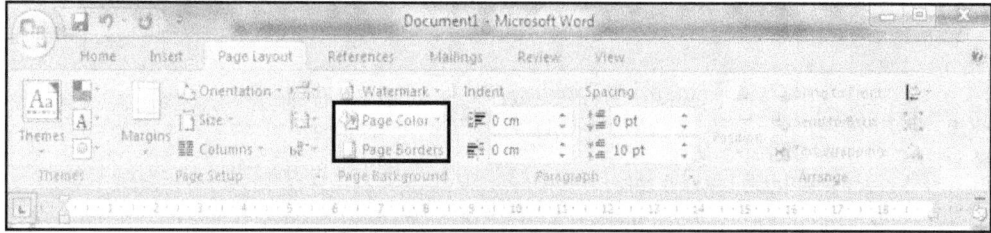

Fig. 3.37: Page border and Color option

Header and Footer Information:
- To insert Header and Footer information such as page numbers, date, or title, first, decide if you want the information in the header (at the top of the page) or in the Footer (at the bottom of the page), then:
  (i) Click the **Insert** Tab on the Ribbon.
  (ii) Click **Header or Footer**.
  (iii) Choose a **style**.

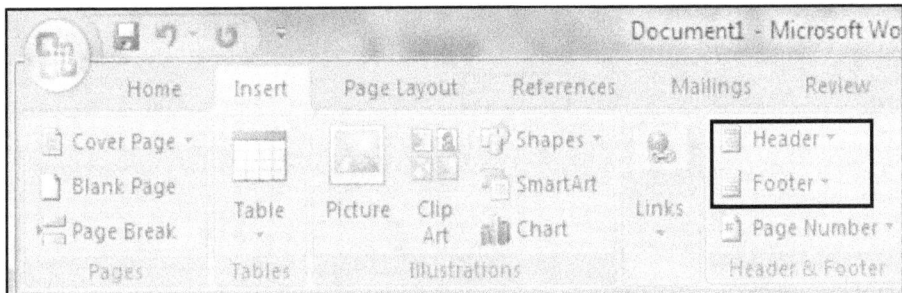

Fig. 3.38: Header and Footer option

Create a Page Break:
- To insert a page break:
    (i) Click the **Page Layout** Tab on the Ribbon.
    (ii) On the Page Setup Group, click the **Breaks Drop Down Menu**.
    (iii) Click **Page Break**.

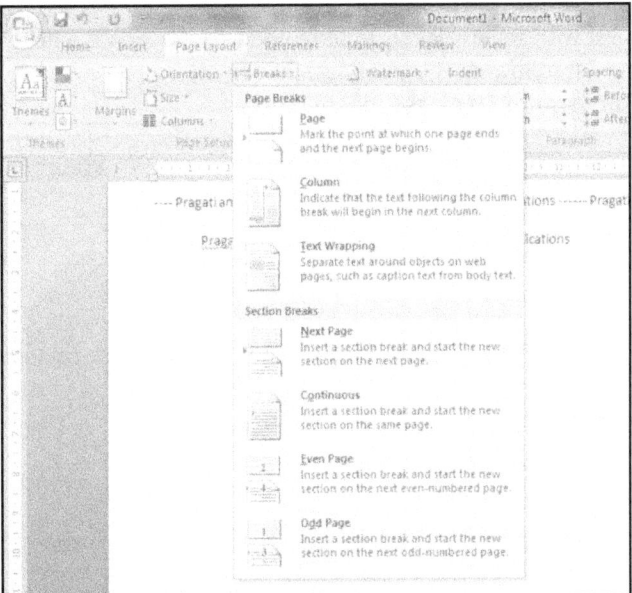

Fig. 3.39: Breaks options

Lists:
- Lists allow you to format and organize text with numbers, bullets, or in an outline.
- **Bulleted and Numbered Lists** Bulleted lists have bullet points, numbered lists have numbers, and outline lists combine numbers and letters depending on the organization of the list.
- To add a list to existing text:
    (i) Select the text you wish to make a list.
    (ii) From the Paragraph Group on the Home Tab, Click the **Bulleted or Numbered Lists** button.

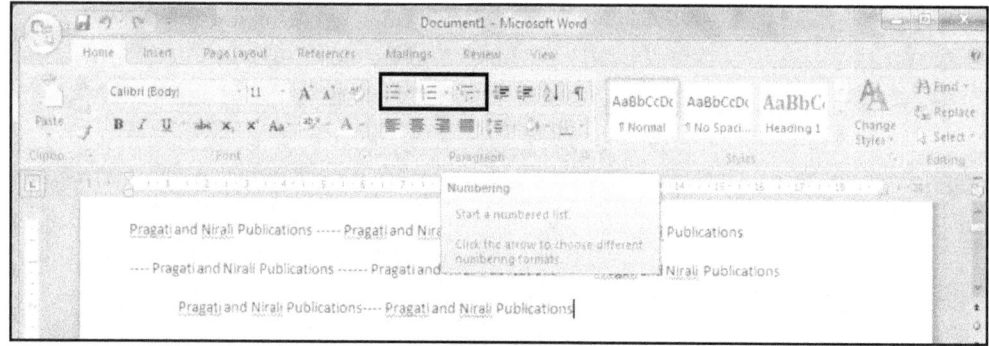

Fig. 3.40

- To create a new list:
    (i) Place your cursor where you want the list in the document.
    (ii) Click the **Bulleted or Numbered** Lists button.
    (iii) Begin typing.

Nested Lists:
- A nested list is list with several levels of indented text. To create a nested list:
    (i) Create your list following the directions above
    (ii) Click the **Increase or Decrease** Indent button

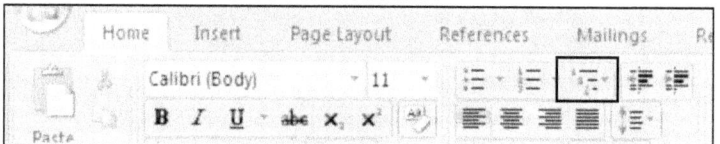

Fig. 3.41

Formatting Lists:
- The bullet image and numbering format can be changed by using the Bullets or Numbering dialog box.
    (i) Select the entire list to change all the bullets or numbers, or Place the cursor on one line within the list to change a single bullet.
    (ii) Right click.
    (iii) Click the **arrow** next to the bulleted or numbered list and choose a bullet or numbering style.

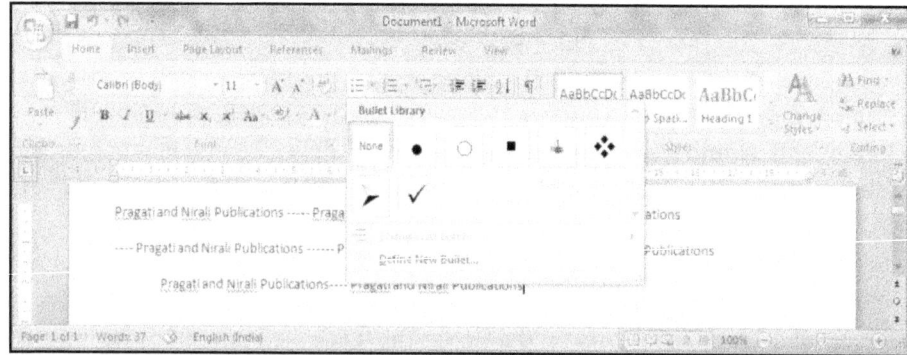

Fig. 3.42: Bullets are numbering option

Working with Shapes:
- You can add a variety of shapes to your document including arrows, callouts, squares, stars, flowchart symbols and more.

To Insert a Shape:
   (i) Select the Insert tab.
   (ii) Click the Shape command.
   (iii) Left-click a shape from the menu. Your cursor is now a cross shape.
   (iv) Left-click your mouse and while holding it down, drag your mouse until the shape is the desired size.
   (v) Release the mouse button.

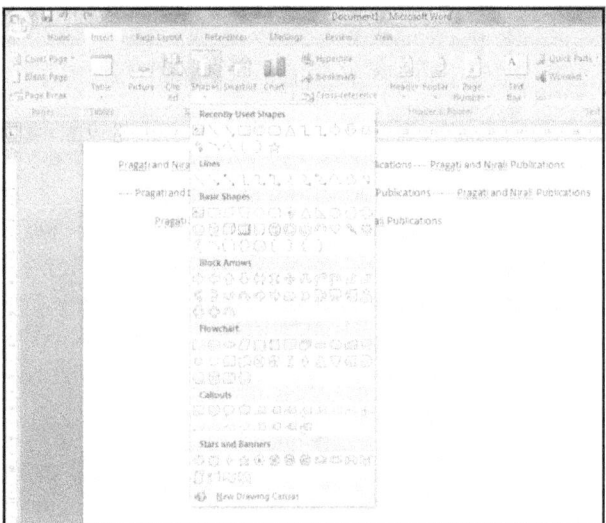

Fig. 3.43: Shapes options

- WordArt allows you to use special effects such as bending, twisting and rotating text in your documents.
- Microsoft Word provides the WordArt feature. WordArt is a way of converting normal text into graphics. WordArt adds special effects to the text. You can insert WordArt, while inserting a particular word in a document.

Adding WordArt in Document:
- Word Art provides a way to add fancy words in your word document. You can document your text in a variety of ways.
- Following are the simple steps to add a WordArt in your document.
   (i) Click in your document where you want to add a WordArt.
   (ii) Click the **Insert tab** and then click **WordArt** option available in Text group, which will display a gallery of WordArt.

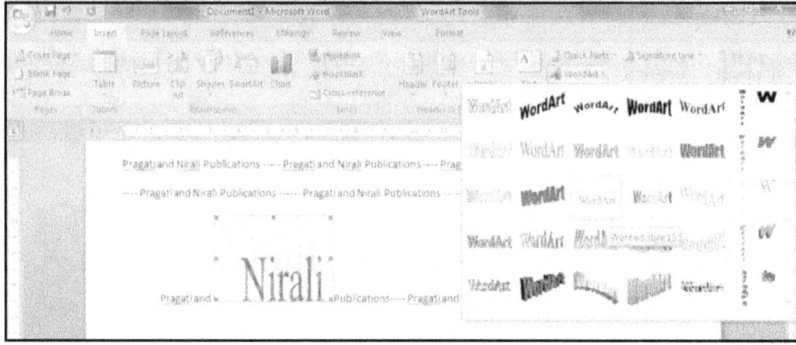

Fig. 3.44: WordArt options

(iii) You can select any of the WordArt style from the displayed gallery by clicking on it. Now you can modify the inserted text as per your requirement and you can make it further beautiful by using different options available.

Mail Merge:
- Mail merge is a useful tool that will allow you to easily produce multiple letters, labels, envelopes and more using information stored in a list, database, or spreadsheet.
- In this lesson, you will learn how to use the mail merge wizard to create a data source and a form letter, and explore other wizard features. Additionally, you will learn how to use the Ribbon commands to access the mail merge tools outside of the wizard.

Fig. 3.45: Mail merge tool

To Use Mail Merge:
(i) Select the Mailings on the Ribbon.
(ii) Select the Start Mail Merge command.

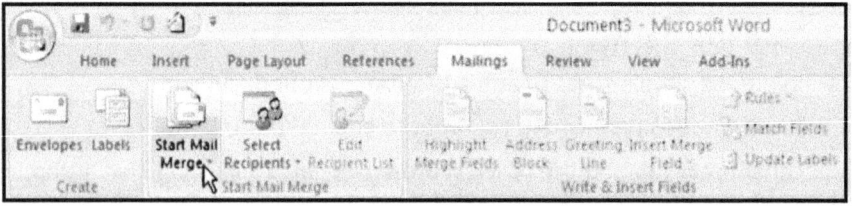

Fig. 3.46: Mail merge option

- Select Step by Step Mail Merge Wizard.
- The Mail Merge task pane appears and will guide you through the six main steps to complete a mail merge. You will have many decisions to make during the process. The following is an example of how to create a form letter and merge the letter with a data list.

Steps 1-3:
- Choose the type of document you wish to create. In this example, select Letters.
- Click Next:Starting document to move to Step 2.
- Select Use the current document.
- Click Next:Select recipients to move to Step 3.
- Select the Type a new list button.
- Click Create to create a data source. The New Address List dialog box appears.
    - Click Customize in the dialog box. The Customize Address List dialog box appears.
    - Select any field you do not need and click Delete.
    - Click Yes to confirm that you wish to delete the field.
    - Continue to delete any unnecessary fields.
    - Click Add. The Add Field dialog box appears.
    - Enter the new field name.
    - Click OK.
    - Continue to add any fields necessary.
    - Click OK to close the Customize Address List dialog box.

To Customize the New Address List:

Fig. 3.47: Customize address list dialog box

- Enter the necessary data in the New Address List dialog box.
    - Click New Entry to enter another record.
    - Click Close when you have entered all your data records.
    - Enter the file name you wish to save the data list as.
    - Choose the location you wish to save the file.

- o Click Save. The Mail Merge Recipients dialog box appears and displays all the data records in the list.
- o Confirm the data list is correct and click OK.
- o Click Next:Write your letter to move to Step 4.

Steps 4-6:
- Write a letter in the current Word document, or use an open, existing document.

To Insert Recipient Data from the List:
- o Place the insertion point in the document where you wish the information to appear.
- o Select Address block, Greeting line, or Electronic postage from the task pane. A dialog box with options will appear based on your selection.

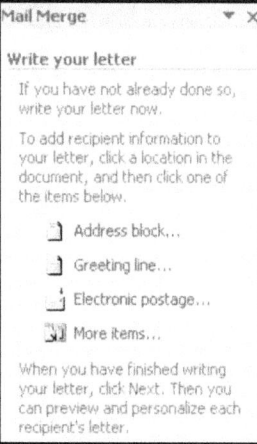

Fig. 3.48: Mail merge recipients dialog box

OR

- Select More Items. The Insert Merge Field dialog box will appear.
  - o Select the field you would like to insert in the document.
  - o Click Insert. Notice that a placeholder appears where information from the data record will eventually appear.
  - o Repeat these steps each time you need to enter information from your data record.
- Click Next: Preview your letters in the task pane once you have completed your letter.
- Preview the letters to make sure the information from the data record appears correctly in the letter.
  - o Click Next: Complete the merge.
  - o Click Print to print the letters.
  - o Click All.
  - o Click OK in the Merge to Printer dialog box.
  - o Click OK to send the letters to the printer.

3.3 Introduction to Desktop Publishing

- Desktop publishing (abbreviated DTP) is the creation of documents using page layout skills on a personal computer.
- When used skillfully, desktop publishing software can produce text and images with attractive layouts and typographic quality comparable to traditional typography and printing, so DTP is also the main reference for digital typography.

What is Desktop Publishing?

- The term Desktop Publishing (DTP) covers a broad range of activities. In it's widest sense, it can mean anything concerned with creating a printed document on a desktop PC.
- Desktop Publishing is anything where you need precise control over the position of text and/or graphics on the printed page.
- However, most simple documents can be handled by a Word Processor and do not require the more advanced facilities of a dedicated DTP application and so we normally refer to Desktop Publishing as anything where you need precise control of the position of text and/or graphics on the printed page.
- Typical DTP candidates include:
    - Books containing diagrams,
    - Newsletters,
    - Advertising Flyers,
    - Leaflets, and
    - Anything that requires multi-column output.
- Desktop Publishing characterizes the fabrication of camera-ready page layouts with the help of a personal computer as well as specific software and periphery (scanners to import templates, printers/ phototypesetters for high quality editions from page layouts).
- DTP is word processing as well as graphics and layout.
    1. DTP enables the creation of high quality technical printed matter such as artwork from the comfort of each computer users desk.
    2. DTP or more precisely the essential (content) components typography and layout, this serves for an improved legibility for the reader as well as a higher acceptance of texts.
    3. The initial scepticism from the pioneer years, dating back to the first 5-10 years since the introduction on the market of the first DTP systems in 1984, reached its current professionalism of software and hardware through a broad acceptance, it also yielded the highly professional printing and type setting industry.
- A good composition by now is an important factor for all types of texts and is of great important for all professions that produce texts based on the effective technical possibilities.

Advantages:
1. **Simplification of work flows:** One person at one workstation can complete the single steps from text production up to its fabrication of printable standard texts. This leads to drastic cost reductions because the complete number of people taking part is reduced.
2. **Speed and Flexibility:** Gives one the possibility to make last minute changes. This advantage is currently being strengthened by the current trend of "Printing on Demand"; here printing high quality final versions are also transferred to electronically supported "End-User" systems.
3. **Controllability of the Printing Process:** When it comes to foreign-languages goods, which translators have a lot to do with, typing errors and other errors can be avoided that could arise due to language and cultural barriers.

Disadvantages:
1. **DTP provides for intensive training:** This affects typographic basic knowledge and a higher necessity for regulation for a professional and uniform configuration "corporate identity."
2. **An individual person needs to combine special knowledge:** From earlier specialised occupations and carryout the orthography, punctuation, and hyphenation having sole responsibility. The available aids, especially for German, for professional use are in most cases insufficiently suited.

DTP Components:
1. **Software:** The new entry in the layout programme, as well as the completion of texts and exports from effective word-processing programmes. The most important products are: Microsoft Word, Word Perfect, Lotus AmiPro, for Apple Macintosh Claris MacWrite Pro etc.
2. **Graphic:** Creation of vector drawings from objects, softrwares like CorelDraw, Micrografx Designer, Visio, MacDraw and others.
    (i) **Diverse:** Pixel photos (Bitmaps) from individual points, generated from MS Word Graphic Editor, MS Paintbrush, Aldus Freehand et.al... Some programmes (Canvas) have the ability to process both vector graphics and Bitmaps.
    (ii) **Special form:** Clipart, that is to say a collection of iconised graphics that are for example treated as specific file types (catalogued with keywords) in Microsoft. All types of graphics can be administered with CorelMosaic.
3. **Layout:** Combination of text (parts) and graphics whereas the presentation does not comply with individual pages but modelled on mounting surfaces of a graphic artist, independent of a specific page or paper format a larger working surface is presented. Most well known programmes are:
    - Adobe (previously known as Aldus) PageMaker (Mac, Windows), mainly applicable for the composition of time consuming printing matters, e.g. notifications, brochures, magazines
    - Ventura Publisher (Windows), mainly for larger quantities (books), and
    - Quarkexpress (specifically for Mac).

Types of Softwares:
- There are four general groups of software used in desktop publishing software most designers need. These types of programs make up the core of your toolbox. Additional utilities, add-ons, and specialty software not covered here can enhance the basic desktop publishing software arsenal. Within some of the four general groups of software are additional sub-categories.

1. **Word Processor:**
- You will use a word processor to type and edit your text including spell and grammar checking. You may even be able to format specific elements on the fly and include those formatting tags when you import text to your page layout program, simplifying some formatting tasks.
- While you can do some fancy, advanced layouts in your word processor software they are best suited to simply working with words, not for page layout. Additionally, if your intent is to have your work commercially printed, word processing file formats are generally not suitable.
- Choose a word processor that can import and export a variety of formats for maximum compatibility with others.
- **Examples:**
    - **(i) Microsoft Word:** Microsoft may be best known for its operating systems. But in the desktop publishing, Web design, and home creativity arena, Microsoft produces several lines such as Microsoft Expression, PowerPoint, Publisher, and Word as well as a number of apps that come with the Windows OS.
    - **(ii) Corel WordPerfect:** Corel Corporation has long been known primarily for its graphics software and digital imaging products. Corel produces products frequently considered strong alternatives to Adobe and Microsoft.

2. **Graphics Software:**
- For most print publishing an illustration program and an image editor are the types of programs needed. Some graphics software programs may incorporate a few features of the other type, but for most professional work you'll need each one.
    - **(i) Illustration:** Illustration or drawing programs work with vector graphics formats and allow more flexibility when creating artwork that is to be resized or must go through multiple edits. Adobe Illustrator is one example.
    - **(ii) Photo/Image Editing:** Image editors, also called paint programs or photo editors work with bitmap images such as photos and scans. Although illustration programs can export bitmaps, photo editors are better for Web images and many special photo effects. Photoshop is a popular example.

3. **Adobe FrameMaker:**
- Adobe FrameMaker enterprise software provides powerhouse publishing for corporate and technical publishing of complex documents for Web, print, and other distribution methods. FrameMaker is a part of the Adobe Technical Communication Suite.
- For desktop publishing that requires that documents be available in print as well as in various formats such as PDF, HTML, or XML, FrameMaker delivers. It is strong on features for the layout and management of long, highly structured documents.

4. **Adobe InDesign:**
- InDesign is the successor to PageMaker, the original desktop publishing software program.
- It is a page layout software program available as a standalone package or in some of the editions of the Adobe Creative Suite.

5. **Adobe PageMaker 7:**
- Not quite on a par with InDesign or QuarkXPress, Adobe PageMaker 7 is still a professional-level page layout application.
- Marketed as a small business/enterprise publishing solution, PageMaker shines just as bright as the similarly-targeted Microsoft Publisher in output but not in price or ease of use.

6. **Microsoft Publisher / Microsoft Office Publisher:**
- Despite its detractors, Microsoft Publisher is a major step up from consumer creative printing programs. For Windows users, it fills the void between price and pro features.
- The Microsoft Office Publisher incarnation moved it more into competition with Adobe PageMaker for the enterprise/small business market and away from the individual consumer. And although not perfect, there were major improvements with the release of Publisher 2010.

3.4 MS-Excel

- Microsoft Excel is an example of a program called a "spreadsheet."
- Spreadsheets are used to organize real world data, such as a check register or a rolodex. Data can be numerical or alphanumeric (involving letters or numbers).
- The key benefit to using a spreadsheet program is that you can make changes easily, including correcting spelling or values, adding, deleting, formatting, and relocating data.

Spreadsheets:
- A spreadsheet is an electronic document that stores various types of data. There are vertical columns and horizontal rows.
- A cell is where the column and row intersect. A cell can contain data and can be used in calculations of data within the spreadsheet.
- An Excel spreadsheet can contain workbooks and worksheets. The workbook is the holder for related worksheets.

Work with Excel:
- The Excel 2007 program window is easy to navigate and simple to use (See Fig. 3.49 and Table 3.2 for the main elements of the program window). It is designed to help you quickly find the commands that you need to complete a task.

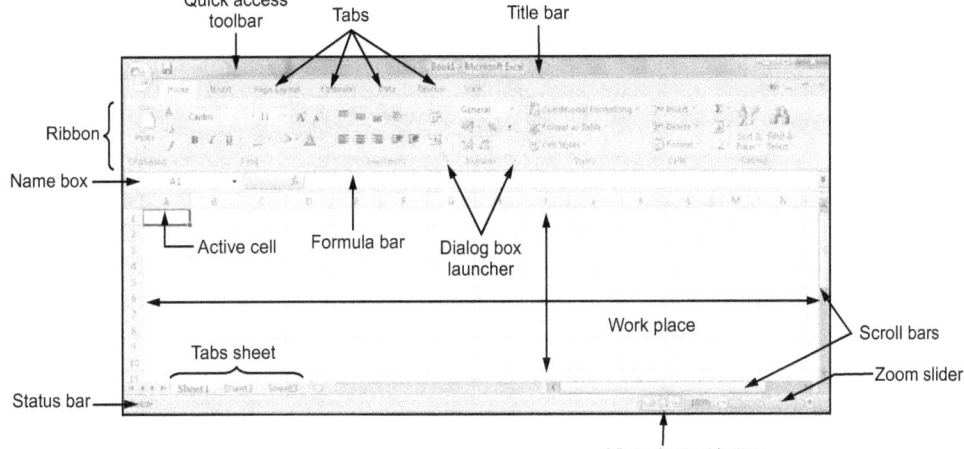

Fig. 3.49: Excel 2007 program window

Table 3.2: Excel 2007 program window elements

Element of Excel Window	Description
Title bar	Displays the name of the workbook and the program.
Minimize, Restore Down/ Maximize and Close buttons	Used to control the program window. Use the Minimize button to hide the window. Use the Restore Down/Maximize button to adjust he size of the window. Use the Close button to exit Excel.
Quick Access toolbar	Contains frequently used commands that are independent of the tab displayed on the Ribbon.
Ribbon	Contains all the commands related to managing workbooks and working with workbook content.
Formula bar	Displays the data or formula stored in the active cell. It can also be used to enter or edit a formula, a function, or data in a cell.
Name box	Displays the active cell address or the name of the selected cell, range or object.
Workbook window	Displays a portion of the worksheet.
Sheet tabs	Each tap represents a different worksheet in the workbook. A workbook can have any number of sheets and each sheet has its name displayed on its sheet tab.
Scroll bars	Used to scroll through the worksheet.
Status bar	Displays various messages as well as the status of the Num Lock, Caps Lock and Scroll Lock keys on the keyboard.
View Shortcuts toolbar	Used to display the worksheet in a variety of views, each suited to a specific purpose.
Zoom Level button and Zoom slider	Used to change the magnification of the worksheet.

Creating a Workbook:
- To create a new Workbook:
    - (i) Click the Microsoft Office **Toolbar**.
    - (ii) Click **New**.
    - (iii) Choose **Blank Document**.

Save a Workbook:
- When you save a workbook, you have two choices: Save or Save As.
- To save a document:
    - (i) Click the **Microsoft Office Button**.
    - (ii) Click **Save**.

Open a Workbook:
- To open an existing workbook:
    - (i) Click the **Microsoft Office Button**.
    - (ii) Click **Open**.
    - (iii) Browse to the workbook.
    - (iv) Click the title of the workbook.
    - (v) Click **Open**.

Entering Data:
- There are different ways to enter data in Excel: in an active cell or in the formula bar.
- To enter data in an active cell:
    - (i) Click in the **cell** where you want the data.
    - (ii) Begin typing.

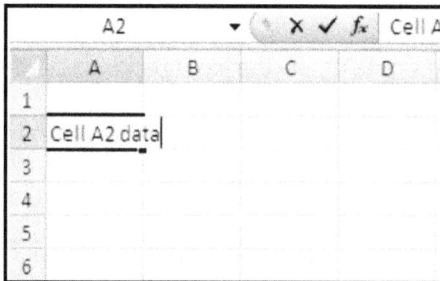

Fig. 3.50: Entering data in Excel

Insert Cells, Rows, and Columns:
- To insert cells, rows, and columns in Excel:
    - (i) Place the cursor in the row below where you want the new row, or in the column to the left of where you want the new column.
    - (ii) Click the **Insert** button on the **Cells** group of the **Home** tab.
    - (iii) Click the appropriate choice: **Cell**, **Row**, or **Column**.

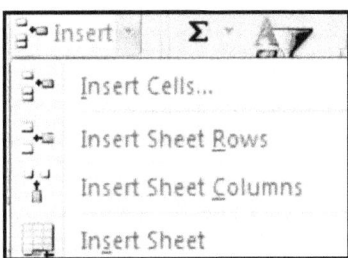

Fig. 3.51: Insert options

Delete Cells, Rows and Columns:
- To delete cells, rows, and columns:
    (i) Place the cursor in the cell, row, or column that you want to delete.
    (ii) Click the **Delete** button on the **Cells** group of the **Home** tab.
    (iii) Click the appropriate choice: **Cell, Row**, or **Column**.

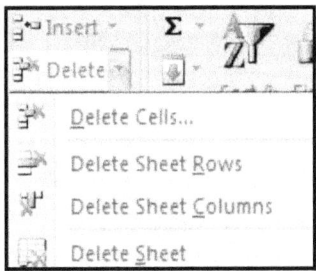

Fig. 3.52: Delete options

Find and Replace:
- To find data or find and replace data:
    (i) Click the **Find & Select** button on the Editing group of the Home tab.
    (ii) Choose **Find** or **Replace**.
    (iii) Complete the **Find What** text box.
    (iv) Click on **Options** for more search options.

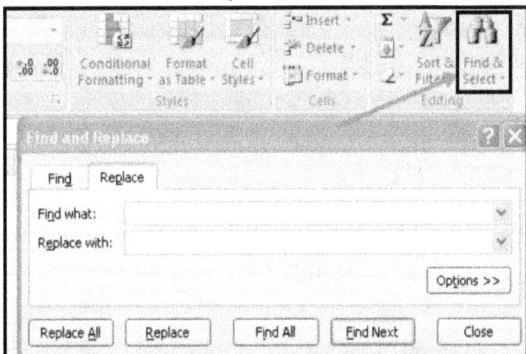

Fig. 3.53: Find and Replace Dialog box

Spell Check:

- To check the spelling:
  (i) On the **Review** tab click the **Spelling** button.

Fig. 3.54: Review options

Excel Formulas:

- A formula is a set of mathematical instructions that can be used in Excel to perform calculations. Formals are started in the formula box with an = sign.

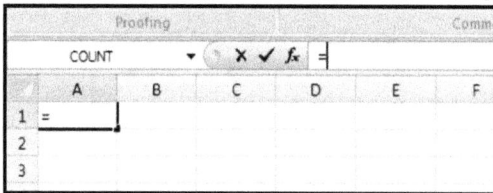

Fig. 3.55: Formula box

- There are many elements to and excel formula.
  - **References:** The cell or range of cells that you want to use in your calculation.
  - **Operators:** Symbols (+, -, *, /, etc.) that specify the calculation to be performed.
  - **Constants:** Numbers or text values that do not change.
  - **Functions:** Predefined formulas in Excel.
- To create a basic formula in Excel:
  (i) Select the cell for the formula.
  (ii) Type = (the equal sign) and the formula.
  (iii) Click Enter.

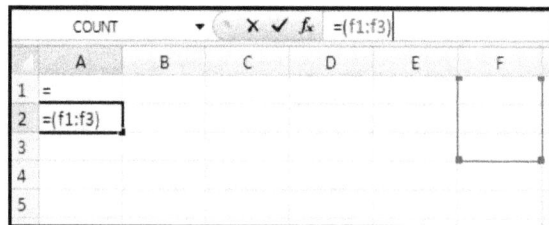

Fig. 3.56: Apply formula on cell

Functions in Excel:

- A function is a built in formula in Excel. A function has a name and arguments (the mathematical function) in parentheses.

- Common functions in Excel:
  - **Sum:** Adds all cells in the argument.
  - **Average:** Calculates the average of the cells in the argument.
  - **Min:** Finds the minimum value.
  - **Max:** Finds the maximum value.
  - **Count:** Finds the number of cells that contain a numerical value within a range of the argument.
- To calculate a function:
  (i) Click the **cell** where you want the function applied.
  (ii) Click the **Insert Function** button.
  (iii) Choose the function.
  (iv) Click **OK**.

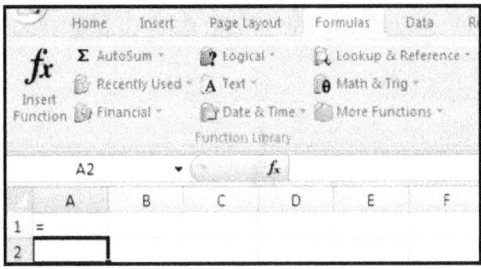

Fig. 3.57: Insert function option

  (v) Complete the Number 1 box with the first cell in the range that you want calculated
  (vi) Complete the Number 2 box with the last cell in the range that you want calculated

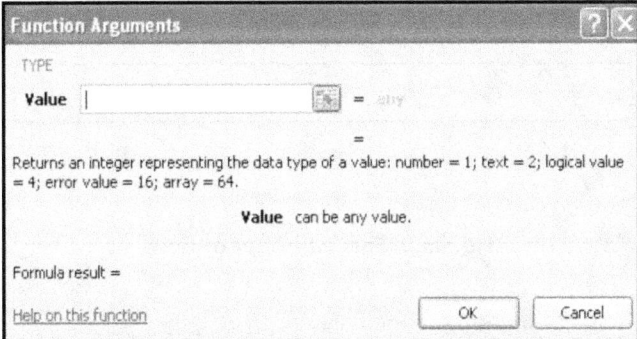

Fig. 3.58: Function arguments dialog

Function Library:
- The function library is a large group of functions on the Formula Tab of the Ribbon. These functions include:
  1. **AutoSum**: Easily calculates the sum of a range.
  2. **Recently Used**: All recently used functions.
  3. **Financial**: Accrued interest, cash flow return rates and additional financial functions.
  4. **Logical**: And, If, True, False, etc.
  5. **Text**: Text based functions.
  6. **Date & Time**: Functions calculated on date and time.
  7. **Math & Trig**: Mathematical Functions.

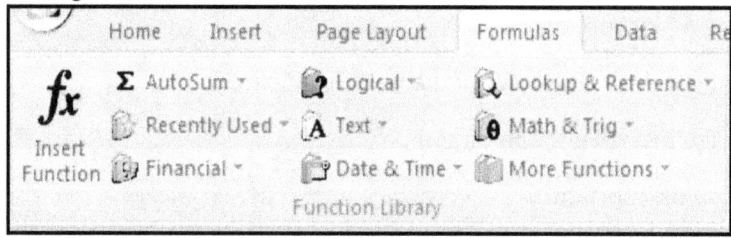

Fig. 3.59: Function library

- Sorting and Filtering allow you to manipulate data in a worksheet based on given set of criteria.

Basic Sorts:
- To execute a basic descending or ascending sort based on one column:
  (i) Highlight the cells that will be sorted.
  (ii) Click the **Sort & Filter** button on the **Home** tab.
  (iii) Click the **Sort Ascending** (A-Z) button or **Sort Descending** (Z-A) button.

Fig. 3.60: Sort and filter options

Custom Sorts:
- To sort on the basis of more than one column:
  (i) Click the **Sort & Filter** button on the **Home** tab.
  (ii) Choose which column you want to sort by first.

(iii) Click **Add Level**.
(iv) Choose the next column you want to sort.
(v) Click **OK**.

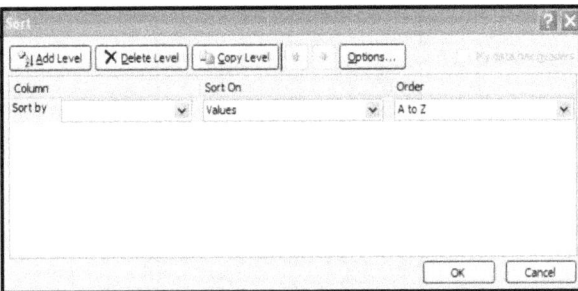

Fig. 3.61: Sort dialog box

Filtering:
- Filtering allows you to display only data that meets certain criteria.
- To filter follow the following steps:
    (i) Click the column or columns that contain the data you wish to filter.
    (ii) On the **Home** tab, click on **Sort & Filter**.
    (iii) Click **Filter** button.
    (iv) Click the **Arrow** at the bottom of the first cell.
    (v) Click the **Text Filter**.
    (vi) Click the **Words** you wish to Filter.

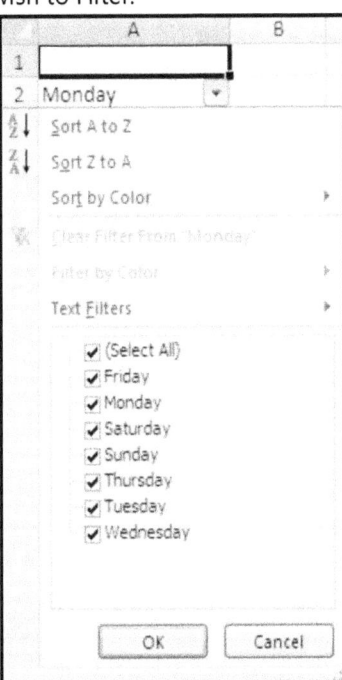

Fig. 3.62: Filtering options

(vii) To clear the filter click the **Sort & Filter** button.
(viii) Click **Clear**.

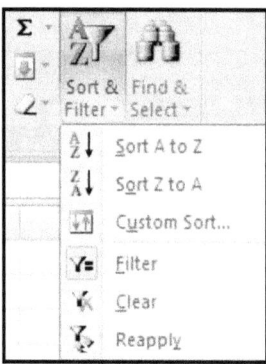

Fig. 3.63: Clear filter

Adding a Picture:
- To add a picture:
    (i) Click the **Insert** tab.
    (ii) Click the **Picture** button.
    (iii) Browse to the picture from your files.
    (iv) Click the **name** of the picture.
    (v) Click **Insert**.
    (vi) To move the graphic, click it and drag it to where you want it.

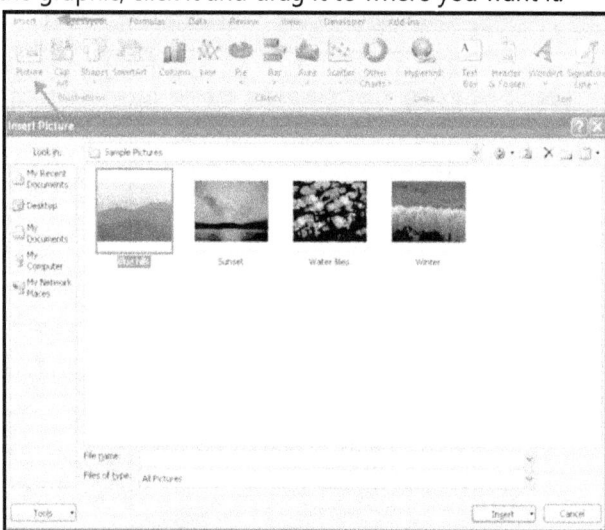

Fig. 3.64: Insert pictures dialog box

Adding Clip Art:
- To add Clip Art:
    (i) Click the **Insert** tab.
    (ii) Click the **Clip Art** button.

(iii) Search for the clip art using the search **Clip Art** dialog box.
(iv) Click the **Clip Art**.
(v) To move the graphic, click it and drag it to where you want it.

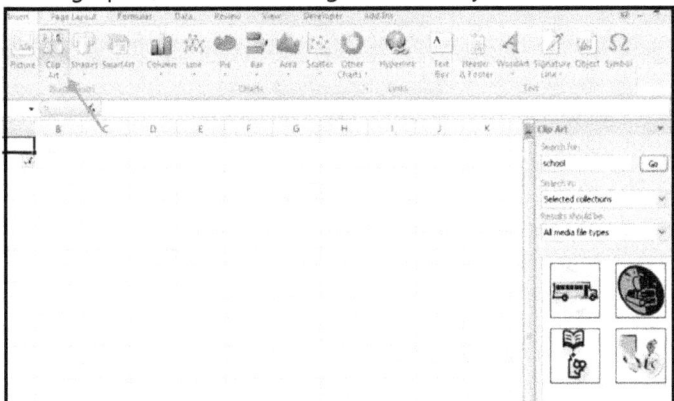

Fig. 3.65: Clip Art option

Adding Shapes:
- To add Shape:
   (i) Click the **Insert** tab.
   (ii) Click the **Shapes** button.
   (iii) Click the shape you choose.

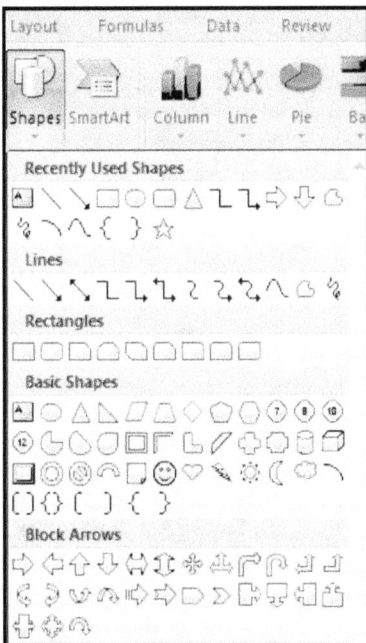

Fig. 3.66: Shapes options

(iv) Click the **Worksheet**.
(v) Drag the cursor to expand the Shape.

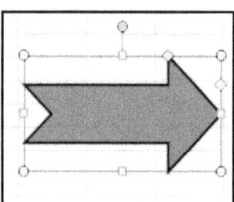

Fig. 3.67: A typical shape

- To format the shapes:
  (i) Click the **Shape**.
  (ii) Click the **Format** tab.

Fig. 3.68: Format options of a shape

Adding SmartArt:
- SmartArt is a feature in Office 2007 that allows you to choose from a variety of graphics, including flow charts, lists, cycles, and processes.
- To add SmartArt follow the following steps:
  (i) Click the **Insert** tab.
  (ii) Click the **SmartArt** button.
  (iii) Click the **SmartArt** you choose.

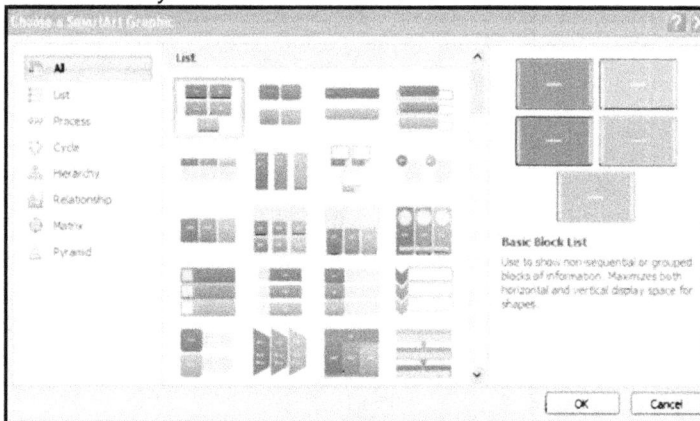

Fig. 3.69: Smart Art dialog box

  (iv) Select the Smart Art.
  (v) Drag it to the desired location in the worksheet.

Charts:
- Charts allow you to present information contained in the worksheet in a graphic format.
- Excel offers many types of charts including. Column, Line, Pie, Bar, Area, Scatter and more. To view the charts available click the Insert Tab on the Ribbon.

Creating a Chart:
- To create a chart:
    (i) Select the **cells** that contain the data you want to use in the chart.
    (ii) Click the **Insert** tab on the Ribbon.
    (iii) Click the type of **Chart** you want to create.

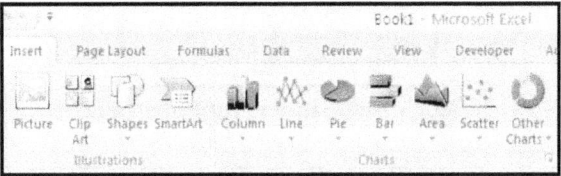

Fig. 3.70: Types of charts on Ribbon

Chart Tools:
- The Chart Tools appear on the Ribbon when you click on the chart. The tools are located on three tabs i.e. Design, Layout, and Format.
- Within the **Design** tab you can control the chart type, layout, styles, and location.

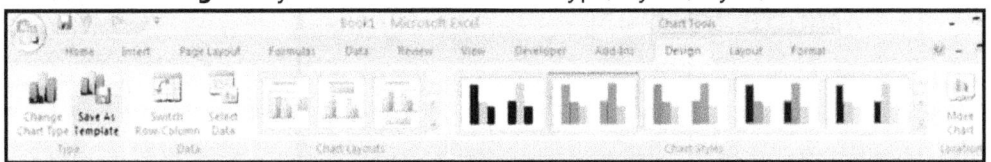

Fig. 3.71: Design tab of chart

- Within the **Layout** tab you can control inserting pictures, shapes and text boxes, labels, axes, background, and analysis.

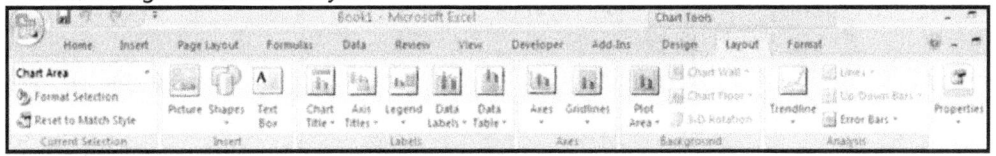

Fig. 3.72: Chart layout tab

- Within the **Format** tab you can modify shape styles, word styles and size of the chart.

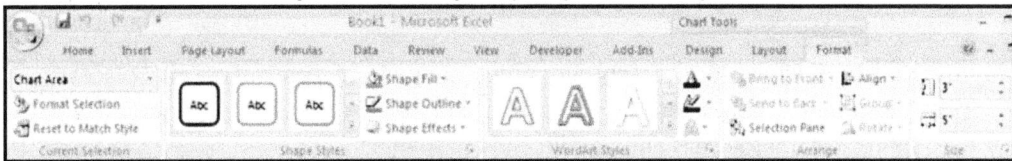

Fig. 3.73: Chart format tab

Modify Fonts:
- Modifying fonts in Excel will allow you to emphasize titles and headings. To modify a font:
    (i) Select the cell or cells that you would like the font applied.
    (ii) On the **Font** group on the **Home** tab, choose the font type, size, bold, italics, underline, or color.

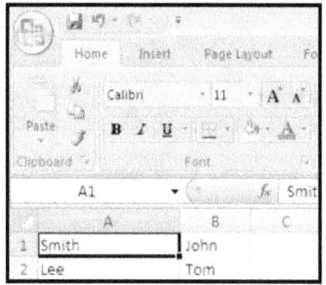

Fig. 3.74: Changing font of a cell

Format Cells Dialog Box:
- In Excel, you can also apply specific formatting to a cell.
- To apply formatting to a cell or group of cells:
  (i) Select the cell or cells that will have the formatting.
  (ii) Click the **Dialog Box** arrow on the **Alignment** group of the **Home** tab.

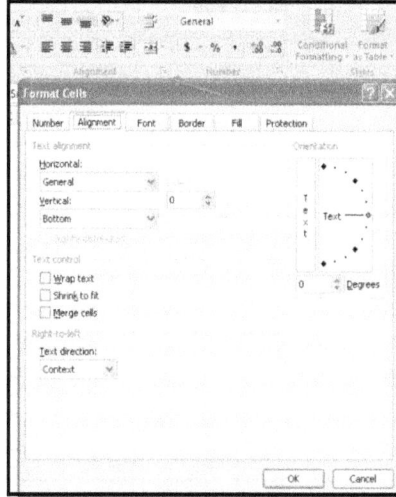

Fig. 3.75: Format cells dialog box

- There are several tabs on this dialog box that allow you to modify properties of the cell or cells.
  (i) **Number:** Allows for the display of different number types and decimal places.
  (ii) **Alignment:** Allows for the horizontal and vertical alignment of text, wrap text, shrink text, merge cells and the direction of the text.
  (iii) **Font:** Allows for control of font, font style, size, color, and additional features.
  (iv) **Border:** Border styles and colors.
  (v) **Fill:** Cell fill colors and styles.

Add Borders and Colors to Cells:
- Borders and colors can be added to cells manually or through the use of styles.
- To add borders manually:
  (i) Click the **Borders** drop down menu on the Font group of the Home tab.
  (ii) Choose the appropriate border.

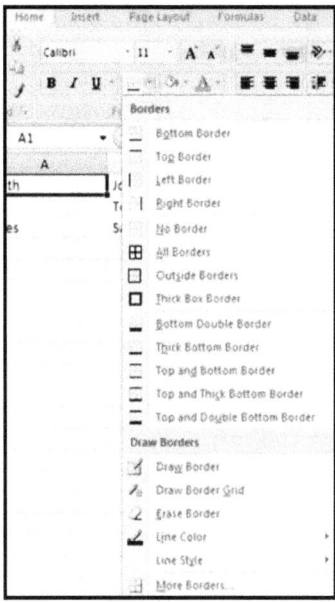

Fig. 3.76: Borders options

- To apply colors manually:
    - (i) Click the **Fill** drop down menu on the **Font** group of the **Home** tab.
    - (ii) Choose the appropriate color.

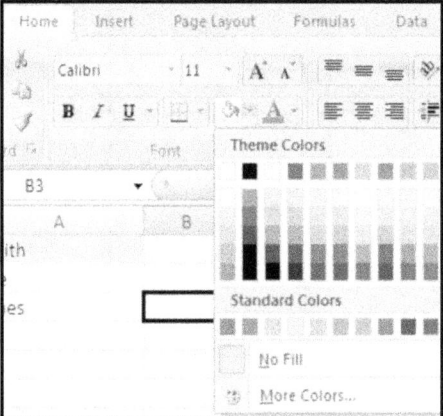

Fig. 3.77: Color options

- To apply borders and colors using styles:
    - (i) Click **Cell** Styles on the **Home** tab.
    - (ii) Choose a style or click **New Cell Style**.

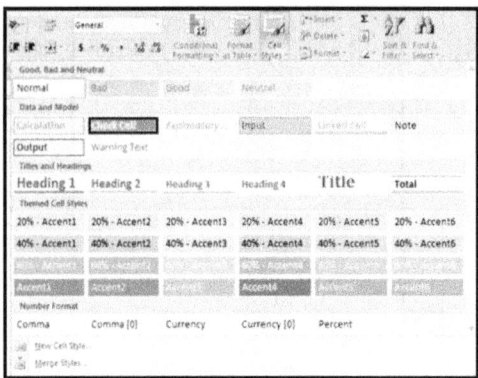

Fig. 3.78: Cell styles

Change Column Width and Row Height:
- To change the width of a column or the height of a row:
    - (i) Click the **Format** button on the **Cells** group of the **Home** tab.
    - (ii) Manually adjust the height and width by clicking **Row Height** or **Column Width**.
    - (iii) To use **AutoFit** click **AutoFit Row Height** or **AutoFit Column Width**.

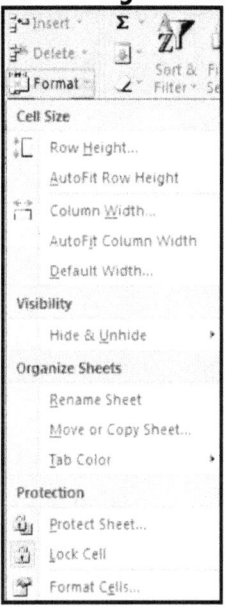

Fig. 3.79: Format cell options

Merge Cells:
- To merge cells select the cells you want to merge and click the Merge & Center button on the Alignment group of the Home tab.
- The four choices for merging cells are:
    - (i) **Merge & Center**: Combines the cells and centers the contents in the new, larger cell.
    - (ii) **Merge Across**: Combines the cells across columns without centering data.
    - (iii) **Merge Cells**: Combines the cells in a range without centering.
    - (iv) **Unmerge Cells**: Splits the cell that has been merged.

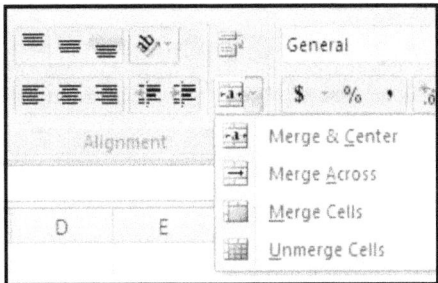

Fig. 3.80: Merge cells options

Align Cell Contents:

- To align cell contents, click the cell or cells you want to align and click on the options within the Alignment group on the Home tab.
- There are several options for alignment of cell contents:
    (i) **Top Align**: Aligns text to the top of the cell.
    (ii) **Middle Align**: Aligns text between the top and bottom of the cell.
    (iii) **Bottom Align**: Aligns text to the bottom of the cell.
    (iv) **Align Text Left**: Aligns text to the left of the cell.
    (v) **Center**: Centers the text from left to right in the cell.
    (vi) **Align Text Right**: Aligns text to the right of the cell.
    (vii) **Decrease Indent**: Decreases the indent between the left border and the text.
    (viii) **Increase Indent**: Increase the indent between the left border and the text.
    (ix) **Orientation**: Rotate the text diagonally or vertically.

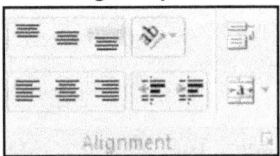

Fig. 3.81: Alignment options

3.5 MS-PowerPoint

- PowerPoint is a complete presentation graphics package. It gives you everything you need to produce a professional-looking presentation.
- PowerPoint offers word processing, outlining, drawing, graphing, and presentation management tools- all designed to be easy to use and learn.
- Fig. 3.82 shows various screen components of MS PowerPoint screen.

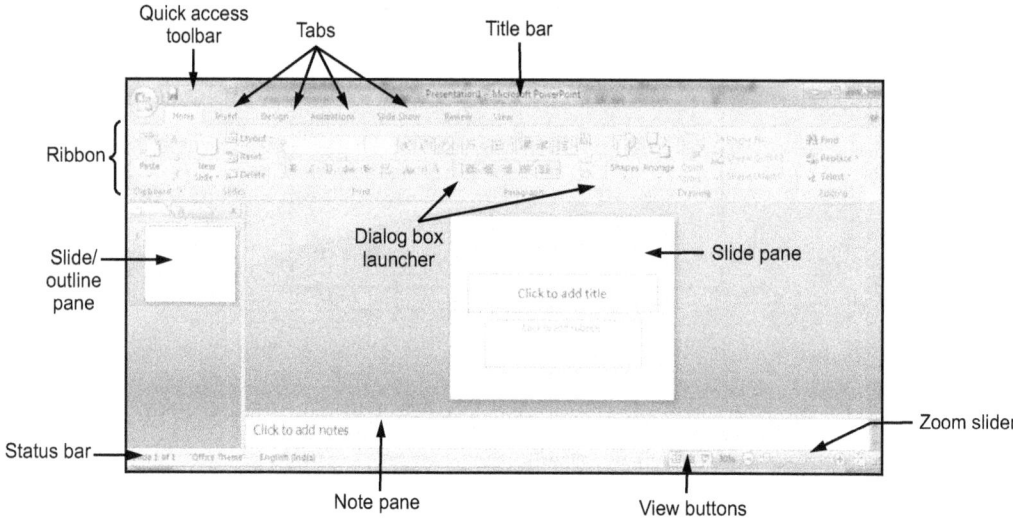

Fig. 3.82: PowerPoint program window

- Table 3.3 shows PowerPoint 2007 Screen Elements.

Table 3.3: PowerPoint 2007 program window element

Screen Element	Description
Ribbon	Organizes commands on tabs, and then groups the commands by topic for performing related presentation tasks.
File tab	Displays a list of commands related to things you can do with a presentation, such as opening, saving, printing, or sharing.
Quick Access Toolbar (QAT)	Displays buttons to perform frequently used commands with a single click. Frequently used commands in PowerPoint include Save, Undo, and Repeat. For commands that *you* use frequently, you can add additional buttons to the Quick Access Toolbar.
Title bar	Displays the name of the presentation and the name of the program. The Minimize, Maximize/Restore Down, and Close window control buttons are grouped on the right side of the title bar.
Ribbon tabs	Display across the top of the Ribbon, and each tab relates to a type of task-related activity within PowerPoint.
Program-level control buttons Groups	Minimizes, restores or closes the program window. Indicate the name of the groups of related commands on each displayed tab.
Slide pane	Displays a large image of the active slide in PowerPoint.

contd. ...

View buttons	A set of commands that control the look of the presentation window.
Notes pane	Displays below the Slide pane and allows you to type notes regarding the active side.
Status bar	A horizontal bar at the bottom of the presentation window that displays the current slide number, number of slides in a presentation, Theme Name, View buttons, and Zoom slider.
Slides/Outline pane	Displays either all of the slides in the presentation in the form of miniature images called thumbnails (Slides tab) or the presentation outline (Outline tab).

Working with PowerPoint Document:

New Presentation or Creating New Document:

- You can start a new presentation from a blank slide, a template, existing presentations, or a Word outline.
- To create a new presentation from a blank slide:
    (i) Click the **Microsoft Office Button**.
    (ii) Click **New**.
    (iii) Click **Blank Presentation**.

Fig. 3.83: Creating new presentation

Save a Presentation:

- When you save a presentation, you have two choices: **Save** or **Save As**.
- To save a document:
    (i) Click the **Microsoft Office Button**.
    (ii) Click **Save**.

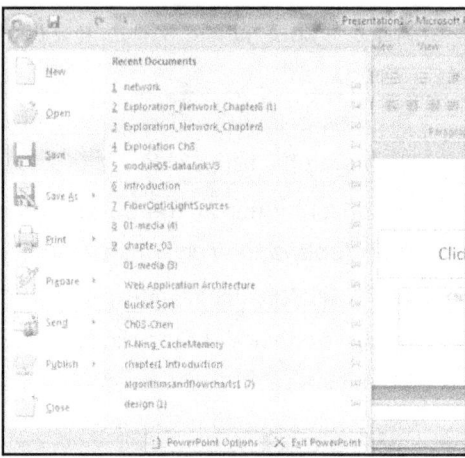

Fig. 3.84: Save options

Add Slides:
- There are several choices when you want to add a new slide to the presentation: Office Themes, Duplicate Selected Slide, or Reuse Slides.
- To create a new slide from Office Themes:
  (i) Select the slide immediately **BEFORE** where you want the new slide.
  (ii) Click the **New Slide** button on the **Home** tab.
  (iii) Click the slide choice that fits your material.

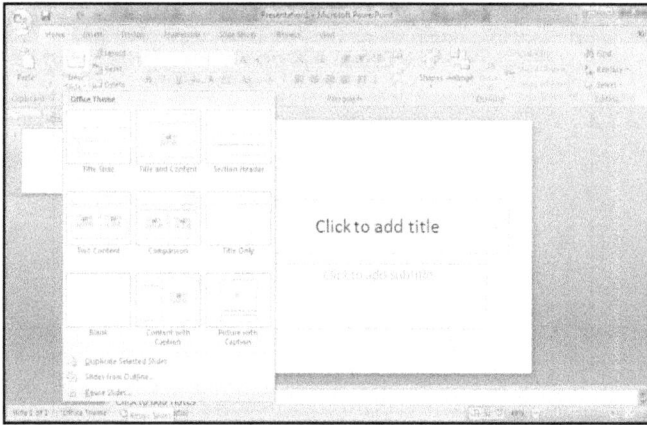

Fig. 3.85: Add slides in PowerPoint

Themes:
- Themes are design templates that can be applied to an entire presentation that allows for consistency throughout the presentation.
- To add a theme to a presentation:
  (i) Click the **Design** tab.
  (ii) Choose one of the displayed **Themes** or click the **Galleries** button.

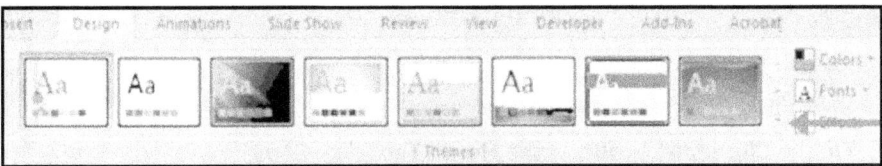

Fig. 3.86: Themes

Enter Text:
- To enter text:
    (i) Select the **slide** where you want the text.
    (ii) Click in a **Textbox** to add text.

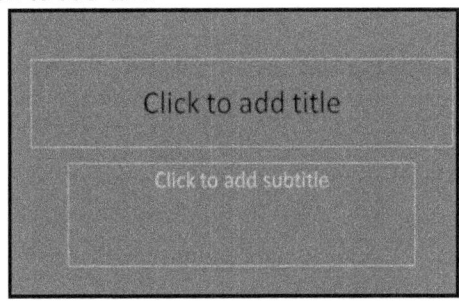

Fig. 3.87: Adding text in slide

- To add a text box:
    (i) Select the **slide** where you want to place the text box.
    (ii) On the **Insert** tab, click **Text Box**.
    (iii) Click on the slide and drag the cursor to expand the text box.
    (iv) Type in the text.

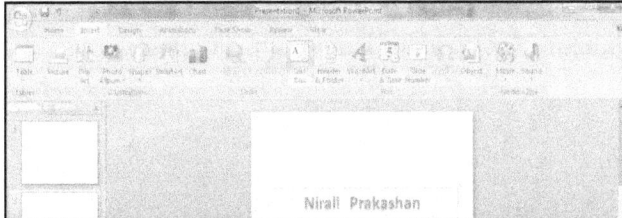

Fig. 3.88: Adding TextBox

Select Text:
- To select the text:
    (i) Highlight the text.

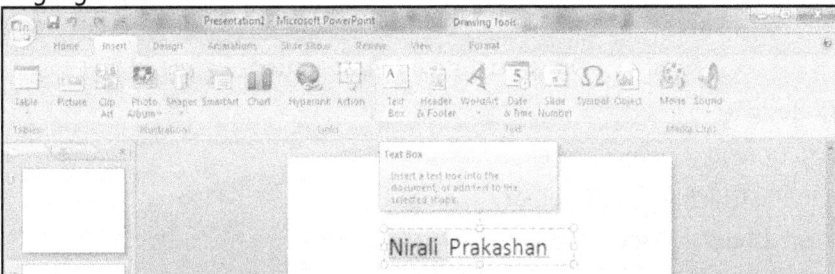

Fig. 3.89

Copy and Paste:

- To copy and paste data:
  - (i) Select the item(s) that you wish to copy.
  - (ii) On the **Clipboard Group** of the **Home Tab**, click **Copy**.
  - (iii) Select the item(s) where you would like to copy the data.
  - (iv) On the **Clipboard** Group of the **Home** Tab, click **Paste**.

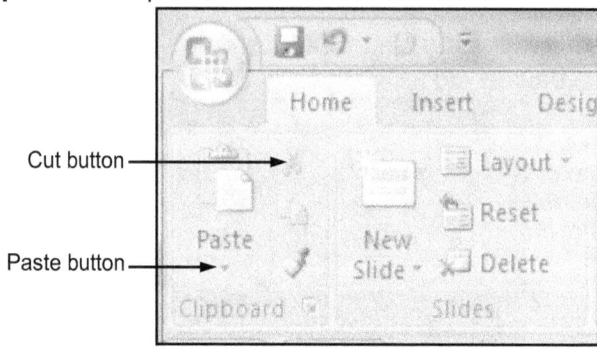

Fig. 3.90: Copy and Paste option

Cut and Paste:

- To cut and paste data:
  - (i) Select the item(s) that you wish to copy.
  - (ii) On the **Clipboard Group** of the **Home** Tab, click Cut.
  - (iii) Select the items(s) where you would like to copy the data.
  - (iv) On the **Clipboard Group** of the **Home** Tab, click **Paste**.

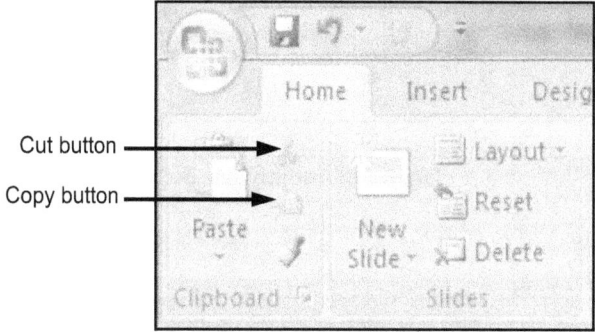

Fig. 3.91: Cut and Paste option

Undo and Redo:

- To undo or redo your most recent actions:
  - (i) On the **Quick Access Toolbar**.
  - (ii) Click **Undo** or **Redo**.

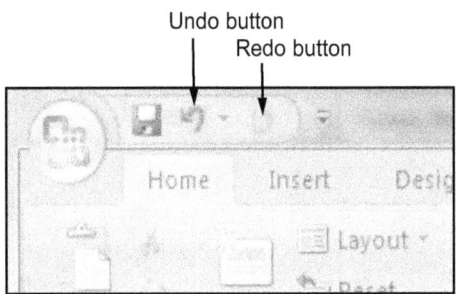

Fig. 3.92: Undo and Redo options

Spell Check:
- To check the spelling in a presentation:
  (i) Click the **Review tab**.
  (ii) Click the Spelling **button**.

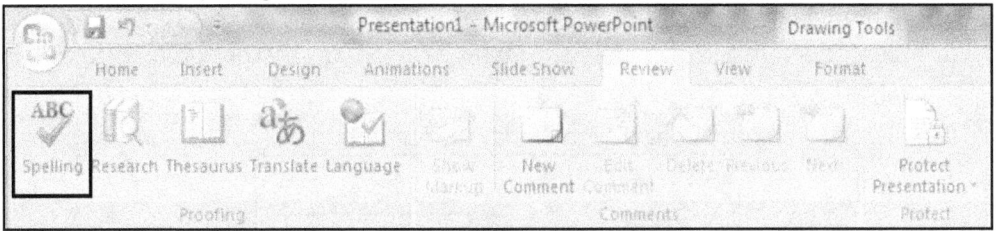

Fig. 3.93: Spell check options

Change Font Typeface and Size:
- To change the font typeface:
  (i) Click the **arrow** next to the font name and choose a font.
  (ii) Remember that you can preview how the new font will look by highlighting the text, and hovering over the new font typeface.

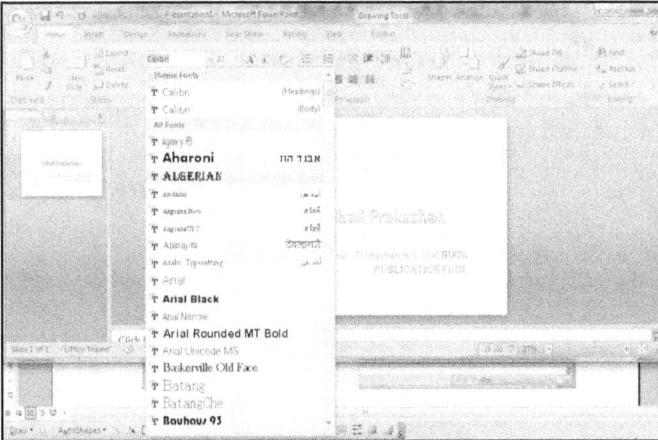

Fig. 3.94: Changing font

- To **change the font size**:
  (i) Click the **arrow** next to the font size and choose the appropriate size, or
  (ii) Click the **increase or decrease** font size buttons.

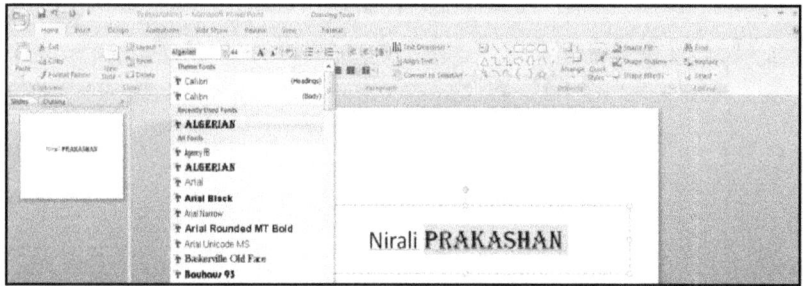

Fig. 3.95: Changing font size

Font Styles and Effects:
- Font styles are predefined formatting options that are used to emphasize text. They include: Bold, Italic, and Underline.
- To add these to text:
  (i) Select the text and click the **Font Styles** included on the Font group of the Home tab or
  (ii) Select the text and right click to display the font tools.

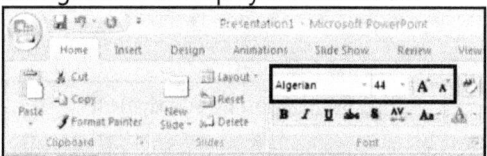

Fig. 3.96: Font styles

Change Text Color:
- To change the text color:
  (i) Select the text and click the **Colors** button included on the Font Group of the Ribbon, or
  (ii) Highlight the text and right click and choose the colors tool.
  (iii) Select the color by clicking the down arrow next to the font color button.

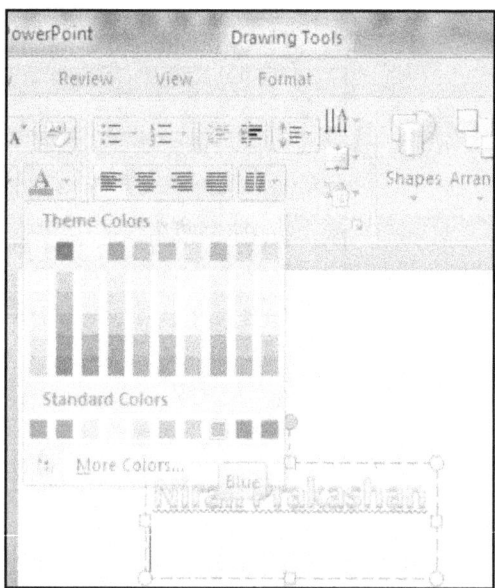

Fig. 3.97: Color options

WordArt:
- WordArt are styles that can be applied to text to create a visual effect.
- To apply Word Art follow the following steps:
    (i) Select the text.
    (ii) Click the **Insert** tab.
    (iii) Click the **WordArt** button.
    (iv) Choose the **WordArt**.

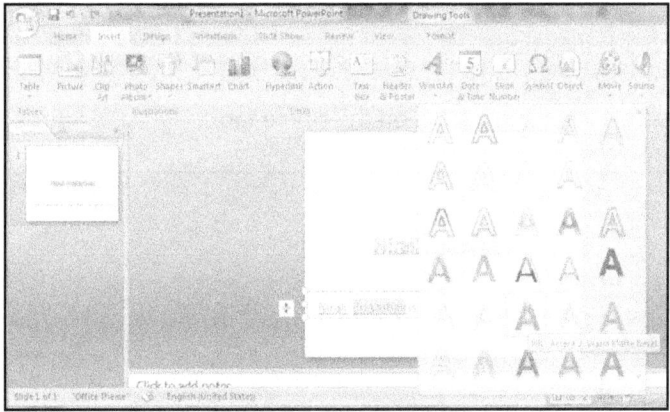

Fig. 3.98: Work Art options

Change Paragraph Alignment:
- The paragraph alignment allows you to set how you want text to appear.
- To change the alignment:
    (i) Click the **Home Tab**
    (ii) Choose the appropriate button for alignment on the Paragraph Group.
        (a) **Align Left:** The text is aligned with your left margin.
        (b) **Center:** The text is centered within your margins.
        (c) **Align Right:** Aligns text with the right margin.
        (d) **Justify:** Aligns text to both the left and right margins.

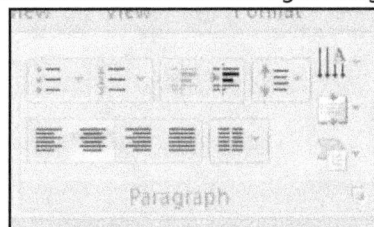

Fig. 3.99: Alignment options

Indent Paragraphs:
- To indent paragraphs, you can do the following:
    (i) Click the **Indent** buttons to control the indent.
    (ii) Click the **Indent** button repeated times to increase the size of the indent.

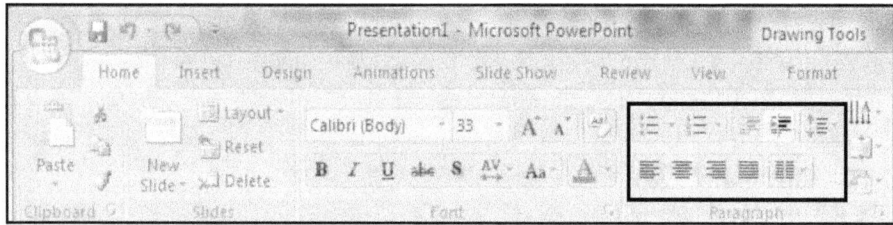

Fig. 3.100: Indent option

Text Direction:
- To change the text direction:
  (i) Select the text.
  (ii) Click the Text Direction button on the Home tab.
  (iii) Click the selection.

Fig. 3.101: Text direction option

Bulleted and Numbered Lists:
- Bulleted lists have bullet points, numbered lists have numbers, and outline lists combine numbers and letters depending on the organization of the list.
- To add a list to existing text:
  (i) Select the text you wish to make a list.
  (ii) Click the **Bulleted or Numbered Lists** button.

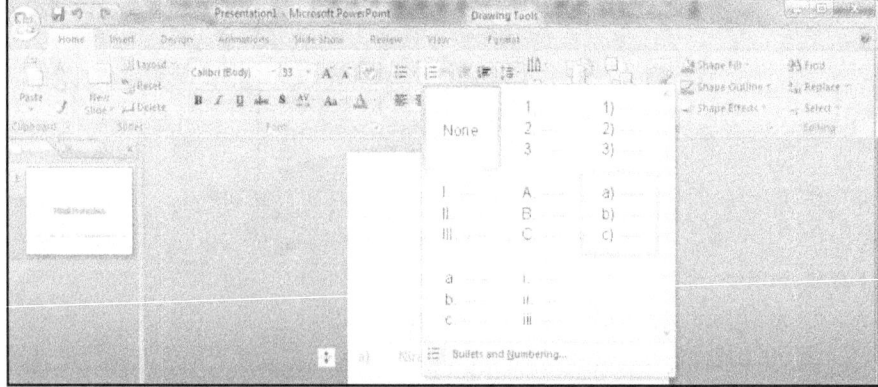

Fig. 3.102: Bulleted or Numbered lists

- To create a new list:
    (i) Place your cursor where you want the list in the document.
    (ii) Click the **Bulleted or Numbered Lists** button.
    (iii) Begin typing.

Nested Lists:
- A nested list is list with several levels of indented text.
- To create a nested list follow the following steps:
    (i) Create your list following the directions above.
    (ii) Click the **Increase or Decrease Indent** button.

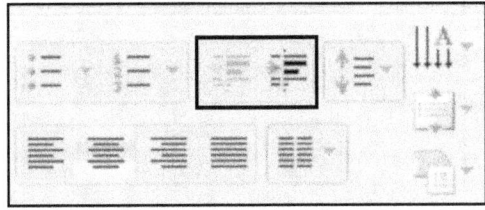

Fig. 3.103: Nested list option

Formatting Lists:
- The bullet image and numbering format can be changed by using the **Bullets or Numbering** dialog box.
    (i) Select the entire list to change all the bullets or numbers, or Place the cursor on one line within the list to change a single bullet.
    (ii) Click the arrow next to the bulleted or numbered list and choose a bullet or numbering style.

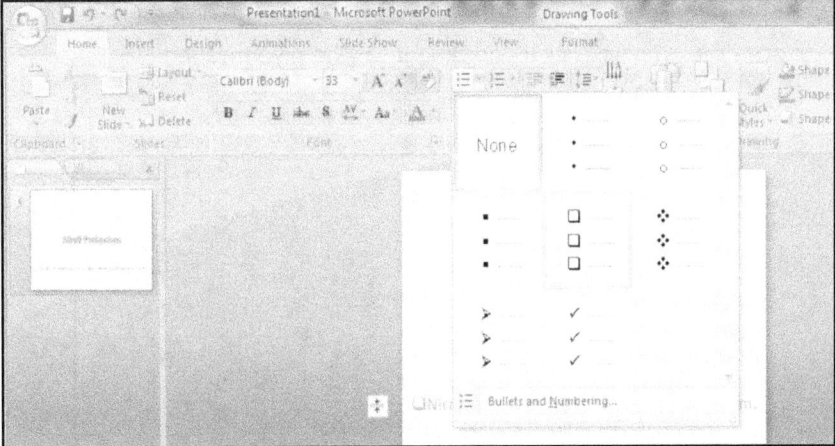

Fig. 3.104: Bullet or Numbering style

Adding Picture:
- To add a picture:
    (i) Click the **Insert** Tab.
    (ii) Click the **Picture** Button.
    (iii) Browse to the picture from your files.
    (iv) Click the **name** of the picture.
    (v) Click **insert**.
    (vi) To move the graphic, click it and drag it to where you want it.

Fig. 3.105: Insert pictures dialog box

Adding Clip Art:
- To add Clip Art:
    (i) Click the **Insert** Tab.
    (ii) Click the **Clip Art** Button.
    (iii) Search for the clip art using the search Clip Art dialog box.
    (iv) Click the **Clip Art**.
    (v) To move the graphic, click it and drag it to where you want it.

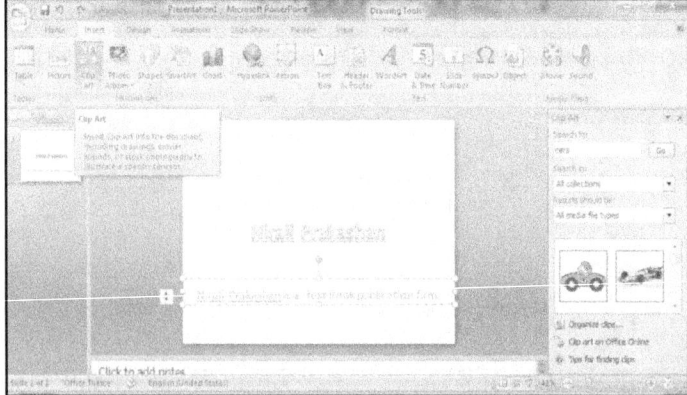

Fig. 3.106: Clip art option

Adding a Shape:
- To add Shapes:
    (i) Click the **Insert** Tab.
    (ii) Click the **Shapes** Button.
    (iii) Click the shape you choose.

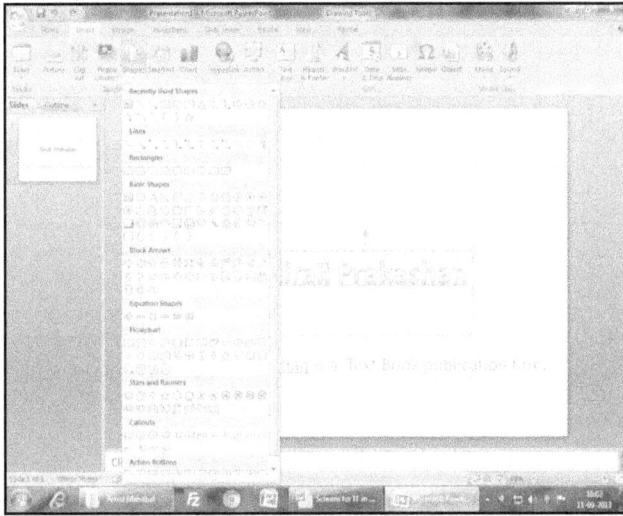

Fig. 3.107: Shapes option

    (iv) Click the **Slide**.
    (v) Drag the **cursor** to expand the Shape.

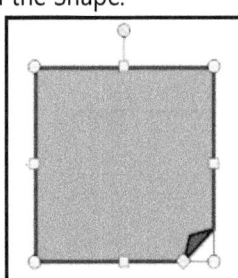

Fig. 3.108: A typical shape

Adding SmartArt:
- SmartArt is a feature in Office 2007 that allows you to choose from a variety of graphics, including flow charts, lists, cycles, and processes.
- To add SmartArt follow the following steps:
    (i) Click the **Insert** Tab.
    (ii) Click the **SmartArt** Button.
    (iii) Click the **SmartArt** you choose.
    (iv) Click the **SmartArt**.
    (v) Drag it to the desired location in the slide.

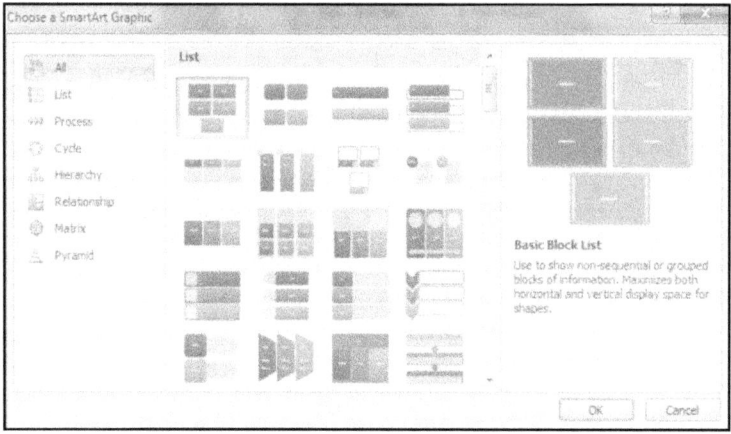

Fig. 3.109: SmartArt dialog box

Creating a Table:
- To create a table:
    (i) Place the cursor on the page where you want the new table
    (ii) Click the **Insert** Tab of the Ribbon
    (iii) Click the **Tables** Button on the Tables Group.
- You can create a table one of four ways:
    (i) Highlight the number of row and columns.
    (ii) Click **Insert Table** and enter the number of rows and columns.
    (iii) Click the **Draw Table**, create your table by clicking and entering the rows and columns.
    (iv) Click Excel **Spreadsheet** and enter data.

Fig. 3.110: Create table options

Charts:
- Charts allow you to present information contained in the worksheet in a graphic format.
- PowerPoint offers many types of charts including: Column, Line, Pie, Bar, Area, Scatter and more.
- To view the charts available click the Insert Tab on the Ribbon.

Fig. 3.111: Chart options

Creating a Chart:
- To create a chart:
    (i) Click the **Insert** tab on the ribbon.
    (ii) Click the type of **Chart** you want to create.
    (iii) Insert the **Data** and **Labels**.

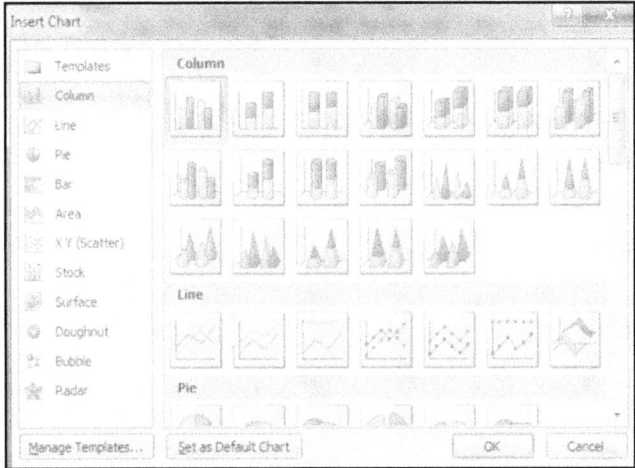

Fig. 3.112: Insert chart dialog box

Slide Transitions:
- Transitions are effects that are in place when you switch from one slide to the next.
- To add slide transitions:
    (i) Select the slide that you want to transition.
    (ii) Click the **Animations** tab.
    (iii) Choose the appropriate animation or click the **Transition** dialog box.

Fig. 3.113: Slide transitions

- To apply the transition to all slides:
    - (i) Click the **Apply to All** button on the **Animations tab**.

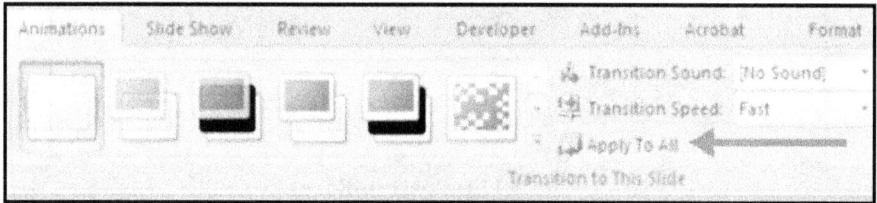

Fig. 3.114: Apply to all option

Slide Animation:

- Slide animation effects are predefined special effects that you can add to objects on a slide.
- To apply an animation effect follow the following steps:
    - (i) Select the object
    - (ii) Click the **Animations** tab on the Ribbon.
    - (iii) Click **Custom Animation**.
    - (iv) Click **Add Effect**.
    - (v) Choose the appropriate effect.

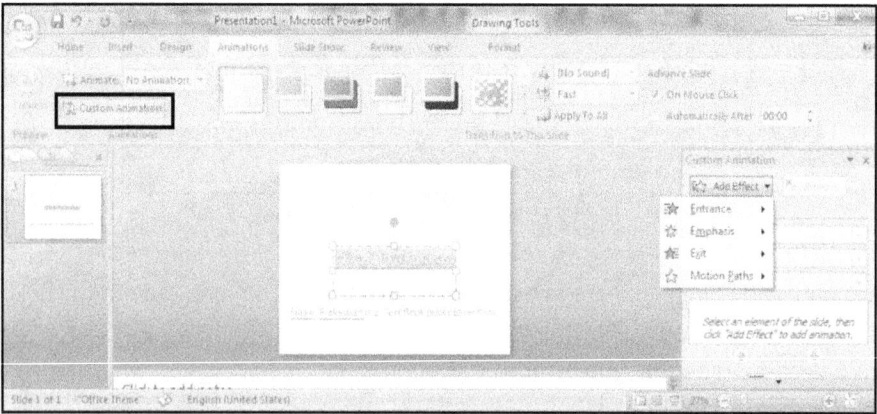

Fig. 3.115: Slide Animation

Animation Preview:

- To preview the animation on a slide:

  (i) Click the **Preview** button on the **Animations** tab.

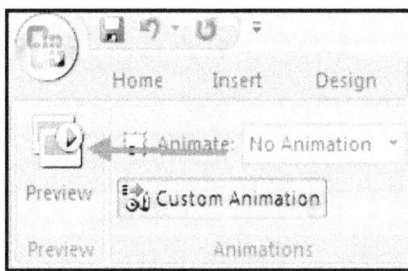

Fig. 3.116: Preview options

Slide Show Options:

- The Slide Show tab of the ribbon contains many options for the slide show. These options include:

  (i) Preview the slide show from the beginning.

  (ii) Preview the slide show from the current slide.

  (iii) Set up Slide Show.

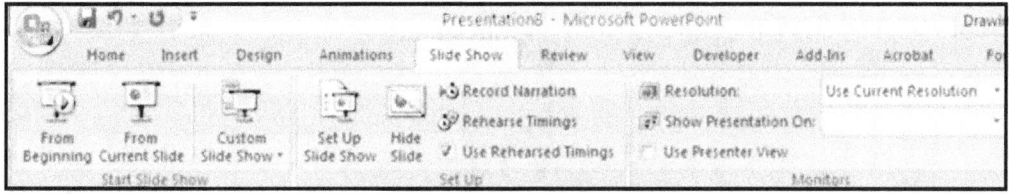

Fig. 3.117: Slide show options

3.6 MS-Access

- Access 2007 is a program that allows you to **create** and **manage** databases.
- Microsoft Access is a database software package. A database is an organized collection of records. Telephone and address books are examples of paper databases. With Access, you can create a computerized database.
- For example, you can use Access to organize the students who attend a school, the courses they take, and the instructors who teach them. After you create an Access database, you can search it, manipulate it, and extract information from it.
- Fig. 3.118 shows access screen component.

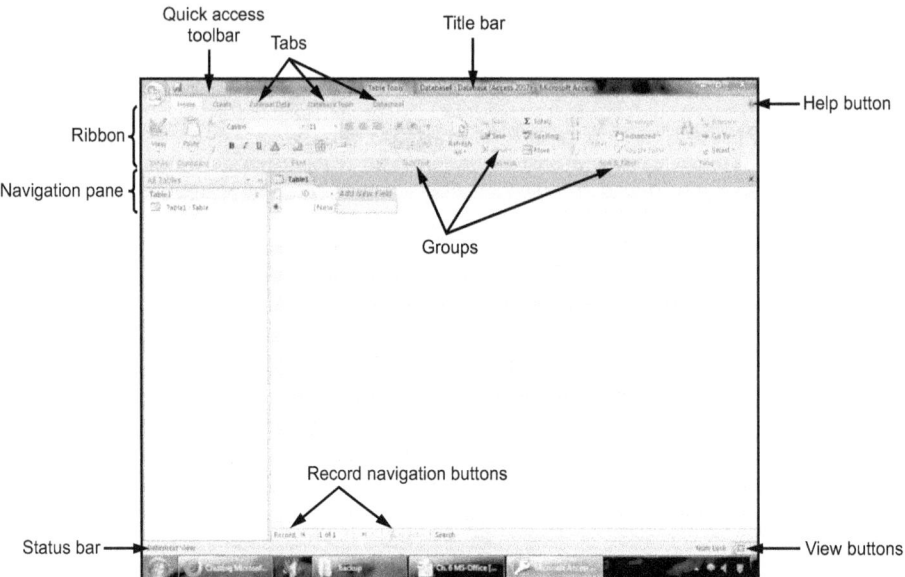

Fig. 3.118

- Before you can begin to use a database, you need to become familiar with the Access window.

1. **Microsoft Office Button:**
- In the upper-left corner of the Access window is the Microsoft Office button. When you click the button, a menu appears. You can use the menu to create a new file, open an existing file, save a file, and perform many other tasks.

Fig. 3.119

2. **The Quick Access Toolbar:**
- Next to the Microsoft Office button is the Quick Access toolbar. The Quick Access toolbar provides you with access to commands you frequently use. By default, Save, Undo, and Redo appear on the Quick Access toolbar.
- You use Save to save an object, Undo to roll back an action you have taken, and Redo to reapply an action you have rolled back.

Fig. 3.120

3. **The Title Bar:**
- The Title bar is located at the top in the center of the Access window.
- The Title bar displays the name of the database on which you are currently working.

Northwind 2007 : Database (Access 2007) - Microsoft Access

Fig. 3.121

4. Ribbon:

- You use commands to tell Access what to do. In Access 2007, you use the Ribbon to issue commands. The Ribbon is located near the top of the Access window, below the Quick Access toolbar. At the top of the Ribbon are several tabs; clicking a tab displays related command groups. Within each group are related **command buttons**.
- You click buttons to issue commands or to access menus and dialog boxes. You may also find a dialog box launcher in the bottom-right corner of a group. When you click the dialog box launcher, a dialog box makes additional commands available.

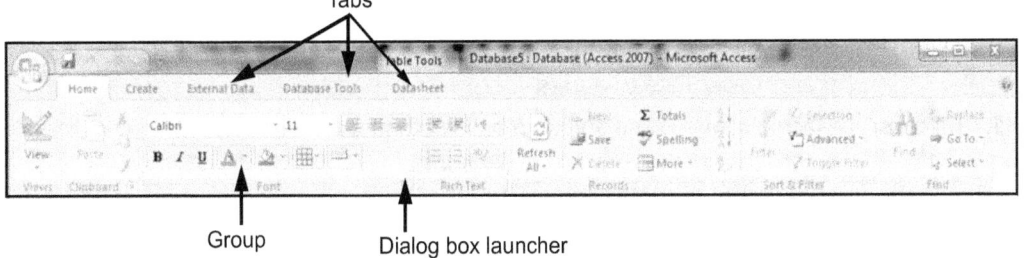

Fig. 3.122

5. Access Objects:

- To view or hide the objects on the Navigation pane as shown in Fig. 3.123.

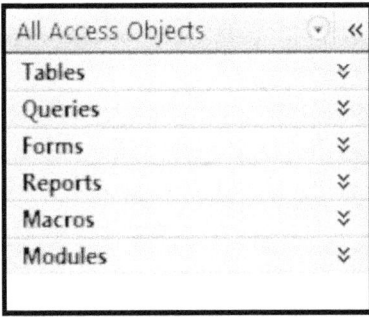

Fig. 3.123

- You click the double down-arrows ⋎ to view objects. The double down-arrows change to double up-arrows ⋏.
- You click the double up-arrows ⋏ to hide objects. The double up-arrows change to double down-arrows ⋎.
- As stated earlier, the Navigation pane stores the objects in your database: tables, queries, forms, reports, macros, and modules. Objects always display with an icon to the right. The icon tells you the object type: table, query, form, report, macro, and module.

Terms	Description
1. Tables	In Access, data is stored in tables. A table is a set of columns and rows, with each column referred to as a field. Each value in a field represents a single type of data. Each row of a table is referred to as a record.
2. Queries	You use queries to retrieve specific data from your database and to answer questions about your data. For example, you can use a query to find the names of the employees in your database who live in a particular state.
3. Forms	Forms give you the ability to choose the format and arrangement of fields. You can use a form to enter, edit, and display data.
4. Reports	Reports organize or summarize your data so you can print it or view it onscreen. You often use reports when you want to analyze your data or present your data to others.
5. Macros	Macros give you the ability to automate tasks. You can use a macro to add functionality to a form, report, or control.
6. Modules	Like macros, modules give you the ability to automate tasks and add functionality to a form, report, or control. Macros are created by choosing from a list of macro actions, whereas modules are written in Visual Basic for Applications.

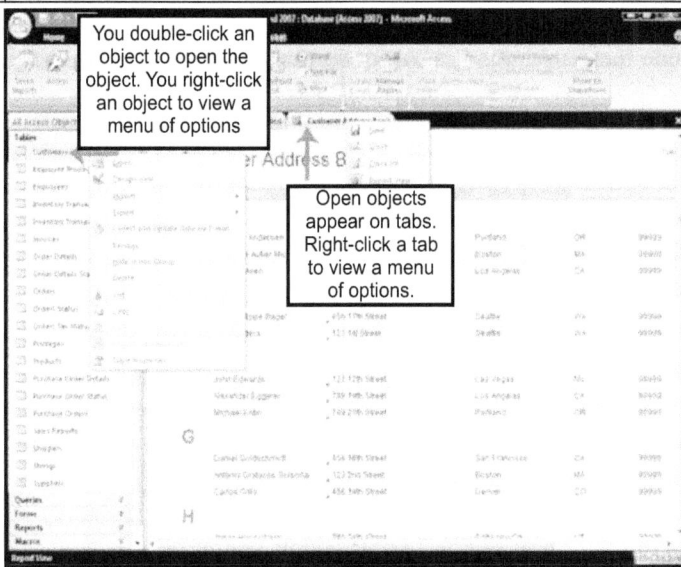

Fig. 3.124

- You double-click an object to open the object. You right-click an object to view a menu of options. You can use the menu to do such things as open objects, rename objects, and delete objects.
- Objects that are open appear on tabs. Right-click a tab to view a menu of options you can perform, such as save the object, close the object, or change the view.

Change Views:
- A view is a way of looking at an object. For example, in Access, data is stored in tables. Two of the possible ways you can view a table are Datasheet view and Design view. You can see the data contained in a table in Datasheet view.

Fig. 3.125

- You can see the design of a table in Design view. When you open an object, buttons appear in the lower-right corner of the Access window. You can use the View button on the Home tab to change views, or you can click the proper button in the lower-right corner of the window.

Creating a Blank Database:
- A blank database is a database with nothing in it. You must create all the tables, forms, reports, queries, and so on. If you cannot find a template that suits your needs, create a blank database.
- After you create the database, Access opens to a datasheet and makes available the tools you need to create objects. Creating tables is the first step in building a database.
- To create a blank database follow the following steps (See Fig. 3.126).

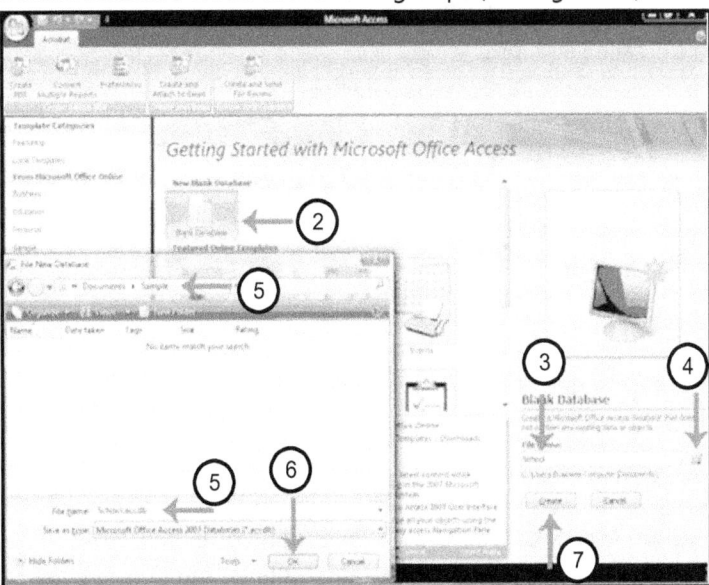

Fig. 3.126

1. Start Access.
2. Click Blank Database.
3. Type the name you want to give your database in the File Name field. Access will automatically append .accdb to the name.
4. Click the Browse button. The File New Database window appears.

5. Locate the folder in which you want to store your database. Note that the name of the file appears in the File Name field.
6. Click OK.
7. Click the Create button. Access creates the database and opens a datasheet with the Table Tools available to you.

What is a Datasheet?
- In Access, data is stored in tables. A datasheet displays the information stored in a table in columns and rows.
- The columns are called fields and the rows are called records. You can use a datasheet to create a table, enter data, retrieve data, and perform other tasks.

Tables in Microsoft Access:
- Tables are the foundation of an Access database. Access stores data in tables.
- A table is a set of columns and rows. Each column is called a field. Within a table, each field must be given a name and no two fields can have the same name. Each value in a field represents a single category of data.
- For example, a table might have three fields: Last Name, First Name, and Phone Number (See Fig. 3.127). The table consists of three columns: one for last name, one for first name, and one for phone number.
- In every row of the table, the Last Name field contains the last name, the First Name field contains the first name, and the Phone Number field contains the phone number. Each row in a table is called a record.

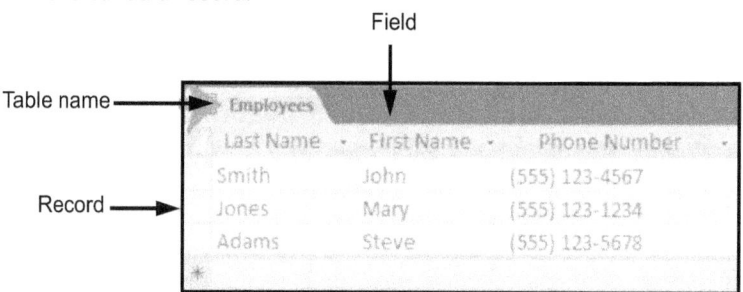

Fig. 3.127

- All of the data in a table should refer to the same subject. For example, all of the data in the Employees table should refer to employees, all of the data in the Students table should refer to students, and all of the data in the Courses table should refer to courses.
- You can view an Access database as a collection of related tables. For example, in a database that contains tables for Employees, Students, and Courses, the Employees table lists the employees, the Students table lists students, and the Courses table lists the courses students can take.
- After Access creates a blank database, it opens in Datasheet view and makes available the tools you need to create a table. Datasheet view displays a table as a set of columns and rows. When you view a blank database for the first time in Datasheet view, you see a column named ID. This column is by default the primary key field.

- A *primary key* is a field or combination of fields that uniquely identify each record in a table. No two records in a table should have the same values in every field. For example, the following should not occur in a table.

Last Name	First Name	City
Smith	John	Jonestown
Smith	John	Jonestown

- In the real world, it is possible to have two people from the same city with the same first and last name. In cases like this, you can use the ID field as the primary key field and use it to make each record unique.
- The ID field has a data type of AutoNumber; as a result, Access automatically creates a unique number for each record in the database. The resulting table will look like the one shown here.

ID	Last Name	First Name	City
1	Smith	John	Jonestown
2	Smith	John	Jonestown

- Access provides several methods for creating a table. One method is to use the Rename option with the Add New Field column label to give each column the field name you want it to have and then to type or paste your data into the table. Field names can include letters, numbers, and spaces and can be up to 64 characters long. When choosing a field name, try to keep it short.
- When you save your table for the first time, Access gives you the opportunity to name your table. Each table name must be unique; hence, two tables in the same database cannot have the same name. The table name should describe the data in the table; can consist of letters, numbers, and spaces; and can be up to 64 characters long. When choosing a table name, try to keep it short.
- You can save a table by clicking the Save button on the Quick Access toolbar or by right-clicking the Tables tab and then choosing Save from the menu that appears.

To add fields to a table:
1. Click the Add New Field column label.
2. Activate the Datasheet tab.
3. Click Rename in the Fields & Columns group.
4. Type the field name.

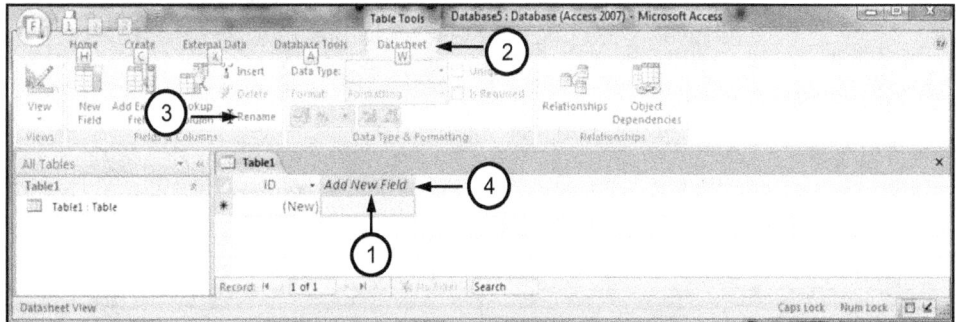

Fig. 3.128

5. Press Enter. Access creates the field.
6. Type the next field name. Access creates the field. Continue until you have created all of the fields in your table.
7. Press Enter without entering a field name to end your entries.

Name and Save a Table:
1. Click the Save button on the Quick Access toolbar. The Save As dialog box appears.
2. Type the name you want to give your table.
3. Click OK. Access names your table.
- After you create a table, you must name and save it.

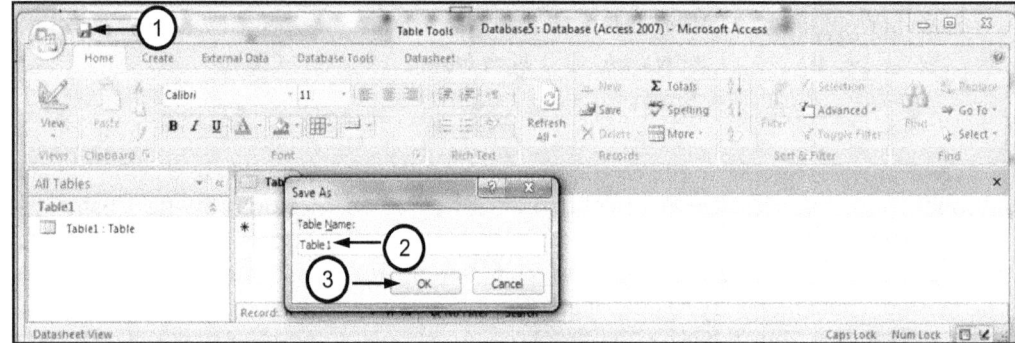

Fig. 3.129

Understanding Data Types:
- In Access, you use data types to specify the type of data each field can capture.
- A field with a data type of text can store alphabetic characters and numbers. Generally speaking, you cannot perform mathematical calculations by using a text field.
- Following table shows various data types used in MS-Access.

Data Type	Use
1. Text	Alphanumeric data. Use for text and for numbers that are not used in mathematical calculations. Use for names, addresses, and other relatively short pieces of text. Can store up to 255 characters.
2. Memo	Long text. Use for long pieces of text, such as notes and long descriptions. Can store up to 64,000 characters.
3. Number	Numeric data. Use for numbers you want to use in mathematical calculations.
4. Date/Time	Use for dates and times.
5. Currency	Use for currency.

contd. ...

6. AutoNumber	Unique sequential numbers or random numbers automatically inserted when you create a record. Use to create a primary key.
7. Yes/No	Logical data. Use when only one of two values is valid. Yes/No, True/False, etc.
8. Hyperlink	Use to store hyperlinks.
9. Attachment	Use to store attachments.
10. OLE Object	Use to attach an OLE object such as a Word document, Excel spreadsheet, or PowerPoint presentation.

Entering Data in Access:

- Microsoft Access is designed to manage information. Access allows you to enter the client's name, address, and phone number- the first time they do an order.
- This information is entered into an Access table designed to hold basic customer information on clients. A table is a list of related information in columns and rows. In a table, each row is called a record and each column is called a field.
- An Access table in Datasheet View looks similar to an Excel spreadsheet, as you can see below.

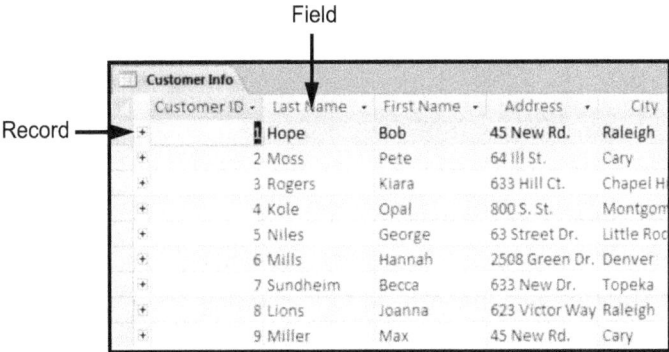

Fig. 3.130: Data in an Access Customer Info Table

- In addition to the table with customer information, you would probably also want a table with information about the products you sell, and a third table to hold data related to specific customer orders. These tables would all be linked together, to help you make the most out of your data.
- Access is called a relational database management program, because the tables are linked, or related, as you can see in the image below.
- In this example, the Customer Info and Orders tables are linked by Customer ID and Book ID.

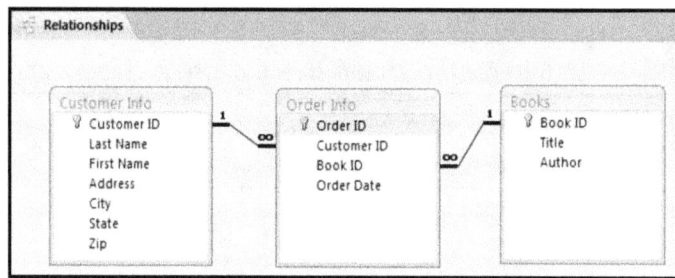

Fig. 3.131: Table relationships diagram in access

Forms in MS-Access:
- An Access 2007 form helps the person entering data know exactly what information to enter.
- Access forms are much like paper forms: you can use them to enter, edit, or display data.
- Forms are based on tables. When using a form, you can choose the format, the arrangement, and which fields you want to display.

Creating a Form:
- Access 2007 has several automatic tools for creating forms. These tools are located in the Forms group on the Create tab in the Ribbon, as shown in Fig. 1.132.

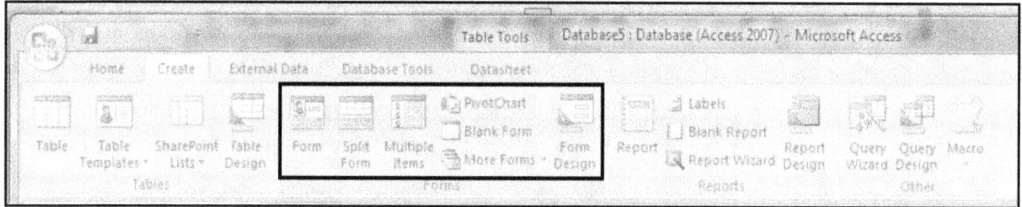

Fig. 3.132: Forms command group

- The Access 2007 forms tools include:
  - The **Form** command makes a basic form, showing a single record at a time.
  - The **Split Form** command creates a form showing one record on top, and includes the datasheet view of entire source table on the bottom.
  - The **Multiple Items** command creates a form that shows all the records at once, which looks very similar to the source table in datasheet view.
  - The **Form Wizard** is hidden under the **More Forms** command. It walks you through the process of creating more customized forms.

Creating Using the Form Button:
- Access can automatically create several types of forms. For example, when you click the Form button on the Create tab, Access places all fields in the selected table on a form.
- If the table has a one-to-many relationship with one other table or query, Access creates a stacked form (the records are displayed in a column) for the primary table and a datasheet for the related table. If there are several tables with a one-to-many relationship, Access does not create the datasheet.

To create a form follow following steps:
1. Open the Navigation pane.
2. Click the table or query on which you want to base your form.
3. Activate the Create tab.
4. Click Form in the Forms group. Access creates a form.

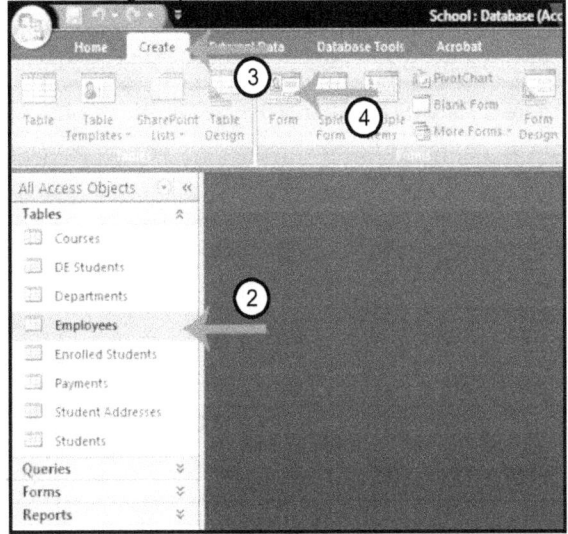

Fig. 3.133

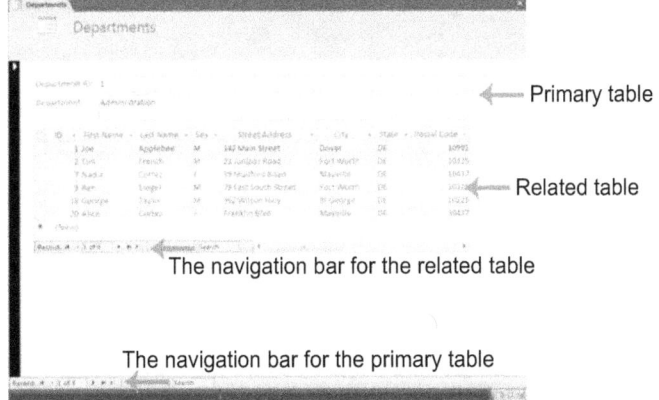

Fig. 3.134

- You can use the Navigation bars to move through the records on a form.

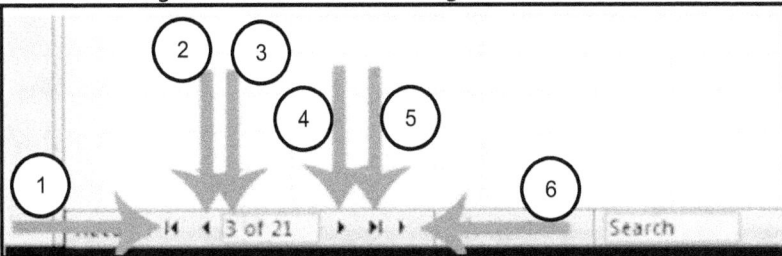

Fig. 3.135

1	Go to First Record
2	Go to Previous Record
3	The Current Record
4	Go to Next Record
5	Go to Last Record
6	Create a New (Blank) Record

Using Forms to Enter Data:
- We can enter data to form by typing the text.
- Populating a database is easy once you have a basic form in place. Record navigation works the same way for forms as it did for tables. The Navigation Bar is located in the bottom left of the object pane.
- The Navigation Buttons work the same way they did for the tables, also. The following picture shows the navigation buttons for a form.

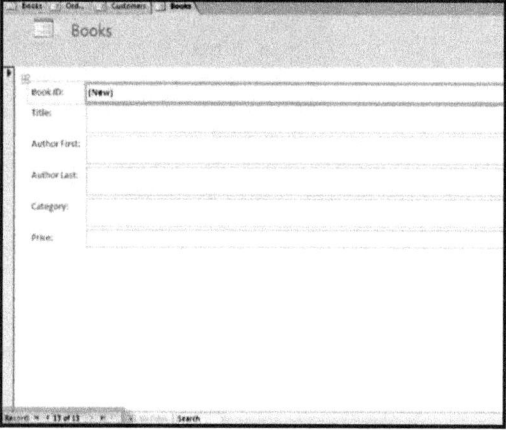

Fig. 3.136: Navigation Buttons

Queries in MS-Access:
- The real power of an Access 2007 database is in the ability to pull data for quick analysis, which is what happens when you run a query.
- Queries allow you to retrieve information from one or more tables based on a set of search conditions you define.

Fig. 3.137

- Access 2007 will display your results in their very own table that you can analyze and manipulate further.
- Queries retrieve information from one or more tables based on a set of search conditions that you set up and then combine that information in a way that is easy for you to analyze.

Using the Query Design Command:
- Once you have planned out your query, you can build and run it using Access 2007's query tools.
- To Build a Query using the Query Design Command follow the following steps:
  (i) Select the Query Design command from the Create tab on the Ribbon.

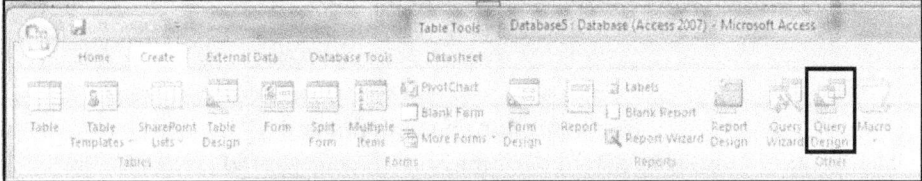

Fig. 3.138: Query Design Command

  (ii) Use the **Show Table** dialog box to select which tables (and/or queries) to include in the query. Our plan called for all three tables.

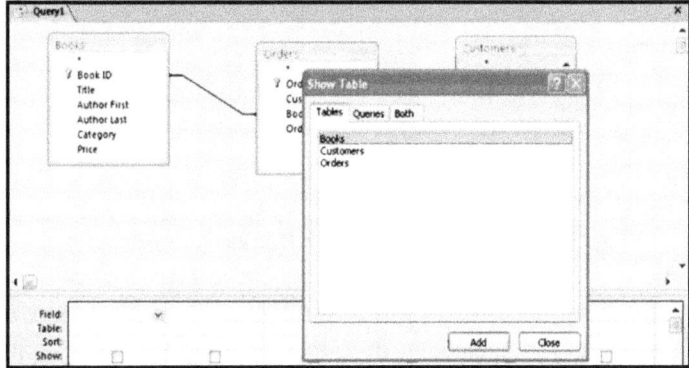

Fig. 3.139: Show Table Dialog Box

  (iii) Drag and drop the fields you want to see in your results to the bottom portion of the query design screen.

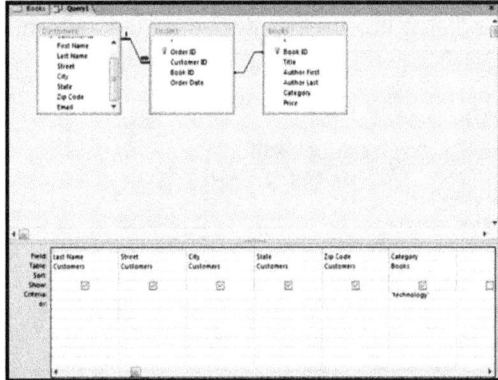

Fig. 3.140: Add Fields to Query Design Screen

- Enter the condition in the **Criteria** row for the condition field. For our query, we typed **Technology** in the cell labeled **Criteria** for the **Category** field. As seen above, Access 2007 puts quotation marks around the term to show it is looking for exactly that term within the designated field.
- Once the condition is set, click **Run!** in the **Results** group on the Ribbon.

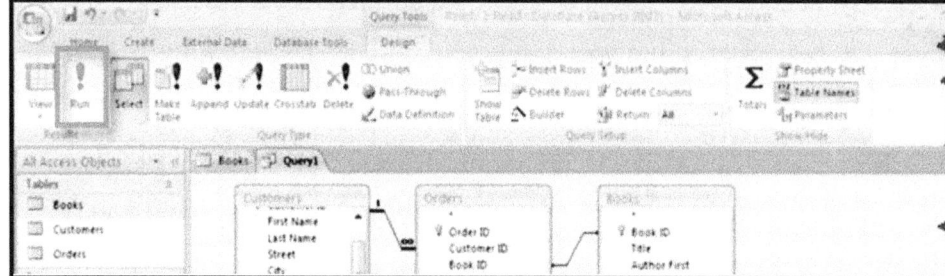

Fig. 3.141: Run Query Command

- Finally, view your results to determine if they match your desired results.

First Name	Last Name	Street	City	State	Zip Code	Category
Jimmy	Smith	123 Hill Top Dr.	Raleigh	NC	21110	Technology
Alex	Hinton	1011 Hodge Ln.	Durham	NC	21113	Technology
Cody	Hayes	65 North St.	Richmond	VA	21119	Technology
Sarah	Allen	12 Jupe Dr.	Phoenix	AZ	21114	Technology
Hillary	Clayton	2516 Newman Dr.	Garner	NC	21108	Technology
Cynthia	Love	7825 Venice Ct.	Topeka	KS	21117	Technology
Alex	Hinton	1011 Hodge Ln.	Durham	NC	21113	Technology
Sarah	Allen	12 Jupe Dr.	Phoenix	AZ	21114	Technology
Alleigh	Gibson	5 West St.	Smithfield	NC	21110	Technology

Fig. 3.142: Customers of Tech Books Query Results

Saving the Query:
- Sometimes you will not need to save your results or your query design. Other times, you may want to keep it to run again later or to modify it slightly. Saving a query is very easy to do.
- To save the query for later use:
  (i) Right click on the query tab.
  (ii) When the **Save As** dialog box opens, give your query a meaningful name.

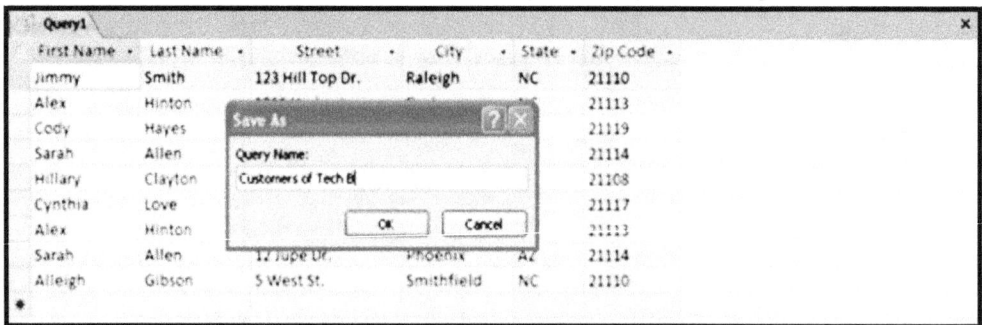

Fig. 3.143: Saving the Query

(iii) Click **OK**.

(iv) The query will now be listed in the object list on the left side of the Access window.

Reports in MS-Access:
- Reports organize and summarize data for viewing online or for printing. A detail report displays all of the selected records. You can include summary data such as totals, counts, and percentages in a detail report.
- Access has several report generation tools that you can use to create both detail and summary reports quickly. This lesson teaches you how to create reports.

Use the Report Button:
- The Report button creates a simple report that lists the records in the selected table or query in a columnar format.

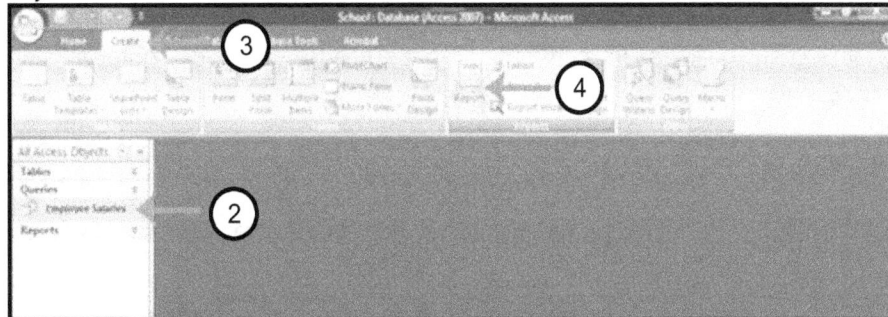

Fig. 3.144

1. Open the Navigation pane.
2. Click the table or query on which you want to base your report.
3. Activate the Create tab.
4. Click the Report button in the Reports group. Access creates your report and displays your report in Layout view. You can modify the report.

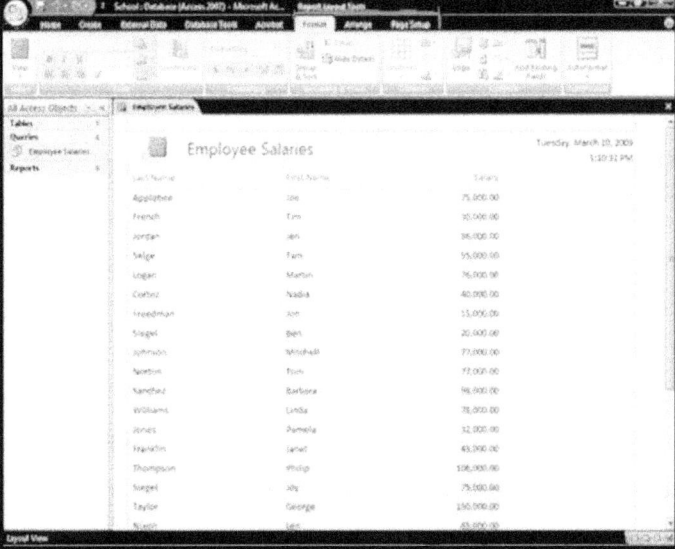

Fig. 3.145

Sections of a Report:

- Fig. 3.146 shows various sections of report in MS-Access which is described below.

1.	Report Header	Appears at the top of the first page and displays the report title.
2.	Page Header	Appears at the top of every page and displays the headings (field labels) for each column.
3.	Page Footer	Appears at the bottom of every page and displays the page number and total number of pages.
4.	Detail Section	Appears between the page header and page footer and displays the records from the table or query.
5.	Report Footer	This section is optional. Appears on the last page of the report and displays summary information such as grand totals.

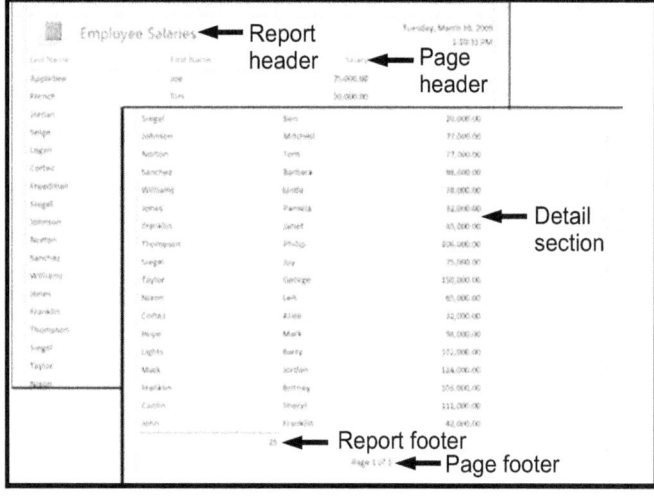

Fig. 3.146

Use the Report Wizard:

- You can also use the Report Wizard to create a report. The Report Wizard provides you with more flexibility than you get by using the Report button.
- You can choose the tables and fields, group the data, sort the data, summarize the data, choose a layout and orientation, apply a style, and title your report.

- Follow the steps shown here to create a report by using the Report Wizard:

  (i) Open the Report Wizard.

Fig. 3.147

  (ii) Activate the Create tab.

  (iii) Click Report Wizard in the Reports group. The Report Wizard appears.

Select tables, queries and fields:

- When using the Report Wizard, you can use fields from multiple tables and/or queries if the tables/queries have a relationship.

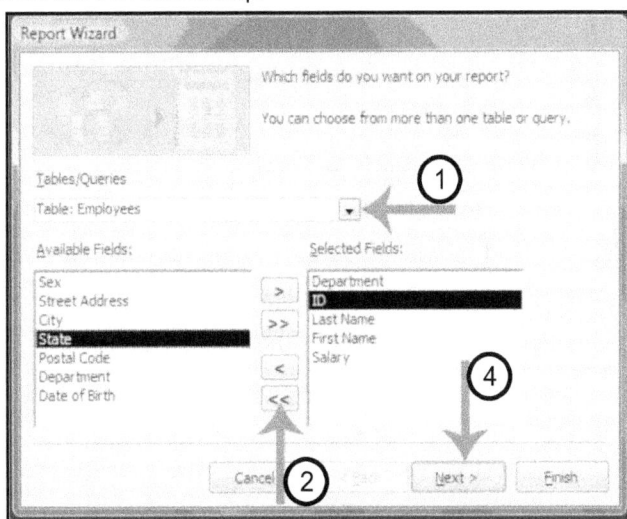

Fig. 3.148

(i) Click the down-arrow next to the Table/Queries field and then click the table from which you want to select fields.

(ii) Click a field and then click the single-right arrow to select a single field, click the double-right arrows to select all fields, click a field and then click the single-left arrow to deselect a single field, or click the double-left arrow to deselect all fields.

(iii) Repeat steps 1 and 2 for each table from which you want to select fields.

(iv) Click Next. The Report Wizard moves to the next page.

Group:

- When using the Report Wizard, you can group data. Grouping puts all of the values in a field into a group based on the field's value. For example, if your data is grouped by the Department field and the records in the Department field have values such as Administration, Computer Science, and English. Access will group all of the data for the Administration department together, all of the data for the Computer Science department together, and all of the data for the English department together.

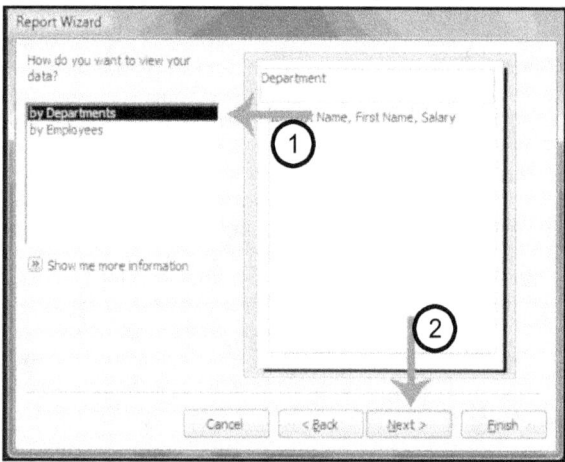

Fig. 3.149

(i) Click to select the field by which you want to group your data. You may not see this page of the wizard if you are selecting data from a single table.

(ii) Click Next. The Report Wizard moves to the next page.

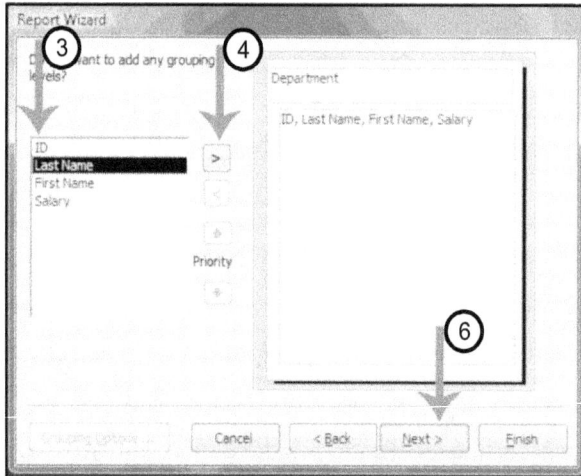

Fig. 3.150

(iii) Click a field you want to group by.

(iv) Click the right-arrow to select a field; click a field and then click the left arrow to deselect a field. Use the up- and down-arrows to change the order of the groupings. If you are only using one table, this may be your first opportunity to select a field to group by.

(v) Repeat steps 3 and 4 for each field you want to group by.

(vi) Click Next. The Report Wizard moves to the next page.

Questions

1. What is meant by MS-Office 2007?
2. Enlist features of MS-Office 2007.
3. What are the components of MS-Office? Explain them in short.
4. What is MS-Word?
5. How to insert table in MS-Word?
6. What are the uses of MS-Word?
7. Explain the following word concepts:
   (i) WordArt
   (ii) ClipArt
   (iii) SmartArt
8. What is MS-Excel?
9. How to create formula in MS-Excel?
10. Explain the following MS-Excel concepts:
    (i) ClipArt
    (ii) Formula
    (iii) Cell alignment
11. What is PowerPoint?
12. Explain the uses of Excel.
13. Write short notes on Bullet and Numbering in PowerPoint.
14. With the help of diagram describe MS-Word screen components.
15. Describe Excel screen with its various components.

16. Explain PowerPoint screen components diagrammatically.
17. What is database?
18. Explain Access 2007 window in detail.
19. How to create tables in MS-Access.
20. How to create database in MS-Access.

Chapter 4...

Introduction to Networking

Contents ...

4.1 Introduction
4.2 Basics of Computer Networks
    4.2.1 Definition
    4.2.2 Goals
    4.2.3 Components of Network
    4.2.4 Advantages and Disadvantages
    4.2.5 Applications
4.3 Network Topology
    4.3.1 Definition
    4.3.2 Types of Network Topologies
        4.3.2.1 Bus Topology
        4.3.2.2 Ring Topology
        4.3.2.3 Star Topology
        4.3.2.4 Mesh Topology
        4.3.2.5 Tree Topology
        4.3.2.6 Hybrid Topology
4.4 Types of Networks
    4.4.1 Local Area Network (LAN)
    4.4.2 Metropolitan Area Network (MAN)
    4.4.3 Wide Area Network (WAN)
4.5 Modes of Communication
    4.5.1 Simplex Mode
    4.5.2 Half-duplex Mode
    4.5.3 Full-duplex Mode
4.6 Transmission Media
    4.6.1 Twisted-Pair (TP) Cable
    4.6.2 Coaxial Cable
    4.6.3 Fiber-Optic Cable
4.7 Protocols and Purpose
    4.7.1 Definition
    4.7.2 Purpose of Protocols
    4.7.3 Elements of Protocol
    4.7.4 Functions of Protocols

4.8 Network Connectivity Devices
- 4.8.1 Repeaters
- 4.8.2 Hubs
- 4.8.3 Switches
- 4.8.4 Bridges
- 4.8.5 Routers
- 4.8.6 Gateways

4.9 Internet Basics
- 4.9.1 Internet
  - 4.9.1.1 Definition
  - 4.9.1.2 What is the Internet?
  - 4.9.1.3 Advantages and Disadvantages
  - 4.9.1.4 Uses of Internet
- 4.9.2 Intranet
  - 4.9.2.1 Definition
  - 4.9.2.2 Advantages and Disadvantages
- 4.9.3 Extranet
  - 4.9.3.1 Definition
  - 4.9.3.2 Advantages and Disadvantages
- 4.9.4 Web Server and Client
- 4.9.5 WWW
  - 4.9.5.1 Definition
  - 4.9.5.2 How does the WWW works?
- 4.9.6 Search Engine
  - 4.9.6.1 Definition
  - 4.9.6.2 Popular Search Engines

4.10 Internet Service Provider (ISP)
- 4.10.1 What is an ISP?
- 4.10.2 How does an ISP Work?
- 4.10.3 ISP Services

- Questions

4.1 Introduction

- A computer network, or simply a network, is a collection of computers and other hardware interconnected by communication channels that allow sharing of resources and information.
- When one process in one device is able to send/receive data to/from one process residing in a remote device, the two devices are said to be networked.

- A network is a group of devices connected to each other. Networks may be classified into a wide variety of characteristics like the medium used to transport the data, communications protocol used, scale, topology, benefit, and organizational scope.
- Communication protocols define the rules and data formats for exchanging information in a computer network, providing the basis for network programming.
- Network means a collection of interconnected computer network of stand-alone computers.
- A computer network is interconnection of various computer systems located at different places. In computer network two or more computers are linked together with a medium and data communication devices for the purpose of communication of data and sharing resources.

4.2 Basics of Computer Networks

- A computer network, often simply referred as network, is a collection of computers and devices connected by communication channels that facilitate communication among users and allow users share resources with other users.
- A network is nothing more than two or more computers connected by a cable or by a wireless connection so that they can communicate and exchange information or data.
- In other words **"network means a collection of interconnected computer network of stand-alone computers".**
- The purpose of a computer network is to link two or more "clients" together in order to exchange information.
- A computer network is defined as "interconnected collection of autonomous computers". Computer are said to be interconnected, if they able to exchange information. Connection is physically established through cables, lasers, microwaves, fiber optics and communication satellite.

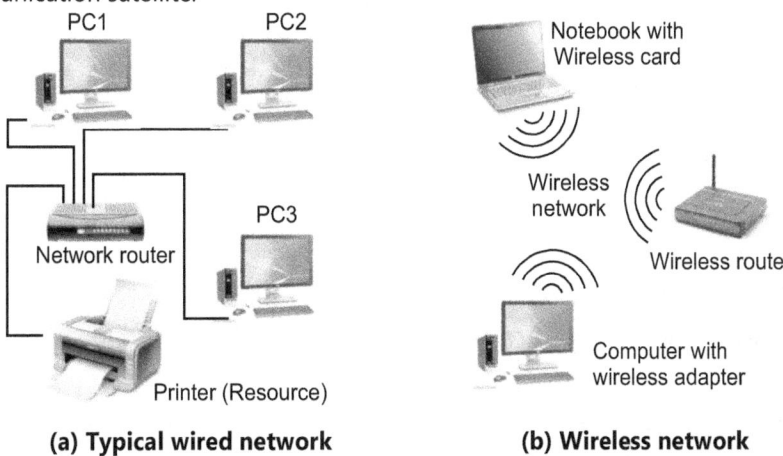

(a) **Typical wired network**   (b) **Wireless network**

Fig. 4.1

- A computer network is interconnection of various computer systems located at different places. In computer network two or more computers are linked together with a medium and data communication devices for the purpose of communication data and sharing resources.
- The computer that provides resources to other computers on a network is known as server. In the network the individual computers, which access shared network resources, are known as nodes.
- The computers on a network may be linked through cables, telephone lines, radio waves, satellites, or infrared light beams.

4.2.1 Definition

- Computer network is "a group of computers connected in same fashion in order to share resources."

OR

- A computer network is a set of electronically connected computers which can share information and resources among themselves.

OR

- A computer network is a group of computer systems and other computing hardware devices that are linked together through communication channels to facilitate communication and resource-sharing among a wide range of users.

OR

- A computer network is a collection of computer systems which can communicate or interact with each other.

OR

- Network is a group of computers and associated peripheral devices connected by a communications channel capable of sharing files and other resources among several users.

Network Services:

1. **File services:** This includes file transfer, storage, data migration, file update, synchronization and achieving.
2. **Printing services:** This service produces shared access to valuable printing derives.
3. **Message services:** This service facilitates e-mail, voice mails and coordinate object oriented applications.
4. **Application services:** This services allows to centralize high profile applications to increase performance and scalability.
5. **Database services:** This involves coordination of distributed data and replication.

How does a Computer Network Works?

- How does one computer send information to another? It is rather simple. Fig. 4.2 below shows a simple network.

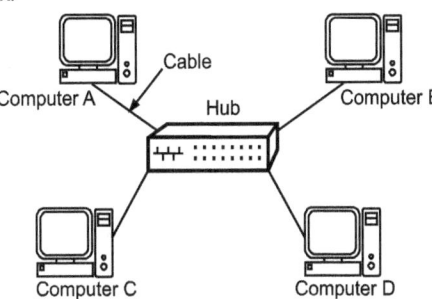

Fig. 4.2: A typical network

- If computer A wants to send a file to Computer B, the following procedure would take place:
    1. Based on a protocol that both computers use, the NIC (Network Interface Card), in Computer A translates the file, (which consists of binary data 1's and 0's) into pulses of electricity.
    2. The pulses of electricity pass through the cable with a minimum (hopefully) of resistance.
    3. The hub takes in the electric pulses and shoots them out to all of the other cables.
    4. Computer B's NIC interprets the pulses and decides if the message is for it or not. In this case, it is, so Computer B's NIC translates the pulses back into the 1's and 0's that make up the file.
- If Computer A sends the message to the network using NetBEUI (NetBIOS Extended User Interface), a Microsoft protocol, but Computer B only understands the TCP/IP protocol, it will not understand the message; no matter how many times Computer A sends it.
- Computer B also would not get the message if the cable is getting interference from the fluorescent lights or if the network card has decided not to turn on today etc.

4.2.2 Goals

- The following are the objectives or goals of the computer networks:
    1. **Resource sharing:** It is the main objective of the computer network. The goal is to provide all the program, date and hardware is available to everyone on the network without regard to the physical location of the resource and the users.
    2. **High reliability:** It is achieved by replicating the files on two or more machines, so in case of unavailability (due to fail of hardware) the other copies can be used.
    3. **Saving money:** Computer organization has helped organization in saving money. This is due to the fact that the small computer has much better price to the

performance ratio comparison than the large computer like mainframe. Mainframe computer are approximately ten times faster that the micro computers, but they cost thousands times more. As a result of this imbalance, organization has preferred to install interconnected micro computer connected to the mainframe computer.

4. **Performance:** Computer network have provided means to increase system performance as the work load increases, (load balancing). In the days of mainframe when the system was full it was to replace with the other large mainframe computer, usually at and expensive rate not convenience for user.

5. **Powerful medium:** Computer network help people who live or work apart to report together. So, when one user prepared some documentation, he can make the document online enabling other to read and convey their opinions. Thus, computer network is a powerful communication medium.

6. **Security:** Only authorized user can access resource in a computer network. Users are authenticated by their user name and password. Hence, it is not possible to access the data without proper account. This increases security.

4.2.3 Components of Network

- A computer network is exchange of data between two computer machines. A computer network is made up of five components. This is shown in Fig. 4.3.

    1. **Sender:** This is the device which sends the data message. It can be a computer, workstation, telephone handset, video camera and so on. Data is in human readable form, gets converted into machine form i.e. 0's and 1's.

    2. **Receiver:** The receiver is the device which receives the message. Again it can be a computer, workstation, telephone handset, television and so on.

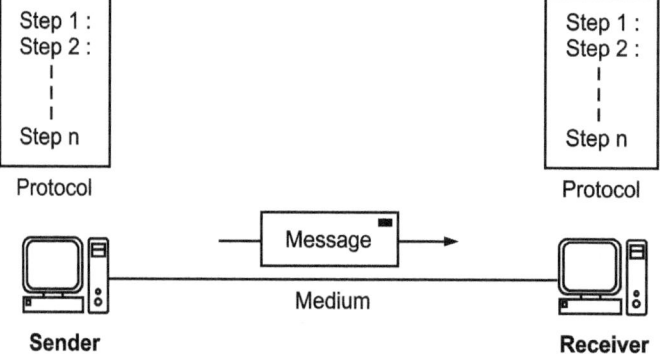

Fig. 4.3: Components of computer network

3. **Message:** The message is nothing but the data or information which is to be communicated. It may have texts, numbers, pictures, sound or video or combination of anything from these.

4. **Medium:** The transmission medium is the physical path by which a message travels from sender to receiver. It may be twisted pair wire, coaxial cable, fiber-optic cable, laser or radio waves and so on. The radio waves may be terrestrial or satellite microwave.
5. **Protocol:** A protocol is a set of rules required for data communication. It represents the agreement between the two communicating devices. Without protocol, we can connect two devices but they cannot communicate with each other.

4.2.4 Advantages and Disadvantages

Advantages of Network:
1. Networking provides the advantage of centralization of data from all the user systems to one system where it can be managed in an easy and better way.
2. Using networking peripherals such as printers can be shared amongst many different users.
3. Communication across the network is cheap and fast.
4. Networking terminals are cheaper than standalone PCs.
5. Using networking software can be shared amongst different users.
6. Networking provides a flexible networking environment. Employees can work at home by using through networks ties through networks into the computer at office.
7. Networking also provides the function of back-up.
8. Networking supports increased storage capacity since there is one or more computers which can easily share files.

Disadvantages of Network:
1. Proper maintenance of a network requires considerable time and expertise.
2. Security threats are always problems with large networks. There are hackers who are trying to steal valuable data of large companies for their own benefit.
3. One major disadvantages of networking is the breakdown of the whole network due to an issue to the server, therefore once established it is vital to maintain it properly to prevent such disastrous breakdowns.
4. Security measures are needed to restrict access to the network.
5. Computer networks are expensive to set up.
6. Since most networks have client/server architecture, the client users lack any freedom, as centralized decision making sometimes hinder how a client wants to user his computer.
7. Networks need efficient handlers i.e. any user with just the basic skills cannot operate/administer a computer network.

4.2.5 Applications

- Some of the network applications of the different fields are discussing below:
  1. **Marketing and Sales:** Marketing professional uses them to collect exchange and analyze data relating to customer needs and product development cycles.

     Sales application includes teleshopping, which uses order entry computers or telephone connected to an order processing network, and online reservation services for railways, hotels, airlines, restaurants, theatre etc.
  2. **Financial services:** It include credit history searches, foreign exchange and investment services and Electronic Fund Transfer (EFT), which allow a user to transfer money without going to bank.
  3. **Manufacturing:** computer networks are used today in many aspects of manufacturing, including the manufacturing processes itself. Two aspects that uses network to provide essential services are Computer Assisted Design (CAD) and Computer Assisted Manufacturing (CAM), both of which allow multiple user to work on a project simultaneously.
  4. **Electronic messaging:** E-mails transfer the messages between two and more users in a network. With this application user can transfer the information in the form of text, picture and voice.
  5. **Directory services:** It allows list of files to be stored in central location to speed up the world wide search operation, For example, search engines like Google, Britannia, and Yahoo etc.
  6. **Information services:** It includes Bulletin Boards and data bank. A 'WWW' site offering the technical specification for a new product in a information services.
  7. **Electronic Data Exchange (EDI):** EDI allows business information (including documents such as purchase orders and services) to be transferred without using paper.
  8. **Teleconferencing:** It allows conference to occur without the participant being in the same location. It includes:
     - (i) **Text conferencing:** Participant communicates through their keywords and computer monitors.
     - (ii) **Voice conferencing:** Participant at a number of locations communicates simultaneously through phone (talk).
     - (iii) **Video conferencing:** Participant can see as well as talk to another.
  9. **Cellular telephone:** Wireless phone communication even while travelling through long distance.
  10. **Cable TV:** This is widest usable thing today throughout the world.

4.3 Network Topology

- A topology is geometric arrangement of computers and its devices in a network.
- The word "topology" comes from topos, which is Greek for "place." Topology is the map of a network i.e. a topology is the layout of connected devices.
- The way in which the elements of a network are mapped or arranged is known as a network topology.
- A topology describes the physical and the logical interconnection between the different nodes of a network.
- Network topologies are classified as physical and logical topologies.
    1. **Physical topology:** It is the physical design of a network including the devices, location and cable installation. A physical topology describes the placement of network nodes and the physical connections between them. This includes the arrangement and location of network nodes and they are connected. Bus topology, star topology, ring topology, tree topology, mesh topology, etc. are the examples of physical topologies.
    2. **Logical topology:** It is also called as signal topology. Logical topology refers to the nature of the paths the signals follow from node to node. Logical topologies are bound to the network protocols that direct how the data moves across a network. Logical topology refers to the paths that messages take to get from one place on the network to another place.

4.3.1 Definition

- The topology of a network is "the geometric representation of the relationship of all the links and linking devices (nodes) in a network".

OR

- Network topology is defined as "the physical interconnection between various elements, such as links and nodes".

OR

- A topology is a "usually schematic description of the arrangement of a network, including its nodes and connecting lines (links)".

4.3.2 Types of Network Topologies

- The way in which the connections are made is called the topology of the computer network.
- A network topology describes the configuration of a network and the physical and logical arrangement of the nodes that form the network.

- Fig. 4.4 shows different categories of topologies in computer network.

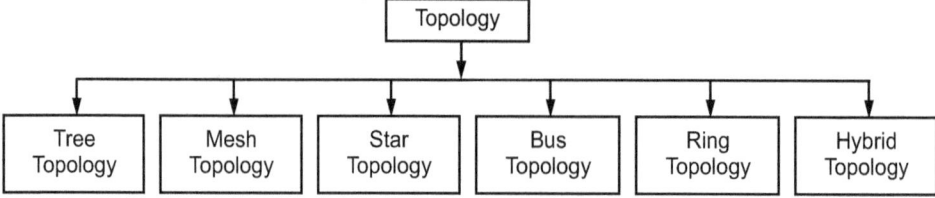

Fig. 4.4: Categories of topologies

4.3.2.1 Bus Topology

- In networking, a topology that allows all network nodes to receive the same message through the network cable at the same time is called as bus topology.
- In this type of network topology, all the nodes of a network are connected to a common transmission medium having two endpoints.
- All the data that travels over the network is transmitted through a common transmission medium known as the bus or the backbone of the network.
- When the transmission medium has exactly two endpoints, the network topology is known by the name, 'linear bus topology'.
- A network that uses a bus topology is referred to as a "Bus Network".

Working:

- Fig. 4.5 shows bus topology.
- The central cable is the backbone of the network and is known as Bus (thus the name). Every workstation or node communicates with the other device through this Bus.

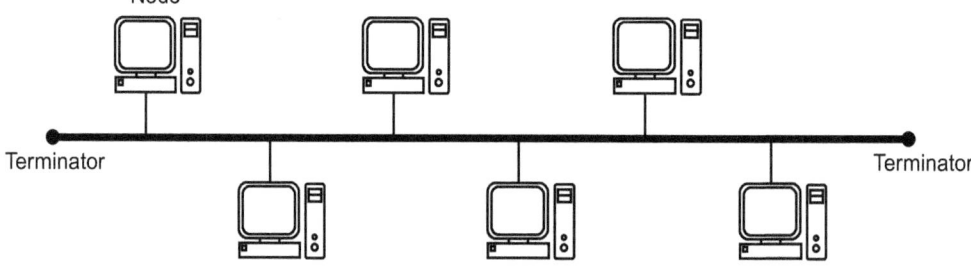

Fig. 4.5: Bus topology diagram

- A signal from the source is broadcasted and it travels to all workstations connected to bus cable. Although the message is broadcasted but only the intended recipient, whose MAC address or IP address matches, accepts it. If the MAC /IP address of machine doesn't match with the intended address, machine discards the signal.
- A terminator is added at ends of the central cable, to prevent bouncing of signals. A barrel connector can be used to extend it.

Advantages of Bus Topology:
1. Easy to install and set-up.
2. It is very easy to connect a computer or peripheral to a bus.
3. Requires less cabling length so cheaper.
4. Any one computer or device being down does not affect the others.
5. Fast as compare to ring topology.
6. Sufficient for small network.
7. Cabling cost is less than other topologies.

Disadvantages of Bus Topology:
1. Can not connect a large number of computers.
2. Difficult faulty isolation. A fault or break in the bus cable stops all transmission. Difficult to identify the problem if the entire network shuts down.
3. Collision may occur.
4. Signal reflection at the taps can cause degradation in quality.
5. Entire network shuts down if there is a break in the main cable.
6. Terminators are required at both ends of the backbone cable.
7. Not meant to be used as a stand-alone solution in a large building.

4.3.2.2 Ring Topology

- Each device in ring topology has a dedicated point-to-point line configuration only with the two devices on either side of it, (Dedicated means that the link carries traffic only between the two devices is connects).
- A network topology that is set-up in circular fashion. In other words all nodes in ring topology are connected in ring structure.
- Each node in this topology contains repeater. A signal passes node to node, until it reaches its destination. If a node receives a signal intended for another node its repeater regenerates the signal and passes it.

Working:
- In a ring network, the data and the signals that pass over the network travel in a single direction. Fig. 4.6 shows a ring topology.
- In ring topology network arrangement, a signal is transferred sequentially using a TOKEN from one node to the next. If a node wants to transmit, it "grabs" the token, attaches data and a destination address to it, and then sends it around the ring.
- The token travels along the ring until it reaches its destination. Once token reaches destination, receiving computer acknowledges receipt with a return message to the sender.
- The sender then releases the token for the token for use by another computer.

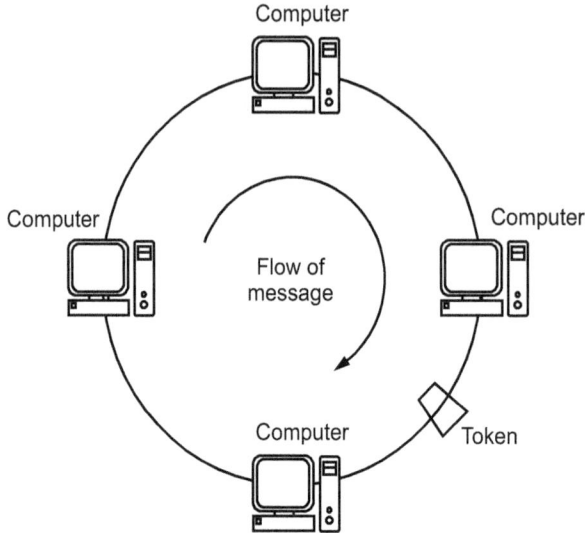

Fig. 4.6: Ring topology

Advantages of Ring Topology:
1. Require less cabling.
2. Less expensive.
3. This type of network topology is very organized. Each node gets to send the data when it receives an empty token. This helps to reduces chances of collision.
4. Each computer has equal access to resources.
5. There is no need for network server to control the connectivity between workstations.
6. Even when the load on the network increases, its performance is better than that of Bus topology.
7. Fault isolation is simplified.

Disadvantages of Ring Topology:
1. Traffic is unidirectional.
2. Network is highly dependent on the wire which connects different components.
3. If one node goes down, it takes down the whole network.
4. Slow in speed.
5. Reconfiguration is required to add one node, whole network must be down first.
6. Difficult for troubleshooting the ring.

4.3.2.3 Star Topology

- Star topology is one topology in which a central unit called a hub or concentrator host a set of network cables that radiate out to each node on the network.
- Unlike Bus topology, where nodes were connected to central cable, here all the workstations are connected to central device i.e. hub or concentrator with a point-to-point connection.
- The data that is transmitted between the network nodes passes across the central hub.

- All the data on the star topology passes through the central device before reaching the intended destination.
- Hub acts as a junction to connect different nodes present in Star Network, and at the same time it manages and controls whole of the network.
- A distributed star is formed by the interconnection of two or more individual star networks.
- The centralized nature of a star network provides a certain amount of simplicity while also achieving isolation of each device in the network.

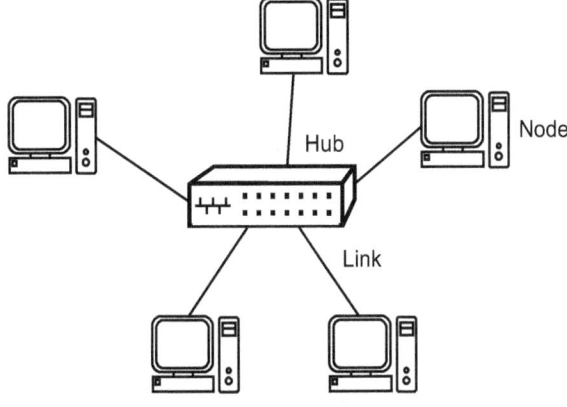

Fig. 4.7: Star topology

Advantages of a Star Topology:
1. Easy to install, reconfigure and wire.
2. Centralized management. It helps in monitoring the network.
3. Robustness i.e. If one link fails, only that link is affected.
4. Fast as compare to ring topology.
5. Multiple devices can transfer data without collision.
6. Eliminates traffic problem.
7. No disruptions to the network then connecting or removing devices.
8. Its easy to detect the failure and troubleshoot it.
9. Supported by several hardware and software venders.

Disadvantages of Star Topology:
1. If central node (hub or switch) goes down then entire network goes down.
2. More cabling is required than bus topology.
3. More expensive than bus topologies because of the cost of the concentrators, (hub or switch).
4. Performance and as well number of nodes which can be added in such topology is depended on capacity of central device.

4.3.2.4 Mesh Topology

- In a mesh network topology, each of the network node, computer and other devices, are interconnected with one another.
- Every node not only sends its own signals but also relays data from other nodes. In fact a true mesh topology is the one where every node is connected to every other node in the network.
- This type of topology is very expensive as there are many redundant connections, thus it is not mostly used in computer networks. It is commonly used in wireless networks.
- Fig. 4.8 shows mesh topology.

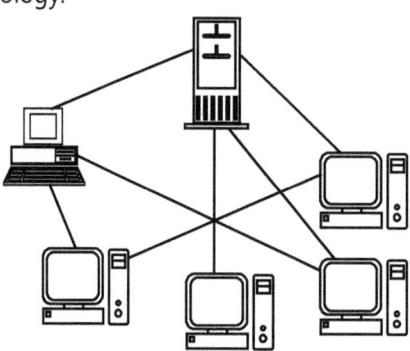

Fig. 4.8: Mesh topology

- A mesh topology employs one of two connection arrangements, full mesh topology or partial mesh topology.
    1. In a **full mesh network**, each network node is connected to every other node in the network. Due to this arrangement of nodes, it becomes possible for a simultaneous transmission of signals from one node to several other nodes.
    2. In a **partially connected mesh network**, only some of the network nodes are connected to more than one node. This is beneficial over a fully connected mesh in terms of redundancy caused by the point-to-point links between all the nodes. The nodes of a mesh network require possessing some kind of routing logic so that the signals and the data travelling over the network take the shortest path during each of the transmissions.

Advantages of Mesh Topology:
1. Each connection can carry its own data load due to dedicated link.
2. Eliminates traffic problem.
3. Mesh topology is robust. If one link becomes unusable, it does not affect other systems.
4. Privacy or Security because of dedicated line.
5. Point-to-point link make fault identification easy.

Disadvantages of Mesh Topologies:
1. More cables are required than other topologies.
2. Overall cost of this network is way too high as compared to other network topologies.
3. Installation and reconfiguration is very difficult because each device must be connected to every other device.
4. Set-up and maintenance of this topology is very difficult.
5. Expensive due to hardware requirements such as cables and input/output ports.

4.3.2.5 Tree Topology

- As its name implies in this topology devices make a Tree structure.
- Tree Topology integrates the characteristics of Star and Bus Topology.
- In Tree Topology, the number of Star networks are connected using Bus. This main cable seems like a main stem of a tree, and other star networks as the branches.
- It is also called Expanded Star Topology.
- Ethernet protocol is commonly used in this type of topology.
- Fig. 4.9 shows tree topology.

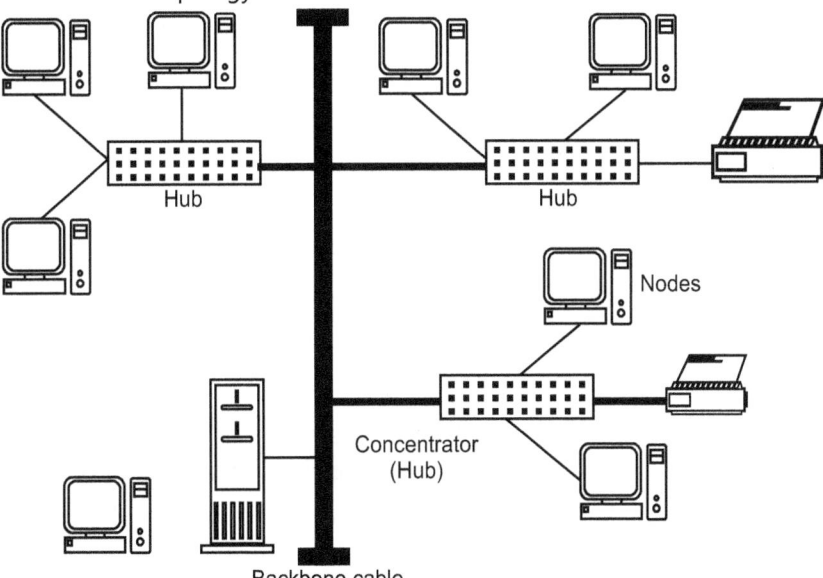

Fig. 4.9: A tree network

- A tree topology can also combines characteristics of linear bus and star topologies. It consists of groups of star-configure workstations connected to a linear bus backbone cable.
- Tree topologies allow for the expansion of an existing network and enable schools to configure a network to meet their needs.

Advantages of Tree Topology:
1. Easy to install and wire.
2. Fast as compare to other topologies.
3. Multiple devices can transfer data without collision.
4. Eliminates traffic problem.
5. Increase the distance of a signal can travel between network devices.
6. No disruptions to the network then connecting or removing devices.
7. Easy to detect faults and to remove parts.
8. Supported by several hardware and software venders.
9. It allows the network to isolate and priorities communications form different computers.
10. Each node in the network having a specific fixed number nodes connected to it at the next lower level hierarchy.

Disadvantages of Tree Topology:
1. Because of its basic structure, tree topology, relies heavily on the main bus cable, if it breaks whole network is crippled.
2. More expensive than bus topologies because of the cost of the concentrators (hub or switch).
3. The cabling cost is more.
4. As more and more nodes and segments are added, the maintenance becomes difficult.
5. Scalability of the network depends on the type of cable used.

4.3.2.6 Hybrid Topology

- Hybrid, as the name suggests, is mixture of two different things. A hybrid topology is combination of two or more network topologies.
- A combination of two or more different topologies makes for a hybrid topology. This combination of topologies is done according to the requirements of the organization.
- The topology that combines more than one topology is called hybrid topology. This topology is used to connect a network that is divided into smaller sections also known as segments.
- Two common examples for Hybrid network are star ring network and star bus network.
    1. A star-ring network consists of two or more star topologies connected using a Multistation Access Unit (MAU) as a centralized hub.
    2. A star-bus network consists of two or more star topologies connected using a bus trunk (the bus trunk serves as the network's backbone).

- Fig. 4.10 shows a hybrid star and bus topologies.

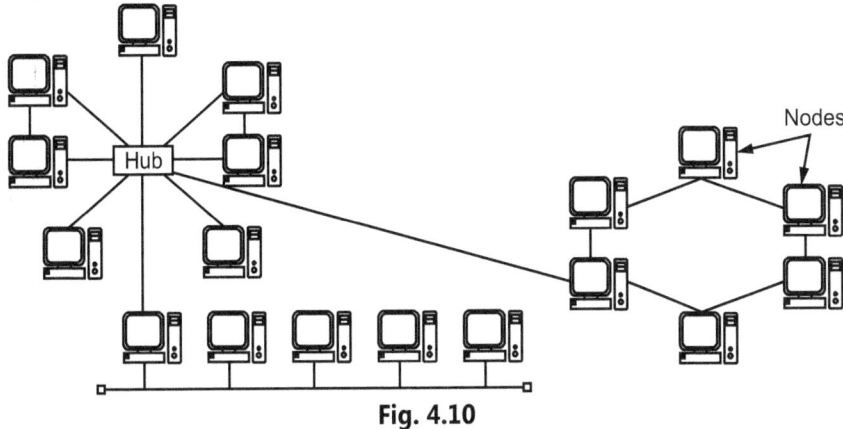

Fig. 4.10

Advantages of Hybrid Topology:
1. Unlike other networks, fault detection and troubleshooting is easy and simple in this type of topology.
2. Its easy to increase the size of network by adding new components, without disturbing existing architecture.
3. Hybrid Network can be designed according to the requirements of the organization and by optimizing the available resources. Special care can be given to nodes where traffic is high as well as where chances of fault are high.
4. Hybrid topology is the combination of two or more topologies, so we can design it in such a way that strengths of constituent topologies are maximized while there weaknesses are neutralized.

Disadvantages of Hybrid Topology:
1. One of the biggest drawback of hybrid topology is its design. Its not easy to design this type of architecture and its a tough job for designers.
2. Configuration and installation process needs to be very efficient.
3. The hubs used to connect two distinct networks, are very expensive. These hubs are different from usual hubs as they need to be intelligent enough to work with different architectures and should be function even if a part of network is down.
4. As hybrid architectures are usually larger in scale, they require a lot of cables, cooling systems, sophisticate network devices, etc.

4.4 Types of Networks

- Fig. 4.11 shows categories or types of computer networks.

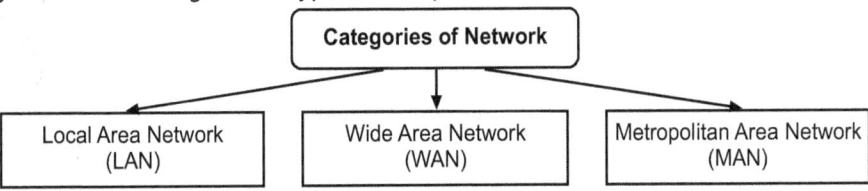

Fig. 4.11: Types of networks

4.4.1 Local Area Network (LAN)

- LAN is a group of computers and associated peripheral devices connected by a communications channel, capable of sharing files and other resources among several users.
- A local area network (LAN) is a computer network that interconnects computers in a limited area (less than 1 km) such as a home, school, computer laboratory, or office building using network media.
- LAN is a group of computes and associated devices that share a common communications line or wireless link.
- LANs are capable of transmitting data at very fast rates, much faster than data can be transmitted over a telephone line; but the distances are limited, and there is also a limit on the number of computers that can be attached to a single LAN.
- LAN have data rate 10 to 100 Mbps.

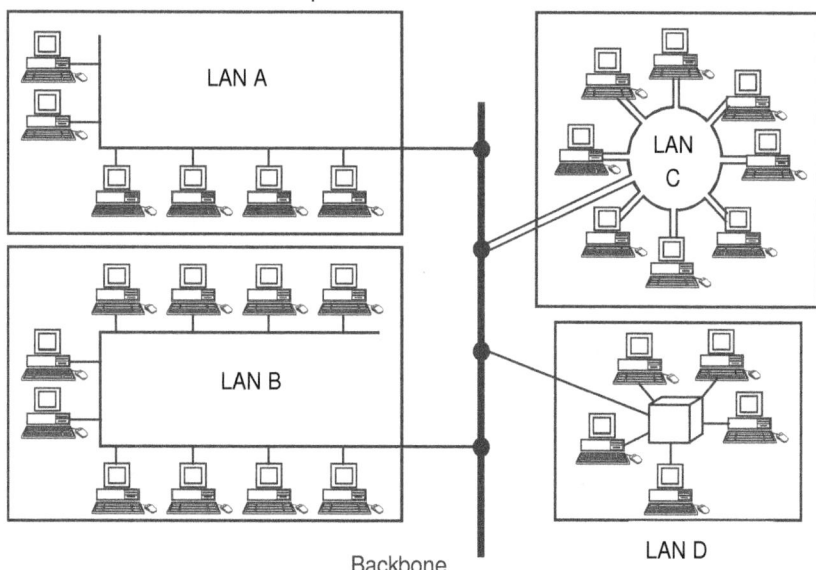

Fig. 4.12: Multiple building LAN (within 1 km distance)

Characteristics of LAN:

1. Every computer has the potential to communicate with any other computers of the network.
2. High degree of interconnection between computers.
3. Easy physical connection of computers in a network.
4. Inexpensive medium of data transmission.
5. High data transmission rate.

Advantages of LANs:
1. Expensive hardware can be shared e.g. laser printers.
2. Network software is cheaper than buying individual packages.
3. Users can access the same files.
4. Messages can be sent between users.
5. A single internet connection can be shared among many users.

Disadvantages of LANs:
1. Quite expensive to set up and maintain.
2. A virus can be easily spread to all the computers on the network.
3. More prone to hacking because of multiple points of access.
4. If the file server goes down, the entire network may go down (star network).
5. Distance and number of computers in a LAN is limited.

Uses of LAN:
1. File transfers and access.
2. Word and text processing.
3. Electronic message handling.
4. Remote database access.
5. Personal computing.
6. Digital voice transmission and storage.

4.4.2 Metropolitan Area Network (MAN)

- Large computer networks that typically span a large city or campus are called Metropolitan Area Networks (MAN).
- MANs geographic scope falls between MAN and LAN.
- MANs provide internet connectivity for LANs in a metropolitan region and connect them to wider area networks like the internet.
- MAN is a public, high-speed network, capable of voice and data transmission over a distance of up to 80 kilometers (50 miles).
- A MAN is smaller than a Wide Area Network (WAN) but larger than a Local Area Network (LAN).
- MAN is designed to extend over an entire city. Multiple local area networks (LANs) that are connected on a campus or industrial complex using a high-speed backbone.
- Multiple networks that are connected within the same city to form a citywide network for a specific government or industry. Any network bigger than a LAN but smaller than a wide area network (WAN) is called as MAN.
- Fiber Distributed Data Interface (FDDI) is a good network technology for building a Metropolitan Area Network (MAN).

- A MAN may be wholly owned and operated by a private company. Number of LANs connected so that resources may be shared LAN-to-LAN as well as device-to-device. (For example: Cable television network).

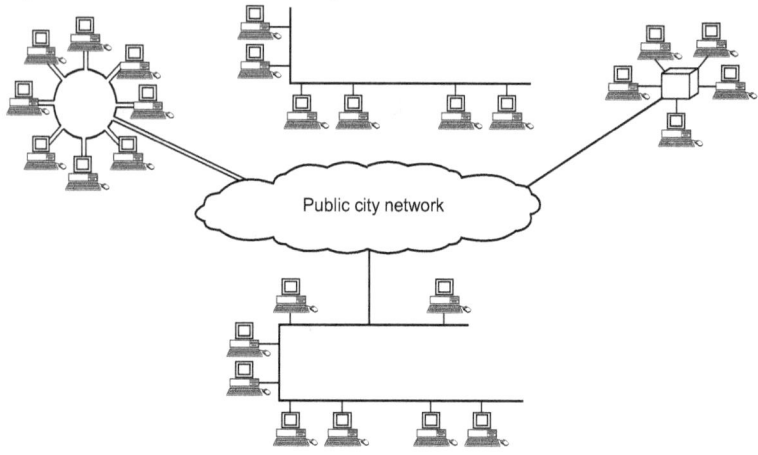

Fig. 4.13: MAN

Advantages:

1. MAN spans large geographical area than LAN.
2. MAN falls in between the LAN and WAN therefore, increases the efficiency of handling data. While at the same time saves the cost attached to establish a wide area network.
3. MAN offers centralized management of data. It enables you to connect many fast LANs together.

4.4.3 Wide Area Network (WAN)

- WAN is a network that connects users across large distances, often crossing the geographical boundaries of cities or states.
- A WAN provides long-distance transmission of data, voice, image, and video information over large geographical areas that may comprise a country, or even whole world.
- A geographically distributed network composed of local area networks (LANs) joined into a single large network using services provided by common carriers.
- Wide area networks are commonly implemented in enterprise networking environments in which company offices are in different cities, states, or countries or on different continents.
- WANs often connect multiple smaller networks, such as Local Area Networks (LANs) or Metropolitian Area Networks (MANs).

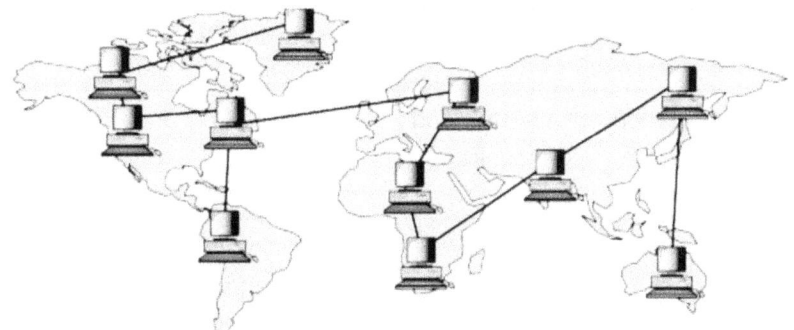

Fig. 4.14: WAN

Advantages of WAN:
1. WAN covers a large geographical area so long distance businesses can connect on the one network.
2. WAN shares software and resources with connecting workstations.
3. Messages can be sent very quickly to anyone else on the network. These messages can have pictures, sounds, or data included with them (called attachments).
4. Expensive things (such as printers or phone lines to the internet) can be shared by all the computers on the network without having to buy a different peripheral for each computer.
5. Everyone on the network can use the same data. This avoids problems where some users may have older information than others.

Disadvantages of WAN:
1. WANs are expensive and generally slow.
2. WANs need a good firewall to restrict outsiders from entering and disrupting the network.
3. Setting up a network can be an expensive and complicated experience. The bigger the network the more expensive it is.
4. Security is a real issue when many different people have the ability to use information from other computers. Protection against hackers and viruses adds more complexity and expense.

Comparison of LAN and WAN:

LAN	WAN
1. LAN is restricted to limited geographical area of few kilometers.	1. WAN covers great distance and operate nationwide or even worldwide.
2. LAN is a privately owned network.	2. WAN can be private or it can be public leased type network.
3. LAN can operate on very high data rates.	3. WAN operates on low data rates.

contd. ...

4. LANs are easy to design and easy to maintain.	4. WAN is not so easy to design and maintain.
5. In a LAN each station can transmit and receive over the communication medium.	5. In WAN each station cannot transmit.
6. The communication medium used for interconnection of LAN is a simple co-axial cable.	6. The communication medium used in WAN can be PSTN or satellite links due to longer distances involved.
7. LAN operates on the principle of broadcasting.	7. WAN operates on the principle of switching.
8. Cost of data transmission in LAN is less than WAN.	8. In WAN cost of data transmission in very high.
9. Transmission a medium is co-axial cable.	9. Transmission medium is satellite links.

Comparison of LAN and MAN:

LAN	MAN
1. A LAN (Local Area Network) is a group of computers and network devices connected together, usually within the same building.	1. A MAN (Metropolitan Area Network) is a larger network that usually spans several buildings in the same city or town.
2. A communication network linking a number of stations in same local area.	2. This network shares the characteristics of packet broadcasting networks.
3. Used Guided Media	3. Use may be Guided or may be Unguided media.
4. LAN generally provides a high-speed 100 Kbps to 100 Mbps. So used for small geographical area.	4. A MAN is optimized for a large geographical area than LAN.
5. LAN is a privately owned network.	5. MAN can be either privately or publicly owned network.
6. These types of networks are usually operated by individuals or organizations. LANs are most commonly used by offices, homes, schools etc.	6. These types of networks are usually operated by the government bodies and large corporations.
7. The most primary technology used for LAN is Ethernet and Token Ring.	7. The IUB network is an example of a MAN.

Comparison of WAN and MAN:

WAN	MAN
1. A **WAN** (Wide Area Network), in comparison to a MAN, is not restricted to a geographical location, although it might be confined within the bounds of a state or country.	1. A MAN (Metropolitan Area Network) is a larger network that usually spans several buildings in the same city or town.
2. A communication network distinguished from a Local Area Network.	2. This network shares the characteristics of packet broadcasting networks.
3. Used Unguided media.	3. Use may be Guided or may be Unguided media.
4. Its long distance communications, which may or may not be provided by public packet network.	4. A MAN is optimized for a large geographical area than LAN.
5. WAN can be private or it can be public leased type network.	5. MAN can be either privately or publicly owned.
6. Wide Area Network (WAN) spans over a wider area. It is basically a collection of several LANs.	6. These types of networks are usually operated by the government bodies and large corporations.
7. The Internet is an example of a worldwide public WAN.	7. The IUB network is an example of a MAN.

4.5 Modes of Communication

- The manner in which data is transmitted from one location to another location is called data flow or data transmission mode.
- There are three ways or modes for transmitting data from one location to another. These are:
  1. Simplex, 2. Half duplex, and 3. Full duplex.

4.5.1 Simplex Mode

- In simplex mode, data is transmitted in only one direction.
- A terminal can only send data and cannot receive it or it can receive data but cannot send it.
- Simplex mode is usually used for a remote device that is meant only to receive. It is not possible to confirm successful transmission of data in simplex mode.
- In simplex mode the flow of information is uni-directional. Hence it is rarely used for data communication.

- Speaker, radio, and television broadcasting are examples of simplex transmission, on which the signal is sent from the transmission to your TV antenna. There is no return signal.
- Keyboard and monitors are also example of simplex mode.

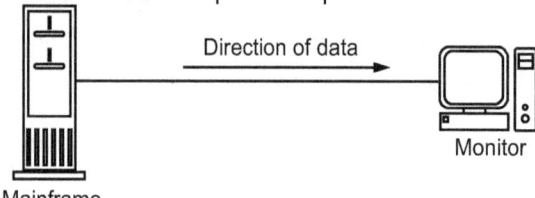

Fig. 4.15: Simplex communication mode

Advantage of simplex mode:
1. Cheapest communication method.
2. Easily programmed on a computer.
3. Easy and simple to use or implement.

Disadvantages of simplex mode:
1. Only allows for communication in one direction.
2. Scope is limited to limited applications.

4.5.2 Half-duplex Mode

- In half duplex mode, data can be transmitted in both directions but only in one direction at a time.
- During any transmission, one is the transmitter and the other is receiver. So each time for sending or receiving data, direction of data communication is reversed, this slow down data transmission rate.
- In half duplex modes, transmission of data can be confirmed.
- Wireless communication is an example of half duplex.
- Fig. 4.16 shows half duplex mode.

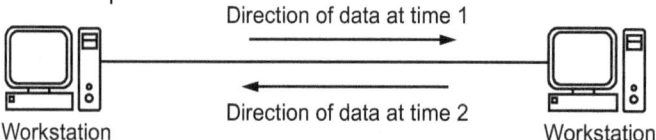

Fig. 4.16: Half-duplex communication mode

Advantages of half duplex mode:
1. Costs less than full duplex.
2. Enables for two way communications.
3. It is possible to perform error detection and request sender to retransmit information.

Disadvantages of half duplex mode:
1. Costs more than simplex.
2. Only one device can transmit at a time.

4.5.3 Full duplex Mode

- In full duplex mode, data can be transmitted in both directions simultaneously. It is a faster mode for transmitting data because no time wasted in switching directions.
- Example of full duplex is telephone set in which both the users can talk and listen at the same time.
- Use of full-duplex line improves the efficiency as the line turn around time required in half-duplex arrangement is eliminated.

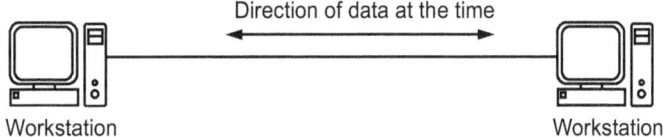

Fig. 4.17: Full-duplex communication mode

Advantage of full duplex mode:
1. Enables for two way communication simultaneously.

Disadvantage of Full duplex mode:
1. Expensive method.

4.6 Transmission Media

- The physical path over which the information flows from transmitter to receiver is called the transmission medium.
- Transmission media is a means by which a communication signal is carried from one system to another.
- The transmission medium is the physical path between transmitter and receiver in a data transmission system.
- A transmission medium can be defined as "anything that can carry information from a source to a destination".
- The transmission medium is usually free space, metallic cable or fiber optic cable.
- Transmission media are the physical infrastructure components that carry data from one computer to another. Transmission media are at the basis of data communications.

Definition:
- We can define transmission medium as "the physical path between transmitter and receiver in a data transmission system."

OR

- Transmission media are the physical pathways that connect computers, other devices, in a computer network.

OR

- Transmission medium is the physical path between transmitter and receiver in a data transmission system.

- Fig. 4.18 shows role of transmission media.

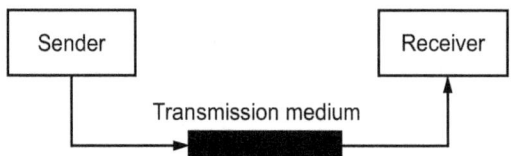

Fig. 4.18: Transmission of data from sender to receiver through a medium

- Fig. 4.19 shows categories of transmission media.

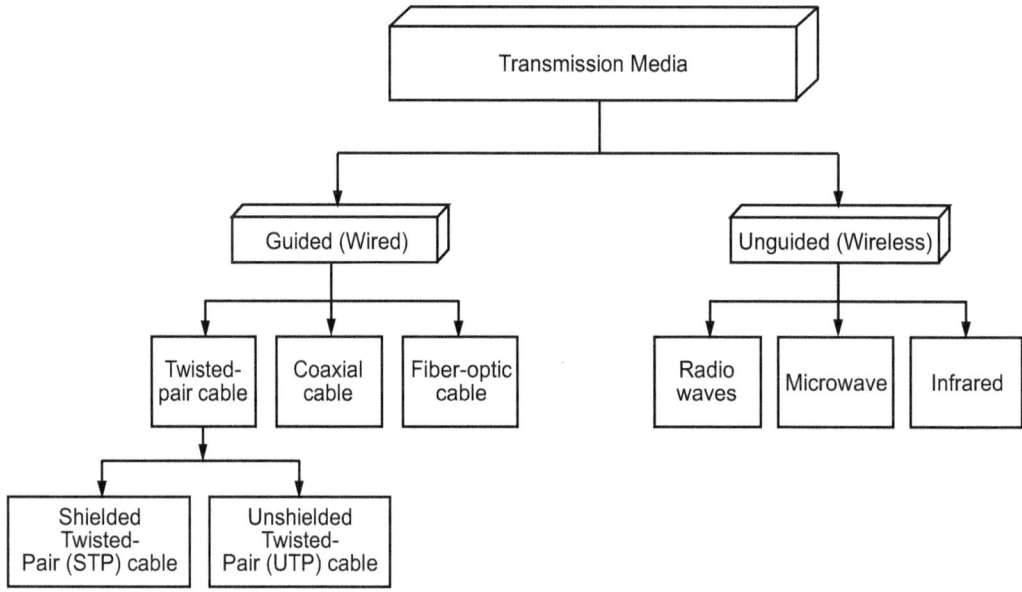

Fig. 4.19: Categories of transmission medium

1. **Guided Media:**
- Guided media are the physical links through which signals are confined to narrow path.
- Guided media is also known as bounded media or wired media or wired communication.
- Guided media are great for use because they offer high speed, good security and low cost. However, some cannot be used for distance (long distance) communication.
- Guided transmission media uses a "cabling" system that guides the data signals along a specific path.
- In other words the data signals are bound by the "cabling" system.
- In guided media cable is the medium through which information usually moves from one network device to another.
- Twisted pair cable and coaxial cable use metallic (copper) conductors that accept and transport signals in the form of electric current.
- Fiber optic cable is a glass or plastic cable that accepts and transports signals in the form of light.

- There are four basic types of guided media as shown in Fig. 4.20.

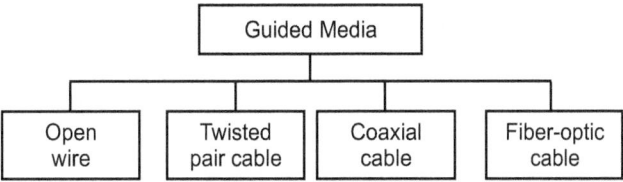

Fig. 4.20: Types of guided media

2. **Unguided Media:**
- In unguided media the data signals are transferred through air.
- Unguided media, also known as wireless communication or unbounded media and it transports electromagnetic waves without using a physical connection.
- Unguided transmission media consists of a means for the data signals to travel but nothing to guide them along a specific path.
- The data signals are not bound to a cabling media.
- Signals are broadcasted through air and thus are available to anyone who has a device capable of receiving them.
- In wireless communication, transmission and reception are achieved using an antenna.
- Transmitter sends out the electromagnetic signal into the medium. Receiver picks up the signal from the surrounding medium.
- Wireless transmission can be divided into three groups: radiowaves, microwave, and infrared waves.

Comparison between Guided Media and Unguided Media:

Guided Media	Unguided Media
1. Guided media also called bounded or wired media.	1. Unguided media also called unbounded or wireless media.
2. Twisted pair wires, coaxial cable, fiber optic cables are the examples of wired media.	2. Radio microwave and infrared light are the examples of wireless media.
3. Additional transmission capacity can be obtained by adding more wires.	3. It is not possible to obtain additional capacity.
4. Wired media lead to discrete network topologies.	4. Wireless media leads to continuous network topologies.
5. Installation is costly, time-consuming and complicated.	5. Installation needs less time and money.
6. Attenuation depends exponentially on the distance.	6. Attenuation is proportional to square of the distance.
7. The signal energy is contained and guided within a solid medium.	7. The signal energy propagates in the form of unguided electromagnetic waves.
8. Used for point-to-point communication.	8. Used for radio broadcasting in all directions.

4.6.1 Twisted-Pair (TP) Cable

- Twisted pair cable is the most common type of cable used in computer networks. It is reliable, flexible and cost effective.
- The wires in Twisted Pair cabling are twisted together in pairs. Each pair would consist of a wire used for the +ve data signal and a wire used for the -ve data signal.
- Any noise that appears on one wire of the pair would occur on the other wire. Because the wires are opposite polarities, they are 180 degrees out of phase
- When the noise appears on both wires, it cancels or nulls itself out at the receiving end.
- Twisted Pair cables are most effectively used in systems that use a balanced line method of transmission: polar line coding (Manchester Encoding) as opposed to unipolar line coding (TTL logic).
- Transmission time is measured in minutes and hours – not milliseconds.

Transmission Characteristics:

1. Requires amplifiers every 5-6 km for analog signals.
2. Requires repeaters every 2-3 km for digital signals.
3. Attenuation is a strong function of frequency.
4. Higher frequency implies higher attenuation.
5. Susceptible to interference and noise.
6. Improvement possibilities.
7. Shielding with metallic braids or sheathing reduces interference.
8. Twisting reduces low frequency interference.
9. Different twist length in adjacent pairs reduces crosstalk.

Physical Description:

- Fig. 4.21 (a) shows physical description of TP cable.

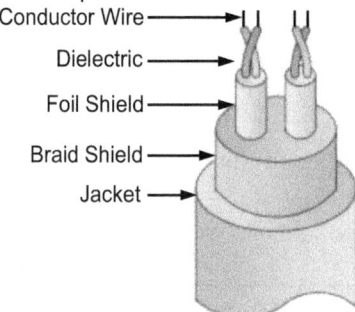

Fig. 4.21 (a)

- Fig. 4.21 shows following parts of twisted pair cable.
    1. **Conductor wire:** Made of copper, copper treated with tin or silver, or aluminum or steel covered with copper.

2. **Dielectric:** Non-conductive material (such as polyethylene or Teflon).
3. **Foil shield:** Made of polypropylene or polyester tape coated with aluminum on both sides, (STP only).
4. **Braid Shield:** Flexible conductive wire braided around the dielectric. Braid may be made of aluminum or bare or treated copper.
5. **Jacket:** Made of polyvinylchloride or polyethylene for nonplenum made of Teflon or Kynar for plenum cable.
- Fig. 4.21 (b) shows frequency ranges for TP cable.

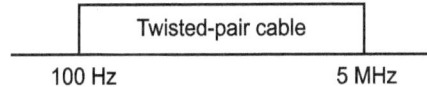

Fig. 4.21 (b): Frequency range for twisted-pair cable

- There are two main categories of twisted pair cable:
  1. Unshielded Twisted Pair (UTP) Cable, and
  2. Shielded Twisted Pair (STP) Cable

Unshielded Twisted Pair (UTP):

- UTP is more common. It can be either voice grade or data grade depending on the condition.
- UTP cable normally has an impedance of 100 ohm. UTP cost less than STP and easily available due to its many use.
- Unshielded Twisted Pair (UTP), illustrated in Fig. 4.22, is the copper media inherited from telephony that is being used for increasingly higher data rates.
- A twisted pair is a pair of copper wires with diameters of 0.4 to 0.8 mm that are twisted together and protected by a thin polyvinyl-chloride (PVC) or Teflon jacket.
- The amount of twist per inch for each cable pair has been scientifically determined and must be strictly observed because it serves a purpose.
- The twisting increases the electrical noise immunity and reduces crosstalk as well as the Bit Error Rate (BER) of the data transmission.
- UTP is a very flexible, low-cost media and can be used for either voice or data communications. Its greatest disadvantage is the limited bandwidth, which restricts long-distance transmission with low error rates.

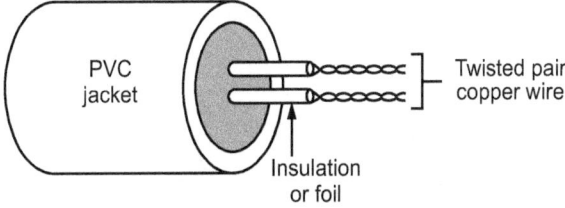

Fig. 4.22: Unshielded Twisted Pair (UTP)

Characteristics:
- (i) Easy to install,
- (ii) High speed capacity,
- (iii) High attenuation,
- (iv) Effective to EMI, and
- (v) 100 meter limit.

Advantages of UTP:
- (i) Easy installation and setup.
- (ii) Capable of high speed for LAN.
- (iii) Low cost.

Disadvantages of UTP:
- (i) Short distance due to attenuation.

Shielded Twisted Pair (STP) Cable:

- It is similar to UTP but has a mesh shielding that's protects it from EMI which allows for higher transmission rate.
- Shielded Twisted Pair (STP), depicted in Fig. 4.23 is a 150Ω composed of two copper pairs. Each copper pair is wrapped in metal foil and then sheathed in an additional braided metal shield and an outer PVC jacket.
- The shielding absorbs radiation and reduces the EMI. As a result, STP can handle higher data speeds than UTP. The main drawback of STP is its high cost, although STP is less expensive than fiber-optic cabling.
- In addition, STP is bulkier than UTP, when poses problem for installations with crowded conduits. Foil Twisted Pair (FTP) or Screened Twisted Pair (ScTP) are variations of original STP.
- They are thinner and less expensive, as they use a relatively thin overall outer shield. STP is used extensively by the telephone company for moving digitized information over distances of 2 km between repeaters, to span the distance of several miles between telephone company switching stations.

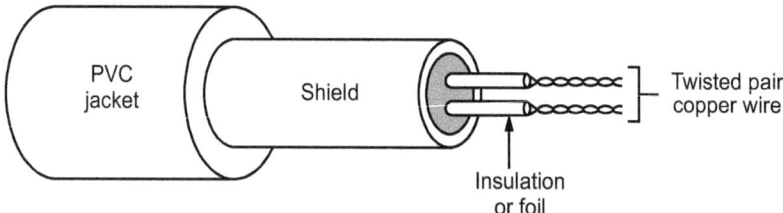

Fig. 4.23: Shielded Twisted Pair (STP)

Characteristics:
  (i) Medium cost,
  (ii) Easy to install,
  (iii) Higher capacity than UTP,
  (iv) Higher attenuation, but same as UTP,
  (v) Medium immunity from EMI, and
  (vi) 100 meter limit.

Advantages of STP:
  (i) It reduces interference.
  (ii) Faster than UTP and coaxial cable.

Disadvantages of STP:
  (i) More expensive than UTP and coaxial cable.
  (ii) More difficult installation and set-up.
  (iii) High attenuation rate.

Comparison of Unshielded and Shielded Twisted Pairs:

Unshielded Twisted Pair (UTP)	Shielded Twisted Pair (STP)
1. Ordinary telephone wire.	1. Shielded with a metallic braid or sheath.
2. Subject to external electromagnetic interference.	2. Reduces interference.
3. Low performance at higher data rates.	3. Better performance at higher data rates.
4. Less expensive.	4. More expensive and difficult to work compared to UTP.
5. Cheaper in cost.	5. Cost is more
6. Easy to install	6. Difficult to install
7. Flexible	7. Not flexible

Advantages:
  1. Reasonable cost.
  2. High speed.
  3. Easy to add additional network devices.
  4. Supports large number of network devices.

Disadvantages:
  1. High attenuation (signal loss) limits individual runs to 100 meters.
  2. Cost is high.
  3. STP can be expensive and difficult to install and setup.
  4. Twisted Pair cables are regarded as being less suitable for high-speed transmissions than coax or fiber optic.

Applications:
1. TP cables are used in telephone lines to provide voice and data channels.
2. The line that connects subscribers to the central telephone office is most commonly UTP cable.
3. The DSL lines that are used by the telephone companies to provide high data rate connections also use high bandwidth capability UTP cable.
4. Local Area Network (LAN) also uses twisted-pair cable.

4.6.2 Coaxial Cable

- Coaxial cable was invented in 1929 and first used commercially in 1941.
- The name "coax" comes from its two-conductor construction in which the conductors run concentrically with each other along the axis of the cable.
- Coaxial cabling has been largely replaced by twisted-pair cabling for local area network (LAN) installations within buildings, and by fiber-optic cabling for high-speed network backbones.
- Coaxial cable (or coax) carries signals of higher frequency ranges than twisted-pair cable. Instead of having two wires, coax has a central core conductor of solid or standard wire (usually copper) enclosed in an insulating sheath, which is, in turn, encased in an outer conductor of metal foil, braid, or a combination of the two (also usually copper).
- Fig. 4.24 shows frequency range of coaxial cable.

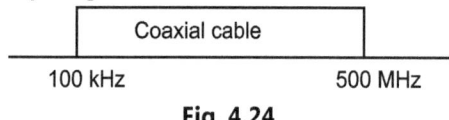

Fig. 4.24

- Coaxial cable (or coax) carries signals of higher frequency ranges than twisted-pair cable.

Transmission Characteristics:
1. Coaxial cable used to transmit both analog and digital signals.
2. It is superior frequency characteristics compared to twisted pair.
3. It can support higher frequencies and data rates.
4. Shielded concentric construction makes it less susceptible to interference and crosstalk than twisted pair.
5. Constraints on performance are attenuation, thermal noise, and intermediation noise.
6. Requires amplifiers every few kilometers for long distance transmission.
7. Usable spectrum for analog signaling up to 500 MHz.
8. Requires repeaters every few kilometers for digital transmission.
9. For both analog and digital transmission, closer spacing is necessary for higher frequencies/data rates.

Physical Description:
- Fig. 4.25 shows construction of coaxial cable.

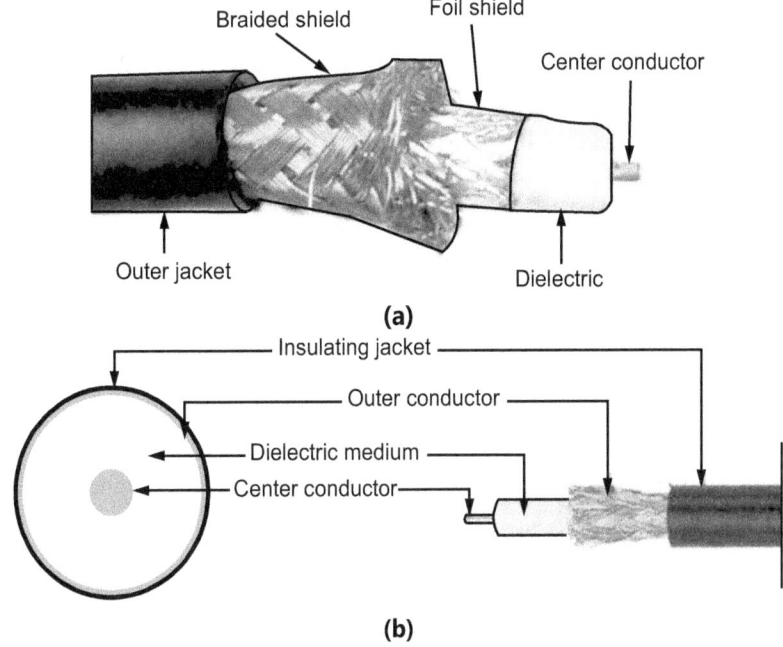

Fig. 4.25

- Each of these components plays a specific role. Let's take a look at each in more detail:

1. **Center Conductor:**
- At the heart of a coaxial cable is a center conductor. Typically constructed of either pure copper (in higher-end cables) or copper-coated steel or aluminum (in less-expensive cables), the center conductor is responsible for transmitting the cable's signal.

2. **Dielectric Insulator:**
- The dielectric insulator's purpose is two-fold; first, it acts as an insulator between the center conductor and the outer braided / foil shielding. Second, it helps physically hold the center conductor in the center of the cable. This is important, as signal loss can occur if the center conductor strays too close to the outer area of the cable. Various materials are commonly used for the dielectric. A few of the more common materials, in order of quality (from best to worst), are below:
  (i) Foamed Polyethylene (FPE)
  (ii) Teflon
  (iii) Polyethylene (PE)
  (iv) Polypropylene (PP)
  (v) Polyvinylchloride (PVC)

3. **Braided Shield:**

   Long copper cables have a tendency to act like antennas, picking up stray signals from the environment. These unwanted signals, known as "interference", disrupt the signal that the cable is supposed to be carrying. Interference tends to come in two different flavors: electromagnetic interference (known as EMI) and radio frequency interference (RFI). EMI interference is often caused by heavy power lines, cell phone signals, etc. A braided shield protects the signal from EMI interference.

   When looking at cable specs, the braided shield will often be expressed in a percent coverage, which often ranges anywhere from 30% to 95% coverage. The higher the coverage, the better the protection.

4. **Foil Shield:**

   Although not always present on coaxial cables, the foil shield serves to protect from RFI interference. Foil shields are almost always made out of aluminum foil, and simply wrap around the inner parts of the cable. Unlike braided shields, which have a percent coverage, foil shields always cover 100%.

5. **Outer Jacket:**

   The outer jacket is generally made out of flexible PVC (polyvinyl chloride) and serves primarily to hold the cable together and protect it from the elements.

Advantages of Coaxial Cable:

1. Low cost due to less total footage of cable, hubs not needed.
2. Lower attenuation than twisted pair.
3. Good immunity to EMI/RFI / Highly insensitive to EMI.
4. Supports high bandwidths.
5. Heavier types of coax are sturdy and can withstand harsh environments.
6. Represents a mature technology that is well understood and consistently applied among vendors.

Disadvantages of Coaxial Cable:

1. Limited in network speed.
2. Limited in size of network.
3. One bad connector can take down entire network.
4. Although fairly insensitive to EMI, coax remains vulnerable to EMI in harsh conditions such as factories.
5. Coax can be bulky.
6. Coax is among the most expensive types of wire cables.

Applications:
1. The use of coaxial cable started in analog telephone networks where a single coaxial network could carry 10,000 voice signals.
2. Later it was used in digital telephone networks where a single coaxial cable could carry digital data up to 600 Mbps.
3. Most common use is in cable TV.
4. Coaxial cabling is often used in heavy industrial environments where motors and generators produce a lot of electromagnetic interference (EMI), and where more expensive fiber-optic cabling is unnecessary because of the slow data rates needed.
5. Another common application of coaxial cable is in traditional Ethernet LANs. Because of its high bandwidth, and consequently high data rate, coaxial cable was chosen for digital transmission in early Ethernet LANs.

4.6.3 Fiber-Optic Cable
- Fiber-optic is a glass cabling media that sends network signals using light.
- Fiber-optic cabling has higher bandwidth capacity than copper cabling, and is used mainly for high-speed network Asynchronous Transfer Mode (ATM) or Fiber Distributed Data Interface (FDDI) backbones, long cable runs, and connections to high-performance workstations.
- A fiber-optic cable is made of glass or plastic and transmits signals in the form of light.
- Light is a form of electromagnetic energy. It travels at its fastest in a vacuum: 3,00,000 kilometers/sec. The speed of light depends on the density of the medium thro, which it is traveling, (the higher the density, the slower the speed).
- Light travels in a straight line as long as it is moving thro a single uniform substance. If a ray of light traveling thro one substance suddenly enters another (more or less dense), the ray changes direction.
- Data transmission over optical fiber has greatly increased over the last few years, although fiber to the desktop has not really caught on as expected.

Transmission Characteristics:
1. Fiber optic cabling can provide extremely high bandwidths in the range from 100 mbps to 2 gigabits because light has a much higher frequency than electricity.
2. The number of nodes which a fiber optic can support does not depend on its length but on the hub or hubs that connect cables together.
3. Fiber optic cable has much lower attenuation and can carry signal to longer distances without using amplifiers and repeaters in between.
4. Fiber optic cable is not atlected by EMI effects and can be used in areas where high voltages are passing by.
5. The cost of tiber optic cable is more compared to twisted pair and co-axial.
6. The installation of fiber optic cables is difficult and tedious.

Construction of Fiber-Optic Cable:

- Optical fiber cable carries light signals instead of electric signal. Fig. 4.26 shows construction of fiber-optic cable.

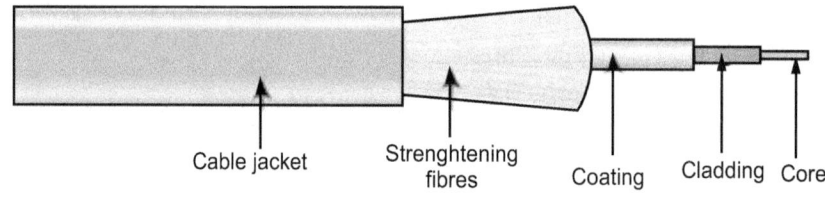

Fig. 4.26

- Fig. 4.26 shows following parts of fiber-optic cable.
  1. **Core:** This is the physical medium that transports optical data signals from an attached light source to a receiving device. The core is a single continuous strand of glass or plastic that's measured in microns (µ) by the size of its outer diameter. The larger the core, the more light the cable can carry.

     All fibre optic cable is sized according to its core's outer diameter. The three multimode sizes most commonly available are 50, 62.5, and 100 microns. Single-mode cores are generally less than 9 microns.

  2. **Cladding:** This is the thin layer that surrounds the fibre core and serves as a boundary that contains the light waves and causes the refraction, enabling data to travel throughout the length of the fibre segment.

  3. **Coating:** This is a layer of plastic that surrounds the core and cladding to reinforce and protect the fibre core. Coatings are measured in microns and can range from 250 to 900 microns.

  4. **Strengthening fibres:** These components help protect the core against crushing forces and excessive tension during installation. The materials can range from Kevlar® to wire strands to gel-filled sleeves.

  5. **Cable jacket:** This is the outer layer of any cable. Most fibre optic cables have an orange jacket, although some types can have black or yellow jackets.

Propagation Modes:

- An optical fiber guides light waves in distinct patterns called modes. Mode describes the distribution of light energy across the fiber.
- There are 2 types of propagation mode in fiber optics cable which are multi-mode and single-mode. These provide different performance with respect to both attenuation and time dispersion. The single-mode fiber optic cable provides the better performance at a higher cost.

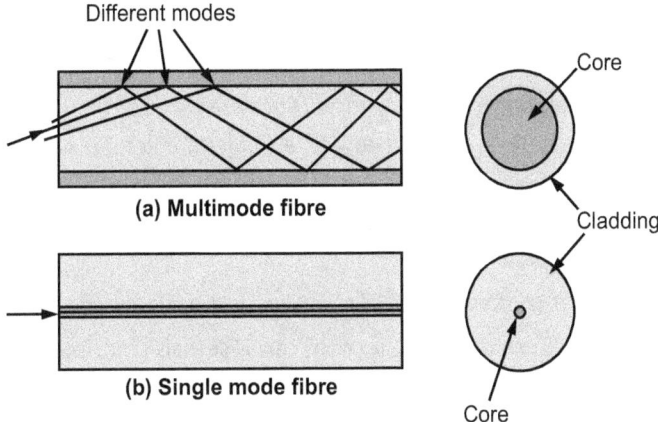

Fig. 4.27

- The number of modes in a fiber optic cable depends upon the dimensions of the cable and the variation of the indices of refraction of both core and cladding across the cross section. There are three principal possibilities which are multi-mode step index, single-mode step index and multi-mode graded index.
- In **multimode fiber**, multiple beams travel in the core in different paths. In multimode fiber, the diameter of core is about 50 microns. Multimode fibers are further categorized into Step index fibers and Graded index fibers.
- **Single mode** uses step-index fiber and a highly focused source of light that limits beams to small range of angles, all close to the horizontal.
- Single **mode cable** is a single stand of glass fiber with a diameter of 8.3 to 10 microns that has one mode of transmission.
- **Step-index multimode fiber** has a large core, up to 100 microns in diameter. As a result, some of the light rays that make up the digital pulse may travel a direct route, whereas others zigzag as they bounce off the cladding.
- A **graded index fiber** has different densities at the core and at the edges. Density is highest at the centre of the core and decreases gradually to its lowest at the edge.

Advantages of fiber-optic cable:
1. **Higher Bandwidth:** Higher data rate than TP and coaxial cable.
2. **Less signal attenuation:** Fiber-optic transmission distance is significantly greater than that of other guided media. A signal can run for 50 km without requiring regeneration. We need repeaters after every 5km for coaxial or TP cable.
3. **Noise resistance:** Because fiber-optic transmission uses light rather than electricity, noise is not a factor. External light, the only possible interference, is blocked from the channel by the outer jacket.
4. **Light weight:** Fiber-optic cables are much lighter than copper cables.

5. **More immune to tapping (or Security):** Fiber-optic cables are more immune to tapping than copper cables. Copper cables create antennas that can easily be tapped.
6. **High data transmission rate:** Optical fiber can carry thousands of times more information than copper wire. For example, a single-strand fiber strand could carry all the telephone conversations in the United States at peak hourn Fiber is more lightweight than copper. Copper cable equals approximately 80 lbs./1000 feet while fiber weighs about 9 lbs./1000 feet.
7. **Reliability**: Fiber is more reliable than copper and has a longer life span.
8. **Long distance:** Fiber optic cable can carry signals for longer distance without repeater than co-axial cable.

Disadvantages of fiber-optic cable:
1. **Installation/maintenance expertise:** Installation and maintenance need expertise that is not yet available everywhere.
2. **Unidirectional:** Propagation of light is unidirectional.
3. **Cost:** Fiber-optic cable is more expensive.
4. **Fragility:** Glass fiber is more easily broken than wire, making it less useful for applications where h/w portability is required.
5. **Limited physical arc of cable of cable:** Bend it too much and it will break!

Applications of fiber-optic cable:
1. Fiber-optic cable is often found in backbone networks because its wide bandwidth is cost-effective. SONET network provides such backbone.
2. Some cable TV companies use a combination of optical-fiber and coaxial cable.
3. Telephone companies also using optical-fiber cable.
4. Local Area Networks (LANs) such as 100BaseFx network (Fast Ethernet) and 1000Base-X also use fiber-optic cable.

Characteristics comparison of Guided Media:

	Twisted Pair	Coaxial Cable	Fiber Optic Cable
1.	It uses electrical signal for transmission.	It uses electrical signal for transmission.	It uses optical signal for transmission.
2.	Affected by EMI and noise.	Less affected by EMI and noise.	Not affected by EMI and noise.
3.	Bandwidth is low which is 3 to 4 MHz.	Bandwidth is high which is 300 to 400 MHz.	Bandwidth is very high which is 2 to 3 GHz.
4.	Used for analog and digital transmission.	Used for analog and digital transmission.	Used for analog and digital transmission.

contd. ...

5.	Supports low data rates upto 4 Mbps.	Supports high data rates upto 400 to 500 Mbps.	Supports very high data rates upto 3 Gbps.
6.	Cost is very less.	Cost is moderate.	More costly.
7.	For long distance communication repeaters are required after every 2 km distance.	For long distance communication repeaters are required after every 1 km distance.	For long distance communication repeaters are required after every 10 km distance.
8.	Signal attenuation is more.	Signal attenuation is moderate.	Signal attenuation is least.
9.	Installation is easiest.	Installation is easy.	Installation is difficult.
10.	Signal to noise ratio is less.	Signal to noise ratio is moderate.	Signal to noise ratio is very high.
11.	Crosstalk is more.	Crosstalk is moderate.	No crosstalk is present.
12.	Losses like copper losses and radiation losses are present.	Losses like copper losses and radiation losses are present.	Losses like microbending and macrobending losses are present.

4.7 Protocols and Purpose

- A protocol is a set of rules that governs data communication.
- A protocol defines what is to be communicated, how it is to be communicated and when it is to be communicated.
- Protocol is very important for networking without protocol communication cannot occur. The sending device cannot just send the data and expect the receiving device to receive and further interpret it correctly.
- A network protocol is a set of rules for communicating between computers. Protocols govern format, timing, sequencing, and error control.
- The sender and the receiver, the two parties in data communication must agree on a common set of rules, i.e. protocols before they can communicate with each other. In networking many protocols are available, some of which are more popular than others.
- A protocol defines:
  1. What is communicated?
  2. How is communicated?
  3. When it is communicated?

4.7.1 Definition

- A protocol is "a set of rules that governs the communications between computers on a network".

OR

- A protocol is a set of rules that govern data communication.

OR

- A protocol is a formal set of rules, conventions and data structure that governs how computers and other network devices exchange information over a network. Network protocols define the rules and procedures for the network communications.

OR

- A set of rules or standards designed to enable computers to connect with one another over a network and to exchange information is called as protocol.

OR

- A protocol is a formal set of conventions governing the format and control of interaction among communicating functional units.

4.7.2 Purpose of Protocols

- In the area of networking, protocols are defined as a set of standard, pre-determined rules and regulations for computers to communicate with each other.
- These protocols define how a computer should establish a connection, how it should be addressed, and how it should transfer the data to the recipient.
- Currently, many networking protocols are used over computer networks for different purposes.
- Following points describe the need of protocols:
    1. **Addressing:** The main purpose of protocol is to provide a significant addressing technique to a network and its elements.
    2. **Network Segmentation:** Protocols provides a facility to break down a network into multiple segments, so that the maximum number of clients (computers) can be interconnected with each other. This process is known as network segmentation or sub-networking.
    3. **Routing:** Routing is the most important requirement of the Internet, which is effectively approached and carried out by protocol. Routing involves communication between two different networks through devices called routers, on a shared common link like WAN (Wide Area Network), Internet, etc.

4.7.3 Elements of Protocol

- A protocol defines the following elements:
    1. **Syntax:** The syntax of protocol defines the structure or format of data. This means that the order in which it is to be sent is decided. A protocol could define that the first 16 bits of a data transmission must always contain the receiver's address.

2. **Semantics:** Protocol semantics defines the interpretation of the data that is being sent. For example: The semantics could define that if the last two bits of the receiver's address field contain a 00, it means that the sender and the receiver are on the same network.
3. **Timing:** Timing refers to an agreement between the sender and the receiver about the data transmission rates and duration.

4.7.4 Functions of Protocols

- A protocol performs the following functions:
    1. **Data sequencing:** It refers to breaking a long message into smaller packets of fixed size. Data sequencing rules define the method of numbering packets to detect loss or duplication of packets, and to correctly identify packets, which belong to same message.
    2. **Data routing:** Data routing defines the most efficient path between the source and destination.
    3. **Data formatting:** Data formatting rules define which group of bits or characters within packet constitute data, control, addressing, or other information.
    4. **Flow control:** A communication protocol also prevents a fast sender from overwhelming a slow receiver. It ensures resource sharing and protection against traffic congestion by regulating the flow of data on communication lines.
    5. **Error control:** These rules are designed to detect errors in messages and to ensure transmission of correct messages. The most common method is to retransmit erroneous message block. In such a case, a block having error is discarded by the receiver and is retransmitted by the sender.
    6. **Precedence and order of transmission:** These rules ensure that all the nodes get a chance to use the communication lines and other resources of the network based on the priorities assigned to them.
    7. **Connection establishment and termination:** These rules define how connections are established, maintained and terminated when two nodes of a network want to communicate with each other.

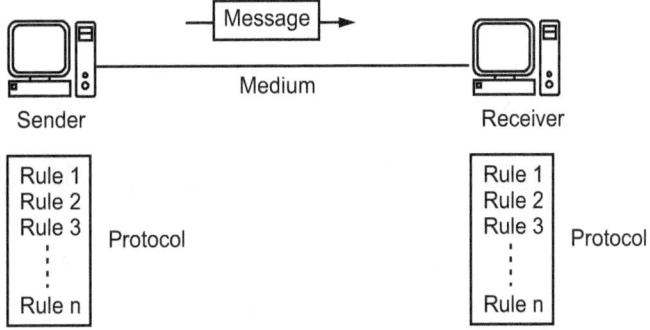

Fig. 4.28: Communication between sender to receiver with protocol

8. **Data security:** Providing data security and privacy is also built into most communication software packages. It prevents access of data by unauthorized users.
9. **Log information:** Several communication software are designed to develop log information, which consists of all jobs and data communications tasks that have taken place. Such information may be used for charging the users of the network based on their usage of the network resources.

- The most common protocols are:
    1. **Ethernet:** The Ethernet protocol is by far the most widely used. Ethernet uses an access method called CSMA/CD (Carrier Sense Multiple Access/Collision Detection). The Ethernet protocol allows for linear bus, star, or tree topologies. Data can be transmitted over wireless access points, twisted pair, coaxial, or fiber optic cable at a speed of 10 Mbps up to 1000 Mbps.
    2. **LocalTalk:** LocalTalk is a network protocol that was developed by Apple Computer, Inc. for Macintosh computers. The method used by LocalTalk is called CSMA/CA (Carrier Sense Multiple Access with Collision Avoidance). The LocalTalk protocol allows for linear bus, star, or tree topologies using twisted pair cable. A primary disadvantage of LocalTalk is speed. Its speed of transmission is only 230 Kbps.
    3. **Token Ring:** The Token Ring protocol was developed by IBM in the mid-1980s. The access method used involves token-passing. In Token Ring, the computers are connected so that the signal travels around the network from one computer to another in a logical ring. A single electronic token moves around the ring from one computer to the next.
    4. **FDDI:** Fiber Distributed Data Interface (FDDI) is a network protocol that is used primarily to interconnect two or more local area networks, often over large distances. The access method used by FDDI involves token-passing. FDDI uses a dual ring physical topology.
    5. **ATM:** Asynchronous Transfer Mode (ATM) is a network protocol that transmits data at a speed of 155 Mbps and higher. ATM works by transmitting all data in small packets of a fixed size; whereas, other protocols transfer variable length packets. ATM supports a variety of media such as video, CD-quality audio, and imaging. ATM employs a star topology, which can work with fiber optic as well as twisted pair cable. ATM is most often used to interconnect two or more local area networks.

4.8 Network Connectivity Devices

- Network connecting devices include all computers, peripherals, interface cards and other equipments needed to perform data-processing and communications within the network.
- A file server stands at the heart of most networks. It is a very fast computer with a large amount of RAM and storage space, along with a fast network interface card.

- The network operating system software resides on this computer, along with any software applications and data files that need to be shared. All of the user computers connected to a network are called workstations.
- Fig. 4.29 shows positions of network devices in OSI model.

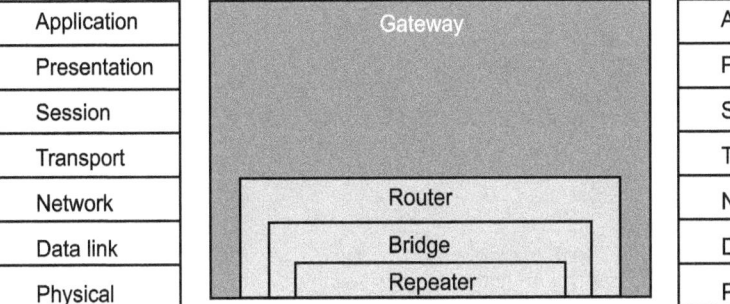

Fig. 4.29: OSI model and position of devices

- A typical workstation is a computer that is configured with a network interface card, networking software and the appropriate cables.
- Workstations do not necessarily need floppy disk drives because files can be saved on the file server. Almost any computer can serve as a network workstation.

4.8.1 Repeaters

- The devices that are used to amplify the signals are called repeaters.
- Repeaters are normally two ports boxes that connect two segments. As a signal comes in one port, it is regenerated and sent out to the other port.
- A repeater (or regenerator) is an electronic device that operates on physical layer of OSI model.

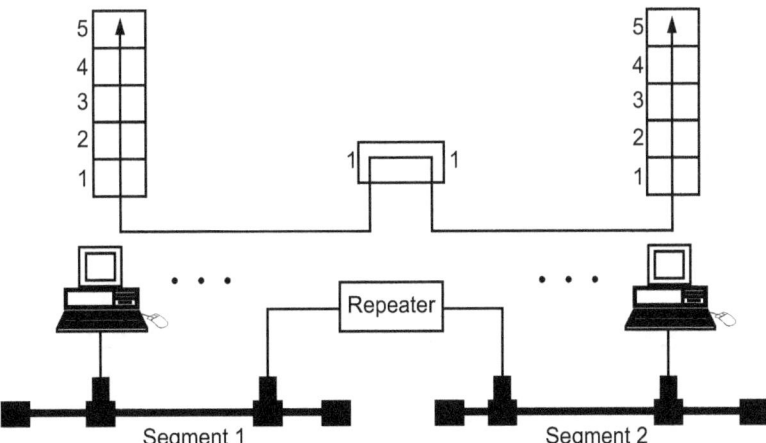

Fig. 4.30: Repeater

- Since, a signal loses strength as it passes along a cable, it is often necessary to boost the signal with a device called a repeater.
- The repeater electrically amplifies the signal it receives and rebroadcasts it.
- Repeaters can be separate devices or they can be incorporated into a concentrator.

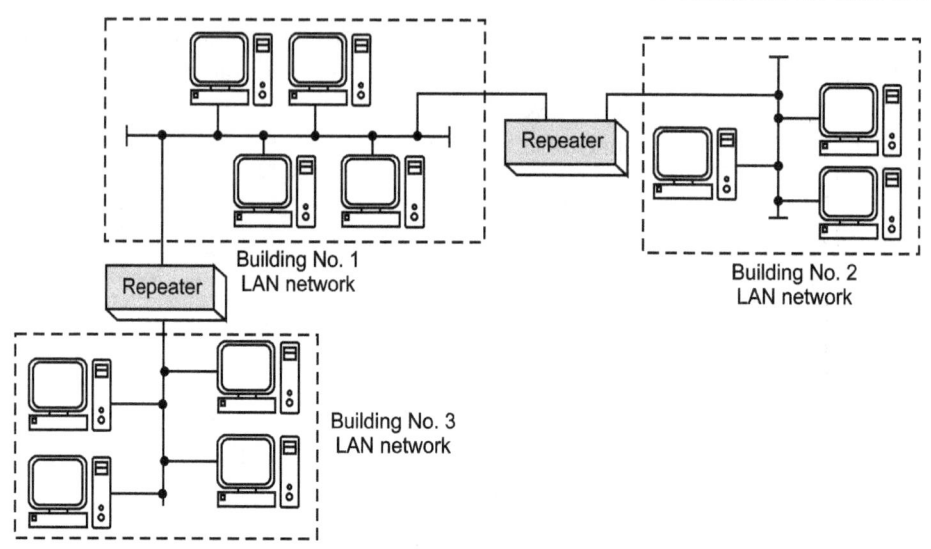

Fig. 4.31: Repeater connected with different LAN

- Repeaters are used when the total length of your network cable exceeds the standards set for the type of cable being used.
- A repeater installed on a link receives the signal before it becomes too weak or corrupted, regenerates the original bit pattern, and puts the refreshed copy back onto the link.
- A repeater allows us to extend the physical length of a network.
- A repeater forwards every frame; it has no filtering capability.
- A repeater is a regenerator, not an amplifier.
- An amplifier cannot discriminate between the intended signal and noise; it amplifies equally everything fed to it.
- A repeater does not amplify the signal; it regenerates it. When it receives a weakened or corrupted signal, it creates a copy bit for bit, at the original strength.

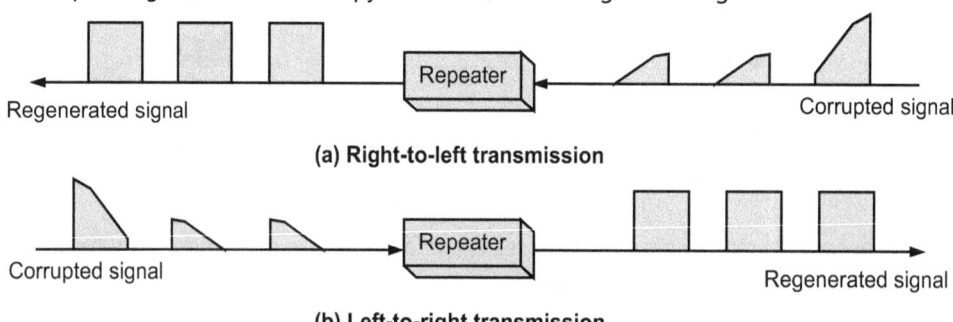

Fig. 4.32: Function of a repeater

Advantages:
1. It passes all traffic in bidirections.
2. It is least expensive for expanding a network.
3. It can connect different types of transmission medias.
4. It can reduce the effect of noise.
5. It can extend the network.
6. It can regenerate the desired information.

Disadvantages:
1. There is a limit to the number of repeaters that can be used to extend a LANs length and topology.
2. They do not examine any destination address and they do not filter or translate any data.
3. Repeater does not support different network architectures.
4. If network traffic is heavy then repeater are not the support.
5. It can operate only in the physical layer.

4.8.2 Hubs

- Networks require a central location, to bring media segment together, called hub.
- A hub is a small rectangular box, often constructed mainly of plastic that receives its power from an ordinary wall outlet.
- A hub joins multiple computers or other network devices together to form a single network segment. On this network segment, all computers can communicate directly with each other.
- Ethernet hubs are by far the most common type, but hubs for other types of networks (such as USB) also exist.
- Originally the term hub is referred to the central part of wheel.
- A hub includes a series of ports that each accepts a network cable.
- Hubs contain four or sometimes five ports (the fifth port being reserved for "uplink" connections to another hub or similar device). Larger hubs contain 8, 12, 16, and even 24 ports.
- The hub or network hub connects computers and devices and sends messages and data from any one device to all the others.
- If the desktop computer wants to send data to the laptop and it sends a message to the laptop through the hub, the message will get sent by the hub to all the computers and devices on the network. Each node/device will check if the message is sent for that device, (See Fig. 4.33).

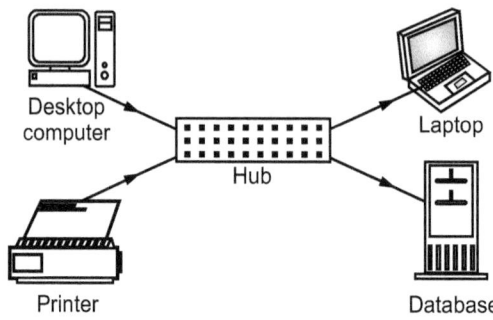

Fig. 4.33

Types of Hubs:

1. Passive Hub:

- As its name suggests, passive hubs are the ones, which does not provide any additional feature except for working just as an interface between the topology.
- Passive hubs provide no signal regeneration. They are simply cables connected together so that the signal is broken out to other nodes without regeneration.
- Passive hubs are not used often today because of loss of cable length that is allowed.
- These types of hubs do not help in rectifying/enhancing the signals they pass the network, in terms they do not help in enhancing the performance of the network/LAN.
- It is very hard to get any help from the passive hubs while troubleshooting in case if there is any fault in the hardware or the network.
- A passive hub simply receives signal(s) on input port(s) and broadcasts it (them) on the output ports without even rectifying it (them).

2. Active Hub:

- Active hub is a type of hub that take active participation in data communication within the network/LAN.
- Active hubs come with various features, such as receiving the signal (data) from the input port and storing it for sometime before forwarding it, this feature allows the hub to monitor the data it is forwarding.
- Active hub act as repeater and regenerates the data signals to all ports.
- Active hubs have no real intelligence to tell weather the signal needs to go all ports that is blindly repeated.

3. Hybrid Hub:

- Hybrid hubs regenerate signals as well as they perform some intelligent path selection.
- Hybrid hub chooses only the port of the device where the signal needs to go, rather than sending the signal along all paths. They also perform some network management functions.

4. Intelligent Hub:
- This hub performs some network management and intelligent path selection.
- Intelligent hubs also be used to create multiple level of hierarchy.
- In this hub all transmission media segment will be used only when a signal sent to a device using that segment.

Advantages of Hub:
1. No need of configuration of a hub.
2. Performance is fast because no processing is done at the hub.
3. Using active hubs we can extend maximum network media distance.

Disadvantages of Hub:
1. Using passive hub limits the maximum media distance.
2. It cannot filter traffic.

4.8.3 Switches
- Switch is a concentrator, a device that provides a central connection point for cables from workstations, servers, and peripherals.
- Most switches are active, that is, they electrically amplify the signal as it moves from one device to another. Switches no longer broadcast network packets as hubs did in the past; they memorize addressing of computers and send the information to the correct location directly.
- Switches can be used to connect single network nodes or entire network segments and in this respect they superficially resemble a cross between a hub and a Bridge.
- Technically, switches work at the Data Link Layer of the OSI Reference Model, and use the MAC address (48 bit Hardware Address) within the frame to determine which node to send the frame to.
- The switch connects the computer network components but it is smart about it. It knows the address of each item and so when the desktop computer wants to talk to the laptop, it only sends the message to the laptop and nobody else as shown in Fig. 4.34.

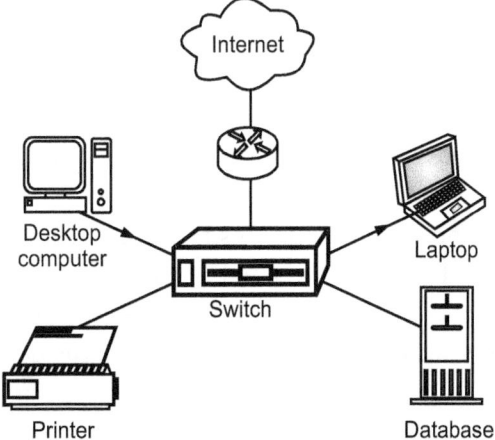

Fig. 4.34

- In order to have a small home network that just connects the local equipment all that is really needed is a switch and network cable or the switch can transmit wireless information that is received by wireless receivers that each of the network devices have.

Types of Switches:
1. **Cut through switch:** It forwards the packets immediately by reading the destination address as soon as they are received and relaying packets to appropriate port with no additional processing.
2. **Store and Forward switch:** It waits until entire packet arrives before forwarding it to its destination. It is a shared memory switch. It has a buffer that stores data coming from ports.

Advantages:
1. Cheaper in cost.
2. Switches give higher throughput.

Disadvantages:
1. Switches required proper designing and configuration.
2. Limited broadcast capacity.
3. Switches are expensive.

4.8.4 Bridges

- Bridge operates in data link layer of the OSI model.
- Bridges are used to connect similar network segments.
- Bridges can divide a large network into smaller segments.
- A bridge has a table used in filtering decisions.
- Bridge generally refers to transparent bridge or learning bridge operation predominate in Ethernet.
- Bridges contain logic that allows them to keep the traffic separate for each segment. Security is provided through this partitioning of traffic.
- Bridges know the physical addresses of all stations connected to it. When frame enters a bridge, the bridge not only regenerates the signal but checks the address of the destination and forwards the new copy only to the segment to which the address belongs.
- In addition to connecting network segments and dissimilar physical media, bridges filter traffic and can connect different network architectures.
- Bridge is more intelligent than the repeater and operates at the Data-Link layer of the OSI model but it is less intelligent than the router, which can determine the best route for each packet to take.
- A bridge is a device that allows you to segment a large network into two smaller, more efficient networks.

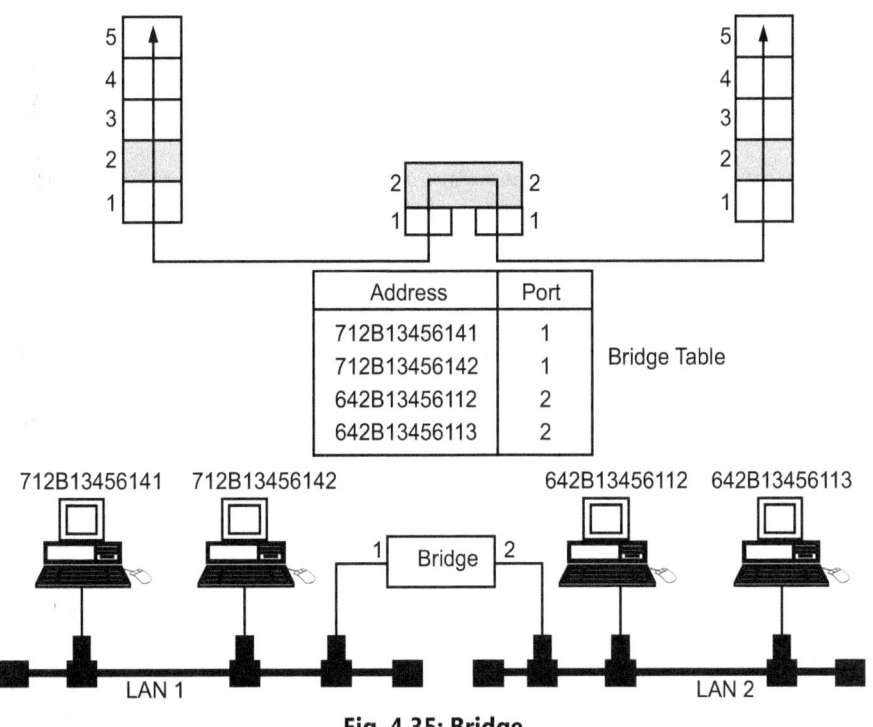

Fig. 4.35: Bridge

- A bridge monitors the information traffic on both sides of the network so that it can pass packets of information to the correct location.
- Most bridges can "listen" to the network and automatically figure out the address of each computer or device on both sides of a bridge.
- Fig. 4.36 shows the address of each computer on both sides of the bridge. The bridge can inspect each message and, if necessary, broadcast it on the other side of the network.
- The bridge manages the traffic to maintain optimum performance on both sides of the network.
- You might say that the bridge is like a traffic cop at a busy intersection during rush hour. It keeps information flowing on both sides of the network, but it does not allow unnecessary traffic through.
- Bridges can be used to connect different types of cabling, or physical topologies. They must, however, be used between networks with the same protocol.
- To select between segments, a bridge must have look-up table that contains the physical address of every station connected to it.

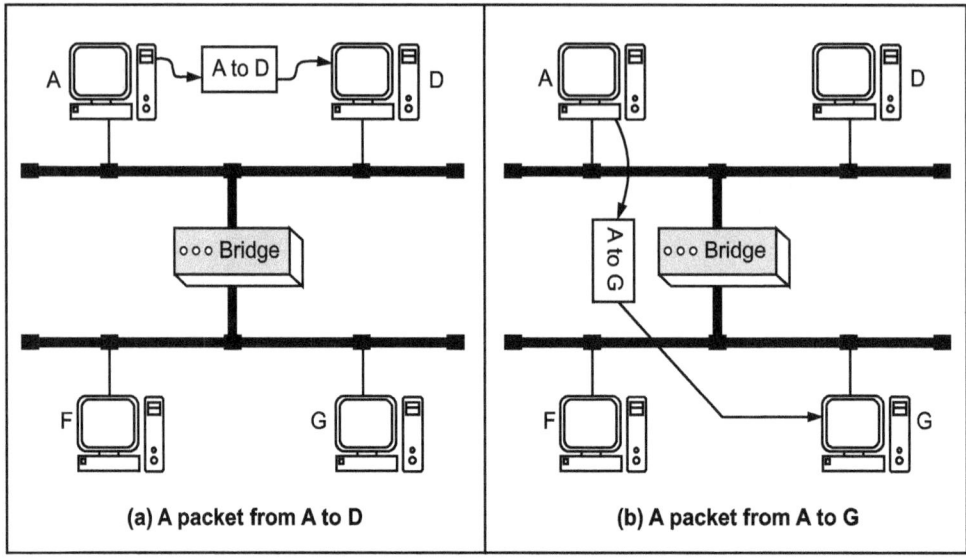

Fig. 4.36: Function of a bridge

Types of Bridges:

1. Simple bridge:
- Simple bridges are the most primitive and least expensive type of bridge.
- A simple bridge links two segments and contains a table that lists the addresses of all the stations included in each of them. Primitive means address must be entered manually.
- Simple bridge links only two segments (LAN).

2. Multiport bridge:
- A Multiport bridge can be used to connect more than two LANs.

3. Transparent bridge:
- A transparent or learning bridge builds its table of station addresses on its own as it performs its bridge functions.
- The bridge is called transparent because its activity is transparent to the network hosts.
- A transparent bridge is a type of network bridge. It interconnects several computers in a network by forwarding packets to hosts.
- A transparent bridge is a bridge whose presence and operation is invisible to hosts on the network.

4. Source routing bridge:
- In source routing, the source of the each packet defines the bridge and LANs through which the packet should go before reaching the destination.
- Source-routing bridges use information provided by the packet's source to determine the path that packet takes.

- In a source routing network, the stations do the majority of the work, whereas in a transparent bridging network, the bridge handles determining the packet's path.
- Source routing bridges do not filter broadcast packets and collisions are not transferred. When it sends it to other segment it needs to reformat the frame so it will be accepted by the other segment (Example: sending from an Ethernet segment to a Token Ring segment).
- In source routing bridge networks, the station that transmits a frame includes, as part of the frame, the route that frame should traverse.

5. **Local bridge:**
- It is a standard type of bridge used to connect network segments of same type and same location.
- It does not modify the data in the packets.
- It simply reads the addresses and pass or discard the packets.

6. **Translation bridge:**
- It connects network segments using different network media or different protocols.
- These bridges not only read addresses but it takes the data link layer frame off the packet to be relayed to other segment and packages them in new frame for transmitting.
- Because of packet manipulation these bridges are slower and expensive.

7. **Remote bridge:**
- It is designed to connect two network segments at distant locations using a WAN link.
- It reduces the amount of traffic passing over WAN link.

Advantages of Bridge:
1. Self configuring.
2. Primitive bridges are often inexpensive.
3. Reduce the size of collision domain by <u>micro segmentation</u> in non switched networks.
4. Transparent to protocols above the MAC layer.
5. Allows the introduction of management/performance information and access control.
6. LANs interconnected are separate and physical constraints such as number of stations, repeaters and segment length do not apply.
7. Helps minimize bandwidth usage.
8. Used to interconnect two LAN.

Disadvantages of Bridge:
1. Does not limit the scope of broadcasts.
2. Does not scale to extremely large networks.

3. Buffering introduces store and forward delays; on average traffic destined for bridge will be related to the number of stations on the rest of the LAN.
4. Bridging of different MAC protocols introduces errors.
5. Because bridges do more than repeaters by viewing MAC addresses, the extra processing makes them slower than repeaters.
6. Bridges are more expensive than repeaters.

4.8.5 Routers

- Routers are devices which can intelligently route network traffic in different ways. Routers are more intelligent bridges.
- Routers operate at a network layer of OSI model.
- Routers are devices which connect two are more networks that use similar protocol. A router consists of hardware and software.
    1. Hardware can be a computer is specific device.
    2. Software consists of special management program that controls flow of data between networks.
- Routers use logical and physical address to connect two or more logically separate network. They make this connection by organizing the large network into logical network segment some times small sub network or subnets.
- Each of these subnets is given a logical address. Data is grouped into packets or block of data.
- Each packet in addition to having a physical device address, has a logical address. The network address allows routers to calculate more accurately and efficiently the path of the computer.
- There are two types of routers:
    1. **Static routers:** This router is hard coded in the routing table. The administrator has to configure and setup all routes manually. Static routing is the process of predefining route paths across data networks and can be used to conserve LAN and WAN bandwidth and optimize processing time.
    2. **Dynamic routers:** Only the first route has to be manually configured. After that additional routes are automatically discovered. The route is decided by the router on the basis of traffic and cost. They use specialized protocols to exchange information.

        Dynamic routing adjusts routing patterns within the network in accordance with varying and uncertain offered traffics, to make better use of spare capacity in the network resulting from dimensioning upgrades or forecasting errors, and to provide extra flexibility and robustness to respond to failures or overloads.

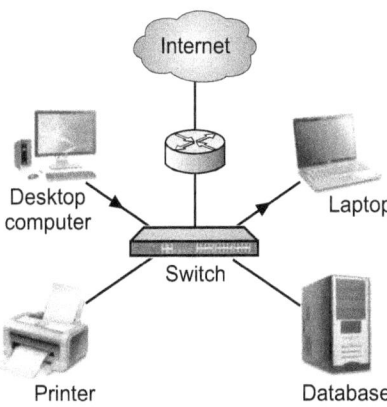

Fig. 4.37

Advantages:
1. Routers are used to interconnect networks i.e. without router, the Internet could not exist.
2. Used to provide connectivity across Wide Area Network (WAN) links.
3. Multiport device i.e. router with multiple slots that can hold different interface cables for other devices.
4. It is used to connect two or more independent network i.e. an Ethernet network connected Token Ring.
5. Diagnose internal or other connectivity problems and trigger alarms.
6. Provide high network fault tolerance through redundant components.

Disadvantages:
1. Routers operate slower than any of the other device because extra decision making is involved.
2. Router do not have ability to stop broadcast packets from being forwarded to other networks.

4.8.6 Gateways
- Gateway is a network device which interconnects two heterogeneous networks.
- Gateway is a connectivity link between two networks that use dissimilar protocols and architecture.
- Gateway receives data from one network and repackages it in destination networks protocol stack. Generally the conversion of protocol is performed at application layer.
- Gateways are devices which connect two or more networks that use different protocols.
- Gateways are similar in function to routes but they are more powerful and intelligent devices.
- A gateway can actually convert data so that network with an application on a computer on the other side of the gateway can use it. For example, a gateway can receive email messages and in one format in convert them into another format.

- Gateway can operate at all seven layer of OSI model. Since, gateway performs data conversion so they are slower in speed and very expensive devices.

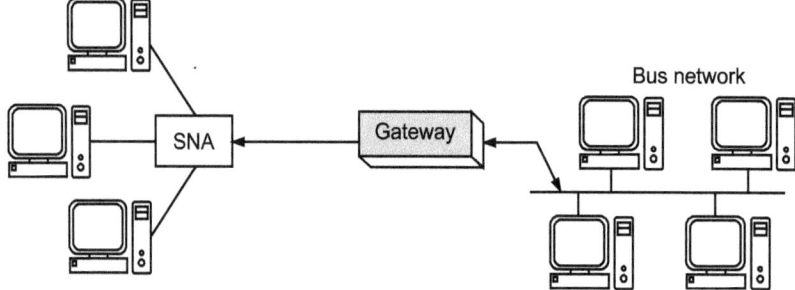

Fig. 4.38: Gateway

- Although gateways are considered to exist at the top of the OSI Reference Model, in reality they can be found at various levels of the model:

    1. **Physical Layer Gateway:** Carries out translation from one speed to another or from one medium to another, i.e. 10 Mbps Ethernet to 100 Mbps Fast Ethernet or UTP to fiber optic (this term is not generally used).

    2. **MAC Gateway:** Translates one MAC protocol to another, i.e. Token Ring to Ethernet or vice versa. These are more commonly referred to as translating and tunneling bridges.

    3. **Architecture Gateway:** Changes the packet from one protocol stack (or architecture) to another, i.e. SNA to TCP/IP, TCP/IP to IPX/SPX or TCP/IP to Appletalk. This is achieved by replacing all the headers from the network layer up to the application layer.

    4. **Application Gateway:** These can translate Application Layer protocols (X.500, X.400) or actual end user applications.

Advantages:

1. Gateway allows communication between two dissimilar network protocol.
2. Typically, gateways are used for one of four purposes as an e-mail gateway, as an IBM host gateway, as an Internet gateways or as a LAN gateway.

Disadvantages:

1. Gateways becomes bottlenecks because the flow of data is slow and the conversion from one data format to another takes time.
2. Gateways are slow because they need to perform intensive conversions.

4.9 Internet Basics

- The internet is a global network connecting millions of computers. In internet more than 100 countries are linked into exchanges of data, news and opinions.
- The internet is a global system of interconnected computer networks that use the standard Internet protocol suite (TCP/IP) to serve billions of users worldwide.
- Internet is a network of networks that consists of millions of private, public, academic, business, and government networks, of local to global scope, that are linked by a broad array of electronic, wireless and optical networking technologies.

4.9.1 Internet

- The internet carries an extensive range of information resources and services, such as the inter-linked hypertext documents of the World Wide Web (WWW) and the infrastructure to support email.
- The internet is a "a worldwide interconnection of computers and computer networks that facilitate the sharing or exchange of information among users".

4.9.1.1 Definition

- The Internet is the largest computer network in the world, connecting millions of computers.

OR

- The Internet, sometimes called simply the Net, is a worldwide system of computer networks - a network of networks in which users at any one computer can, if they have permission, get information from any other computer.

OR

- Internet is an electronic communications network that connects computer networks and organizational computer facilities around the world.

4.9.1.2 What is the Internet?

- The Internet is millions of computers throughout the world, all connected by cables.
- In professional networking diagrams, the Internet is always displayed as a cloud like in Fig. 4.39.
- The cloud is a good analogy because just as a cloud is made up of millions of tiny water droplets, the Internet is made up of millions of computers.
- You connect to the Internet through a device called a modem, and an ISP (Internet Service Provider). Your ISP might be MSN, America Online, Comcast, Juno, or any of several hundred other companies.

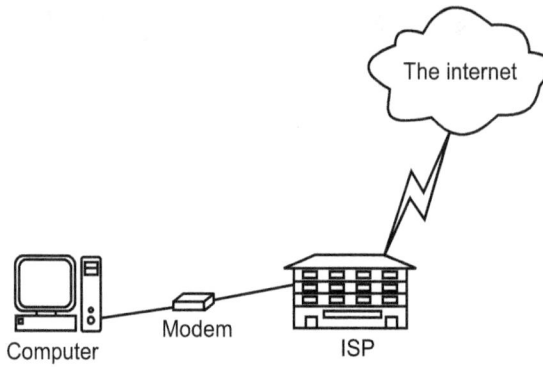

Fig. 4.39

- The term online means "connected to the Internet". When your computer is online, you have access to all the stuff on the Internet, as well as all the stuff on your local hard disk. The term offline means "not connected to the Internet", sort of like snipping the wire that runs from your computer to your ISP. When you are offline, you only have access to the stuff that's on your own hard disk. You cannot get to things on the Internet when you are offline.

- The Internet provides many services, the most popular being e-mail and the World Wide Web (also known as the Web). The program you use to do e-mail is not Windows XP.

4.9.1.3 Advantages and Disadvantages

Advantages:

1. **Easy and cheap communication:** Communicating with friends and loved ones has been easy and simple through e-mail and social communication sites like Facebook and MySpace. You do not have to pay even a single cent just to chat with them because these services are free of charge.

2. **Send small or big files with others easily:** If you have to send a file, for example, a video to your friend who's living in other country, it is not practical nowadays to send him a package with the video cd. Instead, you can send him the video from your e-mail, or upload it in YouTube or other video sharing sites.

3. **Loads of information:** As mentioned earlier, internet has a lot of information that is very essential for the students so they do not have to buy books or go to the library anymore. Search engines like Google and Yahoo! are always available when you need them.

4. **Entertainment:** Entertainment is one of the most popular reasons why many people prefer to surf the internet. There are a lot of games to play, videos to watch, and etc.

5. **Services:** Internet is making our life a lot easier by offering different services like online banking, online booking, hotel reservations, online shopping, and many more.

6. **Earn money:** Aside from entertainment, internet also lets you earn money while at the same time, enjoying what you're doing.
7. **Promote the product:** Internet is one of the best and cheapest ways to promote the business or product.

Disadvantages:
1. **Theft of personal information:** If you use the Internet for online banking, social networking or other services, you may risk a theft to your personal information such as name, address, credit card number etc. Unscrupulous people can access this information through unsecured connections or by planting software and then use your personal details for their benefit. Needless to say, this may land you in serious trouble.
2. **Spamming:** Spamming refers to sending unwanted e-mails in bulk, which provide no purpose and needlessly obstruct the entire system. Such illegal activities can be very frustrating for you as it makes the Internet slower and less reliable.
3. **Virus threat:** Internet users are often plagued by virus attacks on their systems. Virus programs are inconspicuous and may get activated if you click a seemingly harmless link. Computers connected to the Internet are very prone to targeted virus attacks and may end up crashing.
4. **Social disconnect:** Thanks to the Internet, people now only meet on social networks. More and more people are getting engulfed in virtual world and drifting apart from their friends and family. Even children prefer to play online games rather than going out and mingling with other kids. This may hamper a healthy social development in children.

4.9.1.4 Uses of Internet

- Since, the internet has become popular, it is being used for many purposes. Through the help of the World Wide Web (WWW) and websites, the internet has become very useful in many ways for the common man.
- Today internet has brought a globe in a single room. Right from news across the corner of the world, wealth of knowledge to shopping, purchasing the tickets of your favorite movie-everything is at the finger tips.
- Here, is the list of some common uses of internet:
    1. **Email:** By using internet now we can communicate in a fraction of seconds with a person who is sitting in the other part of the world. Today for better communication, we can avail the facilities of e-mail. We can chat for hours with our loved ones. There are plenty messenger services and email services offering this service for free. With help of such services, it has become very easy to establish a kind of global friendship where you can share your thoughts, can explore other cultures of different ethnicity.

2. **Information:** The biggest advantage that internet offering is information. The internet and the World Wide Web has made it easy for anyone to access information, and it can be of any type, as the internet is flooded with information. The internet and the World Wide Web has made it easy for anyone to access information, and it can be of any type. Any kind of information on any topic is available on the Internet.

3. **Business:** World trade has seen a big boom with the help of the internet, as it has become easier for buyers and sellers to communicate and also to advertise their sites. Now a days, most of the people are using online classified sites to buy or sell or advertising their products or services. Classified sites saves you lot of money and time so this is chosen as medium by most of people to advertise their products. We have many classified sites on the web like craigslist, Adsglobe.com, Kijiji, Quicker etc.

4. **Social networking:** Today social networking sites have become an important part of the online community. Almost all users are members and use it for personal and business purposes. It is an awesome place to network with many entrepreneurs who come here to begin building their own personal and business brand.

5. **Shopping:** In today's busy life most of us are interested to shop online. Now a days, almost anything can be bought with the use of the internet. In countries like USA most of consumers prefer to shop from home. We have many shopping sites on internet like amazon.com, Dealsglobe.com etc. People also use the internet to auction goods. There are many auction sites online, where anything can be sold.

6. **Entertainment:** On internet we can find all forms of entertainment from watching films to playing games online. Almost anyone can find the right kind of entertainment for themselves. When people surf the Web, there are numerous things that can be found. Music, hobbies, news and more can be found and shared on the internet. There are numerous games that may be downloaded from the internet for free.

7. **E-commerce:** Ecommerce is the concept used for any type of commercial maneuvering, or business deals that involves the transfer of information across the globe via internet. It has become a phenomenon associated with any kind of shopping, almost anything. It has got a real amazing and range of products from household needs, technology to entertainment.

8. **Services:** Many services are now provided on the internet such as online banking, job seeking, purchasing tickets for the favorite movies, and guidance services on array of topics in the every aspect of life, and hotel reservations and bills paying. Often these services are not available off-line and can cost you more.

9. **Job search:** Internet makes life easy for both employers and job seekers as there are plenty of job sites which connects employers and job seekers.

10. **Dating/Personals:** People are connecting with others through internet and finding their life partners. Internet not only helps to find the right person but also to continue the relationship.

4.9.2 Intranet

- The term Intranet is derived from two words, 'Intra' which means within and 'net' which means group of interconnected computer.
- Intranet is a private computer network that uses Internet protocols and network connectivity to securely share any part of an organization's information or operational systems with its employees.
- An intranet is a private computer network that uses Internet Protocol technologies to securely share any part of an organization's information or network operating system within that organization.
- The term intranet is used in contrast to internet, a network between organizations, and instead refers to a network within an organization.
- Sometimes, the term refers only to the organization's internal website, but may be a more extensive part of the organization's information technology infrastructure.

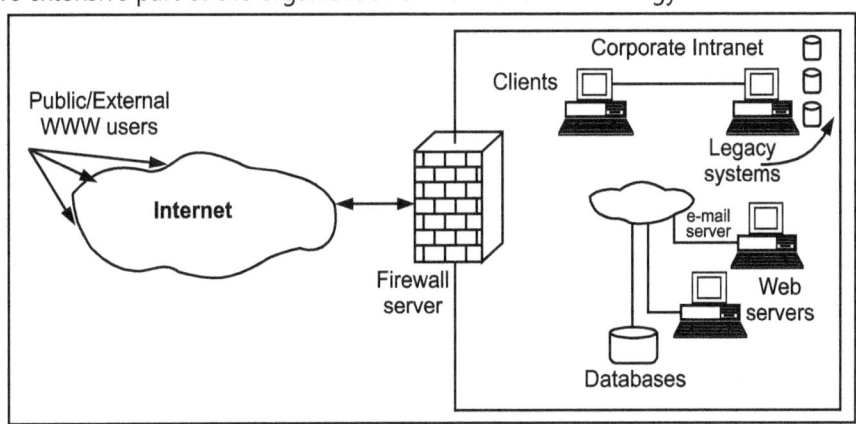

Fig. 4.40: Architecture of Intranet

- It may host multiple private websites and constitute an important component and focal point of internal communication and collaboration. Intranets are being used to deliver tools and applications, e.g., collaboration (to facilitate working in groups and teleconferencing) or sophisticated corporate directories, sales and customer relationship management tools, project management etc., to advance productivity.
- Intranets are also being used as corporate culture-change platforms. For example, large numbers of employees discussing key issues in an intranet forum application could lead to new ideas in management, productivity, quality, and other corporate issues.
- In large intranets, website traffic is often similar to public website traffic and can be better understood by using web metrics software to track overall activity. User surveys also improve intranet website effectiveness.
- Larger businesses allow users within their intranet to access public internet through firewall servers. They have the ability to screen messages coming and going keeping security intact.

- The intranet in the number of the organisations or companies provides the main source of working material, the vehicle for co-operating projects and the preferred reporting, accounting and supply route.

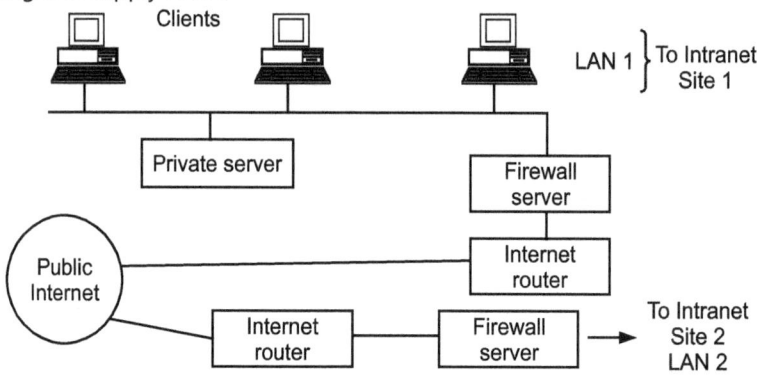

Fig. 4.41: An overview of Intranet

4.9.2.1 Definition

- Intranet is the generic term for a collection of private computer networks within an organization. An intranet uses network technologies as a tool to facilitate communication between people or workgroups to improve the data sharing capability and overall knowledge base of an organization's employees.

OR

- An intranet is a private network that is contained within an enterprise. It may consist of many interlinked local area networks and also use leased lines in the wide area network. Typically, an intranet includes connections through one or more gateway computers to the outside Internet. The main purpose of an intranet is to share company information and computing resources among employees. An intranet can also be used to facilitate working in groups and for teleconferences.

OR

- Internet based computing networks that are private and secure are known as intranet. Intranets are typically used by corporations, government and other organisations. Intranets are based upon Internet standards and provide the means for an organisation to make resources more readily available to its employees online.

4.9.2.2 Advantages and Disadvantages

Advantages:

1. **Workforce productivity:** Intranets can also help users to locate and view information faster and use applications relevant to their roles and responsibilities. With the help of a web browser interface, users can access data held in any database the organization wants to make available, anytime and - subject to security provisions - from anywhere within the company workstations, increasing employees'

ability to perform their jobs faster, more accurately, and with confidence that they have the right information. It also helps to improve the services provided to the users.
2. **Time:** Intranets allow organizations to distribute information to employees on an as-needed basis; Employees may link to relevant information at their convenience, rather than being distracted indiscriminately by electronic mail.
3. **Communication:** Intranets can serve as powerful tools for communication within an organization, vertically and horizontally. From a communications standpoint, intranets are useful to communicate strategic initiatives that have a global reach throughout the organization. The type of information that can easily be conveyed is the purpose of the initiative and what the initiative is aiming to achieve, who is driving the initiative, results achieved to date, and who to speak to for more information. By providing this information on the intranet, staff have the opportunity to keep up-to-date with the strategic focus of the organization. Some examples of communication would be chat, email, and or blogs.
4. **Business operations and management:** Intranets are also being used as a platform for developing and deploying applications to support business operations and decisions across the internet worked enterprise.
5. **Cost-effective:** Users can view information and data via web-browser rather than maintaining physical documents such as procedure manuals, internal phone list and requisition forms. This can potentially save the business money on printing, duplicating documents, and the environment as well as document maintenance overhead.
6. **Ease of publishing:** Intranets are easy and simple to publishing.
7. **Ease of use and People friendly:** Intranets are user friendly and easy and simple to used and understand.
8. **Low maintenance:** Intranet requires less maintenance than other.
9. **Easy to change and Easily customized:** Some modification is intranet are done easily. Intranet customized easily.
10. **Good performance and Well suited for most applications:** Intranet having good performance than other technologies.
11. **Promote common corporate culture:** Every user is viewing the same information within the Intranet.
12. **Enhance collaboration:** With information easily accessible by all authorised users, teamwork is enabled.
13. **Cross-platform capability:** Standards-compliant web browsers are available for Windows, Mac, and UNIX.
14. **Built for one audience:** Many companies dictate computer specifications. Which, in turn, may allow Intranet developers to write applications that only have to work on one browser.

Disadvantages:
1. Intranets can be expensive to maintain within an organization.
2. Collaborative applications for Intranets are not as powerful compared to the ones offered by traditional groupware.
3. Intranets can reduce face to face meetings with clients or business partners.
4. There are limited tools for linking an intranet service to databases or other back-end mainframe-based applications.
5. With intranets, companies have to set up and maintain separate applications such as e-mail and web servers, instead of using one unified system as with groupware.

4.9.3 Extranet
- An extranet is a private network that uses Internet protocols, network connectivity.
- An extranet can be viewed as part of a company's intranet that is extended to users outside the company, usually via the Internet.
- Extranet has also been described as a "state of mind" in which the Internet is perceived as a way to do business with a selected set of other companies Business-to-Business, (B2B), in isolation from all other Internet users.
- In contrast, Business-to-Consumer (B2C) models involve known servers of one or more companies, communicating with previously unknown consumer users.
- Extranet gives the channel to secure communications between intranet and shared portions of the system that are externalized to your business partners. Hence, the term as 'extranet'.
- Extranets will provide a secure gateway for visitors coming in from the outside and gives them controlled access to the portions of data that they have permission to see, modify or publish.
- In some situations, the extranet can also be used to provide access to legacy systems via a web interface or by other means.
- This approach allows business partners to gain access not just to data that is located on the extranet web, but other internal systems that are important to your business relationships.
- An extranet is a private network that uses Internet technology and the public telecommunication system to securely share part of a business's information or operations with suppliers, vendors, partners, customers, or other businesses.
- An extranet can be viewed as part of a company's intranet that is extended to users outside the company.
- Extranets has also been described as a "state of mind" in which the Internet is perceived as a way to do business with other companies as well as to sell products to customers.

- An extranet requires security and privacy. These can include firewall server management, the issuance and use of digital certificates or similar means of user authentication, encryption of messages, and the use of virtual private networks (VPNs) that tunnel through the public network.
- Companies can use an extranet to:
  1. Exchange large volumes of data using Electronic Data Interchange (EDI).
  2. Share product catalogs exclusively with wholesalers or those "in the trade".
  3. Collaborate with other companies on joint development efforts.
  4. Jointly develop and use training programs with other companies.
  5. Provide or access services provided by one company to a group of other companies, such as an online banking application managed by one company on behalf of affiliated banks.
  6. Share news of common interest exclusively with partner companies.
- Fig. 4.42 shows an example of Intranets and Extranets.

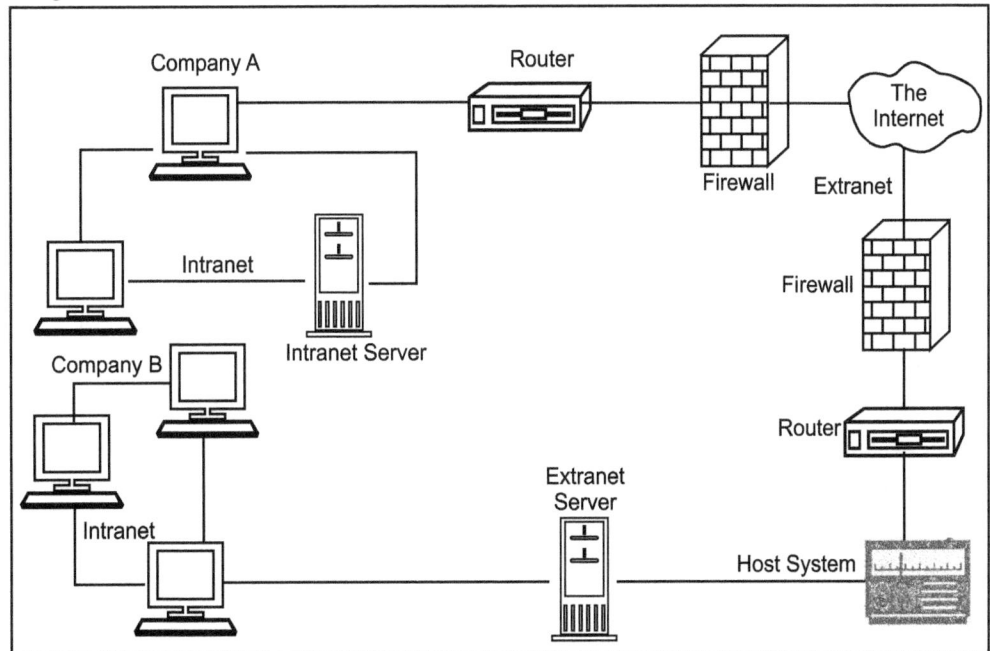

Fig. 4.42

- Extranets are networks that links some of the intranet resources of a company with other organisations and individuals and they enable customers, suppliers, sub-contractors consultants and others to access intranet websites and other company databases.
- Organisations or companies can establish private extranets among themselves or use the Internet as part of the network connections between them.

4.9.3.1 Definition

- An extranet is a private network that uses the Internet protocol and the public telecommunication system to securely share part of a business's information or operations with suppliers, vendors, partners, customers, or other businesses.

  OR

- Extranet refers to a group of websites, belonging to independent entities that are combined together in order to share information.

  OR

- An extranet is a computer network that allows controlled access from the outside for specific business or educational purposes. Extranets are extensions to, or segments of, private intranet networks that have been built in many corporations for information sharing and ecommerce.

  OR

- Extranets are private wide area networks that run on public protocols with the goal of fostering collaboration and information sharing between organisations.

4.9.3.2 Advantages and Disadvantages

Advantages:

1. **Improved productivity:** Extranets can improve organization productivity by automating processes that were previously done manually. For example: reordering of inventory from suppliers). Automation can also reduce the margin of error of these processes.

2. **Saving time:** Extranets allow organization or project information to be viewed at times convenient for business partners, customers, employees, suppliers and other stake-holders. This cuts down on meeting times and is an advantage when doing business with partners in different time zones.

3. **Easy to updation:** Information on an extranet can be updated, edited and changed instantly. All authorized users therefore have immediate access to the most up-to-date information.

4. **Improved relationship:** Extranets can improve relationships with key customers, providing them with accurate and updated information.

Disadvantages:

1. **Expensive:** Extranets can be expensive to implement and maintain within an organization (For example: hardware, software, employee training costs), if hosted internally rather than by an application service provider.

2. **Security problem:** Security of extranets can be a concern when hosting valuable or proprietary information.

3. **High cost:** Extranets can be costly to apply and maintain within an organization.
4. **Protection problem:** One of big problem is the protection of extranets when dealing with precious information. System access should be controlled and checked properly to protect the system and information going into the incorrect hands.
5. **Lack of communication:** Extranets can decrease personal face-to-face contact with clients and business partners. This can cause a lack of communication between employees, clients and organization.

Difference between Intranet and Extranet:

Intranet	Extranet
1. Intranets facilitate sharing of information by people in a single organization.	1. Extranets facilitate sharing of information by individuals in multiple organizations.
2. Intranets are Internet based computing networks that are private and secure, typically used by corporations, government and other organizations are used to make resources more readily available to its employees online.	2. Extranets provide wide area networks that run on public protocols with the goal of fostering collaboration and information sharing between organizations or firms.
3. Intranet is an internet like network within an organization.	3. A network that links selected resources of the intranet of an organization with its customers, suppliers and other business partners, using the Internet or private networks to link the organization's intranets.
4. An intranet is the generic term for a collection of private computer networks within an organization.	4. An extranet is a computer network that allows controlled access from the outside for specific business or educational purposes.
5. Intranet is totally internal to an organization.	5. The Extranet is a way to connect businesses and suppliers to each other securely.
6. The internet is open to the public.	6. An Extranet is private and not open to the public.

contd. ...

7. An intranet is a private network that is contained within an enterprise. It may consist of many interlinked local area networks and also use leased lines in the wide area network.	7. An extranet is a private network that uses Internet technology and the public telecommunication system to securely share part of a business's information or operations with suppliers, vendors, partners, customers, or other businesses.
8. Typically, an intranet includes connections through one or more gateway computers to the outside Internet.	8. An extranet can be viewed as part of a company's intranet that is extended to users outside the company.
9. An intranet uses TCP/IP, HTTP, and other Internet protocols and in general looks like a private version of the Internet. With tunneling, companies can send private messages through the public network, using the public network with special encryption/ decryption and other security safeguards to connect one part of their intranet to another.	9. These can include firewall server management, the issuance and use of digital certificates or similar means of user authentication, encryption of messages, and the use of Virtual Private Networks (VPNs) that tunnel through the public network.
10. The main purpose of an intranet is to share company information and computing resources among employees. An intranet can also be used to facilitate working in groups and for teleconferences.	10. It has also been described as a "state of mind" in which the Internet is perceived as a way to do business with other companies as well as to sell products to customers. An extranet requires security and privacy.
11. Intranet diagram: 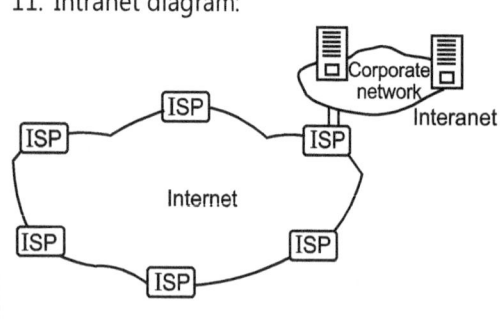	11. Extranet diagram: 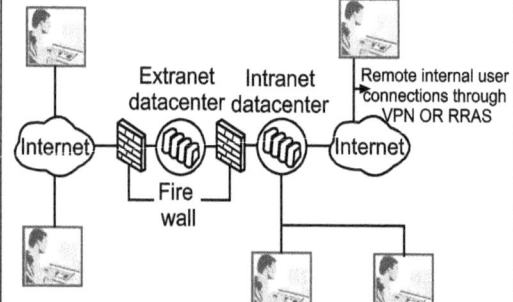

Difference between Intranet and Internet:

Factors	Intranet	Internet
1. Speed	Faster.	Slower.
2. System costs – hardware, software to implement and maintain	Less expensive.	Expensive.
3. Cost to connect/transmit	Economical.	More costly.
4. Information/Knowledge type	Frequently used knowledge; high relevance; in common interest of staff.	May be essential information or knowledge occasionally used
5. Confidentially	Very high and strictly confidential.	Low or moderate generally.
6. Security	Exclusive use to internal users.	Some external websites requires logins and passwords from its restricted users.
7. System failure	System availability is high as system is monitored and attended to.	Unpredictable, systems may be down or not available at certain time periods.
8. Human effort to maintain webpage	Technical staff to ensure system maintenance, control and availability.	Beyond control of intranet technical staff and its general users.
9. Domain knowledge	Trade specific information/ knowledge or central database tend to be put on the intranet.	Knowledge can be beyond trade scope, is trade-related information, or is information that affect trade.
10. Diversity of knowledge	Knowledge diversity is within usable knowledge scope.	Knowledge diversity involves both scopes of usable and unusable knowledge.
11. Temporal consideration	Updated more frequently by internal staff.	Some websites are removed or moved. Some information get outdated.
12. Currency information	Within control of internal web master or database administrator.	Maintenance of information is beyond control.

4.9.4 Web Server and Client

1. Web Server:

- A server is a computer program that provides services to other computer programs (and their users) in the same or other computers.
- A Web Server is a Computer or Combination of computers, which is connected through internet or intranet to serve the clients quests, coming from their web browser.
- It is a large repository of web pages which transfer to the client in response to their request. The client request to the server through protocol such as FTP, HTTP, SMTP etc for their own specific use.
- Every web server has a unique IP address and domain name which identifies that machine on the network.
- A server contains the server software installed on it, which manages the client request and response them.

Fig. 4.43: Web server

- Web server interacts with the client through a web browser. It delivers the web pages to the client and to an application by using the web browser and the HTTP protocols respectively.
- We can also define the web server as the package of large number of programs installed on a computer connected to internet or intranet for downloading the requested files using File Transfer Protocol, serving e-mail and building and publishing web pages.
- Web server provides static content to a web browser by loading a file from a disk and transferring it across the network to the user's web browser. This exchange is intermediated by the browser and the server, communicating using HTTP (HyperText Transfer Protocol).

Working:

- A web server is a specialized type of file server. Its job is to retrieve files from the server's hard drive, format the files for the Web browser, and send them out via the network.
- Web servers are designed to do a great job of sending static content out to a large number of users. The pages delivered by the server are expected to be the same for everyone who visits the server.
- The function of a typical Web server is shown in Fig. 4.44. The user requests a web page. The Web Server finds the web page file in a local directory and sends it back out to the user. When graphic files are requested, the same thing happens. The Web Server finds the requested graphic files and sends them back to the user.

- The web server standards were originally designed to publish static documents on the Internet. There was a limited capability for accessing dynamic content, but this was never intended to support high volume, highly interactive Web applications.

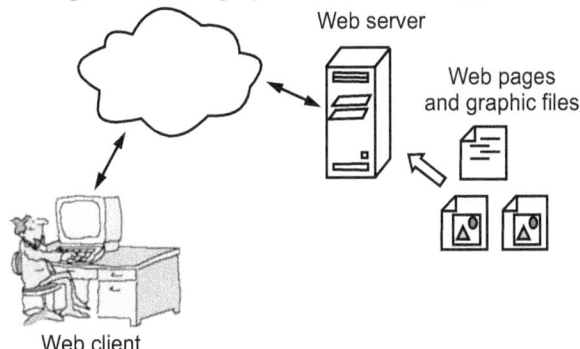

Fig. 4.44: How a Web server works

- Then, as the Internet and Web browsers became popular in the mid-1990's, organizations saw an opportunity to provide web pages that contained dynamic content like stock prices, weather information, inventory levels, and shipping status for a package.
- Web browsers became such a pervasive way to access information that users and organizations desired to access a wide variety of information and applications through their Web browser. So, Web servers had to be extended to allow software application development and access to databases.
- There are many types of web server, Enterprise or organization uses according to their need. Some of the popular category of web servers are:

   (i) **HTTP Server:** It handles HTTP request coming from clients browser and transfer the static pages to client in response to their request. This pages runs of the client browser. It generally contains the static pages.

   (ii) **Application Server:** It is installed database and web servers.

   (iii) **FTP Server:** This type of server is used for file transfer from one machine (Computer) to another using the internet or intranet. It uses File Transfer Protocols to transfer file from one computer to another. Such type of server uses some file transfer policies, authentication, login validation etc.

   (iv) **Apache Tomcat** is popular web server being used today for the implementation of some java technologies. It is a open source software used for implementing web applications.

   (v) **Mail Server:** A Mail Server store and retrieve mail messages from client mail box.

2. **Clients:**
- Independent computers connected to a server are called clients.
- A client is the requesting program or user in a client/server relationship.

- For example, the user of a Web browser is effectively making client requests for pages from servers all over the Web.
- A web client contains two parts: dynamic web pages and the web browser. Dynamic web pages are produced by components that run in the web tier, and a web browser delivers web pages received from the server.
- A web client is also known as a thin client because it does not execute heavy-duty operations such as querying databases, performing complex business tasks, or connecting to legacy applications.
- A web client is actually your browser. It is the browser on you PC/Mac that makes the requests to the remote server. A PC/Mac that uses a web (Client) browser is referred to as a client machine.
- The browser itself is a client in its relationship with the computer that is getting and returning the requested HTML file. The computer handling the request and sending back the HTML file is a server.

4.9.5 WWW

- The term WWW refers to the World Wide Web or simply the Web.
- The World Wide Web consists of all the public websites connected to the internet worldwide, including the client devices (such as computers and cell phones) that access web content.
- The WWW is just one of many applications of the internet and computer networks.
- The World Wide Web is a system of interlinked hypertext documents accessed via the internet. With a web browser, one can view web pages that may contain text, images, videos, and other multimedia, and navigate between them via hyperlinks.
- The World Wide Web is based on technologies like HTML (Hypertext Markup Language), HTTP (Hypertext Transfer Protocol) and Web servers and Web browsers.

4.9.5.1 Definition

- The World Wide Web Consortium (W3C) define WWW as "The World Wide Web is the universe of network-accessible information, an embodiment of human knowledge."

OR

- "An internet-wide distributed hypermedia information retrieval system which provides access to a large universe of documents".

OR

- A technical definition of the World Wide Web is "all the resources and users on the internet that are using the Hypertext Transfer Protocol (HTTP)".

4.9.5.2 How does the WWW Work?

- World Wide Web works on the client-server model.
- A user computer works as a client which can receive and send data to the server.

- When a web page is requested by a user, the browser contacts the requested server (where the website is stored) and by fetching and interpreting the requested files, it displays the web page on the computer screen.
- Information is stored in documents called web pages and the web pages are files stored on computers called Web servers.
- Computers reading the web pages and these web clients view the pages with a program called a web browser.

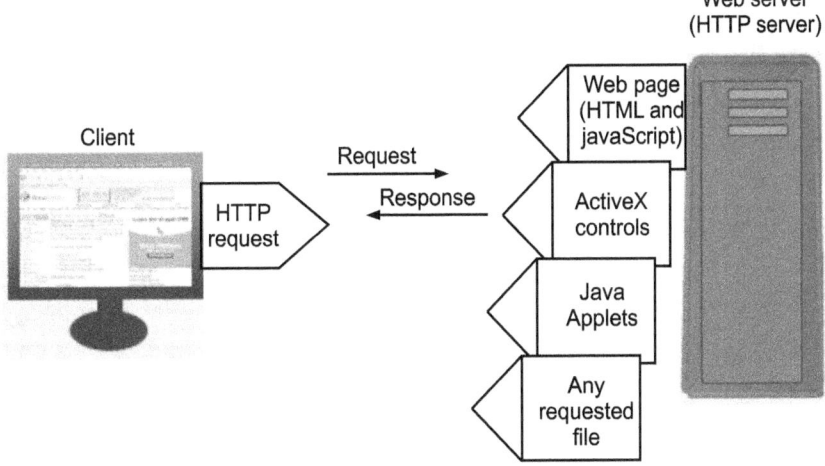

Fig. 4.45: Working of server and client (www client-server model)

4.9.6 Search Engine

- A search engine is a web site that collects and organizes content from all over the internet.
- A web search engine is software code that is designed to search for information on the World Wide Web.
- The search results are generally presented in a line of results often referred to as Search Engine Results Pages (SERP's).
- The information may be a specialist in web pages, images, information and other types of files.
- Some search engines also mine data available in databases or open directories. Unlike web directories, which are maintained only by human editors, search engines also maintain real-time information by running an algorithm on a web crawler.
- Various search engines work, but they all perform three basic tasks:
  1. They **search the Internet or Select pieces of the Internet** based on important words.
  2. They **keep an index of the words** they find, and where they find them.
  3. They **allow users to look for words or combinations of words** found in that index.

- A search engine is a coordinated set of programs that includes:
  1. A spider (also called a "crawler" or a "bot") that goes to every page or representative pages on every website that wants to be searchable and reads it, using hypertext links on each page to discover and read a site's other pages.
  2. **A program that creates a huge index (sometimes called a catalog)** from the pages that have been read.
  3. **A program that receives your search request, compares** it to the entries in the index, and returns results to you.

4.9.6.1 Definition

- We can define a search engine as, "a program designed to help find information stored on a computer system such as the World Wide Web, or a personal computer".

OR

- Search engines are programs that search documents for specified keywords and returns a list of the documents where the keywords were found. A search engine is really a general class of programs, however, the term is often used to specifically describe systems like Google, Bing and Yahoo! Search that enable users to search for documents on the World Wide Web.

OR

- Search engine is a software program that searches a documents and gathers and reports information that contains or is related to specified terms.

4.9.6.2 Popular Search Engines

1. **Google:**
- Google search is a web search engine owned by Google, Inc. (organisation) and is the most used search engine on the web.
- Google receives several hundred million queries each day through its various services.
- Google search was originally developed by Larry Page and Sergey Brin in 1996-1997.

Fig. 4.46: Google search engine (window/view)

2. **Yahoo!:**
- Yahoo! Search is a web search engine, owned by Yahoo!, Inc. and is currently the second largest search engine on the web, after its competitor Google.

- Originally Yahoo! Search started as a web directory of other websites, organized in a hierarchy, as opposed to a searchable index of pages. In the late 1990s, Yahoo! evolved into a full-fledged portal with a search interface and, by 2007, a limited version of selection-based search.
- Yahoo! Search, originally referred to as Yahoo! provided Search interface, would send queries to a searchable index of pages supplemented with its directory of sites. The results were presented to the user under the Yahoo! brand. Originally, none of the actual web crawling and storage/retrieval of data was done by Yahoo! itself.
- In 2001 the searchable index was powered by Inktomi and later was powered by Google until 2004, when Yahoo! Search became independent. Major competitors of Yahoo! Search are: Google Search, Live Search and Ask Search.

Fig. 4.47: Yahoo search engine view

- Searching a web is very easy and simple. For serching a web follow the following steps:
1. Open a search engine like Google.

Fig. 4.48: Google search engine - opened Step 1

2. Then type the web site like pragationline.com.

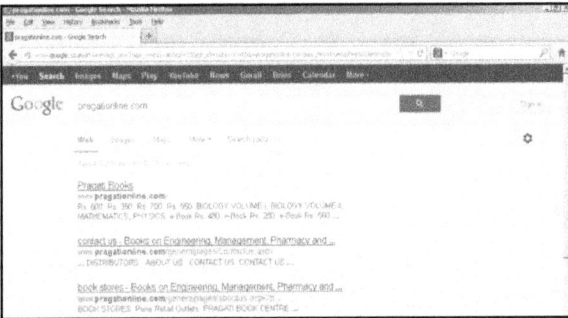

Fig. 4.49: Enter search keywords - Step 2

3. Then click ![button] button which search the website then click pragationline.com which displays following screen:

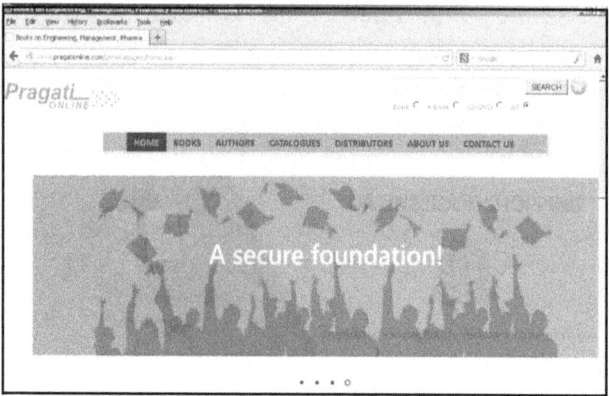

Fig. 4.50: Search results - Step 3

4.10 Internet Service Provider (ISP)

- ISP Short for Internet Service Provider.
- An ISP is a company that provides Internet access to users or subscribers of its service.
- An Internet Service Provider (ISP, also called Internet Access Provider or IAP) is a business or organization that provides consumers or businesses access to the Internet and related services. In the past, most ISPs were run by the phone companies.

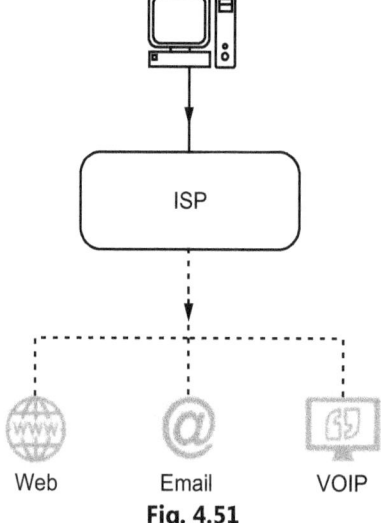

Fig. 4.51

4.10.1 What is an ISP?

- An Internet Service Provider (ISP) is an organisation through which you can arrange Internet access. ISPs are typically commercial or community organisation offering broadband or dial-up access, usually alongwith other services such as, Web hosting and, e-mail etc.

- Internet Service Provider are the agencies that help you connect your computer to the Internet. The first cross-country link through the Internet was established in 1970. But, till date there are many people who are not aware of the working of the world wide web. The answer is the ISP, which connects you to the Internet.
- An Internet Service Provider (ISP) is a company that provides third parties access to the Internet. Many ISP also offer other related services such as Web site design and virtual hosting.

4.10.2 How does an ISP Work?

- Fig. 4.52 shows simple flowchart to help you understand the working of an ISP.

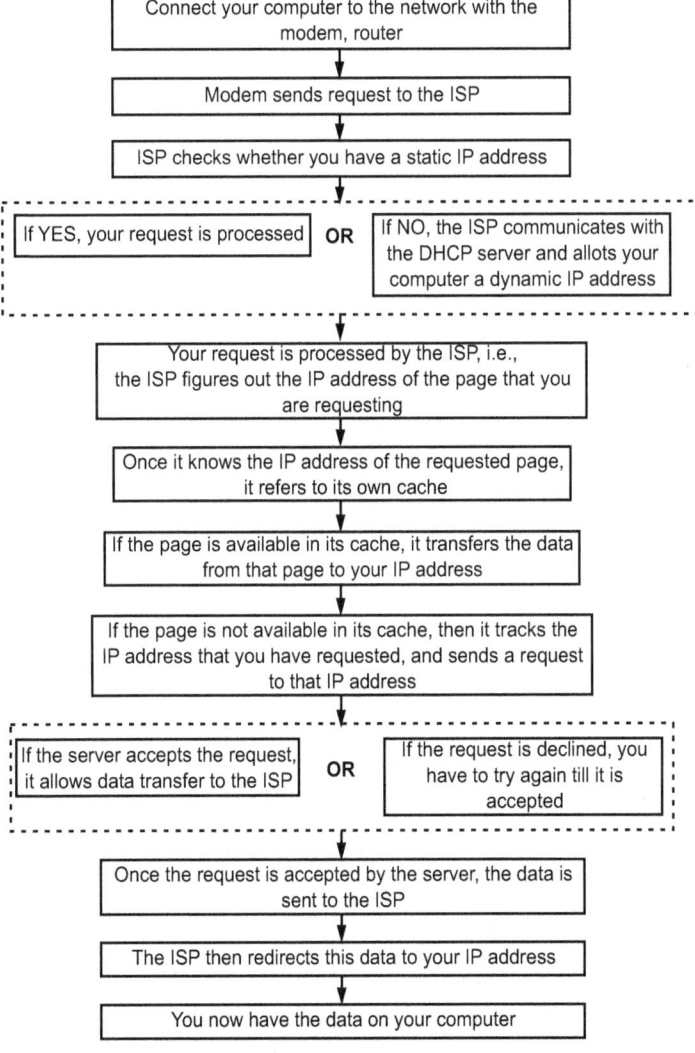

Fig. 4.52

- Let's start with the procedure right from the local computer. Home computers connect to the ISP using telephone cables or broadband Internet connections. Large networks like that of educational institutes connect to the ISP using a D1 line. The way of logging into the ISP is same for both. For connecting to the Internet, you will need a modem and an ISP subscription.
- Let's try to understand the entire procedure in a step-by-step process:
    - The first step is to login into the ISP using the user information provided to you by your ISP. Here, you enter the username, password and telephone number of the ISP.
    - Once, the ISP receives your information in its modem pool, it verifies if you are an authentic user or not.
    - Once, the user authentication process is done, the ISP provides you with a dynamic IP address using the DHCP (Dynamic Host Control Protocol). If you have bought a static IP from your ISP, then this step is not required. However, buying a static IP will cost you a lot.
    - Now, you are allowed to browse any web page through your web browser. When you type in the name of the URL (Uniform Resource Locator) on the address bar, you are actually requesting for the IP address of the server machine, that holds those web pages.
    - The information is received at the modem pool. Once this information is received, the ISP connects the subscriber to the modem pool.
    - The requested server machine is reached through an array of dedicated lines and routers.
    - Once the ISP finds the required IP address, it transfers the requested web pages to the source IP address.
    - Some ISPs store every page that is requested by their users in their own cache. So the next time you request the same page, if it is still in the cache your request is directly fulfilled by the ISP without contacting the server. If the page has been flushed from the cache, the above procedure is repeated.
    - ISPs have large caches and are transferring data to and from hundreds of computers at super fast speeds. A pause in their service can cause losses, and inconvenience to their customers, and their improper functioning can result in the network getting jammed! Hence, it is very important to maintain ISPs properly and have the necessary equipment required to do so. Cooling devices and backup power supplies are among the important components used by an ISP to ensure its smooth operation. These components are of utmost importance for the effective functioning of the ISP.

4.10.3 ISP Services

- Various ISP services are listed below:

1. **Digital Subscriber Line (DSL):**

- To understand DSL, you first need to know a couple of things about a normal telephone line the kind that telephone professionals call **POTS** (Plain Old Telephone Service). One of the ways that POTS makes the most of the telephone company's wires and equipment is by limiting the frequencies that the switches, telephones and other equipment will carry. Human voices, speaking in normal conversational tones, can be carried in a frequency range of 0 to 3,400 Hertz. This range of frequencies is tiny. For example, compare this to the range of most stereo speakers, which cover from roughly 20 Hertz to 20,000 Hertz. And the wires themselves have the potential to handle frequencies up to several million Hertz in most cases.

- The use of such a small portion of the wire's total bandwidth is historical remember that the telephone system has been in place, using a pair of copper wires to each home, for about a century. By limiting the frequencies carried over the lines, the telephone system can pack lots of wires into a very small space without worrying about interference between lines. Modern equipment that sends digital rather than analog data can safely use much more of the telephone line's capacity. DSL does just that.

- **Types of DSL:**

  CDSL: CDSL (Consumer DSL) is a version of DSL, trademarked by Rockwell Corp., that is somewhat slower than ADSL (1 Mbps downstream, probably less upstream) and has the advantage that a "splitter" does not need to be installed at the user's end.

  G.Lite or DSL Lite: G.lite (also known as DSL Lite, splitterless ADSL, and Universal ADSL) is essentially a slower ADSL that does not require splitting of the line at the user end but manages to split it for the user remotely at the telephone company. This saves the cost of what the phone companies call "the truck roll." G.Lite, officially ITU-T standard G-992.2, provides a data rate from 1.544 Mbps to 6 Mpbs downstream and from 128 Kbps to 384 Kbps upstream. G.Lite is expected to become the most widely installed form of DSL.

  HDSL: HDSL (High bit-rate Digital Subscriber Line), one of the earliest forms of DSL, is used for wideband digital transmission within a corporate site and between the telephone company and a customer. The main characteristic of HDSL is that it is symmetrical: an equal amount of bandwidth is available in both directions. HDSL can carry as much on a single wire of twisted-pair cable as can be carried on a T1 line (up to 1.544 Mbps) in North America or an E1 line (up to 2.048 Mbps) in Europe over a somewhat longer range and is considered an alternative to a T1 or E1 connection.

IDSL: IDSL (ISDN DSL) is somewhat, of a misnomer since it's really closer to ISDN data rates and service at 128 Kbps than to the much higher rates of ADSL.

RADSL: RADSL (Rate-Adaptive DSL) is an ADSL technology from Westell in which software is able to determine the rate at which signals can be transmitted on a given customer phone line and adjust the delivery rate accordingly. Westell's FlexCap2 system uses RADSL to deliver from 640 Kbps to 2.2 Mbps downstream and from 272 Kbps to 1.088 Mbps upstream over an existing line.

SDSL: SDSL (Symmetric DSL) is similar to HDSL with a single twisted-pair line, carrying 1.544 Mbps (U.S. and Canada) or 2.048 Mbps (Europe) each direction on a duplex line. It's symmetric because the data rate is the same in both directions.

UDSL: UDSL (Unidirectional DSL) is a proposal from a European company. It's a unidirectional version of HDSL.

VDSL: VDSL (Very high data rate DSL) is a developing technology that promises much higher data rates over relatively short distances (between 51 and 55 Mbps over lines up to 1,000 feet or 300 meters in length). It's envisioned that VDSL may emerge somewhat after ADSL is widely deployed and co-exist with it. The transmission technology (CAP, DMT, or other) and its effectiveness in some environments is not yet determined. A number of standards organizations are working on it.

x2/DSL: x2/DSL is a modem from 3 Com that supports 56 Kbps modem communication, but is upgradeable through new software installation to ADSL when it becomes available in the user's area. 3 Com calls it "the last modem you will ever need".

2. **Asymmetric Digital Subscriber Line (ADSL):**

- ADSL technology is asymmetric. It allows more bandwidth downstream-from an NSP's central office to the customer site-than upstream from the subscriber to the central office.

- This asymmetry, combined with always-on access (which eliminates call setup), makes ADSL ideal for Internet/intranet surfing, video-on-demand, and remote LAN access. Users of these applications typically download much more information than they send.

Questions

1. Define the term Internet.
2. What is meant by Extranet?
3. What is Intranet? State its advantages.
4. What are the advantages and disadvantages of internet?
5. State advantages and disadvantages of internet.
6. What is internet? What are its uses?
7. What is meant by search engine?
8. Enlist most popular search engines.
9. With the help of diagram describe working of WWW.
10. What is network topology?
11. Define Bus topology?
12. Define Ring topology.
13. Explain bus topology with suitable diagram.
14. Explain star topology with suitable diagram.
15. Explain briefly ring topology.
16. With neat diagram explain mesh topology.
17. Explain hybrid topology.
18. State advantages and disadvantages of ring topology.
19. Describe tree topology.
20. State the advantages and disadvantages of bus topology.
21. State the advantages and disadvantages of star topology.
22. State the advantages and disadvantages of tree topology.
23. State the advantages and disadvantages of mesh topology.
24. Describe network topology. State any four topologies.
25. Compare hub and switch.
26. With the help of neat diagram describe the working of routers. Also enlist types of routers.
27. With the help of neat diagram describe the functioning of gateway.
28. Explain hybrid topology in detail. Also compare star and ring topology.
29. What is hub? List the types of hub.
30. What is repeater? Explain in detail.
31. What is bridge? Explain its different types in detail.
32. List the categories of transmission media.

33. List the types of guided media.
34. List the types of unguided media.
35. Define fiber optic.
36. Draw and explain the unshielded twisted pair cable.
37. Explain shielded twisted pair cable.
38. Describe with suitable diagram of coaxial cable. State its advantages.
39. Explain the different propagation modes.
40. Enlist the two advantages and two disadvantages of optical fiber.
41. Compare UTP and STP cable.
42. What is ISP? Explain in detail.
43. Write short note on:
    (i) Web server
    (ii) Web client.

Chapter 5...

Introduction to R.D.B.M.S.

Contents ...

5.1 Introduction
5.2 Introduction to R.D.B.M.S.
    5.2.1 Definition
    5.2.2 Characteristics
    5.2.3 Features
    5.2.4 Components of R.D.B.M.S.
    5.2.5 Difference between D.B.M.S. and R.D.B.M.S.
    5.2.6 Examples of D.B.M.S. and R.D.B.M.S. Softwares
    5.2.7 Advantages of R.D.B.M.S.
    5.2.8 Disadvantages of R.D.B.M.S.
    5.2.9 Keys of R.D.B.M.S.
5.3 Normalization
    5.3.1 Purpose of Normalization
    5.3.2 Steps of Normalization
    5.3.3 Advantages
    5.3.4 Disadvantages
    5.3.5 Normal Forms
        5.3.5.1 First Normal Form (1NF)
        5.3.5.2 Second Normal Form (2NF)
        5.3.5.3 Third Normal Form (3NF)
5.4 Entity Relationships
    5.4.1 Features
    5.4.2 Components
    5.4.3 Examples
5.5 Use of Simple SQL Commands
    5.5.1 Introduction to SQL
    5.5.2 Data Types
    5.5.3 SQL Languages and their Commands
        5.5.3.1 Data Definition Language (DDL)
        5.5.3.2 Data Manipulation Language (DML)
        5.5.3.3 SQL Queries
- Questions

5.1 Introduction

- Data is the collection of facts stored in the database.
- Data is a representation of facts, concepts, or instructions in a formalized manner suitable for communication, interpretation, or processing by humans or by automated means.
- The term data can be defined as "a set of isolated and unrelated raw facts with an implicit meaning".
- Database is a collection of data.
- A database is a collection of interrelated data that are stored in controllable and retrievable form. The collection represents static information of a group of related data that collectively makes sense. In this way, the information can be stored and retrieved quickly with ease using databases.
- The database is used to store information useful to an organization. Database contains information about one particular enterprise or an organization.
- A database is a collection of related data elements such as, Tables (entities), Columns (fields or attributes), Rows (records).

Definition of Database:

- A database is an application that manages data and allows fast storage and retrieval of that data.

OR

- A database is a data structure that stores organized information.

OR

- A database is a collection of information that is organized so that it can easily be accessed, managed, and updated.
- Databases are organized by fields, records and files. These are described briefly as follows:
    1. **Fields:** It is the smallest unit of the data that has meaning to its users and is also called data item or data element. Name, Address and Telephone number are examples of fields. These are represented in the database by a value.
    2. **Records:** A record is a collection of logically related fields and each field possesses a fixed number of bytes and is of fixed data type.
    3. **Files:** A file is a collection of related records.

Database Management System (D.B.M.S.):

- A Database Management System (D.B.M.S.) is an integrated set of programs used to create and maintain a database.
- A D.B.M.S. is a collection of interrelated data and a set of programs to access those data. The collection of data is usually referred as the database, contains information relevant to an enterprise.

- The primary goal of a D.B.M.S. is to provide a way to store and retrieve the database information in convenient and efficient manner.
- A Database Management System (D.B.M.S.) is a computer program for managing a permanent, self-descriptive repository of data. This repository of data is called a database and is store in one or more files.

Examples:
1. **Manufacturing company:** Which stores product_id, name, price etc., data.
2. **Bank:** Which stores customers banking data such as cust_name, balance, acc_no. etc.
3. **Hospital:** Which stores data such as Dr_name, Patient_name, Admit_date, discharge_date etc.
4. **University:** Which stores data such as college_name, address, courses, staff-details etc.

- Some of the popular relational database management systems include:
    1. Microsoft Access,
    2. Microsoft SQL Server,
    3. MySQL, and
    4. Oracle.

Definition of D.B.M.S.:
- A Database Management System [D.B.M.S.] is a software system that allows user to define, manipulate and process the data in a database, in order to produce meaningful information.

OR

- D.B.M.S. is a collection of data (database) and programs to access that data. The goal of D.B.M.S. is to store, retrieve, and display information (attribute).

OR

- A database management system (D.B.M.S.) is system software used to manage the organization, storage, access, security and integrity of data in a structured database.

Functions of a D.B.M.S.:
1. Data definition - How data is to be stored and organised.
2. Database Creation - Storing data in a defined database
3. Data Retrieval - Querying and reporting
4. Updating - Changing the contents of the database.
5. Programming user facilities for system development.
6. Database revision and restructuring
7. Database Integrity control
8. Performance monitoring.

Applications of D.B.M.S.:

1. **Banking:** For customer information, accounts loans and banking transactions.
2. **Airlines:** For reservations and schedule information. Airlines were among the first to use database in a geographically disturbed manner-terminals situated around the world accessed the central database system through phone lines and other data networks.
3. **Universities:** For student information, course registrations and grades.
4. **Credit card transactions:** For purchases on credit cards and generation of monthly statements.
5. **Telecommunications:** For keeping records of calls made, generating monthly bills, maintaining balances on prepaid calling cards and storing information about the communication networks.
6. **Finance:** For storing information about holdings, sales and purchase of financial instruments such as stocks and bonds.
7. **Sales:** For customer, product and purchase information.
8. **Manufacturing:** For management of supply chain and for tracking production of items in factories, inventories of items in warehouses/stores and orders for items.
9. **Human Resources:** For information about employees, salaries, payroll taxes and benefits and for generation of paychecks.
10. **Web Based Services:** For taking web users feedback, responses, resource sharing etc.
11. **E-commerce:** Integration of heterogeneous information sources (for example, catalogs) for business activity such as online shopping, booking of holiday package, consulting a doctor, etc.
12. **Education:** Schools and colleges use databases for course registration, result, and other information.

5.2 Introduction to R.D.B.M.S.

- R.D.B.M.S. stands for **R**elational **D**ata**B**ase **M**anagement **S**ystem.
- R.D.B.M.S. is the basis for SQL, and for all modern database systems like MS SQL Server, IBM DB2, Oracle, MySQL, and Microsoft Access.
- A Relational database management system (R.D.B.M.S.) is a database management system (D.B.M.S.) that is based on the relational model as introduced by E. F. Codd.

5.2.1 Definition

- A simple definition of R.D.B.M.S. is: "It is a database management system where the data are organized as tables of data values and all the operations on the data work on the these tables"

OR

- A relational database management system is a database management system used to manage relational databases.

OR

- R.D.B.M.S. is a type of database management system (D.B.M.S.) that stores data in the form of related tables.

5.2.2 Characteristics

- Various characteristics of R.D.B.M.S. are:
    1. **Data abstraction:** Relational abstraction enhances program-data independence.
    2. **Self-describing data:** Metadata describing structure of data stored together with data.
    3. **Concurrency:** Supporting shared concurrent access (transactions).
    4. **Support for multiple views:** External users can be provided with different views of the data.
    5. **Security:** Privacy/Confidentiality, Integrity, Availability, Accountability.

5.2.3 Features

- Features of R.D.B.M.S. are listed below:
    1. Provides data to be stored in tables.
    2. Persists data in the form of rows and columns.
    3. Provides facility primary key, to uniquely identify the rows.
    4. Creates indexes for quicker data retrieval.
    5. Provides a virtual table creation in which sensitive data can be stored and simplified query can be applied, (views).
    6. Sharing a common column in two or more tables (primary key and foreign key).
    7. Provides multi user accessibility that can be controlled by individual users.

5.2.4 Components of R.D.B.M.S

- Various components of R.D.B.M.S. are as shown in Fig. 5.1.

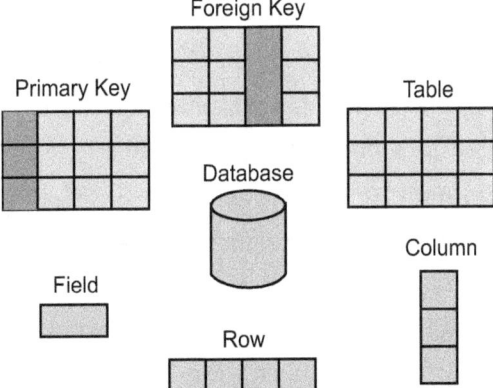

Fig. 5.1: Relational database components

- A **Table** is a basic storage structure of an R.D.B.M.S. and consists of columns and rows. A table represents an entity. For example, the E_DEPT table stores information about the departments of an organization.

- A record, also called a row of data, is each individual entry that exists in a table. A **Row** is a combination of column values in a table and is identified by a primary key. Rows are also known as **records**. For example, a row in the table E_DEPT contains information about one department.

- A column is a vertical entity in a table that contains all information associated with a specific field in a table. A **Column** is a collection of one type of data in a table. Columns represent the attributes of an object. Each column has a column name and contains values that are bound by the same type and size. For example, a column in the table E_DEPT specifies the names of the departments in the organization.

- Every table is broken up into smaller entities called fields. A **Field** is an intersection of a row and a column. A field contains one data value. If there is no data in the field, the field is said to contain a NULL value.

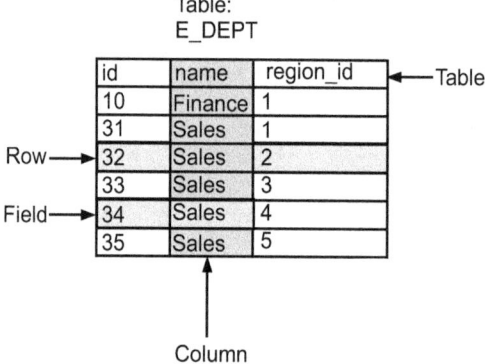

Fig. 5.2: Table, Row, Column and Field

- A **Primary key** is a column or a combination of columns that is used to uniquely identify each row in a table. For example, the column containing department numbers in the E_DEPT table is created as a **primary key** and therefore, every department number is different. A primary key must contain a value. It cannot contain a NULL value.

- A **Foreign key** is a column or set of columns that refers to a primary key in the same table or another table. You use foreign keys to establish principle connections between, or within, tables. A foreign key must either match a primary key or else be NULL. Rows are connected logically when required. The logical connections are based upon conditions that define a relationship between corresponding values, typically between a primary key and a matching foreign key. This relational method of linking provides great flexibility as it is independent of physical links between records.

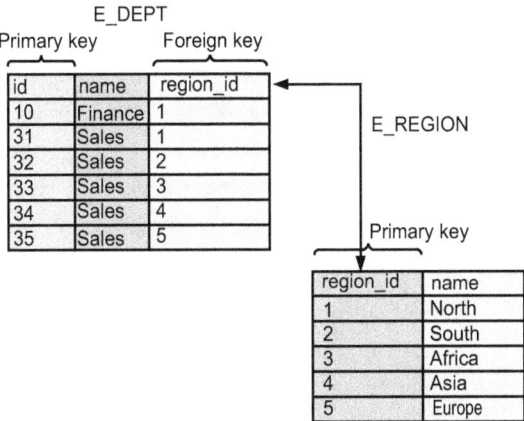

Fig. 5.3: Primary and Foreign key

5.2.5 Difference between D.B.M.S. and R.D.B.M.S.

D.B.M.S.	R.D.B.M.S.
1. D.B.M.S. stands for DataBase Management System.	1. R.D.B.M.S. stands for Relational DataBase Management System.
2. In D.B.M.S. no relationship concept.	2. It is used to establish the relationship concept between two database objects, i.e. tables.
3. It supports single user only.	3. It supports multiple users.
4. It treats Data as files internally.	4. It treats data as Tables internally.
5. It supports 3 rules of E.F. Codd out off 12 rules.	5. It supports minimum 6 rules of E.F. Codd.
6. It requires low software and hardware requirements.	6. It requires high softwares and hardware requirements.
7. D.B.M.S. is used for simpler business applications.	7. R.D.B.M.S. is used for more complex applications.
8. In D.B.M.S. normalization process will not be present.	8. R.D.B.M.S. fully supports normalization.
9. FoxPro, IMS are examples.	9. SQL-Server, Oracle are examples.

5.2.6 Examples of D.B.M.S. and R.D.B.M.S. Softwares

- Various D.B.M.S. and R.D.B.M.S. softwares are listed below:
    1. **FoxPro:** FoxPro is a database management system. It means that using this software we can handle the data in different way.
    2. **Microsoft Access:** Microsoft Access is a database management system from Microsoft that combines the relational Microsoft Jet Database Engine with a graphical user interface and software-development tools.

3. **MySQL:** MySQL is a fast, easy-to-use R.D.B.M.S. used being used for many small and big businesses. MySQL handles a large subset of the functionality of the most expensive and powerful database packages.,
4. **Microsoft SQL Server:** Microsoft SQL Server is a relational database management system developed by Microsoft. As a database, it is a software product whose primary function is to store and retrieve data as requested by other software applications, be it those on the same computer or those running on another computer across a network (including the Internet).
5. **Oracle:** Oracle is a fourth generation relational database management system. In general, a database management system (D.B.M.S.) must be able to reliably manage a large amount of data in a multi-user environment so that many users can concurrently access the same data. All this must be accomplished while delivering high performance to the users of the database.
6. **FileMaker Pro:** FileMaker Pro is easy to use database software for the Mac, Windows and other platforms. It is particularly useful to Mac users because the Access database program is not part of Microsoft Office for the Mac.
7. **IBM DB2:** IBM's DB2 is a relational database management system, DB2 is a collection of computer software programs that perform this particular type of task. DB2 is designed to make the storage and analysis of data easier.
8. **Ingres:** Ingres is open source relational database management system that helps in reducing down the various IT costs and on the other hand provides the class features that can be expected from the high level database.
9. **SQlite:** SQLite is an embedded relational database engine. Its developers call it a self-contained, serverless, zero-configuration and transactional SQL database engine. SQLite is used in Solaris 10 and Mac OS operating systems, iPhone or Skype.

5.2.7 Advantages of R.D.B.M.S.
- Various advantages of R.D.B.M.S. are listed below:
    1. **Data Structure:** The table format is simple and easy for database users to understand and use. R.D.B.M.S. provide data access using a natural structure and organization of the data. Database queries can search any column for matching entries.
    2. **Multi-User Access:** R.D.B.M.S. allow multiple database users to access a database simultaneously. Built-in locking and transactions management functionality allow users to access data as it is being changed, prevents collisions between two users updating the data, and keeps users from accessing partially updated records.
    3. **Privileges:** Authorization and privilege control features in an R.D.B.M.S. allow the database administrator to restrict access to authorized users, and grant privileges to individual users based on the types of database tasks they need to perform. Authorization can be defined based on the remote client IP address in combination with user authorization, restricting access to specific external computer systems.

4. **Network Access:** R.D.B.M.S. provide access to the database through a server daemon, a specialized software program that listens for requests on a network, and allows database clients to connect to and use the database. Users do not need to be able to log in to the physical computer system to use the database, providing convenience for the users and a layer of security for the database. Network access allows developers to build desktop tools and Web applications to interact with databases.

5. **Speed:** The relational database model is not the fastest data structure. R.D.B.M.S. advantages, such as simplicity, make the slower speed a fair trade-off. Optimizations built into an R.D.B.M.S. and the design of the databases, enhance performance, allowing R.D.B.M.S. to perform more than fast enough for most applications and data sets. Improvements in technology, increasing processor speeds and decreasing memory and storage costs allow systems administrators to build incredibly fast systems that can overcome any database performance shortcomings.

6. **Maintenance:** R.D.B.M.S. feature maintenance utilities that provide database administrators with tools to easily maintain, test, repair and back up the databases housed in the system. Many of the functions can be automated using built-in automation in the R.D.B.M.S., or automation tools available on the operating system.

7. **Language:** R.D.B.M.S. support a generic language called "Structured Query Language" (SQL). The SQL syntax is simple, and the language uses standard English language keywords and phrasing, making it fairly intuitive and easy to learn. Many R.D.B.M.S. add non-SQL, database-specific keywords, functions and features to the SQL language

8. **Consistency:** Data is guarantees to be consistent. Irrespective of the number of Custom Web Design simultaneously accessing it. An R.D.B.M.S. always implements suitable locking mechanisms to prevent data inconsistency. A transaction either goes through fully or not at all i.e. it is either "committed "or "rolled back".

9. **Recoverability:** Irrespective of the type of failure, it is always possible to recover the data base upto the most recent consistent state. This means that if recovery measures are correctly implemented you would not lose all days work. And thus no need to reenter.

10. **Distributability:** Database can be distributed in more than one physical location. Irrespective of this, application's view of the database remains same as though it is in a single location. Applications need not undergo any change if the distribution of the data changes.

11. **Support for IV (4th) generation languages:** R.D.B.M.S. support 4GL. Today, there is even a standard 4GL in the structured query Language (SQL) form. The main difference between 4GLs and 3GLs is that in the former the user needs to specify what is required and not how it has to be done.

5.2.8 Disadvantages of R.D.B.M.S.
- Disadvantages of R.D.B.M.S. are listed below:
    1. Possibility of poor design and implementation.
    2. Relational databases do not have enough storage area to handle data such as images, digital and audio/video.
    3. The requirement that information must be in tables where relationships between entities are defined by values.
    4. **Cost:** One disadvantage of relational databases is the expensive of setting up and maintaining the database system. In order to set up a relational database, you generally need to purchase special software so it increases cost
    5. **Abundance of Information:** Advances in the complexity of information cause another drawback to relational databases. Relational databases are made for organizing data by common characteristics. Complex images, numbers, designs and multimedia products defy easy categorization leading the way for a new type of database called object-relational database management systems. These systems are designed to handle the more complex applications and have the ability to be scalable.
    6. **Structured Limits:** Some relational databases have limits on field lengths. When you design the database, you have to specify the amount of data you can fit into a field. Some names or search queries are shorter than the actual, and this can lead to data loss.
    7. **Isolated Databases:** Complex relational database systems can lead to these databases becoming "islands of information" where the information cannot be shared easily from one large system to another. Often, with big firms or institutions, you find relational databases grew in separate divisions differently.

5.2.9 Keys of R.D.B.M.S.
- Every table must have some columns or combination of columns which uniquely identify each row in the table. For that we require a key.
- A key is simply a field used to identify a record. In other words, a key is relation of subset of attributes with following properties:
    1. The value of key is unique for each tuple.
    2. No data redundancy.

1. **Primary Key:**
- The candidate key that you choose to identify each row uniquely is called the primary key. In the table Employee, if you choose Empid# to identify rows uniquely, Empid# is the primary key.

Employee

Empid#	Empname	Salary
1437	Kalaiselvi	5000
1337	Meena	5000
1137	Diana	5000

2. Candidate Key:

- The attribute which posses the unique identification property in a relation is called as candidate key.
- We can define "an attribute in a table that uniquely identifies a row is called a candidate key".
- There can be more than one candidate keys in a relation. Candidate key should have following things:

  (a) It must be unique

  (b) A candidate key's value must exist. It cannot be null.

  (c) The value of the candidate key must be stable. It's value cannot change outside the control of the system. In customer table, various employees were working and having unique identification number called as social security number (SSN)

Customer name	SSN	Basic
John	001-256	₹ 14,000
Martin	005-123	₹ 2,000
Paster	008-200	₹ 1,000
Mary	101-401	₹ 18,000
Johns	102-030	₹ 48,000

Candidate key

3. Alternate Key:

- A candidate key that is not chosen as a primary key is an alternate key. In the table Purchase If you choose Serial# as the primary key, Itemcode is the alternate key. It is important that you understand that a primary key is the only sure way to identify the rows of a table.
- Hence, an alternate key may have the value NULL. A NULL value is not to be permitted in a primary key since it would be difficult to uniquely identify rows containing NULL values.

Purchase

Serial#	Itemcode	Price
01437	1454	500
01438	1667	500
01439	1777	500

4. Composite Key:

- In certain tables, a single attribute cannot be used to identify rows uniquely and a combination of two or more attributes is used as a primary key. Such keys are called composite keys.
- Consider the following table, customer, which is used to maintain the purchase made by various customers.

Customers

Custcode	Productcode	Quantity
c0147	P454	50
c0148	P777	55
c0147	P777	20

- You can see all values are not unique for any of the attributes. However, a combination of Custcode and Productcode results in all unique values. Hence, the combination can be used as a composite primary key.

5. Foreign Key:

- If any key in a given relation has reference to the value of a primary key of some other relation then it is called as foreign key.
- Foreign key can have duplicate values it is used to search a record from two relations.

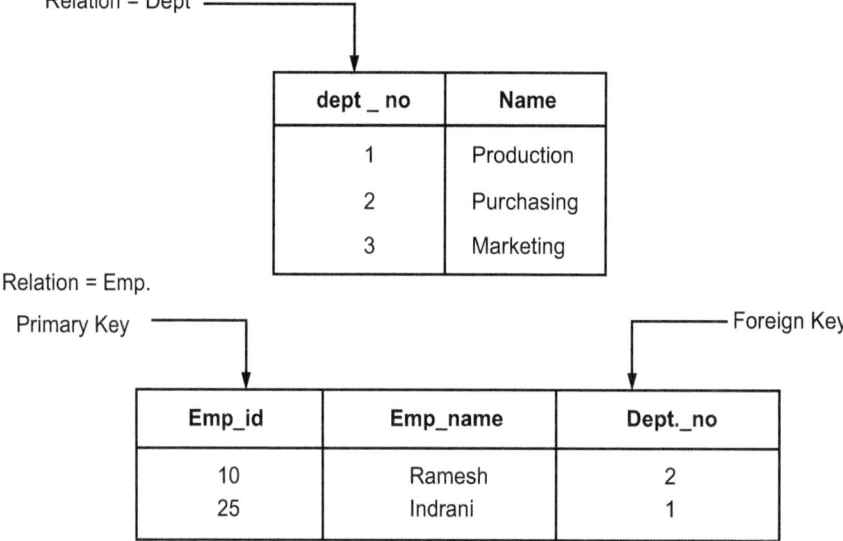

6. Super Key:

- Super key is a set of one or more attributes which taken collectively allows us to identify uniquely an entity in the entity set.

Integrity Rules:

- Data integrity ensures that the data entered into the database by the user is checked for its correctness as is the data that is supposed to go into the database.
- Thus, the data gets automatically validated when it is entered as per the instructions or commands of the designer and by this way R.D.B.M.S. ensures that the application is of a high degree of data security and integrity.
- R.D.B.M.S. ensures data integrity through automatic validation of data using integrity constraints. The integrity constraints are non-procedural constructs and by just specifying those, the designer can automate the validation process at the time of data entry.
- Popular integrity constraints are NOT NULL, UNIQUE, PRIMARY KEY, FOREIGN KEY and CHECK constraints.
- Data integrity falls into the following categories:
    1. **Entity integrity:** Entity integrity ensures that each row can be uniquely identified by an attribute called the primary key. The primary key cannot have a NULL value.
    2. **Domain integrity:** Domain integrity refers to the range of valid entries for a given column. It ensures that there are only valid entries in the column.
    3. **Referential integrity:** Referential integrity ensures that for every value of a foreign key, there is matching value of the primary key.

5.3 Normalization

- Data normalization is a process of refining database structures to improve the speed at which data can be accessed and to increase database integrity.
- Normalization is the process of efficiently organizing data in a database.
- There are two goals of the normalization process:
    1. Eliminating redundant data (for example, storing the same data in more than one table) and
    2. Ensuring data dependencies.
- Normalization is a technique that can be applied to data to ensure that a set of tables is derived that contains no redundant data.
- Normalization is a process of simplifying the relationship between data elements in a record. It is the transformation of complex data stores to a set of smaller, stable data structures.
- Normalized data structures are simpler, more stable and are easier to maintain. Normalization can therefore be defined as a process of simplifying the relationship between data elements in a record.

5.3.1 Purpose for Normalization

- We normalize the relational database management system because of the following reasons:
    1. To structure the data so that there is no repetition of data, this helps in saving space.
    2. To permit simple retrieval of data in response to query and report requests.
    3. To simplify the maintenance of the data through updates, insertions and deletions.
    4. To reduce the need to restructure or reorganize data when new application requirements arise.
    5. Minimize data redundancy i.e. no unnecessarily duplication of data.
    6. To make database structure flexible i.e. it should be possible to add new data values and rows without reorganizing the database structure.
    7. Data should be consistent throughout the database i.e. it should not suffer from following anomalies.
        (i) **Insert Anomaly:** Due to lack of data i.e., all the data available for insertion such that null values in keys should be avoided. This kind of anomaly can seriously damage a database
        (ii) **Update Anomaly:** It is due to data redundancy i.e. multiple occurrences of same values in a column. This can lead to inefficiency.
        (iii) **Deletion Anomaly:** It leads to loss of data for rows that are not stored else where. It could result in loss of vital data.

5.3.2 Steps of Normalization

- Systems analysts should be familiar with the steps in normalization, since this process can improve the quality of design for an application.
- Starting with a data store developed for a data dictionary the analyst normalizes a data structure in three steps. Each step involves an important procedure to simplify the data structure.
- It consists of basic three steps:
    1. First Normal form, which decomposes all data, groups into two-dimensional records.
    2. Second Normal Form, which eliminates do not fully depend on the primary key of the record.
    3. Third Normal Form, which eliminates any relationships that, contain transitive dependencies.

- Fig. 5.4 shows steps of normalization.

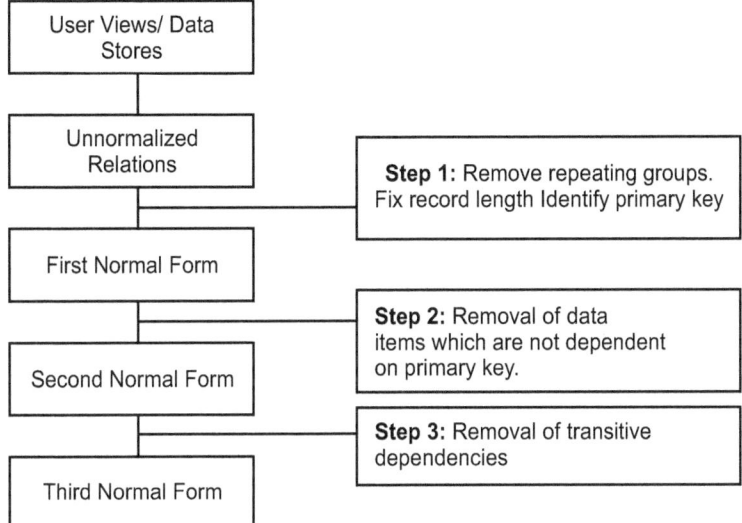

Fig. 5.4: Steps of normalization

5.3.3 Advantages

- Advantages of normalization are listed below:
    1. Avoids data modification (INSERT/DELETE/UPDATE) anomalies
    2. Greater flexibility in getting the expected data in atomic granular
    3. Fewer null values and less opportunity for inconsistency
    4. A better handle on database security
    5. Increased storage efficiency
    6. Easier to maintain data structure i.e. it is easy to perform operations and complex queries can be easily handled.
    7. Normalization minimizes data duplication.

5.3.4 Disadvantages

- Disadvantages of normalization are listed below:
    1. Requires much more CPU, memory, and I/O to process thus normalized data gives reduced database performance
    2. Requires more joins to get the desired result.
    3. Maintenance overhead. The higher the level of normalization, the greater the number of tables in the database.

5.3.5 Normal Forms

5.3.5.1 First Normal Form (1NF)

- **Definition:** "A relation is said to be in 1NF if the values in the domain of each attribute of the relation are atomic i.e. only one value associated with each attribute. A database system is in 1NF if every relation in the system is in 1NF".

- The first rule of data normalization states that you should make a separate table for each set of related columns and give each table a primary key. Databases that hold to this first rule of normalization are said to be in the First Normal Form (1NF).
- The first rule of data normalization is to eliminate repeating groups of data in a data table.
- The basic improvement the analyst should make to such a record structure is to design the record structure so that all records in the file are of fixed length.
- A repeating group, that is, the reoccurrence of a data item or group of data items within a record, is actually another relation. This is removed from the record and treated as an additional record structure, or relation.
- First Normal Form -Employee Record:

Emp. No.	Name	Emp. Details	Salary	Bank Details	Income Tax Details
A01	Jose				
A02	Joseph				

Emp. No.	MMYY	Net Paid
A01	195	3600
A01	196	3800
A01	197	3600
A01	198	3500
A02	199	6000

- As mentioned above the first normal form is carried out by removing the repeating group. In this case we remove the Annual salary earned items and include them in anew file or relation called Annual Salary earned record. Employee number is still the primary key in the employee record. A combination of employee number and MMYY is the primary key in the annual salary earned record.
- We thus form two record structures of fixed length: Employee record consisting of Employee no., employee name, employee details (department code, grade, date of joining, exit code and exit date), bank details (bank c ode, bank name, address, employees A/C no).
- Annual salary earned record consisting of - employee no., month & year (MMYY) and net paid.

- In the attributes mentioned above, the firstNormal form must not contain repeated groups. Here the repeated groups are products. When the Invoice Attribute is in 1st Normal Form, the tables would be:

Invoice_Master	Invoice_Item
Invoice_code	**Invoice_No**
Inv_date	**item_code**
Order_code	ORD_qty
Order_qty	Cust
Cust_code	Ord_value
Cust_name	description
Address	
Invoice_value	

- The attributes that are indicated as bold denote primary key.

5.3.5.2 Second Normal Form (2NF)

- **Definition:** "A relation r is in Second Normal Form (2NF) if and only if it is in 1NF and every non-key attribute (non prime attribute) is fully functionally dependent on the primary key".
- The second rule of data normalization states that if a column depends only on part of a multivalued key, you remove it to a separate table.
- The second normal form is achieved when every data item in a record that is not dependent on the primary key of the record should be removed and used to forma separate relation.
- The PF department ensures that only one employee in the state is assigned a specific PF number. This is called a one-to-one relation. The PF number uniquely identifies a specific employee; an employee is associated with one and only one PF number.
- Thus, if you know the Employee no., you can determine the PF number. This is functional dependency. Therefore a data item is functionally dependant if its value is uniquely associated with a specific data item.
- **Employee Record:**

Emp. No.	Name	Emp. Details	Salary	A/c. No.	Bank Code	Income Tax Details
A01	Jose			SB2152	01	
A02	Joseph			SB3212	03	

Annual Safety Earned Record

Emp. No.	MMYY	Net Paid
A01	195	3600
A01	196	3800
A01	197	3600
A01	198	3500
A02	199	6000

Bank Record

Code	Name	Address
01	SBI	Chennai
03	Canara	Madurai

- The three record structures that are created are:
    1. **Employee record** consisting of: _Employee no., employee name employee details (department code, grade, date of joining, exit code and exit date), bank details (bank code, bank name, address, employees A/C no.)
    2. **Annual salary earned record** consisting of - employee no., month & year (MMYY) and net paid
    3. **Bank record** consisting of: bank c ode, bank name and bank address. All the attributes of this relation are **fully dependent** on Bank c ode.
- A table in Second Normal Form must indicate that all the attributes, which are not dependent of primary key, must be removed. The table in Second Normal Form will be

Invoice_Master	Invoice_Item	Item_Master
Invoice_code	Invoice_No	Item_code
Inv_date	Item_code	description
Order_code	Rate	
Cust_code	Ord_value	
Cust_name		
Address		
Invoice_value		

- There are no changes in the Invoice details.

5.3.5.3 Third Normal Form (3NF)

- "A relation is in third normal for (3NF) if and only if it is in 2NF and every nonkey attribute (non prime attribute) is non-transitively dependent dependent on the primary key. Transitivity means if $\alpha \to \beta$ holds and $\beta \to \gamma$ holds, then $\alpha \to \gamma$ holds. No transitive dependencies implies no mutual dependencies i.e. none of the attributes are functionally dependent on any combination of the other attributes. Such independence implies that each can be updated independently of all the rest.

- The third rule of data normalization states that if a column does not fully describe the index key, that column should be moved to a separate table. In other words, if the columns in your table do not really need to be in this table, they probably need to be somewhere else. Databases that follow this rule are known to be in the Third Normal Form (3NF) i.e. Eliminate Columns Not Dependent on the Primary Key.
- The third normal form indicates that there must not be any dependency between non-key attributes. Resolving the above we get

Invoice_Master	Invoice_Item	Item_Master
Invoice_code	Invoice_No	Item_code
Inv_date	Item_code	description rate
Order_code	description	
Invoice_value	Ord_qty	
	Ord_value	

Order_Cust	Customer_Master
Order_code	cust_code
Cust_code	cust_name
Order_date	address

- Third normal form is achieved when transitive dependencies are removed from a record design. Some of the non-key attributes are dependent not only on the primary key but also on a non-key attribute. This is referred to as a transitive dependency.

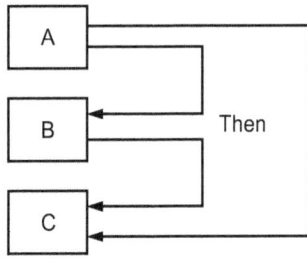

Fig. 5.5

- Conversion to third normal form removes transitive dependence by splitting the relation into two relations.

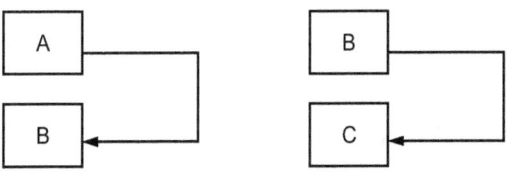

Fig. 5.6

- Reason for concern. When there is a transitive dependence, deleting A will cause deletion of B and C as well.
    - A, B and C are three data items in a record.
    - If C is functionally dependent on B and.
    - B is functionally dependent on A.
    - Then C is functionally dependent on A.
    - Therefore, a transitive dependency exists.
- There are no transitive dependencies, so it is also in third normal form.

5.4 Entity Relationships

- Entity Relationship (E–R) modeling is a design tool. It is a graphical representation of the database system which provides a high-level conceptual data model and supports the user's perception of the data.
- The overall logical structure of a database can be expressed graphically by an E–R diagram.

5.4.1 Features

1. The E-R diagram used for representing E-R Model can be easily converted into Relations (tables) in Relational Model.
2. The E-R Model is used for the purpose of good database design by the database developer so to use that data model in various D.B.M.S..
3. It is helpful as a problem decomposition tool as it shows the entities and the relationship between those entities.
4. It is inherently an iterative process. On later modifications, the entities can be inserted into this model.
5. It is very simple and easy to understand by various types of users and designers because specific standards are used for their representation.

5.4.2 Components

- The overall logical structure of a database can be expressed graphically by an E–R diagram, which is built up from the following components.
    1. **Rectangles** (▭) : Which represents entity sets
    2. **Ellipse** (⬭) : Which represents attributes
    3. **Diamonds** (◇) : Which represents relationships among entity sets.
    4. **Lines** (─────) : Which link attributes to entity sets and entity sets to relationships.

1. Entities:

- An entity is any object in the system that we want to model and store information about database.
- Individual objects are called entities. An entity instance is a specific value of an entity.
- Entities are the basic building blocks of relational database design.
- An entity defines any person, place, thing or concept for which data will be collected. Some examples of entities include the following:
  - **Person**: student, teacher
  - **Place:** classroom, building
  - **Thing:** computer, lab equipment
- Groups of the same type of objects are called entity types or entity sets.
- Entities are represented by rectangles.

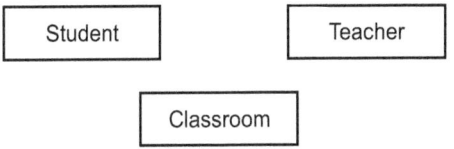

Fig. 5.7: Entity

- There are two types of entities; weak and strong entity.

2. Entity set:

- Entity set is a set of entities of the same type that share the same properties or attributes.
- Entity sets need not be disjoint.
- The set of all students is defined as entity set student.

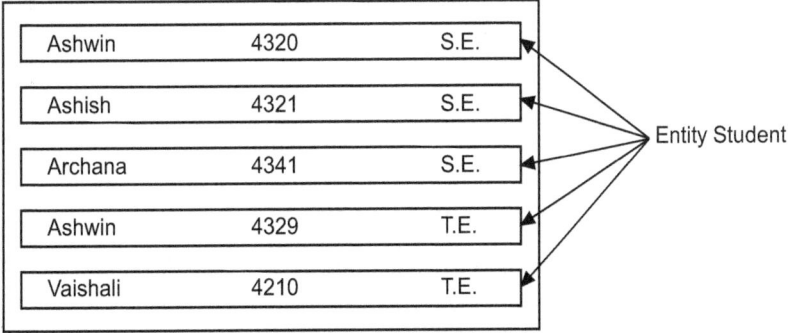

Student entity set

Fig. 5.8: Entity set

3. Attributes:

- All the data relating to an entity is held in its attributes.
- An attribute is a property of an entity.
- Each attribute can have any value from its domain.

- An attribute is a property of an entity that differential if from other entities and provides information about the entity. An attribute type is a property of an entity type.
- For example, the attributes of the entity Student are Course Name, Course Number and Gender. In an ER diagram, you represent attributes as ellipses and label them with the name of the attribute.

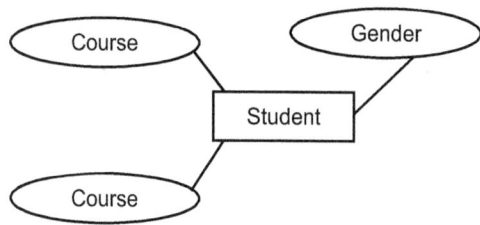

Fig. 5.9: Attributes

- The second major data-modelling concept that you must understand is that of attributes.
- Attributes are additional characteristics or information defined for an entity.
- Each entity within an entity type:
  - May have any number of attributes.
  - Can have different attribute values than that in any other entity.
- Have the same number of attributes. Attributes can be:

  (i) Simple and composite attribute:
  - Simple attribute that consist of a single atomic value.
  - A composite attribute is an attribute that can be further subdivided. For example the attribute ADDRESS can be subdivided into street, city, state and zip code.
  - A simple attribute cannot be subdivided. For example, the attribute age, sex, etc. are simple attributes.
  - In composite attribute value not atomic.

  (ii) Single valued and multi valued attributes:
  - A single valued attribute can have only a single value.
  - For example, a person can have only one 'date of birth', 'age' etc. That is a single valued attribute can have only single value.
  - But it can be simple or composite attribute. That is 'date of birth' is a composite attribute, 'age' is a simple attribute. But both are single valued attributes.
  - Multivalued attribute can have multiple values for instance a person may have multiple phone numbers, multiple degrees etc.
  - Multivalued attributes are shown by a double line connecting to the entity in the E-R diagram.

(iii) Derived attributes:
- The value for the derived attribute is derived from the stored attribute.
- For example, 'Date of birth' of a person is a stored attributed. The value for the attribute 'AGE' can be derived by subtracting the 'Date of Birth' (DOB) from the current date. Stored attribute supplies a value to the related attribute.
- An attribute that's value is derived from a stored attribute is called as derived attribute. Example: age, and its value is derived from the stored attribute Date of Birth.

(iv) Null attribute:
- Null value is used when an entity does not have a value for an attribute.
- Null can also designate that an attribute is unknown i.e. missing or not known.
- All attributes are shown in Fig. 5.10.

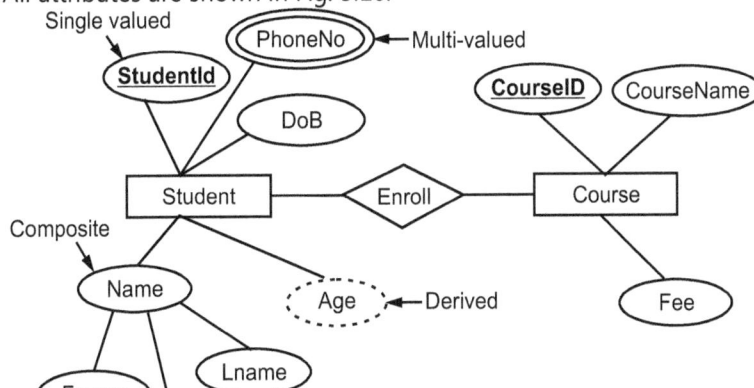

Fig. 5.10: E-R diagram with types of attributes

4. Weak and Strong Entity Sets:
- The entity sets that does not have sufficient attributes to define the primary key are called weak entity sets.
- The entity sets that have sufficient attributes to define the primary key are called strong entity sets.
- In such case the weak entity sets has to be dependent on strong entity sets.
- Strong entity is also called identifying or owner entity set. The relationship that is associating weak entity set with strong entity set is called identifying relationship.
- The identifying relationship is many to one from the weak entity set to the identifying entity set and the sharing of the weak entity set in the relationship is total.
- The weak entity does not have any primary key but a discriminator (set of attributes) in weak entity set is used to distinguish among the rows.
- The primary key of weak entity set is combination of primary key of strong entity set and discriminator of weak entity set.

- The weak entity is denoted by double rectangle ⬜.
- The identifying relationship is denoted by double diamond ◇.
- The total participation of weak entity set is denoted by double line ═══.
- The discriminator is underlined by dash line - - - - - - - -.
- For example, consider the relation loan (loan no, amount) and payment (pno, pdate, pamt).

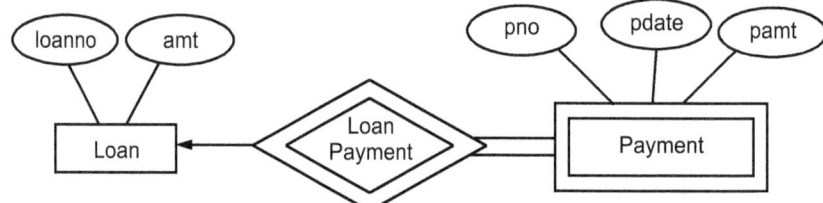

Fig. 5.11: E-R diagram with a weak entity set

5. Keys:
- A key is a data item that allows us to uniquely identify individual occurrences or an entity type.
- A candidate key is an attribute or set of attributes that uniquely identifies individual occurrences or an entity type.
- An entity type may have one or more possible candidate keys, the one which is selected is known as the **primary key**.
- A composite key is a candidate key that consists of two or more attributes.
- The name of each primary key attribute is underlined.

6. Relationships:
- A relationship type is a meaningful association between entity types.
- A relationship is an association of entities where the association includes one entity from each participating entity type.
- Relationship types are represented on the E–R diagram by a series of lines.
- The relationship is placed inside a diamond, For example, managers manage employees:

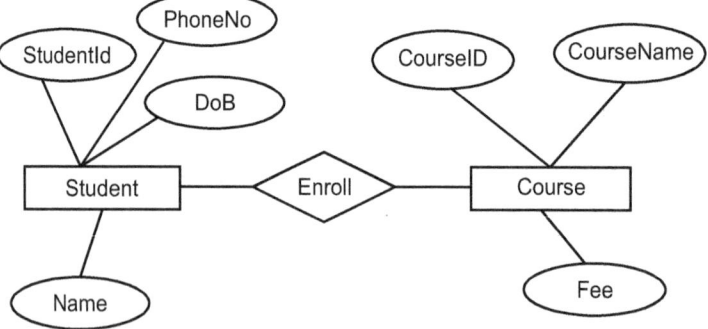

Fig. 5.12: Notation for relationships

7. Relationship Set:
- It is a set of relationships of same type.
- Formally, it is mathematical relation on n ≥ 2 (possibly non distinct) entity sets.
  If $E_1, E_2, ..., E_n$ are entity sets, then a relationship set R is a subset of $\{(e_1, e_2, ..., e_n) \mid e_1 \in E_1, e_2 \in E_2 \; e_n \in E_n\}$ where $(e_1, e_2, ..., e_n)$ is a relationship.
  Consider the following two entity sets.
  Account = {acc_no., balance, type}
  Customer = {name, city, social_security}

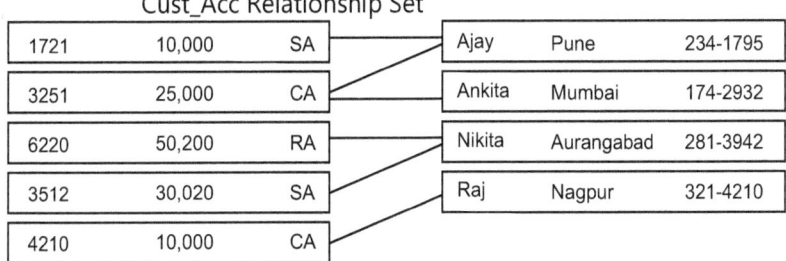

Fig. 5.13: Relationship Set

- Binary Relationship Set relates two entity sets. n-ary Relationship Set relates 'n' number of entity sets. n-ary relationship set can be replaced by binary relationship set.

8. Degree of a Relationship:
- The number of participating entities in a relationship is known as the degree of the relationship.
- If there are two entity types involved it is a binary relationship type as shown in Fig. 5.14.

Fig. 5.14: Binary Relationships

- If there are three entity types involved it is a ternary relationship type as shown in Fig. 5.15.

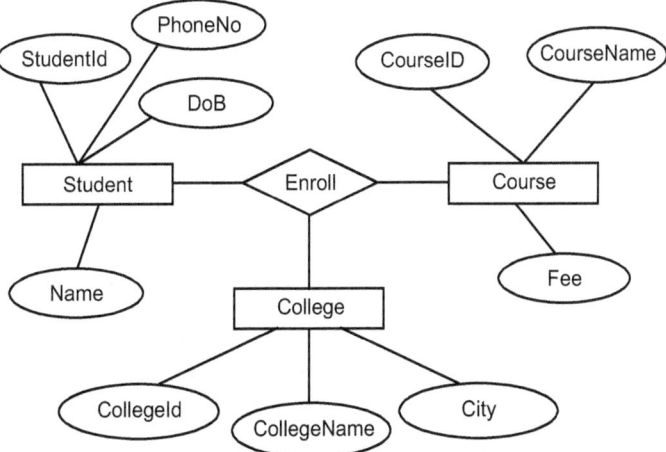

Fig. 5.15: Ternary relationship

- It is possible to have a n-ary relationship (For example, quaternary or unary).
- Unary relationships are also known as a recursive relationship as shown in Fig. 5.16.

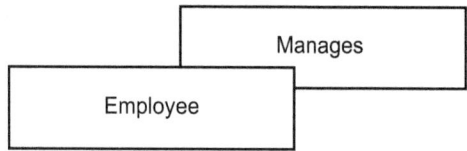

Fig. 5.16: Recursive relationship

- It is a relationship where the same entity participates more than once, in different roles.
- In the example above we are saying that employees are managed by employees.
- If we wanted more information about who manages whom, we could introduce a second entity type called manager.

9. **Mapping Cardinalities:**

- Mapping cardinality or cardinality ratio expresses the number of entities to which another entity can be associated via a relationship set. Mapping cardinalities are most useful in describing binary relationship sets.

   (i) **One-to-One:** An entity in 'A' is associated with at most one entity in 'B' and an entity in 'B' is associated with at most one entity in 'A'.

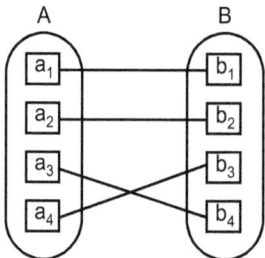

Fig. 5.17: One-to-One

One Customer has an account in the bank and account belongs to only one customer, so it is a one to one (1:1) relationship as shown in Fig. 5.18.

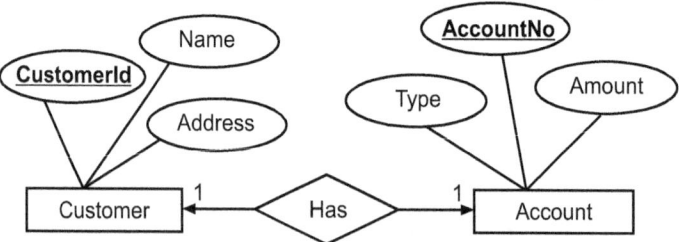

Fig. 5.18: One-to-one relationship example

(ii) One-to-Many: An entity in 'A' is associated with any number of entities in 'B'. An entity in 'B' however, can be associated with at most one entity in 'A'.

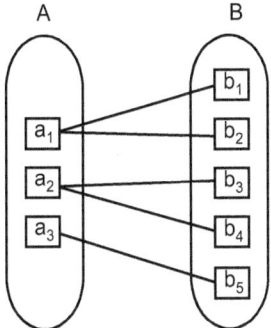

Fig. 5.19: One-to-Many

One customer has many accounts of different types in the bank, but each account has only one customer, so it is a one to many (1:m) relationship as shown in Fig. 5.20.

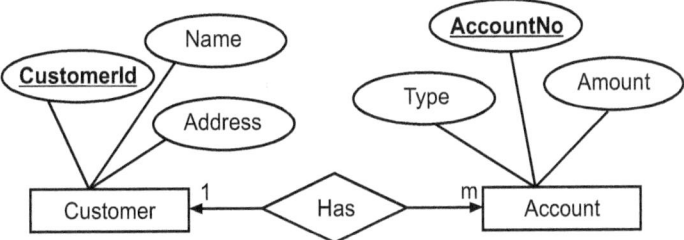

Fig. 5.20: One-to-many relationship example

(iii) Many-to-One: An entity in 'A' is associated with atmost one entity in 'B'. An entity in 'B' however can be associated with any number of entities in 'A'.

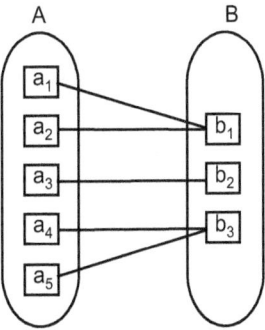

Fig. 5.21: Many-to-One

Many customers may have same account type, so it is a many to one (m:1) relationship as shown in Fig. 5.22.

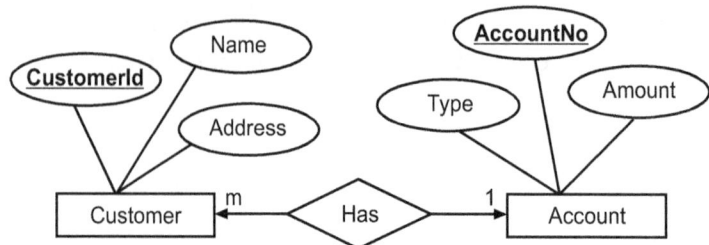

Fig. 5.22: Many-to-one relationship example

(iv) Many-to-Many: An entity in 'A' is associated with any number of entities in 'B' and an entity in 'B' is associated with any number of entities in 'A'.

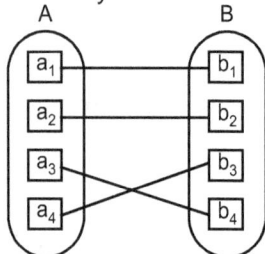

Fig. 5.23: Many-to-many

One customer has many accounts and account belongs to many customers, so it is a many to many (m:m) relationship as shown in Fig. 5.24.

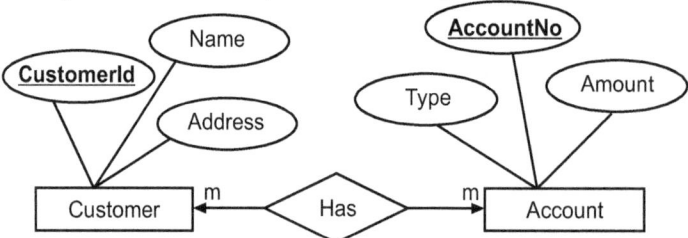

Fig. 5.24: Many-to-many relationship example

5.4.3 Examples

Example 1: *Draw an E-R diagram for order processing system where a person can give order for many items by specifying its quantity.*

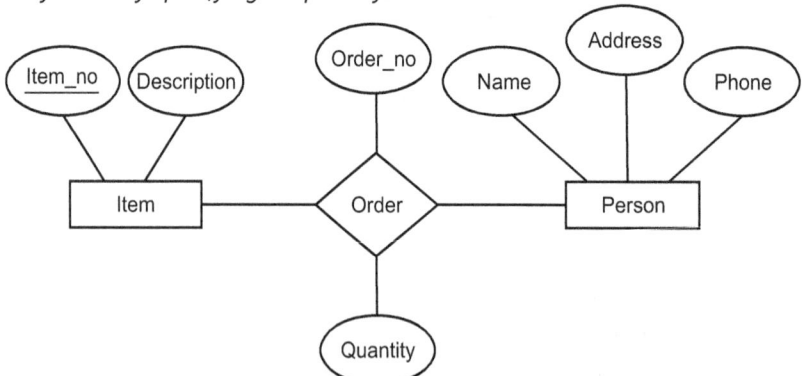

Example 2: *Assume you are to compose database requirements of a wholesale dealer for audio, video consumer equipment from different manufacturers. Customers are the various retail outlets (Retailers). Wholesaler extends credit to old customers (retailers). Draw E-R model.*

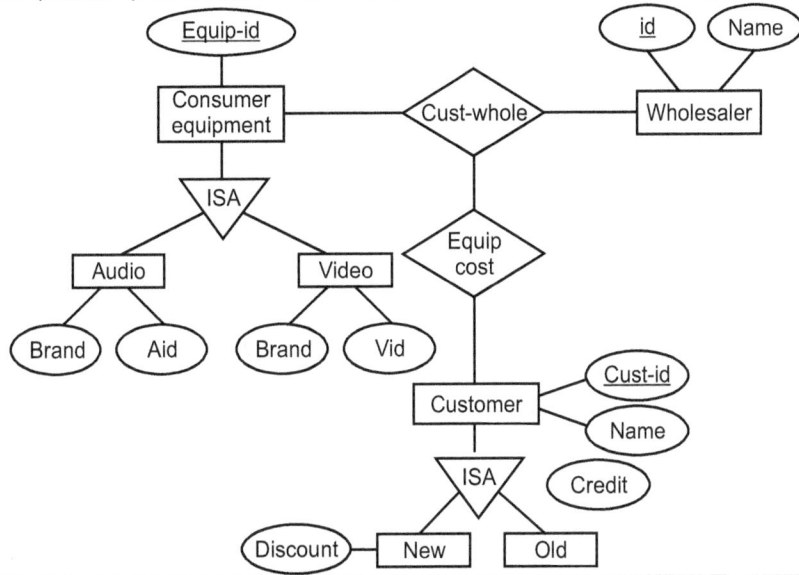

Example 3: *Consider a trucking company which is responsible for picking up shipments for warehouses of a retail chain and delivery the shipments to the individual store location. A truck may carry several shipments in a single trip and deliver it to multiple stores. Draw an E-R diagram for truck-shipment system.*

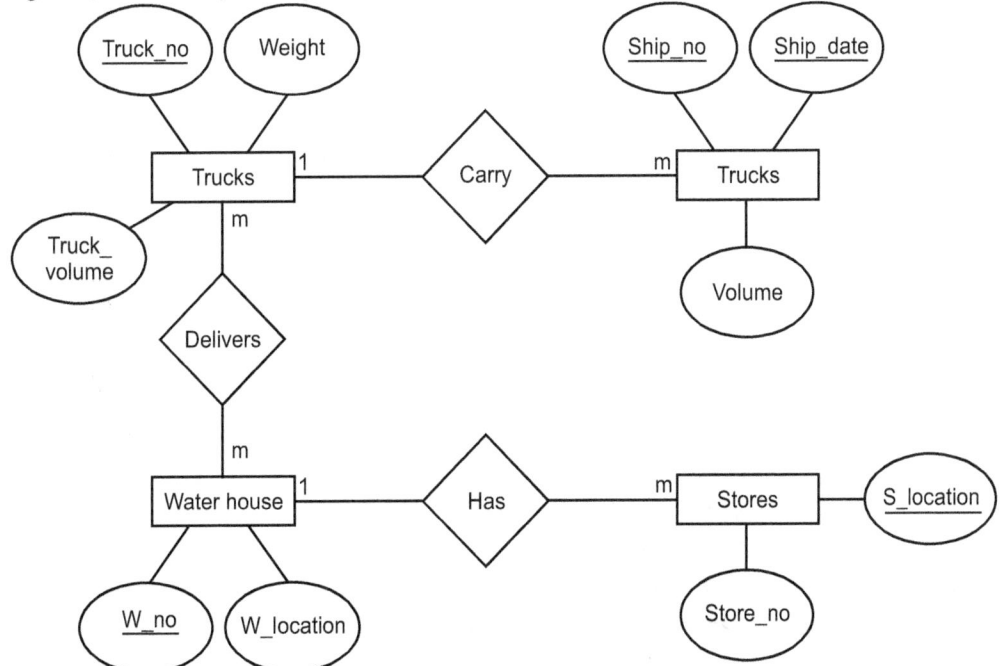

Example 4: *Draw an E-R diagram for airlines reservation system. Here a passenger can book ticket from personal for a flight on some date.*

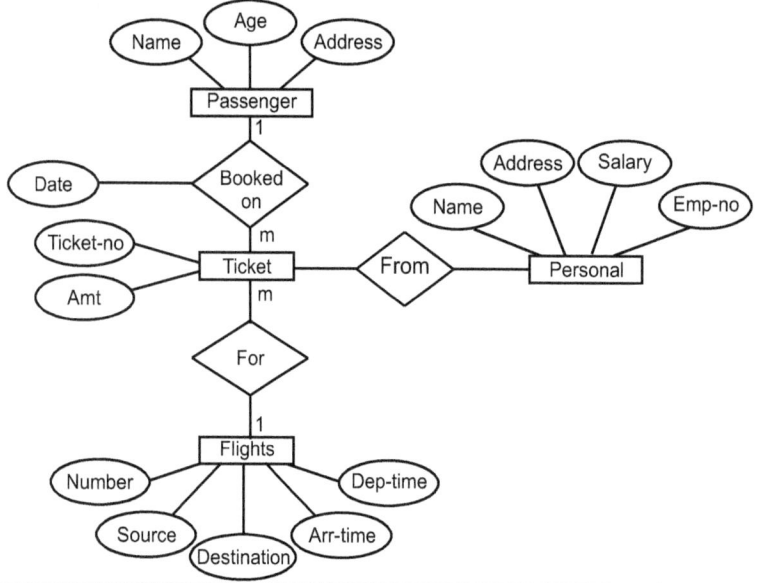

Example 5: *Construct an E-R diagram for a car insurance company that has a set of customers. Each customer owns one or more cars. Each are has associated with more cars. Each can has associated with zero to any number of recorded accidents.*

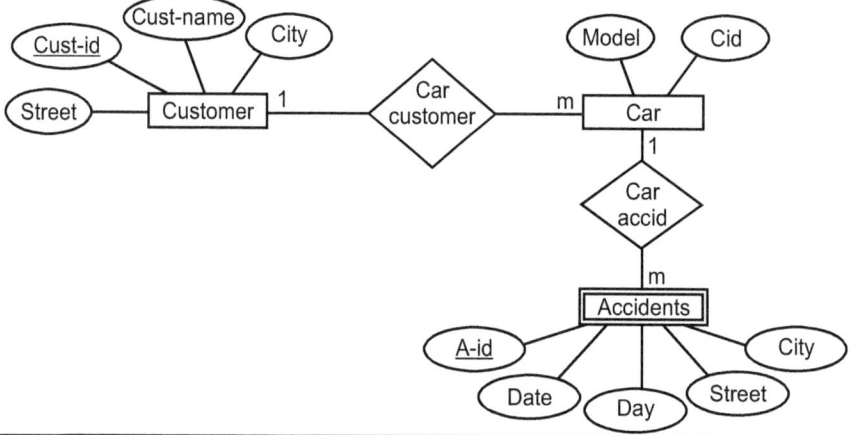

Example 6: *A movie studio wishes to institute a database to manage their files of movies actors and directors. The following facts are relevant.*
  (i) *Each actor has appeared in many movies.*
  (ii) *Each director has directed many movies.*
  (iii) *Each movie has one director and one or more actors.*
  (iv) *Each actor and director may have several addresses.*
  Draw E-R diagram.

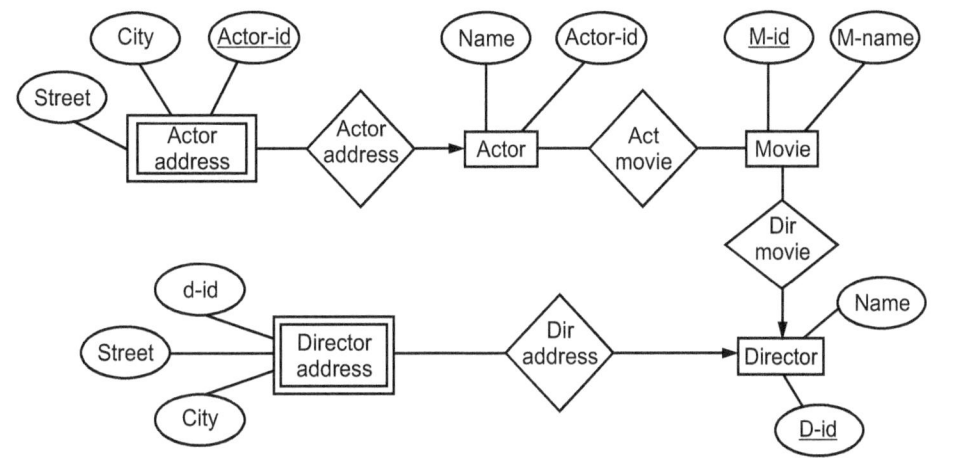

Example 7: *Construct an E-R diagram for a hospital with a set of patients and a set of medical doctors. Associate with each patient a log of the various tests and examination conducted.*

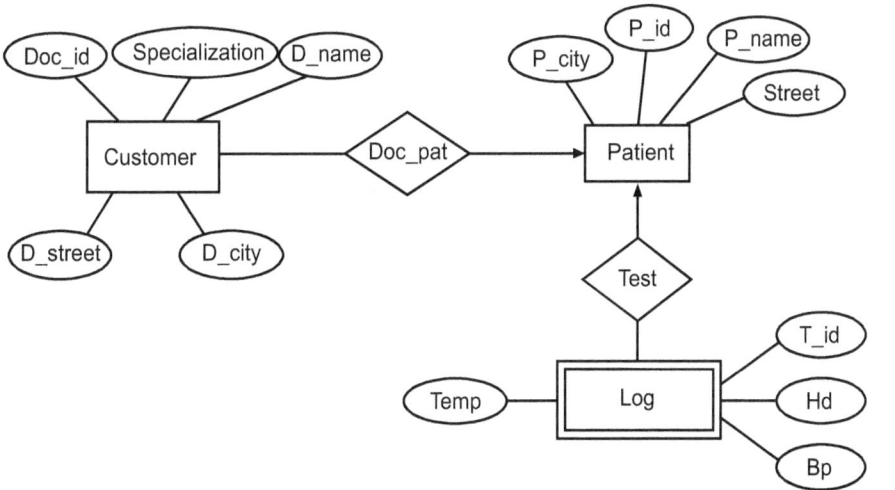

5.5 Use of Simple SQL Commands

5.5.1 Introduction to SQL

- SQL (Structured Query Language) is a database language for querying and modifying relational databases.
- It was developed by IBM Research in the mid 1970's and standardized by ANSI in 1986. It is also pronounced as "Sequel".
- SQL is a Structured Query Language and is the industry standard language to define and manipulate the data in Relational Database Management System.

Why SQL?

- SQL allow users to access data in relational database management systems.
- SQL allow users to describe the data.
- SQL allow users to define the data in database and manipulate that data.
- SQL allow to embed within other languages using SQL modules, libraries & pre-compilers.
- SQL allow users to create and drop databases and tables.
- SQL allow users to create view, stored procedure, functions in a database.
- SQL allow users to set permissions on tables, procedures, and views

SQL Architecture:

- When you are executing an SQL command for any R.D.B.M.S., the system determines the best way to carry out your request and SQL engine figures out how to interpret the task.
- There are various components included in the process. These components are Query Dispatcher, Optimization engines, Classic Query Engine and SQL query engine etc. Classic query engine handles all non-SQL queries but SQL query engine won't handle logical files.
- Fig. 5.25 shows SQL architecture.

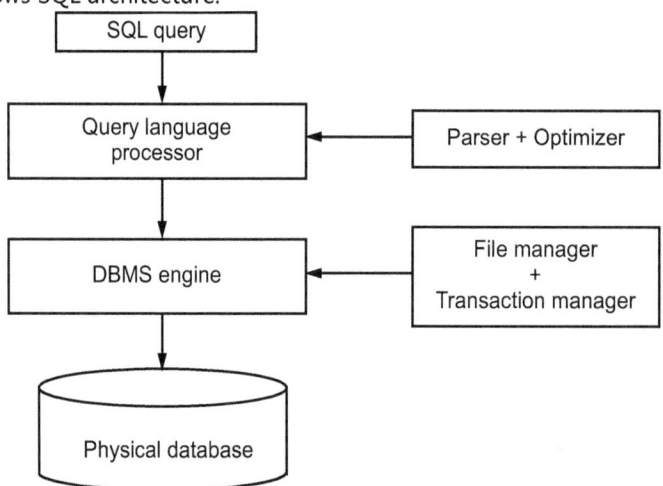

Fig. 5.25: SQL architecture

Types of SQL Languages:

Sr. No.	Classifications	Description	Commands
1.	DDL (Data Definition Language)	Is used to define the structure of a table, or modify the structure.	CREATE, ALTER, DROP, TRUNCATE, RENAME
2.	DML (Data Manipulation Language)	Is used to manipulate with the data.	INSERT, UPDATE, DELETE

contd. ...

3.	DCL (Data Control Language)	Is used to restrict or grant access to tables.	GRANT, REVOKE
4.	TCL (Transaction Control Language)	Is used to complete fully or undo the transactions.	COMMIT, SAVEPOINT, ROLLBACK.
5.	Queries	Is used to select records from the tables or other objects.	SELECT.

5.5.2 Data Types

- Each literal or column value manipulated by Oracle has a datatype. A value's datatype associates a fixed set of properties with the value.

1. **Character Datatypes:**

   (i) Char(n): Char datatype is a fixed length character data of length n bytes. Default size is 1 byte and it can hold a maximum of 2000 bytes. Character datatypes pad blank spaces to the fixed length if the user enters a value lesser than the specified length.

   Syntax: `Char(n)`

   Example: `X char(4)` stores upto 4 characters of data in the column X.

   (ii) Varchar2(size): Varchar2 datatypes are variable length character strings. They can store alpha-numeric values and the size must be specified. The maximum length of varchar2 datatype is 4000 bytes. Unlike char datatype, blank spaces are not padded to the length of the string. So, this is more preferred than character datatypes since it does not store the maximum length.

   Syntax: `Varchar2(Size)`

   Example: `X varchar2(10)` stores upto 10 characters of data in the column X.

2. **Numeric datatypes:**

   (i) Number: The number datatypes can store numeric values where p stands for the precision and s stands for the scale. The precision can range between 1 to 38 and the scale ranges from –84 to 127.

   Syntax: `Number (p, s)`

   Example:

   `Sal number` : Here the scale is 0 and the precision is 38.

   `Sal number(7)` : Here the scale is 0 and the number is a fixed point number of 7 digits.

   `Sal number(7, 2)` : Stores 5 digits followed by 2 decimal points.

3. **DATE datatype:**

   Date datatype is used to store data and time values. The default format is DD-MM-YY. The valid data for a date datatype ranges from January 1, 4712 BC to December 31, 4712 AD. Date datatype stores 7 bytes one each for century, year, month, day, hour, minute and second.

4. RAW Datatype:

RAW datatype stores binary date of length n bytes. The maximum size is 255 bytes. "Specifying the size is a must for this datatype".

Syntax: Raw(n)

5. LONG Datatype:

Stores character data of variable length upto 2 Gigabyte(GB) or $2^{s1} - 1$.

6. LOB Datatypes:

In addition to the above datatypes, Oracle 8 supports LOB datatypes. LOB is the acronym for LARGE OBJECTS. The LOB datatypes stores upto 4 GB of data. This datatype is used for storing video clippings, large images, history documents etc. LOB datatypes can be

(i) CLOB : Character Large Objects (Internal LOB)

(ii) BLOB : Binary Large Objects (Internal LOB)

(iii) BFILE : Binary File (External LOB)

5.5.3 SQL Languages and their Commands

5.5.3.1 Data Definition Language (DDL)

- A DDL is a language used to define data structures within a database.
- It is typically considered to be a subset of SQL, the Structured Query Language, but can also refer to languages that define other types of data.
- A Data Definition Language has a pre-defined syntax for describing data. For example, to build a new table using SQL syntax, the CREATE command is used, followed by parameters for the table name and column definitions.
- The DDL can also define the name of each column and the associated data type.

DDL Commands:

1. Create table command:

The SQL CREATE TABLE statement is used to create a new table.

Syntax:

```
CREATE TABLE table_name(
   column1 datatype,
   column2 datatype,
   column3 datatype,
   .....
   columnN datatype,
   PRIMARY KEY( one or more columns )
);
```

Following is an example which creates a CUSTOMERS table with ID as primary key and NOT NULL are the constraints showing that these fileds can not be NULL while creating records in this table:

```
SQL> CREATE TABLE CUSTOMERS(
     ID      INT             NOT NULL,
     NAME    VARCHAR (20)    NOT NULL,
     AGE     INT             NOT NULL,
     ADDRESS CHAR (25) ,
     SALARY  DECIMAL (18, 2),
     PRIMARY KEY (ID)
);
```

2. **DESC Command:**

   The table structure can be described by using Describe command.

   Syntax: `DESC table_name;`

   Example: `DESC CUSTOMERS;`

   `SQL> DESC CUSTOMERS`

Field	Type	Null	Key	Default	Extra
ID	int(11)	NO	PRI		
NAME	varchar(20)	NO			
AGE	int(11)	NO			
ADDRESS	char(25)	YES		NULL	
SALARY	decimal(18,2)	YES		NULL	

   `5 rows in set (0.00 sec)`

3. **ALTER Command:**

- The ALTER TABLE statement is used to add or drop columns in existing table.

   Syntax:

   ```
   ALTER TABLE tabe_name ADD column_name datatype;
   ALTER TABLE tabe_name DROP COLUMN column_name;
   ```

Person:

LastName	FirstName	Address
Johnson	Kari	RTO Road 20

Example: To add a column named "City" in the "Person" table:

   `ALTER TABLE Person ADD City varchar2(10);`

Result:

LastName	FirstName	Address	City
Johnson	Kari	RTO Road 20	

Example: To drop the "Address" column in the "Person" table:

```
ALTER TABLE Person DROP (address);
```

Result:

LastName	FirstName	City
Johnson	Kari	

To modify the "Address" column in the "Person" table:"

```
ALTER TABLE Person modify (Address varchar2(10))'
```

4. **DROP TABLE Command:**
- A table and its rows can be deleted by issuing the command drop table.

    Syntax: `Drop table table_name;`

    Example: Drop table Person;

5. **Truncate Commands:**
- Truncate table command is used to delete the whole rows of the table. The structure of table remains as it is. You can add new data to the table again.

    Syntax: `Truncate table table_name;`

    Example: `Truncate table Person;`

5.5.3.2 Data Manipulation Language (DML)

- DML used to retrieve, store, modify, delete, insert and update data in database.

1. **INSERT INTO Command:**
- The SQL INSERT INTO Statement is used to add new rows of data to a table in the database.

    Syntax:
    ```
    INSERT INTO TABLE_NAME (column1, column2, column3,...columnN)]
    VALUES (value1, value2, value3,...valueN);
    ```
    Here column1, column2, ..., columnN are the names of the columns in the table into which you want to insert data.

- Following statements would create six records in CUSTOMERS table:
    ```
    INSERT INTO CUSTOMERS (ID,NAME,AGE,ADDRESS,SALARY)
    VALUES (1, 'Ramesh', 32, 'Ahmedabad', 2000.00 );

    INSERT INTO CUSTOMERS (ID,NAME,AGE,ADDRESS,SALARY)
    VALUES (2, 'Amar', 25, 'Delhi', 1500.00 );
    ```

```
INSERT INTO CUSTOMERS (ID,NAME,AGE,ADDRESS,SALARY)
VALUES (3, 'kaushik', 23, 'Kota', 2000.00 );

INSERT INTO CUSTOMERS (ID,NAME,AGE,ADDRESS,SALARY)
VALUES (4, 'Chaitali', 25, 'Mumbai', 6500.00 );

INSERT INTO CUSTOMERS (ID,NAME,AGE,ADDRESS,SALARY)
VALUES (5, 'Hardik', 27, 'Bhopal', 8500.00 );

INSERT INTO CUSTOMERS (ID,NAME,AGE,ADDRESS,SALARY)
VALUES (6, 'Komal', 22, 'MP', 4500.00 );
```
- You can create a record in CUSTOMERS table using second syntax as follows:
```
INSERT INTO CUSTOMERS
VALUES (7, 'Akbar', 24, 'Indore', 10000.00 );
```
- All the above statement would product following records in CUSTOMERS table:

ID	NAME	AGE	ADDRESS	SALARY
1	Ramesh	32	Ahmedabad	2000.00
2	Amar	25	Delhi	1500.00
3	Kaushik	23	Kota	2000.00
4	Chaitali	25	Mumbai	6500.00
5	Hardik	27	Bhopal	8500.0
6	Komal	22	MP	4500.0
7	Akbar	24	Indore	10000.00

2. **Update Command:**
- The SQL UPDATE Query is used to modify the existing records in a table.
- You can use WHERE clause with UPDATE query to update selected rows otherwise all the rows would be effected.

    Syntax: `UPDATE table_name`
    `SET column1 = value1, column2 = value2...., columnN = valueN`
    `WHERE [condition];`
- Consider CUSTOMERS table is having following records:

ID	NAME	AGE	ADDRESS	SALARY
1	Ramesh	32	Ahmedabad	2000.00
2	Amar	25	Delhi	1500.00
3	Kaushik	23	Kota	2000.00
4	Chaitali	25	Mumbai	6500.00
5	Hardik	27	Bhopal	8500.0
6	Komal	22	MP	4500.0
7	Akbar	24	Indore	10000.00

- Following is an example which would update ADDRESS for a customer whose ID is 6:
    ```
    SQL> UPDATE CUSTOMERS
    SET ADDRESS = 'Pune'
    WHERE ID = 6;
    ```
- Now CUSTOMERS table would have following records:

ID	NAME	AGE	ADDRESS	SALARY
1	Ramesh	32	Ahmedabad	2000.00
2	Amar	25	Delhi	1500.00
3	Kaushik	23	Kota	2000.00
4	Chaitali	25	Mumbai	6500.00
5	Hardik	27	Bhopal	8500.0
6	Komal	22	Pune	4500.0
7	Akbar	24	Indore	10000.00

- If you want to modify all ADDRESS and SALARY column values in CUSTOMERS table, you do not need to use WHERE clause and UPDATE query would be as follows:
    ```
    SQL> UPDATE CUSTOMERS
    SET ADDRESS = 'Pune', SALARY = 1000.00;
    ```
- Now CUSTOMERS table would have following records:

ID	NAME	AGE	ADDRESS	SALARY
1	Ramesh	32	Pune	1000.00
2	Amar	25	Pune	1000.00
3	Kaushik	23	Pune	1000.00
4	Chaitali	25	Pune	1000.00
5	Hardik	27	Pune	1000.00
6	Komal	22	Pune	1000.00
7	Akbar	24	Pune	1000.00

3. **DELETE Command:**
- The SQL DELETE Query is used to delete the existing records from a table.
- You can use WHERE clause with DELETE query to delete selected rows, otherwise all the records would be deleted.

    Syntax:
    ```
    DELETE FROM table_name
    WHERE [condition];
    ```

- Consider CUSTOMERS table is having following records:

ID	NAME	AGE	ADDRESS	SALARY
1	Ramesh	32	Ahmedabad	2000.00
2	Amar	25	Delhi	1500.00
3	Kaushik	23	Kota	2000.00
4	Chaitali	25	Mumbai	6500.00
5	Hardik	27	Bhopal	8500.0
6	Komal	22	MP	4500.0
7	Akbar	24	Indore	10000.00

- Following is an example which would DELETE a customer whose ID is 6:

    SQL> DELETE FROM CUSTOMERS
    WHERE ID = 6;

- Now CUSTOMERS table would have following records:

ID	NAME	AGE	ADDRESS	SALARY
1	Ramesh	32	Ahmedabad	2000.00
2	Amar	25	Delhi	1500.00
3	Kaushik	23	Kota	2000.00
4	Chaitali	25	Mumbai	6500.00
5	Hardik	27	Bhopal	8500.0
7	Akbar	24	Indore	10000.00

- If you want to DELETE all the records from CUSTOMERS table, you do not need to use WHERE clause and DELETE query would be as follows:

    SQL> DELETE FROM CUSTOMERS;

    Now CUSTOMERS table would not have any record.

5.5.3.3 SQL Queries

SQL SELECT Statement:
- The SELECT statement is used to select data from a table. The tabular result is stored in a result table.
- SQL SELECT Statement is used to fetch the data from a database table which returns data in the form of result table. These result tables are called result-sets.
- The basic syntax of SELECT statement is as follows:

    SELECT column1, column2, columnN FROM table_name;

- Here column1, column2...are the fields of a table whose values you want to fetch. If you want to fetch all the fields available in the field then you can use following syntax:

    SELECT * FROM table_name;

- Consider CUSTOMERS table is having following records:

ID	NAME	AGE	ADDRESS	SALARY
1	Ramesh	32	Ahmedabad	2000.00
2	Amar	25	Delhi	1500.00
3	Kaushik	23	Kota	2000.00
4	Chaitali	25	Mumbai	6500.00
5	Hardik	27	Bhopal	8500.0
6	Komal	22	MP	4500.0
7	Akbar	24	Indore	10000.00

- Following is an example which would fetch ID, Name and Salary fields of the customers available in CUSTOMERS table:

    SQL> SELECT ID, NAME, SALARY FROM CUSTOMERS;

- This would produce following result:

ID	NAME	SALARY
1	Ramesh	2000.00
2	Amar	1500.00
3	Kaushik	2000.00
4	Chaitali	6500.00
5	Hardik	8500.0
6	Komal	4500.0
7	Akbar	10000.00

- If you want to fetch all the fields of CUSTOMERS table then use the following query:

    SQL> SELECT * FROM CUSTOMERS;

- This would produce following result:

ID	NAME	AGE	ADDRESS	SALARY
1	Ramesh	32	Ahmedabad	2000.00
2	Amar	25	Delhi	1500.00
3	Kaushik	23	Kota	2000.00
4	Chaitali	25	Mumbai	6500.00
5	Hardik	27	Bhopal	8500.0
6	Komal	22	MP	4500.0
7	Akbar	24	Indore	10000.00

WHERE Clause:
- The SQL WHERE clause is used to specify a condition while fetching the data from single table or joining with multiple table.
- If the given condition is satisfied then only it returns specific value from the table. You would use WHERE clause to filter the records and fetching only necessary records.

    Syntax: `SELECT column1, column2, columnN`

    `FROM table_name`

    `WHERE [condition]`

- Consider CUSTOMERS table is having following records:

ID	NAME	AGE	ADDRESS	SALARY
1	Ramesh	32	Ahmedabad	2000.00
2	Amar	25	Delhi	1500.00
3	Kaushik	23	Kota	2000.00
4	Chaitali	25	Mumbai	6500.00
5	Hardik	27	Bhopal	8500.0
6	Komal	22	MP	4500.0
7	Akbar	24	Indore	10000.00

- Following is an example which would fetch ID, Name and Salary fields from the CUSTOMERS table where salary is greater than 2000:

    `SQL> SELECT ID, NAME, SALARY`

    `FROM CUSTOMERS`

    `WHERE SALARY > 2000;`

    This would produce following result:

ID	NAME	SALARY
4	Chaitali	6500.00
5	Hardik	8500.0
6	Komal	4500.0
7	Akbar	10000.00

- Following is an example which would fetch ID, Name and Salary fields from the CUSTOMERS table for a customer with name **Hardik**. Here it is important to note that all the strings should be given inside single quotes ('') where as numeric values should be given without any quote as in above example:

    `SQL> SELECT ID, NAME, SALARY`

    `FROM CUSTOMERS`

    `WHERE NAME = 'Hardik';`

- This would produce following result:

ID	NAME	SALARY
5	Hardik	8500.00

Operators in SQL:

- An operator is a reserved word or a character used primarily in an SQL statement's WHERE clause to perform operation(s), such as comparisons and arithmetic operations.
- Operators are used to specify conditions in an SQL statement and to serve as conjunctions for multiple conditions in a statement.

  1. **SQL Arithmetic Operators:** Assume variable a holds 10 and variable b holds 20 then:

Operator	Description	Example
+ (Addition)	Adds values on either side of the operator	a + b will give 30
– (Subtraction)	Subtracts right hand operand from left hand operand	a - b will give -10
* (Multiplication)	Multiplies values on either side of the operator	a * b will give 200
/ (Division)	Divides left hand operand by right hand operand	b / a will give 2
% (Modulus)	Divides left hand operand by right hand operand and returns remainder	b % a will give 0

  2. **SQL Comparison Operators:** Assume variable a holds 10 and variable b holds 20 then:

Operator	Description	Example
=	Checks if the value of two operands are equal or not, if yes then condition becomes true.	(a = b) is not true.
!=	Checks if the value of two operands are equal or not, if values are not equal then condition becomes true.	(a != b) is true.
<>	Checks if the value of two operands are equal or not, if values are not equal then condition becomes true.	(a <> b) is true.
>	Checks if the value of left operand is greater than the value of right operand, if yes then condition becomes true.	(a > b) is not true.

contd. ...

<	Checks if the value of left operand is less than the value of right operand, if yes then condition becomes true.	(a < b) is true.
>=	Checks if the value of left operand is greater than or equal to the value of right operand, if yes then condition becomes true.	(a >= b) is not true.
<=	Checks if the value of left operand is less than or equal to the value of right operand, if yes then condition becomes true.	(a <= b) is true.
!<	Checks if the value of left operand is not less than the value of right operand, if yes then condition becomes true.	(a !< b) is false.
!>	Checks if the value of left operand is not greater than the value of right operand, if yes then condition becomes true.	(a !> b) is true.

3. **SQL Logical Operators:** Here is a list of all the logical operators available in SQL.

Operator	Description
ALL	The ALL operator is used to compare a value to all values in another value set.
AND	The AND operator allows the existence of multiple conditions in an SQL statement's WHERE clause.
ANY	The ANY operator is used to compare a value to any applicable value in the list according to the condition.
BETWEEN	The BETWEEN operator is used to search for values that are within a set of values, given the minimum value and the maximum value.
EXISTS	The EXISTS operator is used to search for the presence of a row in a specified table that meets certain criteria.
IN	The IN operator is used to compare a value to a list of literal values that have been specified.
LIKE	The LIKE operator is used to compare a value to similar values using wildcard operators.
NOT	The NOT operator reverses the meaning of the logical operator with which it is used. Eg. NOT EXISTS, NOT BETWEEN, NOT IN etc. **This is negate operator.**
OR	The OR operator is used to combine multiple conditions in an SQL statement's WHERE clause.
IS NULL	The NULL operator is used to compare a value with a NULL value.
UNIQUE	The UNIQUE operator searches every row of a specified table for uniqueness (no duplicates).

Order By Clause:

- The SQL ORDER BY clause is used to sort the data in ascending or descending order, based on one or more columns. Some database sorts query results in ascending order by default.

    Syntax: `SELECT column-list`
    `FROM table_name`
    `[WHERE condition]`
    `[ORDER BY column1, column2, .. columnN] [ASC | DESC];`

- Consider CUSTOMERS table is having following records:

ID	NAME	AGE	ADDRESS	SALARY
1	Ramesh	32	Ahmedabad	2000.00
2	Khilan	25	Delhi	1500.00
3	Kaushik	23	Kota	2000.00
4	Chaitali	25	Mumbai	6500.00
5	Hardik	27	Bhopal	8500.0
6	Komal	22	MP	4500.0
7	Muffy	24	Indore	10000.00

- Following is an example which would sort the result in ascending order by NAME and SALARY:

    `SQL> SELECT * FROM CUSTOMERS`
    `ORDER BY NAME, SALARY;`

- This would produce following result:

ID	NAME	AGE	ADDRESS	SALARY
4	Chaitali	25	Mumbai	6500.00
5	Hardik	27	Bhopal	8500.00
3	Kaushik	23	Kota	2000.00
2	Khilan	25	Delhi	1500.00
6	Komal	22	MP	4500.00
7	Muffy	24	Indore	10000.00
1	Ramesh	32	Ahmedabad	2000.00

- Following is an example which would sort the result in descending order by NAME:

    `SQL> SELECT * FROM CUSTOMERS`
    `ORDER BY NAME DESC;`

- This would produce following result:

ID	NAME	AGE	ADDRESS	SALARY
1	Ramesh	32	Ahmedabad	2000.00
7	Muffy	24	Indore	10000.00
6	Komal	22	MP	4500.00
2	Khilan	25	Delhi	1500.00
3	Kaushik	23	Kota	2000.00
5	Hardik	27	Bhopal	8500.00
4	Chaitali	25	Mumbai	6500.00

Group By Clause:

- The SQL GROUP BY clause is used in collaboration with the SELECT statement to arrange identical data into groups.
- The GROUP BY clause follows the WHERE clause in a SELECT statement and precedes the ORDER BY clause.

Syntax: SELECT column1, column2

FROM table_name

WHERE [conditions]

GROUP BY column1, column2

ORDER BY column1, column2

- Consider CUSTOMERS table is having following records:

ID	NAME	AGE	ADDRESS	SALARY
1	Ramesh	32	Ahmedabad	2000.00
2	Khilan	25	Delhi	1500.00
3	Kaushik	23	Kota	2000.00
4	Chaitali	25	Mumbai	6500.00
5	Hardik	27	Bhopal	8500.00
6	Komal	22	MP	4500.00
7	Muffy	24	Indore	10000.00

- If you want to know the total amount of salary on each customer, then GROUP BY query would be as follows:

SQL> SELECT NAME, SUM(SALARY) FROM CUSTOMERS

GROUP BY NAME;

- This would produce following result:

NAME	SALARY
Chaitali	6500.00
Hardik	8500.00
Kaushik	2000.00
Khilan	1500.00
Komal	4500.00
Muffy	10000.00
Ramesh	2000.00

- Now let us has following table where CUSTOMERS table has following records with duplicate names:

ID	NAME	AGE	ADDRESS	SALARY
1	Ramesh	32	Ahmedabad	2000.00
2	Ramesh	25	Delhi	1500.00
3	Kaushik	23	Kota	2000.00
4	Kaushik	25	Mumbai	6500.00
5	Hardik	27	Bhopal	8500.00
6	Komal	22	MP	4500.00
7	Muffy	24	Indore	10000.00

- Now again, if you want to know the total amount of salary on each customer, then GROUP BY query would be as follows:

    ```
    SQL> SELECT NAME, SUM(SALARY) FROM CUSTOMERS
    GROUP BY NAME;
    ```

- This would produce following result:

NAME	SALARY
Hardik	8500.00
Kaushik	8500.00
Komal	4500.00
Muffy	10000.00
Ramesh	3500.00

SQL Aggregate Functions:

- SQL has a lot of built-in functions for counting and calculations. The syntax for built-in SQL functions is:

    ```
    SELECT function(column) FROM table;
    ```

Aggregate functions operate against a collection of values, but return a single value.

Function	Description
1. AVG(column)	Returns the average value of a column.
2. COUNT(column)	Returns the number of rows (without a NULL value) of a column.
3. COUNT(*)	Returns the number of selected rows.
4. MAX(column)	Returns the highest value of a column.
5. MIN(column)	Returns the lowest value of a column.
6. SUM(column)	Returns the total sum of a column.

SQL Having Clause:

- The HAVING clause enables you to specify conditions that filter which group results appear in the final results.
- The WHERE clause places conditions on the selected columns, whereas the HAVING clause places conditions on groups created by the GROUP BY clause.
- The following is the position of the HAVING clause in a query:

    ```
    SELECT
    FROM
    WHERE
    GROUP BY
    HAVING
    ORDER BY
    ```

- The HAVING clause must follow the GROUP BY clause in a query and must also precede the ORDER BY clause if used.
- The following is the syntax of the SELECT statement, including the HAVING clause:

    ```
    SELECT column1, column2
    FROM table1, table2
    WHERE [ conditions ]
    GROUP BY column1, column2
    HAVING [ conditions ]
    ORDER BY column1, column2
    ```

- Consider CUSTOMERS table is having following records:

ID	NAME	AGE	ADDRESS	SALARY
1	Ramesh	32	Ahmedabad	2000.00
2	Khilan	25	Delhi	1500.00
3	Kaushik	23	Kota	2000.00
4	Chaitali	25	Mumbai	6500.00
5	Hardik	27	Bhopal	8500.00
6	Komal	22	MP	4500.00
7	Muffy	24	Indore	10000.00

- Following is the example which would display record for which similar age count would be more than or equal to 2:

    SQL > SELECT *

    FROM CUSTOMERS

    GROUP BY age

    HAVING COUNT(age) >= 2;

- This would produce following result:

ID	NAME	AGE	ADDRESS	SALARY
2	Khilan	25	Delhi	1500.00

String Functions:

- SQL string functions are used primarily for string manipulation. The following table details the important string functions:

Name	Description
ASCII()	Return numeric value of left-most character
BIN()	Return a string representation of the argument
BIT_LENGTH()	Return length of argument in bits
CHAR_LENGTH()	Return number of characters in argument
CHAR()	Return the character for each integer passed
CHARACTER_LENGTH()	A synonym for CHAR_LENGTH()
CONCAT_WS()	Return concatenate with separator
CONCAT()	Return concatenated string
CONV()	Convert numbers between different number bases
ELT()	Return string at index number

contd. ...

EXPORT_SET()	Return a string such that for every bit set in the value bits, you get an on string and for every unset bit, you get an off string
FIELD()	Return the index (position) of the first argument in the subsequent arguments
FIND_IN_SET()	Return the index position of the first argument within the second argument
FORMAT()	Return a number formatted to specified number of decimal places
HEX()	Return a string representation of a hex value
INSERT()	Insert a substring at the specified position up to the specified number of characters
INSTR()	Return the index of the first occurrence of substring
LCASE()	Synonym for LOWER()
LEFT()	Return the leftmost number of characters as specified
LENGTH()	Return the length of a string in bytes
LOAD_FILE()	Load the named file
LOCATE()	Return the position of the first occurrence of substring
LOWER()	Return the argument in lowercase
LPAD()	Return the string argument, left-padded with the specified string
LTRIM()	Remove leading spaces
MAKE_SET()	Return a set of comma-separated strings that have the corresponding bit in bits set
MID()	Return a substring starting from the specified position
OCT()	Return a string representation of the octal argument
OCTET_LENGTH()	A synonym for LENGTH()
ORD()	If the leftmost character of the argument is a multi-byte character, returns the code for that character
POSITION()	A synonym for LOCATE()
QUOTE()	Escape the argument for use in an SQL statement
REGEXP	Pattern matching using regular expressions

contd. ...

REPEAT()	Repeat a string the specified number of times
REPLACE()	Replace occurrences of a specified string
REVERSE()	Reverse the characters in a string
RIGHT()	Return the specified rightmost number of characters
RPAD()	Append string the specified number of times
RTRIM()	Remove trailing spaces
SOUNDEX()	Return a soundex string
SOUNDS LIKE	Compare sounds
SPACE()	Return a string of the specified number of spaces
STRCMP()	Compare two strings
SUBSTRING_INDEX()	Return a substring from a string before the specified number of occurrences of the delimiter
SUBSTRING(), SUBSTR()	Return the substring as specified
TRIM()	Remove leading and trailing spaces
UCASE()	Synonym for UPPER()
UNHEX()	Convert each pair of hexadecimal digits to a character
UPPER()	Convert to uppercase

SQL Joins:

- The SQL Joins clause is used to combine records from two or more tables in a database.
- A JOIN is a means for combining fields from two tables by using values common to each.
- Consider following two tables, (a) CUSTOMERS table is as follows:

ID	NAME	AGE	ADDRESS	SALARY
1	Ramesh	32	Ahmedabad	2000.00
2	Amar	25	Delhi	1500.00
3	Kaushik	23	Kota	2000.00
4	Chaitali	25	Mumbai	6500.00
5	Hardik	27	Bhopal	8500.00
6	Komal	22	MP	4500.00
7	Akbar	24	Indore	10000.00

- (b) Another table is ORDERS as follows:

OID	DATE	CUSTOMER_ID	AMOUNT
102	2009-10-08 00:00:00	3	3000
100	2009-10-08 00:00:00	3	1500
101	2009-11-2 00:00:00	2	1560
103	2008-05-28 00:00:00	4	2060

- Now let us join these two tables in our SELECT statement as follows:

  ```
  SQL> SELECT ID, NAME, AGE, AMOUNT
  FROM CUSTOMERS, ORDERS
  WHERE  CUSTOMERS.ID = ORDERS.CUSTOMER_ID;
  ```

- This would produce following result:

ID	NAME	AGE	AMOUNT
3	Kaushik	23	3000
3	Kaushik	23	1500
2	Amar	25	1560
4	Chaitali	25	2060

- Here it is noteable that the join is performed in the WHERE clause. Several operators can be used to join tables, such as =, <, >, <>, <=, >=, !=, BETWEEN, LIKE, and NOT; they can all be used to join tables. However, the most common operator is the equal symbol.
- There are different type of joins available in SQL these are listed below:

1. **Inner Join:**

- Returns rows when there is a match in both tables. The most frequently used and important of the joins is the INNER JOIN. They are also referred to as an EQUIJOIN.
- The INNER JOIN creates a new result table by combining column values of two tables (table1 and table2) based upon the join-predicate. The query compares each row of table1 with each row of table2 to find all pairs of rows which satisfy the join-predicate. When the join-predicate is satisfied, column values for each matched pair of rows of A and B are combined into a result row.

   Syntax:

   ```
   SELECT table1.column1, table2.column2...
   FROM table1
   INNER JOIN table2
   ON table1.common_filed = table2.common_field;
   ```

- Consider following two tables, (a) CUSTOMERS table is as follows:

ID	NAME	AGE	ADDRESS	SALARY
1	Ramesh	32	Ahmedabad	2000.00
2	Amar	25	Delhi	1500.00
3	Kaushik	23	Kota	2000.00
4	Chaitali	25	Mumbai	6500.00
5	Hardik	27	Bhopal	8500.00
6	Komal	22	MP	4500.00
7	Akbar	24	Indore	10000.00

- (b) Another table is ORDERS as follows:

OID	DATE	CUSTOMER_ID	AMOUNT
102	2009-10-08 00:00:00	3	3000
100	2009-10-08 00:00:00	3	1500
101	2009-11-20 00:00:00	2	1560
103	2008-05-20 00:00:00	4	2060

- Now let us join these two tables using INNER JOIN as follows:

    SQL> SELECT ID, NAME, AMOUNT, DATE
        FROM CUSTOMERS
        INNER JOIN ORDERS
        ON CUSTOMERS.ID = ORDERS.CUSTOMER_ID;

- This would produce following result:

ID	NAME	AMOUNT	DATE
3	Kaushik	3000	2009-10-08 00:00:00
3	Kaushik	1500	2009-10-08 00:00:00
2	Amar	1560	2009-11-20 00:00:00
4	Chaitali	2060	2008-05-20 00:00:00

2. **Left Join:**

- Returns all rows from the left table, even if there are no matches in the right table.
- The SQL LEFT JOIN returns all rows from the left table, even if there are no matches in the right table. This means that if the ON clause matches 0 (zero) records in right table, the join will still return a row in the result, but with NULL in each column from right table.
- This means that a left join returns all the values from the left table, plus matched values from the right table or NULL in case of no matching join predicate.

Syntax:
```
SELECT table1.column1, table2.column2...
FROM table1
LEFT JOIN table2
ON table1.common_filed = table2.common_field;
```
Here given condition could be any given expression based on your requirement.

- Consider following two tables, (a) CUSTOMERS table is as follows:

ID	NAME	AGE	ADDRESS	SALARY
1	Ramesh	32	Ahmedabad	2000.00
2	Amar	25	Delhi	1500.00
3	Kaushik	23	Kota	2000.00
4	Chaitali	25	Mumbai	6500.00
5	Hardik	27	Bhopal	8500.00
6	Komal	22	MP	4500.00
7	Akbar	24	Indore	10000.00

- (b) Another table is ORDERS as follows:

OID	DATE	CUSTOMER_ID	AMOUNT
102	2009-10-08 00:00:00	3	3000
100	2009-10-08 00:00:00	3	1500
101	2009-11-20 00:00:00	2	1560
103	2008-05-20 00:00:00	4	2060

- Now let us join these two tables using LEFT JOIN as follows:
```
SQL> SELECT ID, NAME, AMOUNT, DATE
     FROM CUSTOMERS
     LEFT JOIN ORDERS
     ON CUSTOMERS.ID = ORDERS.CUSTOMER_ID;
```
- This would produce following result:

ID	NAME	AMOUNT	DATE
1	Ramesh	NULL	NULL
2	Amar	1560	2009-11-20 00:00:00
3	Kaushik	3000	2009-10-08 00:00:00
3	Kaushik	1500	2009-10-20 00:00:00
4	Chaitali	2060	2008-05-20 00:00:00
5	Hardik	NULL	NULL
6	Komal	NULL	NULL
7	Akbar	NULL	NULL

3. Right join:

- This join returns all rows from the right table, even if there are no matches in the left table.
- The SQL RIGHT JOIN returns all rows from the right table, even if there are no matches in the left table. This means that if the ON clause matches 0 (zero) records in left table, the join will still return a row in the result.but with NULL in each column from left table.
- This means that a right join returns all the values from the right table, plus matched values from the left table or NULL in case of no matching join predicate.

    Syntax: `SELECT table1.column1, table2.column2...`
    `FROM table1`
    `RIGHT JOIN table2`
    `ON table1.common_filed = table2.common_field;`

- Consider following two tables, (a) CUSTOMERS table is as follows:

ID	NAME	AGE	ADDRESS	SALARY
1	Ramesh	32	Ahmedabad	2000.00
2	Amar	25	Delhi	1500.00
3	Kaushik	23	Kota	2000.00
4	Chaitali	25	Mumbai	6500.00
5	Hardik	27	Bhopal	8500.00
6	Komal	22	MP	4500.00
7	Akbar	24	Indore	10000.00

- (b) Another table is ORDERS as follows:

OID	DATE	CUSTOMER_ID	AMOUNT
102	2009-10-08 00:00:00	3	3000
100	2009-10-08 00:00:00	3	1500
101	2009-11-20 00:00:00	2	1560
103	2008-05-20 00:00:00	4	2060

- Now let us join these two tables using RIGHT JOIN as follows:

    `SQL> SELECT  ID, NAME, AMOUNT, DATE`
    `FROM CUSTOMERS`
    `RIGHT JOIN ORDERS`
    `ON CUSTOMERS.ID = ORDERS.CUSTOMER_ID;`

- This would produce following result:

ID	NAME	AMOUNT	DATE
3	Kaushik	3000	2009-10-08 00:00:00
3	Kaushik	1500	2009-10-08 00:00:00
2	Amar	1560	2009-11-20 00:00:00
4	Chaitali	2060	2008-05-20 00:00:00

4. **Full Join:**
- This join returns rows when there is a match in one of the tables.
- The SQL FULL JOIN combines the results of both left and right outer joins. The joined table will contain all records from both tables, and fill in NULLs for missing matches on either side.

    Syntax: `SELECT table1.column1, table2.column2...`

    `FROM table1`

    `FULL JOIN table2`

    `ON table1.common_filed = table2.common_field;`

- Consider following two tables, (a) CUSTOMERS table is as follows:

ID	NAME	AGE	ADDRESS	SALARY
1	Ramesh	32	Ahmedabad	2000.00
2	Amar	25	Delhi	1500.00
3	Kaushik	23	Kota	2000.00
4	Chaitali	25	Mumbai	6500.00
5	Hardik	27	Bhopal	8500.00
6	Komal	22	MP	4500.00
7	Akbar	24	Indore	10000.00

- (b) Another table is ORDERS as follows:

OID	DATE	CUSTOMER_ID	AMOUNT
102	2009-10-08 00:00:00	3	3000
100	2009-10-08 00:00:00	3	1500
101	2009-11-20 00:00:00	2	1560
103	2008-05-20 00:00:00	4	2060

- Now let us join these two tables using FULL JOIN as follows:

    `SQL> SELECT ID, NAME, AMOUNT, DATE`

    `FROM CUSTOMERS`

    `FULL JOIN ORDERS`

    `ON CUSTOMERS.ID = ORDERS.CUSTOMER_ID;`

- This would produce following result:

ID	NAME	AMOUNT	DATE
1	Ramesh	NULL	NULL
2	Amar	1560	2009-11-20 00:00:00
3	Kaushik	3000	2009-10-08 00:00:00
3	Kaushik	1500	2009-10-20 00:00:00
4	Chaitali	2060	2008-05-20 00:00:00
5	Hardik	NULL	NULL
6	Komal	NULL	NULL
7	Akbar	NULL	NULL
3	Kaushik	3000	2009-10-08 00:00:00
3	Kaushik	1500	2009-10-08 00:00:00
2	Amar	1560	2009-11-20 00:00:00
4	Chaitali	2060	2008-05-20 00:00:00

- If your Database does not support FULL JOIN like MySQL does not support FULL JOIN, then you can use **UNION ALL** clause to combile two JOINS as follows:

```
SQL> SELECT  ID, NAME, AMOUNT, DATE
     FROM CUSTOMERS
     LEFT JOIN ORDERS
     ON CUSTOMERS.ID = ORDERS.CUSTOMER_ID
UNION ALL
     SELECT  ID, NAME, AMOUNT, DATE
     FROM CUSTOMERS
     RIGHT JOIN ORDERS
     ON CUSTOMERS.ID = ORDERS.CUSTOMER_ID
```

5. **Self join:**
- It is used to join a table to itself, as if the table were two tables, temporarily renaming at least one table in the SQL statement.
- The SQL SELF JOIN is used to join a table to itself, as if the table were two tables, temporarily renaming at least one table in the SQL statement.

    Syntax: SELECT a.column_name, b.column_name...

    FROM table1 a, table1 b

    WHERE a.common_filed = b.common_field;

Here WHERE clause could be any given expression based on your requirement.

- Consider following two tables, (a) CUSTOMERS table is as follows:

ID	NAME	AGE	ADDRESS	SALARY
1	Ramesh	32	Ahmedabad	2000.00
2	Amar	25	Delhi	1500.00
3	Kaushik	23	Kota	2000.00
4	Chaitali	25	Mumbai	6500.00
5	Hardik	27	Bhopal	8500.00
6	Komal	22	MP	4500.00
7	Akbar	24	Indore	10000.00

- Now let us join this table using SELF JOIN as follows:

```
SQL> SELECT   a.ID, b.NAME, a.SALARY
     FROM CUSTOMERS a, CUSTOMERS b
     WHERE a.SALARY < b.SALARY;
```

- This would produce following result:

ID	NAME	SALARY
2	Ramesh	1500.00
2	Kaushik	1500.00
1	Chaitali	2000.00
2	Chaitali	1500.00
3	Chaitali	2000.00
6	Chaitali	4500.00
1	Hardik	2000.00
2	Hardik	1500.00
3	Hardik	2000.00
4	Hardik	6500.00
6	Hardik	4500.00
1	Komal	2000.00
2	Komal	1500.00
3	Komal	2000.00
1	Akbar	2000.00
2	Akbar	1500.00
3	Akbar	2000.00
4	Akbar	6500.00
5	Akbar	8500.00
6	Akbar	4500.00

6. Cartesian join:

- This join returns the cartesian product of the sets of records from the two or more joined tables.
- The CARTESIAN JOIN or CROSS JOIN returns the cartesian product of the sets of records from the two or more joined tables. Thus, it equates to an inner join where the join-condition always evaluates to True or where the join-condition is absent from the statement.

    Syntax: SELECT table1.column1, table2.column2...

    FROM table1, table2 [, table3]

- Consider following two tables, (a) CUSTOMERS table is as follows:

ID	NAME	AGE	ADDRESS	SALARY
1	Ramesh	32	Ahmedabad	2000.00
2	Amar	25	Delhi	1500.00
3	Kaushik	23	Kota	2000.00
4	Chaitali	25	Mumbai	6500.00
5	Hardik	27	Bhopal	8500.00
6	Komal	22	MP	4500.00
7	Akbar	24	Indore	10000.00

- (b) Another table is ORDERS as follows:

OID	DATE	CUSTOMER_ID	AMOUNT
102	2009-10-08 00:00:00	3	3000
100	2009-10-08 00:00:00	3	1500
101	2009-11-20 00:00:00	2	1560
103	2008-05-20 00:00:00	4	2060

- Now let us join these two tables using INNER JOIN as follows:

    SQL> SELECT ID, NAME, AMOUNT, DATE

    FROM CUSTOMERS, ORDERS;

- This would produce following result:

ID	NAME	AMOUNT	DATE
1	Ramesh	3000	2009-10-08 00:00:00
1	Ramesh	1500	2009-10-08 00:00:00
1	Ramesh	1560	2009-11-20 00:00:00
1	Ramesh	2060	2008-05-20 00:00:00
2	Amar	3000	2009-10-08 00:00:00
2	Amar	1500	2009-10-08 00:00:00
2	Amar	1560	2009-11-20 00:00:00
2	Amar	2060	2008-05-20 00:00:00
3	Kaushik	3000	2009-10-08 00:00:00
3	Kaushik	1500	2009-10-08 00:00:00
3	Kaushik	1560	2009-11-20 00:00:00
3	Kaushik	2060	2008-05-20 00:00:00
4	Chaitali	3000	2009-10-08 00:00:00
4	Chaitali	1500	2009-10-08 00:00:00
4	Chaitali	1560	2009-11-20 00:00:00
4	Chaitali	2060	2008-05-20 00:00:00
5	Hardik	3000	2009-10-08 00:00:00
5	Hardik	1500	2009-10-08 00:00:00
5	Hardik	1560	2009-11-20 00:00:00
5	Hardik	2060	2008-05-20 00:00:00
6	Komal	3000	2009-10-08 00:00:00
6	Komal	1500	2009-10-08 00:00:00
6	Komal	1560	2009-11-20 00:00:00
6	Komal	2060	2008-05-20 00:00:00
7	Akbar	3000	2009-10-08 00:00:00
7	Akbar	1500	2009-10-08 00:00:00
7	Akbar	1560	2009-11-20 00:00:00
7	Akbar	2060	2008-05-20 00:00:00

Questions

1. Define database.
2. What is meant by D.B.M.S. and R.D.B.M.S.
3. Listout various feature of R.D.B.M.S.
4. Define R.D.B.M.S. Enlist characteristics of R.D.B.M.S.
5. With the neat diagram explain components of R.D.B.M.S.
6. Enlist properties of R.D.B.M.S. with suitable diagram.
7. State advantages of R.D.B.M.S.
8. Give limitations of R.D.B.M.S.
9. What are the different types of keys used in R.D.B.M.S.?
10. Discuss integrity Rule of R.D.B.M.S.
11. Explain the term primary key.
12. Explain the term referential integrity rule.
13. Explain the term candidate key.
14. Write short note on: Foreign key.
15. Describe database normalization.

16. Why we required normalization.
17. Define 1NF with suitable example.
18. Define 2NF with suitable example.
19. Define 3NF with suitable example.
20. Explain entity relationships using its symbols.
21. Define the following terms:
    (a) Entities, (b) Relationship, and (c) Attribute.
22. Write short note on: mapping cardianality
23. Explain SQL with its different languages.
24. Describe following terms:
    (a) Joins, (b) DML, (c) SQL operators, and (d) DDL.
25. Draw an E-R for hospital which includes various entities, attributes and relationship such as Doctors, (Doc_id, Doc_add, Doc_name), Hospital (Hos_name, Hos_address, Hos_id), Patient (Pat_id, Pat_name, Pat_gender, Pat_add); Hos_workers (HosW_id, HosW_name, HosW_add) etc.
26. Draw a E-R diagram for university which includes courses, branches, student, colleges information etc.
27. An insurance agent sells insurance policies to clients. Policies can be of different types such as vehicle insurance, life insurance, accident insurance etc. The agent collects monthly premiums on the policies in the form of cheques of local banks. Appropriate attributes must be assumed for various entities such as agents, vehicles, policy.
    Draw an E-R model for above system. Your E-R model should take advantage of extended E-R notation where relevant.
28. Following information is maintained manually in a library.
    Books (Accession_number, name, authors, price, book_type, publisher)
    Borrowers (membership_no., name, address,
        category, max_no of books that can be issued,
        Accession_number of books borrowed)
    The following constraints are observed:
    (i) Each book has unique accession-number.
    (ii) A book may have more than one author.
    (iii) There may be more than one copy of a book.
    (iv) The category of borrower determines the max. Number of books that may be issued to borrower.
        Draw E-R diagram for above statement.
29. Explain strong and weak entity with example.
30. What is relationship? Explain relationship set in detail.
31. Write short note on:
    (i) Group by clause, (ii) Having clause, and (iii) Order by clause.

F.Y.B.B.A. (SEMESTER - II) : BUSINESS INFORMATICS
QUESTION PAPER (2013 PATTERN)

Time : 3 Hours   October 2014   Max. Marks : 80

Instructions: *Solve Any 3 Questions from No. 2 to Question No. 5.*

Q.1 Write short notes (Any four):   [20]
(a) WWW
Ans. Refer to Section 4.9.5.
(b) ROM
Ans. Refer to Section 1.7.1.2.
(c) Files.
Ans. Refer to Section 1.6.2.
(d) Notepad
Ans. Refer to Section 3.1.
(e) MS-ACCESS
Ans. Refer to Section 3.6.

Q.2 (a) What is Computer? Explain the Block diagram of Computer.   [10]
Ans. Refer to Sections 1.1.1 and 1.3.
(b) What do you mean by an Input device? Explain any two Input devices.   [10]
Ans. Refer to Section 1.8.1.

Q.3 (a) Explain Operating System? Explain the services provided by an O.S.   [10]
Ans. Refer to Sections 2.1 and 2.1.7.
(b) Perform the following: [10]
(i) $(15)_{10} = (?)_8$, (ii) $(10111010)_2 = (?)_{16}$, (iii) $(583)_{10} = (?)_8$, (iv) $(111011101110)_2 = (?)_{16}$, (v) $(10101)_2 = (?)_{10}$
Ans. (i) 17
(ii) BA
(iii) 1107
(iv) EEE
(v) 21

Q.4 (a) What are the difference between primary memory and secondary memory?   [10]
Ans. Refer to Section 1.7.1 and 1.7.2.
(b) What is Normalization? Explain the goals of Normalization.   [10]
Ans. Refer to Section 5.3.

Q.5 (a) Explain the following DOS commands with example.   [10]
(i) Dir (ii) Type (iii) Cls (iv) Format (v) Date
Ans. (i) Refer Section 2.4.2.1 (Point 11).
(ii) Refer Section 2.4.2.1 (Point 47).
(iii) Refer Section 2.4.2.1 (Point 3).
(iv) Refer Section 2.4.2.2 (Point 28).
(v) Refer Section 2.4.2.1 (Point 9).
(b) Explain SQL statements with example: (i) DELETE (ii) ALTER   [10]
Ans. (i) Refer to Section 5.5.3.2.
(ii) Refer to Section 5.5.3.1.

Business Informatics   Question Papers

Time : 3 Hours   **April 2015**   Max. Marks : 80

Instructions: *Solve Any 3 Questions from No. 2 to Question No. 5.*

Q.1 Write short notes (Any four):   [20]
(a) Printer
Ans. Refer to Section 1.8.2.3
(b) RAM
Ans. Refer to Section 1.7.1.1.
(c) Files.
Ans. Refer to Section 2.3.1.
(d) Notepad
Ans. Refer to Section 3.1.
(e) Windows Explorer.
Ans. Refer to Section 2.3.

Q.2 (a) What is Computer? Explain the types of Computer.   [10]
Ans. Refer to Sections 1.1.1 and 1.1.4.
(b) What is input device? Explain any two input devices.   [10]
Ans. Refer to Section 1.8.1.

Q.3 (a) What is ISP? Explain its role.   [10]
Ans. Refer to Section 4.10.
(b) Perform the following: [10]
(i) $(712)_{10} = (?)_8$, (ii) $(10101)_2 = (?)_{10}$, (iii) $(CA)_{16} = (?)_{10}$, (iv) $(010100)_2 = (?)_8$, (v) $(30245)_8 = (?)_2$

Ans. (i) 1310
(ii) 21
(iii) 202
(iv) 24
(v) $(11000010100101)_2$

Q.4 (a) What is Computer Networks? Explain the types of Networks.   [10]
Ans. Refer to Sections 4.1 and 4.4.
(b) What is Normalization? Explain the 1st Normal form.   [10]
Ans. Refer to Sections 5.3 and 5.3.5.1.

Q.5 (a) Explain following DOS commands with example.   [10]
(i) Mkdir (ii) Edit (iii) Attrib (iv) Format (v) Time
Ans. (i) Refer Section 2.4.2.1 (Point 32).
(ii) Refer Section 2.4.2.2 (Point 20).
(iii) Refer Section 2.4.2.2 (Point 4).
(iv) Refer Section 2.4.2.2 (Point 28).
(v) Refer Section 2.4.2.1 (Point 46).
(b) Explain SQL statements with example: (i) SELECT (ii) INSERT   [10]
Ans. (i) Refer to Section 5.5.3.3.
(ii) Refer to Section 5.5.3.2.

Business Informatics   P.3   Question Papers

Time : 3 Hours   **October 2015**   Max. Marks : 80

Q.1 Write short notes on (Any four): [20]
(a) Web Server
Ans. Refer to Section 4.9.4.
(b) Protocols
Ans. Refer to Section 4.7.
(c) Windows Explorer
Ans. Refer to Section 2.3.3.
(d) Plotter
Ans. Refer to Section 1.8.2.4.
(e) ISP
Ans. Refer to Section 4.10.

Q.2 (A) What is computer and explain the characteristics of computer. [10]
Ans. Refer to Sections 1.1.1 and 1.2.
(b) What is memory? Explain the types of memory. [10]
Ans. Refer to Section 1.7.

Q.3 (A) Explain the modes of communication in detail. [10]
Ans. Refer to Section 4.5.
(B) Solve the following: [10]
(a) $(CA)_{16}$ = $(?)_{10}$, (b) $(7B46)_{16}$ = $(?)_8$, (c) $(9F2)_{16}$ = $(?)_8$, (d) $(127)_{16}$ = $(?)_{10}$, (e) $(83A5)_{16}$ = $(?)_8$
Ans. (a) 202
(b) 75506
(c) 4762
(d) 295
(e) 101645

Q.4 (A) What is computer networks? Explain its goals. [10]
Ans. Refer to Sections 4.2 and 4.2.2.
(B) Explain normalization? Explain its goals. [10]
Ans. Refer to Section 5.3.

Q.5 (A) Explain following DOS commands with example: [10]
(a) CLS, (b) Attrib, (c) Edit, (d) Ger, (e) Help
Ans. (a) CLS: Refer Section 2.4.2.1 (Point 3).
(b) Attrib: Refer Section 2.4.2.2 (Point 4).
(c) Edit: Refer Section 2.4.2.2 (Point 20).
(d) Ver: Refer Section 2.4.2.1 (Point 48).
(e) Help: Refer Section 2.4.2.2 (Point 29).
(B) Explain SQL statements with example: (i) DROP (ii) CREATE [10]
Ans. (i) DROP: Refer to Section 5.5.3.1.
(ii) CREATE: Refer to Section 5.5.3.1.

www.ingramcontent.com/pod-product-compliance
Lightning Source LLC
Chambersburg PA
CBHW060317240426
43661CB00059B/2797